MW00560710

FATHER JOSEPH FESSIO, S.J.

CORNELIUS MICHAEL BUCKLEY, S.J.

Father Joseph Fessio, S.J.

~

California Blackrobe

With a foreword by
George Weigel

IGNATIUS PRESS   SAN FRANCISCO

Cover design by Enrique J. Aguilar

© 2024 by Ignatius Press, San Francisco
All rights reserved
ISBN 978-1-62164-617-4 (PB)
ISBN 978-1-64229-265-7 (eBook)
Library of Congress Control Number 2024940273
Printed in the United States of America ∞

CONTENTS

PUBLISHER'S NOTE

Terror is not something Father Joseph Fessio knows well—certainly not as part of his priestly ministry. But there he was, about to jump out of a plane. With a parachute, to be sure, but also with his fully engaged fear of heights. Jesuits are not supposed to aspire to "high office" in the Church, but they are supposed to accept it if they must. In this case, the troposphere called—high indeed. A soul was at stake and a deal was a deal. What else was a Jesuit to do?

Read on to learn the answer.

But first, how we got here. When Mark Middendorf, then president of Lighthouse Catholic Media (now president of Ave Maria University), proposed this biography, Father Fessio didn't want it written. Mark, however, can be very persuasive, and though Father is founder and editor of Ignatius Press, he was overruled by the rest of us. Full transparency: for years, some of us at Ignatius had been trying to figure out how to get such a biography written. It's a strange and important story. Mark Middendorf, as is often so with him, found the precise mechanism to make things happen.

After few initial missteps on our part, Jesuit Father Cornelius Buckley—historian, author, translator, and, most importantly, a close priest friend from Father Fessio's earliest years as a Jesuit—was asked to write this book. He agreed, wrote hard, rewrote harder and mischievously, and here we are.

That is how this book came to be. Well, sort of. Father Fessio first had to live its story. And live it he did. As readers will discover, this book is an entertaining, enlightening, and inspiring account of some of what God has done with the genetic-cultural blend of Italian, German, and French (Vendée) that is Joseph Dean Fessio, S.J.

Along the way, readers will follow the so-called Silent Generation and its uneasy transition into the Age of the Boomer, with the cultural upheaval of the sixties and the ecclesiastical turmoil following Second Vatican Council. They will make their way through the jungle of postconciliar confusion: the crises of Catholic doctrine, Catholic higher education, and the sacred liturgy, among other things. At the same time, this is also the story of the renaissance of Catholic publishing, the Catechism of the Catholic Church, and the trimming of the sails of Peter's Barque under Pope Saint John Paul II, Benedict XVI, and Francis.

Father Fessio was in the middle of all of that and more. A great man of the Church and a loyal son of Saint Ignatius, he thrived in many ways during those profoundly challenging times. Under the circumstances of the last six decades, he has been an *agent provocateur* of the Holy Spirit against the Iron Rule of the Zeitgeist, fighting for the true, the good, the beautiful, and especially the Holy, and helping fellow Catholics sort things out, all for the greater glory of God and love of the Church.

—Mark Brumley
President, Ignatius Press

FOREWORD

In the retrospect of over half a century, it now seems clear that the great debate at the Second Vatican Council was not between "reformers" and "traditionalists", or, in media terms, "liberals" and "conservatives". Rather, it was a debate within the reformist camp of theologians who played a crucial role in shaping the Council's sixteen documents. That debate continues to roil the Catholic Church well into the twenty-first century.

At the beginning of Vatican II, the reformers were all committed to the vision of the Catholic future laid out by Pope John XXIII in his opening address to the Council on October 12, 1962: Vatican II was to lead the Church out of what Hans Urs von Balthasar had called its "bastion" mentality, finding fresh ways to present the truths of the Catholic faith in order to re-energize the Church for its mission of evangelization. As the Council unfolded, however, deep fault lines opened up in the reformist camp over how that renewal should take place.

On one side, there were theologians who sought to develop the Church's self-understanding and proclamation in continuity with the Church's tradition, finding fresh insights by drawing on the Bible, the Fathers of the Church, and the medieval masters. On the other were found theologians in thrall to various forms of modern thought: men and women who imagined that theology could build a new Catholic intellectual edifice with scant reference to the wisdom of the past, but with a close eye on contemporary intellectual trends. This division within the reformist camp during the Council would eventually produce two contending, and in some respects incompatible, interpretations of the Council: was Vatican II a council of reform through the organic development of the Catholic tradition, or was it a council making a decisive break with that tradition as it had long been understood?

George Weigel is Distinguished Senior Fellow of the Ethics and Public Policy Center in Washington, D.C., and the biographer of Pope Saint John Paul II.

In the years immediately following the Council, theological book-making in the Anglosphere was dominated by publishers committed to the idea that Vatican II had marked a rupture with the Catholic past. The singular accomplishment of Father Joseph Fessio, S.J., the subject of this winsome biography was to reverse that trend. Fessio did that by founding Ignatius Press, typically misunderstood as a "conservative" publishing house, but in fact the publisher that brought into the English-speaking world the work of some of the most creative, innovative theologians of the twentieth century. Thanks to his own educational experience in Europe, Father Fessio knew that there were immense intellectual and spiritual riches to be explored in the theological work of such men of genius as Henri de Lubac, S.J., the aforementioned von Balthasar, and Joseph Ratzinger—an exploration that could underwrite the Church's proclamation of Jesus Christ as the answer to the question that is every human life. In establishing Ignatius Press in 1978, Father Fessio made those riches available throughout the Anglosphere, whereas they had previously been accessible only to those fluent in French and German. And in doing so, Fessio helped shape a profound theological renewal that informs the living parts of the Church in the twenty-first century English-speaking world.

Where real theology is being done in the Catholic Anglosphere today, books published by Father Fessio and Ignatius Press will be found in a theologian's library. Thus it is no exaggeration to suggest that the *ressourcement* theology of de Lubac, von Balthasar, Ratzinger, and others is alive and thriving in the twenty-first-century English-speaking Church—informing the new evangelization for which John XXIII hoped and that John Paul II proclaimed—because a California blackrobe decided to make available in English the theology that had shaped the teaching of Vatican II in its two key documents: the Dogmatic Constitution on Divine Revelation (*Dei Verbum*) and the Dogmatic Constitution on the Church (*Lumen Gentium*).

It may or may not have been Mark Twain who observed that "no good deed goes unpunished", but the phrase certainly fits the dramatic life of the Reverend Dr. Joseph Dean Fessio, S.J. His efforts with Ignatius Press, with the University of San Francisco's St. Ignatius Institute, and with other enterprises aimed at strengthening the intellectual foundations of contemporary Catholicism did not sit well with the progressive ecclesiastical establishment, not least within Fessio's own Society of Jesus.

Progressive Catholicism has the unhappy habit of praising diversity while working assiduously, and sometimes brutally, to snuff out deviations from its orthodoxies, whether in theology, higher education, liturgy, or pastoral practice. Father Fessio declined to be cowed by this progressive authoritarianism and suffered from it, even while he remained true to his Jesuit vow of obedience. And by standing firm for what he believed to be the truth of things, he built an enduring legacy that will outlast the record of his persecutors and critics. And for one simple reason: over more than a half-century of consecrated religious life, Joseph Fessio has lived in and through the Lord's promise in John 8:32: "The truth will set you free."

Living in the truth may not make for a comfortable life; it will usually make for controversy. But as Saint Ignatius Loyola knew, living in the truth—especially the truth of Christ—is the royal road to happiness and ultimately to beatitude. Craggy personality and all, Father Joseph Fessio seems to me the kind of Jesuit that Saint Ignatius envisioned: a deeply pious, swashbuckling intellectual and evangelical entrepreneur, determined to set the world ablaze with the fire the Lord Jesus sought to kindle on earth. The Church of the twenty-first century owes a great debt of gratitude to Father Fessio for being that kind of Jesuit—and now to Father Cornelius Michael Buckley for bringing his friend to life in these robust pages.

—George Weigel

PREFACE

This biography owes its origin to the day, some years ago, when Mr. Mark Brumley, the president of Ignatius Press, asked me to compose something publishable about the Jesuit who began the Press in 1978 and whose presence continues to hover over it advantageously to the present time. I accepted the request, but it is the people who populate the following pages who are the real authors. They, and a symbol or two, work together to describe the many accomplishments, failures, disappointments, and successes of the Reverend Joseph Dean Fessio, S.J. But from the very beginning, I felt there was something missing, something intangible that was still needed to define the Fessio élan, something that permeated his activities, his standard of what is right, proper, and decorous; something seemly, more concrete for the observer to grasp. I finally came to the conclusion that it was the notion of the *preux*.

The meaning of the term in French is "gallant, valiant, doughty", usually associated with the characteristics of the knight-errant of chivalric lore, and it is Cervantes' Don Quixote who, in his various quests, incarnates that meaning in the fullest sense. Then there was Voltaire, who in his *Dictionnaire Philosophique* described Saint Ignatius of Loyola as Don Quixote without a horse. Voltaire had been taught by the Jesuits and disliked them intensely, but he seemed to admire Loyola because he lived out the quixotic *preux* ideal in his endeavors.[1] The philosopher Miguel de Unamuno, too, wrote a long study comparing his fellow Basque Saint Ignatius with Don Quixote de la Mancha, citing so many episodes of their respective lives.[2] Citing Ignatius' first biographer, Pedro de Ribadeneira, S.J., Unamuno writes, "Loyola was very warm in constitution and very choleric, though he eventually overcame his choler, preserving the

---

[1] *The Works of Voltaire*, ed. E. R. DuMont, trans. William F. Fleming, vol. 5, *Philosophical Dictionary* (Part 3) (New York: St. Hubert Guild, 1901), 138–42.

[2] Miguel de Unamuno, *Our Lord Don Quixote*, trans. Anthony Kerrigan. (Princeton, N.J.: Princeton University Press, 1976).

vigor and enterprise that this characteristic supplies." *Voilà*, there we have it: Don Quixote, Saint Ignatius, and Joseph Fessio. Well, not quite. There is one more character associated with the term: P. G. Wodehouse's Bertie Wooster, who is prodigiously well-equipped to fall into traps designed by well-meaning foes. But whatever the result of his mischief-making, Bertie Wooster, as the French philosopher Rémy Brague observes, is always the gentleman, before both friend and enemy. The reason, as Bertie confesses, is that it is "the preux thing to do".[3] So the formula of my concoction is: take a shot of Quixote, a shot of Ignatius, and a shot of Wooster; mix together; shake thoroughly and pour out slowly to get that *esprit* of the classic Father Joseph Fessio. Read ahead to see if I am not right.

My personal memories of past events have a large part in recounting this saga of Father Joseph Fessio. Conversations also contributed greatly in weaving together the Fessio drama, particularly my James Boswell–like exchanges with the Samuel Johnson–esque founder of Ignatius Press. A number of these conversations were spontaneous, off-the-cuff bandies, but others were proper interviews. Some serious readers might reasonably find fault that the author sometimes fails to give the source of his findings. "Where are the footnotes?!" The reason for this unfortunate situation is that the archival materials of the Saint Ignatius Institute (1974–2002) and Ignatius Press are not yet formally organized or codified. Letters, emails, news articles, and announcements are stuffed together in boxes at the San Francisco headquarters of the Press. Hopefully, the day will come when this very rich collection will receive the attention it deserves.

Finally, I hasten to thank many who have made this project possible, including Mark Middendorf, Carolyn Lemon, Anne Nash, Vivian Dudro, and especially Thomas Jacobi, without whose professional expertise and charitable ability this book would never have appeared.

—Cornelius Michael Buckley, S.J.

---

[3] One example of Bertie's use of *preux*: P. D. Wodehouse, *Joy in the Morning* (New York: W. W. Norton, 2011), 37. For an analysis of the concept, see Rémi Brague, "God as a Gentleman", *First Things*, February 2019, pp. 39–44.

FROM BIRTH TO THE CALL

Those who know the Reverend Joseph Dean Fessio, S.J., today would never suspect he had such a provenance. He likes to say: "I was born on an island in the San Francisco Bay that begins with 'A'." Then he will add: "I should think people would respond with the question: 'Angel Island?' That's the obvious answer. But they don't. Most pause and then ask, 'Hmm, Alcatraz?'" Alcatraz! During that bleak age when he was born, Alcatraz was a sexist prison that discriminated against women. So what would make people say Alcatraz? Here is a suggestion. *Alcatraz* is the Spanish word for "pelican", and as the old limerick goes: "A wonderful bird is the pelican, / His bill will hold more than his bellican. / He can take in his beak / Food enough for a week, / But I'm damned if I see how the hellican."[1] Is it possible that the pelican is a kind of metaphor for Father Joseph Fessio and that some intuition, however subconscious, in those attempting to divine his place of birth might answer: "Alcatraz"? In the absence of Freud, one might keep in mind this query while reading the pages that follow. They attempt to describe a plethora of projects that the Reverend Fessio has been able to scoop up while keeping them all separate with the instinct of a structural engineer. Meanwhile, the Reverend Fessio pulls us away from speculation about a pelican and answers the original question by declaring that his birth took place in "the city of Alameda"; many people do not know that Alameda is an island, and few of those on the west side of the Bay would concede that it is a city. Distractions aside, that happy event took place at the Alameda Naval Hospital on January 10, 1941.

---

[1] Penned by D. L. Merritt in 1913. See Obituary, "D. L. Merritt, Wrote Limerick on Pelican", *New York Times*, January 11, 1972, https://www.nytimes.com/1972/01/11/archives/d-l-merritt-wrote-limerick-on-pelican.html.

Five years later, after the war had ended and his father was discharged from the service, the family moved around a bit and finally settled down in a middle-class cul-de-sac in Menlo Park, California, which was then a sleepy town and is today near the heart of the so-called Silicon Valley. Young Joseph's sole sibling was a brother, Vincent Joseph (he was born on VJ Day), who was six years younger and has since died. "We didn't talk much", Joe once said in passing. "He was not interested in sports, religion, or anything intellectual."

Their father, Giuseppe Deano Fassio, was born of poor Italian immigrant parents, who had settled in the copper mine area of Wyoming. When Giuseppe was twelve, his father died in a wagon accident when his horse startled at a train whistle. His mother subsequently remarried George Boskovich and eventually moved to Salt Lake City, where Joseph Boskovich, as he was now named, graduated from East High School with a baseball scholarship to Stanford University. Some time after graduation, he decided to go back to his original name, with modifications. Giuseppe stayed Joseph, Deano was changed to Dean, and Fassio, which sounded too ethnic, became Fessio. After graduation from Stanford, he played ball in the Pacific Coast League with Jackie Robinson. Eventually he became a salesman with the Flying Tiger Line, the leading cargo airline in the States, and then an officer in the U.S. Navy. After the war, he became a sales manager in one of the divisions of the Pan American Airways.

It was only recently that Father Fessio discovered his mother's family background. Thanks to the genealogical investigation of an unknown woman in DeSoto, Missouri, he learned that Mrs. Fessio was a member of the Govreau family, and so he was invited, with a number of invitees throughout the country, to participate in a reunion of the extensive Govreau clan. It was at this get-together that Joe heard that the first recorded Govreau left France for Quebec in 1704 and then, following the route marked out in 1673 by the Jesuit Père Jacques Marquette, settled in the territory that eventually became the state of Missouri. Knowing that there was some French blood pumping through his veins, however diluted, was a cause of delight for Father Fessio. If his mother, Florence Adele Miller, who was reared in Los Angeles, was aware of her family's origins, she did not communicate it to her son. "We weren't a very close family", he recalled, and after both boys had left home, the parents separated—divorce an unthinkable option—but they remained on close terms, his father renting an apartment a few streets from the family home.

If neither one of Joe's parents was emotionally expressive, both were intellectually gifted and athletically inclined, and so from a young age Joe demonstrated he had the genes of self-reflection and an inclination to be a baseball player, a hunter, and a fisherman. However, one of his earliest and bitterest memories was when the fathers of all his friends would come to the Little League baseball games to cheer their sons on, but never once did his own father, a one-time college baseball star, show up to support him. He remembers this disappointment caused him to shed silent tears. The wounded young boy was destined to play some baseball in high school and college, enough to convince himself that he was good, sometimes even very good, but never outstanding.

There was one instance that has remained engraved on his memory. He was in college, a member of the Santa Clara University baseball team, and he claimed he was happy because he had batted over .400. "We had not very many games and I got some lucky hits", he recalled. "I had one really great game. It was with Stanford, at the sunken diamond at Stanford, playing the freshman team. And my dad went to Stanford, played ball at Stanford, and he worked in Palo Alto at the time, but he didn't come to the game. I went four for five with a home run and five RBIs. We won the game 10 to 9. My dad wasn't there. . . . I just felt betrayed." Joe later tried to make an excuse for his father's lack of affirmation by asserting: "He was a good man, he did a lot of good things, but you know there was a distance there. Who knows how much I'm responsible for it because I was probably an uncommunicative kid or a kid who didn't appreciate things."

Although Joe gave up playing college baseball, he nourished the habit of following with enthusiastic interest all types of athletic contests. It is *the* recreational diversion that remains with him to this day. It was also just about this time in his life when another wedge pounded further the separation between father and son. Joe was beginning to date, and Joe, Sr., casually offered him some unsolicited fatherly advice: "Look, you know, you should take some condoms just in case." I said, "Dad, what are you saying? I'm not going to do that!" The seeds of nobility and integrity were already planted, and they gave promise of bringing forth a rich harvest.

From his earliest days, Joe attended the local public grade schools, but when it was time for high school, he enrolled at Bellarmine College Preparatory, a 640-student all-boys school in San Jose conducted by the Jesuits, an academic and sports powerhouse to this day. So, for the next four years, he made a daily round-trip commute from Menlo Park to San Jose. The fact that he was able to do homework on the twenty-miles-plus train trip argues well that even at that age he had exceptional powers of concentration and a will power to choose only those means that would acquire for him a desired end. This ability became an essential part of his personality, and it grew concomitantly with the other strengths of character to become even stronger in the intervening years. A regular conductor on the train had two Jesuit sons, Jim and Joe Devlin, who would have important roles in the future formation of young Fessio. In retrospect, he sees Bellarmine as effecting a key influence in his faith, morals, and intellectual life, if only because of the friends he met there. "Looking back on [my days at Bellarmine]," he says, "I tell parents this today too, that one of the most important things for their children when they're of high-school age is to have good companions, to make good friends from good families because that's where you're going to get your influence, from your peers." Some of the friends he made at Bellarmine are still his close friends, especially Barry Christina and John Kiely. But he also attributes his academic, spiritual, and social formation to his Jesuit teachers. "I think there's only four classes I had during my four years [at Bellarmine] that were not taught by Jesuits." Although Bellarmine still prospers, the average boy graduates today without ever having had a single Jesuit teacher.

For Joe, the most impressive member of the Jesuit pack was Father Gerald Flynn, who taught freshman English and Latin classes. He remembers him as "a tall, thin, rather severe Irish Jesuit. Wore a cassock, as they all did in those days." During the first week or two, he slapped a kid for laughing in class. "Almost knocked him out. Then he made him the gradekeeper." On reflection, Joe recalls that the kid had obviously had leadership qualities from the beginning; Father Flynn was a master at recognizing talents and temperaments in the students. He always carried a doughnut-round pillow with him, presumably because he suffered from hemorrhoids. "He was an athletic guy. He would toss that tube from the door onto his chair. It was a pretty good shot actually." Father Flynn had a printed form of special rules for study that the parents of each student had to sign. One part read: "Your son is going to have a half-hour homework at least for every one of his six classes, and if he tells you he doesn't have homework he's lying to you. He's not to watch television, to do anything until he finishes his homework. . . . And it's all to be done in a fountain pen, no ball-point pen, no pencils." In Father Fessio's words, Father Flynn "was the most beloved teacher in that school because he took an interest in every one of us. . . . If you were on the lowest level basketball team, he'd say, 'Oh, I saw you get in the fourth quarter; that was a nice pass you threw.'" (Imagine what today's media would do to a Father Flynn!) "But he taught us, and he taught me, how to study." After freshman year, students kept their same assigned seats for the next three years. Joe sat behind two young men who entered the Jesuits immediately after graduation, Lynn Farwell and Peter Filice (seating was alphabetical in those days). He would follow three years later, but not without some adventures with cars and girls.

When he was fifteen—that is, in 1956—and had completed his freshman year at Bellarmine, he put together the money he had earned that summer and purchased a 1941 Buick convertible that was not running properly. He learned enough about it to fix it up, which speaks well for his potential mechanical as well as entrepreneurial talents, and he practiced driving up and down the road that ended the cul-de-sac on which he lived. Then he sold it, and on the day before his sixteenth birthday, he bought a 1948 Studebaker convertible, in which he promptly drove down to the local California motor vehicle department, took, and passed his test for a driver's license.

Early the next morning, he spun down to Bellarmine for class and then back to Menlo Park to practice for an upcoming debate contest with his partner. The partner must have been an exceptional debater, for he talked Joe into driving thirty miles or so up to San Francisco to see a Bellarmine–Riordan basketball game. But they could not go without another friend, another willing classmate, and so they drove down to pick him up, but pulling away from his house, the confident, newly licensed driver backed up into a mailbox and knocked it over before speeding away—a preview of repeated dramas in the years to come. After the game, the adventurous threesome started off for home, but the gas gauge warned that they would never make it unless they attended to its warning to them, and so Joe pulled into a gas station, where he confidently flashed his parents' Shell Oil credit card (how he got it is another matter) and told the attendant, "Fill up the tank." Then suddenly he stopped. He realized his parents would get the bill and know that he had been in San Francisco, and so, reclaiming the card, the three of them scratched up enough cash to pay the adjusted bill. They then managed to get the pitch-black convertible onto the four-lane, two-way Bayshore Highway and fly south. Halfway home, flashing red lights appeared out of nowhere behind them. Joe pulled over, and the highway patrolman asked to see his license. License? He explained it was his sixteenth birthday and that he passed the test to drive that very morning, but he had to confess he only had a temporary license. "You were speeding", the officer said. "But the speedometer said just sixty", replied the expert debater. "[Expletive]! You were going over eighty, and because you lied to me I'm giving you a ticket." Joe had to confess to his parents how he had spent his sixteenth birthday, and the judge ordered him to have his mother drive him to the juvenile detention center for six weekends in a row for safe-driving instructions. From start to finish, the episode raises some questions: Where were the parents of this adolescent child as the drama unfolded, and did their continuing absence have an influence on this teenager's development? Were such adventures exceptional or ordinary among his Bellarmine peers? For Joe, such queries were probably easily suppressed, for now he had to attend those weekend classes on safe driving and thereby forfeit spending time with his new girlfriend.

There is something of the aura of Dulcinea del Toboso about the several girls who glided in and out of the life of Don José Fessio before he closed the door on dating and opened another leading to an adventurous life as a Jesuit. Dulcinea at this phase assumed the form of a seventeen-year-old named Rosemary, who had a sister named Kathleen. After being grounded (the consequence of the Studebaker convertible episode), Joe had eventually been allowed to drive again. "And so," he said to Rosemary, "let's take a drive." She agreed. "We got in the car. Convertible, summer night, full

moon, Sand Hill Road was in those days an old, almost kind of rural road. We're driving up, and I pull over, and we sit there and talk.
I put my arm around her, and we hear this *ahem, ahem*. Her sister
had hidden in the back seat. She was just trying to figure out what
we were doing. [Kathleen] eventually entered the convent. I don't
know if she stayed in the convent, but she entered the convent."
What he did remember, however, was that on that night the convertible made a hasty retreat down Sand Hill Road and dropped off
Dulcinea-for-the-night and her uninvited chaperone at the doorstep
of their home. At the time, one of Joe's part-time summer jobs was
with the mortgage division of the Prudential Insurance Company,
sending off letters to clients written on the Prudential letterhead
stationery. After the uneventful date, Joe recalled that he wrote "as
a spoof" a letter to Rosemary, "Using language that you use with
clients, the big man behind the desk and all that. She just took
terrible offense at that and she never spoke to me after that."

The next summer, two part-time jobs kept him busy twelve hours
a day. One was with a city water department and the other with
a construction crew. He learned to operate a tractor and earned
sufficient cash to exchange the Studebaker convertible for an MG
convertible that he painted gray and red. By then the role of lovely
Dulcinea had gone to another young woman, one he noticed walking into an apartment near where he was digging a ditch at work.
"Somehow in those days before Facebook, and Twitter, and Google
and everything, I found out what her name was or what her phone
number was", Father Joseph recalled. He thought of her continuously, idealizing her. "And basically I asked her out. And she said,
well, we need to talk to my parents. You know, those were the
days!" Parental permission was cautiously granted. But now, what
to do? Where to go? Fishing? The smelt were running, so Joe and
his date, armed with a large net, zipped over to the San Mateo coast
to engage in the local sport of scooping up these evasive, slippery
creatures that come to shore with a wave, quickly lay their eggs,
and then slide back out in the same wave. It was always a challenge
divining which wave would be the smelt's preference. But Joe lived
on challenges. The two stood near the shore watching empty waves
come in and swish out. Finally, he yelled: "They're running." Before many onlookers he and his lady fair rushed toward an oncoming, smelt-less wave. She pirouetted sweetly and he followed with

élan. Then "she went flat on her face in the sand, very embarrassing." Still, it did provide a nice show for the crowd. Nevertheless, "that was that date. . . . Nothing ever really came of that."

Neither vain efforts to comprehend the psychology of women nor miscalculations of smelt-mating patterns were enough to unman this high school senior. His dreams were not shattered forever; they were simply put on hold. But the frustration of it all seemed at the moment to draw him back to his earlier love: speeding in cars with reckless abandon on the highway. He tells that on one occasion at this time, 1958, he was driving his parents' '56 Buick to Bellarmine. It was evening, and he was on the same Bayshore Highway where, on his sixteenth birthday, the Studebaker convertible crisis had unfolded. Before entering the highway, he came to a stoplight. I just roared through the stoplight. You know how kids do. . . . I was going 60 or 70 miles an hour, and there was this crossroad at a kind of angle. This car came across the highway—didn't stop—right in front of me. . . . I slammed on the brakes, and the car started to skid, so I tried to turn the wheel I skidded all the way across the front of the oncoming two lanes, and then I turned the wheel back and skidded all the way back across those two lands, back across my two lanes, and then back going in the right direction. . . . No cars. The cars behind me had not caught up with me yet . . . and there were no cars in front of me. One is tempted to see some prognostic symbolism in this hair-raising episode, some foreshadowing of his later life when fast-moving events will never be fast enough to catch up with him and reorientation will come to him as second nature.

After Bellarmine, the seventeen-year-old Joe Fessio chose to enroll as a boarding student at another Jesuit institution, the nearby Santa Clara University, where he would major in engineering. Not in electrical engineering, he was quick to add. "It was way too abstruse for me. I wanted to test materials, concrete and steel, stone and lumber, that sort of thing." With the exception of a very small scholarship from the Bank of America, he paid all his tuition with the money he had earned during the summer months, working long hours at part-time jobs that demanded much from his intellectual and physical strength. And what his employers demanded he gave back in spades. (Of course, tuition was not as high then as it is today.)

At the end of his first quarter he received the first B in his academic career, and this, he admits, was because he had neglected to put into practice Father Flynn's dicta and spent too much time proving that he was "just one of the boys". On one occasion, he and his roommate, Bill Beasley, absented themselves from an obligatory university convocation, and, since the doors of the students' rooms on their assigned floor were always left unlocked, they entered every room and dabbed all of the light globes with a kind of red paint. When the students returned, they found their rooms aglow in a soft rouge fog. Foolishly, the miscreants left their own room untouched. As a result, they had to pay a high price exacted by a horde of revenge-seeking peers. Against the rules, Joe cooked in his room, kept a pet cat (which he eventually threw out of the window), and orchestrated other pranks that made him blush in later years. Video games had yet to make their noxious presence felt, but there were seductive card games—pedro freshman year, pinochle sophomore year, and bridge junior year—enticing him and his buddies away from their books.

At the same time, there was an enterprise that he took seriously because it put needed money into his pockets, and it was another venture that attests to his inborn talent for making capital out of matters at hand. Across from the university there was a bar where anyone could come in and place bets on big upcoming weekend football games throughout the country. Seeing that the barkeeper made easy cash, Joe and another student set up a similar betting operation, adding coverage of some lesser-known community college contests as an enticement. The results of well-advertised college games could be found in the daily newspapers, but community college football scores in places like Arkansas, Kentucky, and Alabama were more difficult to find, seeing as they posted only in the local papers. So Joe would get on the phone at night and talk to a lonely telephone operator in one of the towns where the games were played and find out the score. The winnings were handsome, but short-lived. "It wasn't a big racket or anything," he was quick to emphasize, "but it was a nice little source of income." Nice indeed! But in another area of gambling, he had to admit defeat. One of his student friends, a young man from Las Vegas, challenged him to a series of poker games. Joe lost every single game, and the more he lost, the more he wanted to win. He was convinced his opponent had some method, and he was determined to find out what it was. At last, his money ran out, and he had to admit defeat. "How did you manage to do it?" he asked the Las Vegas conqueror. "Well, Joe, I watched you carefully. Each time you got a good hand, you swallowed." Joe went to bed that night broke and, what was worse, crestfallen. At the same time, he determined that in the future, when fortune smiled on him, he would hold his cards close to his chest and refrain from swallowing. As we shall see, this resolve served him well.

Although the need for money kept him hard at work during the summer break, Joe would never let it—or anything else—interfere with a project, however extravagant, to which he had set his mind. For example, at the end of their sophomore year, he and two of his college companions, Tom Kearns and Bob Helmholz, decided to ride their bikes from Chicago to Santa Clara, and Joe and Bob made it all the way to the finish line, riding 2,700 miles in twenty-seven days. (Tom Kearns met with an accident early on in the venture and had to withdraw.) How Joe's spidery legs could pump a newly purchased ten-speed French bike so far and in so short a time invites contemplation. The bike, or, if you prefer, the surrogate convertible—his Rocinante—is common among bicyclists today, but it was a rare jewel in the late 1950s—well equipped to meet the uneven roads, mud-drenched paths, and continuous wind that beat against the rider heading west. But the first challenge that faced Joe was how to get the bike and its rider to the starting line. The solution was a quintessential Fessio maneuver. He got his father, a former employee at the cargo-only airline Flying Tigers, to have him hired at the company with a one-dollar-a-year salary. Now, as an employee, he was entitled to take his bicycle with him on a free flight from San Francisco to Chicago. The plane was equipped with shelves on which were placed thin mattresses, and so Joe was able to stretch out and sleep all the way to his destination. It rivalled traveling on Air Force One.

Since this bicycle ride was to be a Fessio sally into the unexpected, there were adventures at almost every turn. When the two valiant heroes arrived in Newcastle, Wyoming, in the pouring rain, they set out to find some dry corner for the night. On their quest along the streets and squares, they encountered the local sheriff. After a brief interview, he decided they were deserving of consideration and said, "We've got a couple of guys in the city jail here, but I'll put them in the county jail and let you guys take their cell." Agreed.

In another episode, when they reached Yellowstone one evening, he and Bob laid out their sleeping bags on a picnic table, where they tucked in their tired bodies for the night. The following morning, a nearby camper pulled out his Polaroid camera that showed the two sleepers and an uninvited bear sniffing them out. There was a repeat performance of this act near the Grand Tetons, where, under similar circumstances, a mama bear's breath awakened our sleeping hero. After a short eye-to-eye, nose-to-nose contact, she climbed down from the table's bench and, seemingly unimpressed, made a blasé exit, spooring on with cub in tow, leaving a shivering knight limp with terror, hopeful that encounters of a more pleasant nature were in store. Several days later, the two pumped into San Francisco on burned-out bikes, exchanged a 1960 version of a high five, congratulated themselves on their success and then rode off to their homes for a long shower and the beginning of the fall semester.

In November 1960, Joe, now a junior, plotted out an audacious quest for the Thanksgiving vacation. He and a classmate companion decided they would raft down the Sacramento River from its source, continue along the San Francisco Bay, and eventually wind up near Santa Clara. He figured it would be a 200-mile trip, and the two would travel about four miles an hour in a portable blow-up raft they would pack along with them. Total: fifty hours. So they could easily make it back in time for Monday morning classes. They began Wednesday, scrambling into a boxcar around midnight near the Santa Clara railroad station and traveling, raggedy and almost freezing, to Roseville, near Sacramento. They vaulted onto a boxcar heading north, and when, sometime later, the train slowed down at Dunsmuir, above Shasta Dam, they leapt off undaunted into the blackness, landed, got their bearings, and finally rolled out their sleeping bags on someone's front lawn. But tired as they were and late as it was, they were not ready for sleep. They were so close to the coming adventure, so buoyed up by excitement. They plotted out how they would float down the river into Devil's Canyon, that legendary narrow space between two towering cliffs where the racing waters swallowed up motorboats and all types of conventional sailing craft. But on their inflated raft, they would fly along the crest of the foaming flow, touch lightly on the waters that plunged into the rock crevasses, and then finally slide gently into the widening stream. How the thought of these daredevil exploits spurred them on! At last, in the light of the morning, the Sacramento River at Dunsmuir lay lazily exposed before them. "It's about five feet wide and about a foot deep", Joe recalls.

Wounded but not defeated, they hiked to the highway, where they stuck out their thumbs and got a ride in a truck that promptly had a blowout. Parting company with the driver, they hitchhiked farther until the sun began to set. It was then that they met the river again below the dam. It had been a dry year, and water was let out sparingly from the Shasta Dam into the slow-flowing Sacramento, so they figured they could sleep in the raft as it slowly slid downstream. More sober than before, they unpacked the raft, blew it up, flapped it on the water, and jumped aboard. But eventually, the cold forced them to take refuge on a small island where, wrapped with less than sleepwear, they shivered into their sleeping bags. Early the next morning, they dipped their oars into the waters and paddled all day, grateful for the tired ripple that guided them wearily, winding through Devil's Canyon to Red Bluff, some thirty miles from where they began. Here they determined they would never make it back to Santa Clara in time for their Monday-morning class. Then Joe remembered there was a classmate who lived in Red Bluff and had driven up to spend Thanksgiving with his family. Could they hitch a ride back with him? Sure they could, and this they did. So much for another hazardous Fessio exploit. But far from feeling as Nietzsche might have felt after a disappointing night at a casino, he was buoyed up.

The following December, Joe went to a basketball game one evening with three of his buddies, two of whom were players on the Santa Clara Bronco squad, and four senior high school girls. They had arranged beforehand that after the contest they would go to a party at the house of one of the players. During the game, Joe made it a point to sit close to one of girls—Nancy was her name—and later at the party he confided to her his newborn ambition. It had come to him while reading William Lederer and Eugene Burdick's best-selling novel *The Ugly American*, wherein a fictional U.S. engineer goes to Southeast Asia for purposes idealistic. Two episodes in the story particularly captivated Joe's attention. First, there is a description of the engineer watching the native women struggle to keep heavy jugs of water balanced on their heads as they make their laborious trek day after day up from the river into the town.

The scene inspires the fictional engineer to contrive some means to better their lot. He remembers an old World War II jeep he had seen abandoned on a nearby roadside. Finding it, he tears out its engine and converts it into a water pump, using a bicycle to power the pistons. He then takes the assembled device down to the river's edge, where he persuades one of the village women to sit on the bike and pedal. The result: the piston pump coughs up a flow of water that streams up through a pipe into the village. Later on, the hero engineer notices that a good number of the native women are permanently stooped over, and he attributes this condition to the short-stick brooms they seem to have constantly in hand. So he designs a long-stick model, which he has duplicated and distributed throughout the village, thus solving the problem. "And so that's what I want to do", Joe confided to Nancy through the din of the party going on around them. Joe had found his model, his preceptor within the pages of a best seller. "I'd like to take what we've learned in America—our techniques, our accomplishments— and help people improve their lives, give them the chance to earn their living and make it on their own." But, he added, that was not enough. Spiritual nourishment was also necessary. "So I want to be a lay missionary with an engineering background. My idea is to go some place, probably South America, and work on dams and roads and other types of construction while, at the same time, doing missionary work, teaching catechism. You understand?" Yes, indeed, she was a sympathetic listener, and as he continued, she squeezed in closer to hear better what he was saying. "From a man's point of view, there are three things you need in order to be happy: a solid religious commitment, a good job, and a good wife. I have the first one; the second will be easy to get—I have been blessed with ample intelligence and a good education. But now I am looking for the third leg on this stool."

The party was getting wilder, and his buddies started demanding his attention. Drinking was then—as it is now—a pivotal part of college social life, but Joe had contempt for alcohol and judged harshly those who differed from his evaluation of its benefits. "They drink what tastes terrible, act stupid, and then the next morning barf on the floor" was his considered judgment of his fuddling buddies. So he was always the "designated driver" at social events. He did not drink, and he did not smoke. When he was about ten, he had tucked a pack of his mother's cigarettes into his pocket and sneaked them into school. "I tried to smoke one at recess. It was terrible. I tell people now that I gave up smoking when I was in the fifth grade." But we have digressed, leaving Nancy back at the party to chew on Joe's dreams of dams and construction work in Latin America. Let us leave her there for a while as she considers this prospect of becoming the third leg of the stool, with its inbuilt lifetime warranty for happiness, and let us also put on the back burner Joe's progress on those first and second legs: religion and work. What better diversion for us than another adventure from the life of that redoubtable Santa Clara Bronco, Joseph Fessio.

Christmas vacation came about a few weeks after his intimate exchanges with the Lady Nancy, and college people know that if Christmas vacation puts a hold on academic work, it intensifies extracurricular activities, especially sports events. That year the Broncos had a record-breaking schedule and were invited to play tournament games in various cities in New York and New England. Joe had to attend. His good friend Barry Christina was on the team. He had to be there for Barry. That is what friendship means. Since his father worked for Pan American, he was entitled to a free roundtrip ticket from San Francisco to New York. But the problem was that at that date the airline did not have flights available from San Francisco to New York—a mere inconvenience that would not stop any authentic knight-errant. Nothing would. After all, Barry was his friend. And so he got a ticket on a flight from San Francisco to London and then on another flight from London to New York. Joe was present to see Barry play and to congratulate him afterward. He then got on a return flight to London and then from London to San Francisco, making it possible for him to be back at Santa Clara in time to celebrate the coming of the New Year.

Ever since the basketball party earlier in the previous month, Nancy had often been in his thoughts, especially during those long, lonely hours he had spent flying halfway around the world. "Because she was intelligent, attractive, generous, and a devout Catholic," he recalls telling himself, "she fit the description of being that third leg on the stool." Not a very romantic image for a knight-errant, but Nancy did not seem to be affected. During the following months, they went out on a few dates, and each time Joe discovered more in her that was admirable. Later, in the spring, the whole group got together before Mardi Gras for a big celebration. Joe rode to the affair with his friend Bill Beasley at the wheel, and later, as the two rode back to Santa Clara, Joe noticed his friend was surprisingly quiet, morose. After some probing he found out the reason why: at the party Bill's girlfriend had told him she was entering the convent. "And did I give him any sympathy?" recalled his traveling friend. "No! I mocked him. I laughed at him. I said, 'That's the kind of a girl you pick—a nun!' I was brutal." That's what friends are for! Two weeks later, Joe confessed, Lent seemed to be dragging on and on. He needed a break. So he convinced himself that since Sundays were exempt from the Lenten calendar, he would ask Nancy out for Sunday dinner. She accepted, and, after engaging in the customary desultory chatter that is called for on such occasions, she waited for dessert to say: "Joe, I have decided to enter the convent."

An eerie stillness enveloped the surroundings. He sat there dazed and numb. It was difficult for him to discern which reaction was the greater: shock over what she said, or anger because of anticipated reactions from Bill and his other friends when they learned why she had jilted him and left him flat on the floor—like a spent boxer spread out on the mat. Whatever it was, he would not acknowledge defeat. He had won debating contests in high school and was considered a sharp-tongued arguer, a successful public speaker. He would do his homework, read about vocations, the committed celibate life. He would convince her to change her mind. And so, once again he prepared himself to sally forth, fully armed, to meet, confront, and destroy another windmill.

Lent crept on. Then, late on Holy Thursday night, sitting alone on the floor of the empty engineering lab mulling over all that he had read, he stood up—he remembers the experience vividly—and yelled out, "I am going to become a priest!" He had to tell Nancy. It was the *preux* thing to do. Bertie Wooster would have recognized it as an epochal moment. He then jumped into his MG and raced over to Nancy's house. She did not answer the bell. It was late. She might have already gone to bed. But he kept knocking at her window. Finally she appeared. "Nancy," he cried, "I have found the solution. I am going to join the Jesuits! I am going to become a priest!"

Of course, it was easier said than done. But, as we have seen, once

Joe Fessio sets his mind on attaining an objective, there is no obstacle in his way that cannot be contested and overcome. He immediately applied to be accepted as a novice in the Society of Jesus. Family, friends, and even some Jesuits advanced the argument that it would be better for him and for the Jesuits if he were to obtain his degree and then enter the novitiate. Such arguments were mere quixotic fancies in the way. By the end of the academic semester, his petition for acceptance into the order was granted. His father hesitated, but took his decision in stride, and his mother, who was now a devout Catholic, was delighted. But they asked him, as a last hurrah, to accompany his fourteen-year-old brother on an extensive trip visiting such faraway places as Hawaii, Tahiti, the Philippines, and Thailand. It was the first summer since he was a freshman in high school that he did not work, and he profited much from his travel.

By all appearances, Joseph Fessio seemed to have made a hurried decision to pursue a vocation to the priesthood, going, in but a matter of hours, from the desire to be a married man to a desire to embrace a celibate life. But as Sweet Little Buttercup in Gilbert and Sullivan's *H.M.S. Pinafore* observed, "Things are seldom what they seem." When we watch a wave suddenly break and rush to shore, we fail to take into account the time, the space, and the energy it took for the wind to blow on the water, making it build up, crest, and finally crash. Thus was the build-up of Brother Joseph Fessio's journey to the Jesuit novitiate at Los Gatos, California. "The wind blows where it wills, and you hear the sound of it, but you do not know where it comes from or where it goes; so it is with every one who is born of the Spirit" (Jn 3:8).

The pedagogical plan of the Lord was to reveal his call to Joe slowly, forcefully, but secretly, with unexpected splashes of humor. Joe recollects that early in high school, he wrestled with questions not normal for boys his age, questions like "How do I know there is a God? My parents tell me Jesus is God. What if they were Buddhists, would Buddha be God?" It is surprising how through reasoning he came to resolve for himself such queries, and how inclined he was at this period in his life toward prayer, how it entranced and thrilled him. Even as a high schooler, in addition to cars and girls, he took a special interest in books on apologetics, and what he learned there deepened that prayer, encouraged him to make visits to the Blessed Sacrament in the students' chapel, be more attentive at Mass, and say the rosary. At Santa Clara, these pious practices were deepened: he made it a practice to attend daily Mass, and he regularly signed up for the First Friday all-night adoration devotions. At the same time, his philosophy and theology classes ran in tandem with his devotional performances. Then there were revelations more recondite than real. I recall his once saying that the only vivid memory of his First Communion was the Sister telling him that every time he genuflected before the Blessed Sacrament he should say "Jesus, I adore you", and it is a habit he has maintained to this day. And there was the yeast-like presence of gratitude that prevailed in so much of his thinking. "[In my first year at Bellarmine,] I began to realize how lucky I was. I mean, I could have been born in some other century and died before I got out of the womb. . . . Here I am born in America where I'm free, I have an education, I've a home, I've got friends. I mean, look at all I have. I didn't choose it. I didn't choose my genes, I didn't choose my land of birth, I didn't choose anything until later on; it was all given to me. . . . I had to give something back." I also recall his saying that while at Santa Clara, he would sometimes see a cassocked priest walking up and down on the paths in the Mission garden reading his breviary. It made a fleeting but strong impression on his memory. The priest was not a university professor, but one of the Jesuits who served the local parish and lived in the university community. He was considered a bit quirky, and I am sure that his fellow Jesuits would consider it miraculous that Father Frank Frugoli had a quiet but real influence on one of the brightest students in the college, an effect more powerful than that of the university Jesuits (with the exception of one, whom we will meet in the next chapter). Symbols can be more persuasive than words. The two—Fessio and Frugoli—did not even meet until much later.

Sitting there alone in the engineering lab on Holy Thursday, knitting all of these separate threads of his background together, it was easy, quite natural for Joe to transform his way of thinking about service: the inner question "What do I want to do for God?" became "What does God want me to do for him?" The new question was an epiphany, and the answer was clear. And Joe, being Joe, translated the abstract into the concrete, the plan into action, and prepared himself to sally forth, fully armed, to meet new challenges. It was the *preux* thing to do.

2

JESUIT NOVITIATE

After the travels with his brother, Joe entered the novitiate at Los Gatos, California, September 8, 1961, and was unceremoniously bunched up with the other eighty-two first- and second-year novices. The two-year novitiate experience was destined to become a force of singular consequence for his future development, combining as it did a retreat of quiet solitude with boot-camp-like regimentation. From 5:00 A.M. to 9:30 P.M., every moment of the day was ordered and balanced between prayer, study, work, meals, play, and recreation. Silence and obedience prevailed. The regime was designed to emphasize the need of structure in one's life, and organization and discipline were the tools to create it. This was, of course, an era before Facebook, Twitter, texting, computers, iPods, and iPhones, but even then, at the novitiate there were no radios, television sets, or newspapers. Shortly after his entrance, each man made the Spiritual Exercises designed by Saint Ignatius of Loyola, the knightly founder of the Society of Jesus. This was a regimented drill conducted over a period of thirty days of strict silence for training and disciplining the mind and will to praise, glorify, love, and serve God and neighbor; to be obedient to one's superior, while being incorporated into a family-like structure; to be of assistance to the most needy; and to serve the Church. It was a totally Christocentric experience, the foundation upon which the Jesuit life was designed to be constructed.

Then, and during the next two years, Brother Fessio, as he was designated, read daily portions from the three-volume opus *The Practice of Christian and Religious Perfection* by the Jesuit author Alphonsus Rodriguez. To this day, Father Fessio remembers how much he disliked reading it, but he probably was not geared to appreciate the subtle wit (*agudeza*) and irony contained in some of Rodriguez' "sundry examples" of pious wisdom. After all, Rodriguez was a contemporary of Baltasar Gracián, S.J., whose book *The Art of Worldly Wisdom* has remained a classic to this very day. Rodriguez' opus was considered indispensable for the formation of the Jesuit *esprit* at the time when Brother Fessio was attempting to adapt to the novitiate life. Short family visits were allowed the novices once a month. Contact with others—"externs"—was discouraged, but conversations between the novices during work and recreation were carried on with vigor, alternating at designated times between English and Latin. Sports were part of the routine. Novices were *assigned* to play basketball, softball, baseball, or handball, and there was a large outdoor pool for swimming.

The first Jesuits who came to Los Gatos, almost ninety years before the arrival of Brother Fessio, planted grapes and set up a winery, and so the hills and lowlands around the novitiate building were covered with vines. There were also extensive vineyards beyond the novitiate, making the two or more months of grape harvest a special time for the novices. Brother Fessio was in his glory during this season, challenging anyone who was foolhardy enough to compete with him in emptying boxes of grapes into hoppers, then running with the fifty-pound load and dumping it into a one-ton-capacity metal cube container, before rushing back for another load. After a day of silence in the sunbaked fields, the novices would climb up onto flatbed trucks and chug back along dusty roads, and then, to the mystification of onlookers, they bumped along the streets of the town holding on to the guardrails of the trucks with one hand and their rosaries with the other. As they neared the novitiate gatepost, they would break out singing the "Salve Regina". Thanks to Rodriguez, Saint Ignatius, and excessive loads of grapes, Brother Fessio was never in better spiritual and physical shape. Obviously, this was a different era in the American church and state, the age before Vatican II and the Sexual Revolution.

After two years in the novitiate, he pronounced his vows, simple in form, solemn in effect, and moved to another part of the same building, the juniorate. Here he studied works of classical literature with an emphasis on Latin and Greek authors. Since he had done exceptionally well in his four years of Latin and two of Greek at Bellarmine, he was able to sail through the juniorate studies in just one year, rather than the customary two. Then, in 1964, he boarded a train bound for Spokane, Washington, for studies in philosophy at Mount St. Michael's, a Jesuit scholasticate considered to be one of the finest houses of Jesuit studies in the world, chiefly because of its library. In the early 1950s, the famous French philosopher Étienne Gilson paid a visit to the Mount, after which he declared, "I cannot think of a better place to study philosophy in all of North America because of what the Mount has in its library collection."

We have seen that Joe's main academic interest while at Santa Clara had been engineering; however, for an engineer, he took exceptional interest in philosophy, chiefly because of the Jesuit Austin Fagothey. In later years, Father Fessio singled out Father Fagothey as one of the best teachers he had ever had, the author of an ethics textbook, *Right and Reason*, which Father Fessio claims has never been surpassed. Though the young man did not recognize it at the time, Father Fagothey became a compass for the reckless Joe Fessio in discerning what was right and reasonable at that critical period of his Jesuit development. He put into practice Gracián's dictum, "Know or listen to those who know." The result was that his academic advisers at Mount St. Michael's, recognizing his interest and exceptional ability in philosophy, recommended that he put aside his earlier love affair with concrete, iron, steel, nuts, and bolts and pursue the study of philosophy. This he did. After a two-year stint at the Mount, Joe moved down to Gonzaga University, where in May 1967 he received his M.A. in philosophy. The subtle, seductive "spirit of Vatican II" had already begun to waft amid the coniferous groves and around the shady hills of this local Jesuit *akademos*, and, like the lotus eaters Odysseus encountered, young Mr. Fessio surrendered somewhat to its charms. There is an extant photo of him and a few of his peers dressed in their cassocks and holding up a sign declaring, "We Are the New Breed." The photo is iconic of the period: incongruous, contradictory, inviting satire. So, modestly holding an M.A. degree in one hand and boldly waving Teilhard de Chardin's *The Phenomenon of Man* in the other, Mr. Joseph Fessio, S.J., reported to the Department of Philosophy at Santa Clara University in the fall of 1967, ready to confront new challenges and eager to encounter new adventures.

From the outset, this 6′3″ bellyless Jesuit, with ropelike arms attached to Cro-Magnon hands and with a face that could easily fit as a background passerby in a Titian painting, made an impression on the Santa Clara students, with whom he lived and taught, and on the members of the Jesuit community, whose enthusiasm was—well, apathetic, to put it charitably. He and I arrived at the university for an assignment at the same time—he to teach in the Philosophy Department, a Jesuit of six years; I, a priest of five years, to teach in the History Department. These were the 1967 days, the time of the Beatles, Cesar Chavez, Joan Baez, *Bonnie and Clyde*, *The Good, the Bad and the Ugly*, and *Cool Hand Luke*; of Patty Hearst, the Berrigan Brothers, student riots, and the "Third Way" for "the Jesuits of the future". Most of the teaching Fathers at the university vested themselves in cassocks while carrying out their assigned tasks, but a small fraction—the more adventurous—were beginning to appear dressed in suit and Roman collar. From the very beginning of his arrival, young Mr. Fessio donned casual "civilian" clothes, with a big cross hanging from his neck, perhaps identifying him with either the poor or the New Breed, depending on one's predilection. As the months rolled on, his attire evolved, and, by 1969, it screamed out his message, thanks to the Fu Manchu moustache and beard he attempted with modest success to cultivate and to the guitar that hung casually alongside the cross from his neck. The students flocked to him, some seeing in him the embodiment of independence from whatever at the time was regarded as the most oppressive force in society, others regarding him as the personification of what some considered Vatican II's definition of the relevant apostle, unafraid to reach out to the world.

A number of the graver Fathers in the Jesuit community appraised him in all of his regalia with a shrug—one more case of the deadly virus infecting the Church in general and the Society of Jesus in particular. This same virus was manifesting itself in other examples: the talk of some influential Jesuits in houses of study calling for a radical change in community life, the swelling number of men and women committed to celibacy taking on wives and husbands, nuns going from veils and heavy clothing to dangling earrings and miniskirts. At the time, the enigmatic Jesuit president of the university, Father Patrick Donohoe, seemed to tolerate Mr. Fessio's diablerie with a shrug and smile, while disregarding the Fathers' quips at the dinner table about "that arrogant young man".

The Father Superior of the Jesuit community, Father Raymond F. Copeland, was also customarily a silent listener, so refraining from speaking his mind regarding Mr. Fessio was not a challenging task for him. Father Copeland was laconic by nature, and when he did speak, it was like a character out of an eighteenth-century English novel. So it was when, in 1967, he said of Fessio: "I should like to have a stockade erected into which that young man would be consigned." His words were cryptic, reminiscent of those spoken by King Henry II about Thomas à Becket, and seeing as he was the superior of the Jesuit community, they were downright daunting.

Mr. Fessio was a faithful teacher, but in his own words he was not an outstanding one. Whereas he had no trouble connecting with his students on a social level, he did meet opposition on the intellectual. He has a vivid memory of a disconnection he once had with the spokesman for some of his students: "Oh, Mr. Fessio, that is logical thinking", the young man said. "That's Western thinking. [In the East] they think differently . . . they're more intuitive, they don't accept the principle of noncontradiction." He was referring to the philosophical axiom that two contradictory statements cannot be true, in the same sense and at the same time. If A is B, then one cannot say that A is not B in the same respect and time. This fundamental principle cannot be proved. It must be assumed, and the spokesman for the students wouldn't accept that. "Little do you realize", argued the teacher, "that denying the principle of noncontradiction is in itself contradictory, since you are certain the principle is false and not also true." Mr. Fessio tried to convince them by using their own arguments. "But he and they were already set in their own opinions." He was more inclined to let them go. He admits he had neither the patience of a Socrates nor the forbearance of a Father Fagothey. He was more a pioneer than a settler, and so he soon found other challenges.

It seemed that everywhere in those days the liturgy was in a state of constant flux. The two or three self-defined expert liturgists on campus constituted what was more like an Orwellian "herd of independent minds" when it came to devising homegrown Masses. Meanwhile, the older Fathers plodded on, some confused, some angry, while the few outspoken self-styled liturgists, all of whom eventually left the Society, and some of whom left the Church, were rocketed high by the "spirit of Vatican II". Like abstaining from meat on Fridays, Mass vestments were a thing of the past, and the canon prayers, it was decreed, should be adapted to fit the malleable needs of the congregation. For canonical readings, Saint

Paul was respectably retired, while Kahlil Gibran humbly took his place; and in the back room of the mission, Vedic prayers shimmered up to some vague mystery of existence. It is easy today to be critical of such goings-on, but those priests who were involved with such liturgies were sincere and believed they were doing what the Spirit directed. If God willed the salvation of all, it was hard to see how he would restrict himself to Jesus alone, much less to liturgical dictates. Wasn't Catholicism too narrow? Could not one read in the documents of Vatican II that the Spirit had also rested on Buddha, Confucius, and other holy men of different cultures and that in the future all religions would converge, since there are many paths to the same God, paths expressed in different terms throughout history? Some of these men later "discerned" that the Spirit was inspiring them to leave the priesthood; some have since died, and some we shall meet in the following chapters.

When we arrived at Santa Clara, there was a 10 P.M. Sunday Mass offered on limited occasions in one or another of the campus dorms. It soon got "Fessio-fied" and relocated to the mission church. I would be the celebrant, but I could never excuse myself from wearing the proper vestments or from reciting the prescribed canonical prayers and obligatory readings, and Mr. Fessio agreed. He would not have had it otherwise. But looking back more than fifty years later, there were some oddities that Father Fessio would be slow to endorse today. In fact, he would rant against them. For instance, during the scriptural readings of the Mass, Mr. Fessio would flash pictures from a projector—one slide following after another in rapid succession—on the wall of the darkened mission church. These slides were designed to complement the text, but they also bore the aura of a light show. The homily was then given in an almost blacked-out setting. Meanwhile, we managed to get all of the pews removed from the back half of the mission church, much to the bafflement of some, enabling the students to pack in seated comfy-like on the floor during the celebration. Boozy, hip-moving guitar music was strummed, sometimes accompanied by a soft drumbeat and sung with superlatively stupid lyrics, while slides were left projected on the wall during the Offertory and Canon of the Mass. The number of student participants was always extraordinary. One night, well-intentioned members of the campus ministry floated balloons down from the choir loft in order to lift up the spirit of the congregants. We thanked them for their ecumenical spirit. We never disparaged the campus ministers, but we asked them not to interfere again, and this caused some misunderstanding.

Unfortunately, some of the older Fathers made no distinction between the Fessio Masses, those of the campus ministry, and backroom liturgies—a confusion that generated bad feelings within the Jesuit community. Despite all our good intentions, I have often wondered how many of the participants at those Masses practice their faith today, and even if they do, how about their millennial children? But I want to emphasize the fact that, however humbling the memory of these bizarre Masses might be, and however much the spirit of puerility mixed with apostolic endeavor, Mr. Fessio was never drawn into the popular current of destroying the long-cherished rubrics of the Mass.

One so-called "Fessibuck" production at the university was Project 50. It began one day when Mr. Fessio, feeling somewhat unfulfilled by his classroom commitments, sallied forth on another quest. This journey in search of adventure took him to the office of the supervisor of public grade schools in the poorer, east-side district of the neighboring town of San Jose. "Look," he recalled telling the startled man, "I want you to get together with your teachers of the eighth graders and make a list of fifty students, and here are the two criteria: number one, these teachers are convinced that these students have college ability, and, number two, they think that they'll probably drop out of high school. . . . They can be black, Hispanic, white, Asian, I don't care." So Fessio got his list of the fifty carefully selected eighth-grade boys and girls who were either not confident of their talent or not convinced of the importance of a college education for themselves and for their community. He then recruited eighteen college students and a few Jesuit scholastics who believed that education was important and wanted to share that belief with the students. This group became the counselors. Meanwhile, Mr. Fessio convinced the university of the importance of the program, and the administration generously opened up the coffers to support it. Next, an intensified six-week course of studies was drawn up that included remedial reading, composition, mathematics, drama, and history. The students and counselors would live together in a campus residence hall. The seventh week was spent at the Jesuit vacation villa in the Sierra Nevada foothills, a week of relaxation, swimming, movie watching, and games.

One unique feature of the program was the manner in which the courses were presented. For example, there was "Land Grant Week" during which time the students were taught the primary functions of the surveyor's transit. They were then taken out to fields to survey and "claim" a plot of land. Mathematic principles were needed for this exercise. At the same time, they were introduced to a bit of local history, since the land they were standing on was once claimed in the same manner. Mission Santa Clara, founded in 1777, is at the center of the university, and the students got to know the history of the mission very well. They also learned that just as the settlers had to write an essay describing their desired claim, so the students were expected to write a letter to an imaginary governor describing their claimed acquisition and advising him how they would develop their land for their own economic advantage and for the benefit of the community. This part of the program stressed the importance of understanding the different functions of the imagination and reason, of developing an appreciation of history and culture, of being conversant with the basic principles of capitalism and the need to know how to express oneself in good spoken and written English. The week was also designed to build up self-confidence, and so each student was expected to read his letter before small peer groups. Results were far from ideal, but these were eighth graders from backgrounds where encouragement to learn was lacking. I recall how one student wrote he would build a grocery store on his hopefully acquired property, explaining how and where he would obtain the merchandise, to whom he would sell it, how many employees he would have to hire, and what kind of realistic profit he would expect from the transaction. The counselors who heard him congratulated him warmly.

I remember we acquired, free of charge—a long story—an old, abused Greyhound bus, which was both challenging and indispensable in transporting the students to various places of interest. We also used the moot court in the law school building for debates and mock court trials, visited art museums, formed various sports teams, and produced the play *A Raisin in the Sun*. The last week at Applegate, the Jesuits' vacation villa, was the delightful culmination

of the seven-week experience, especially for those students who had
never seen a pine tree or touched a horse. But it was not the end of
the program. By exception, thanks to the supportive policy of the
public high school where most of our students were now enrolled
as freshmen, we were able to get their grades or progress reports,
and the Project 50 counselors regularly conducted night study halls
and encouraged the attendance of those having trouble. Mr. Fessio left Santa Clara in May 1969, and I followed shortly after, but
not before sponsoring a second year of the Project 50 experience
in June. The university supported its survival for a few years following our departure, but it was never exactly the same, for two
reasons. First, it became more La Raza-oriented and, secondly, it
lost its religious dimension, the essential force of the experiment.
Every night the counselors of the original Project 50 had gathered
for Mass, and although we did not explicitly mention religion to
the students, we prayed for them and did not hesitate to let them
know that the directors and the counselors were inspired primarily
by religious, not social, much less racial motivations. We all professed our belief that education was important, and we wanted to
share our belief with the students for their sake and for the sake of
their communities, which we hoped they would acquire the necessary tools to serve. In one of his visits to San Jose, Cesar Chavez
learned about Project 50 and sent his approval and encouragement.
Finally, Mr. Fessio had the foresight to understand the enormous
pastoral significance of introducing students to the truth, and they
were inclined to accept more easily the principle of noncontradiction than the few self-appointed rebels among the collegians.

There were other activities he plotted out at the time, and they
met with amazing success. One was a students' pilgrimage based
on the famous *Pèlerinage des Étudiants à Chartres*, undertaken each
year from Paris to Chartres. For the selected, limited number of
Santa Clara students, the point of departure was to be the mission
church at Soledad and the point of arrival, the mission church at
San Juan Bautista. Highway traffic forced the point of departure to
be changed to the Old Coach Road, a short distance from Soledad
and a modest substitute for Paris. Mr. Fessio plotted out the two-
day route, obtaining permission from ranchers in this Steinbeck
country to walk through their properties and to use their barns and
fields for Mass, eating, resting, and a sleeping stopover. His ability

to reconnoiter the terrain, provide food and drink for the thirty or so pilgrims, and to plot out the unmarked route through fields and over hills was admirable, although not surprising, given his ability to step up to the plate in facing a challenge. And that challenge was real. All had to be hurriedly planned between preparing for and giving classes. The theme chosen for meditation and prayer along the silent walk was "Vocation", and we used an adaptation of the dialogue between Usbek and Rica in Montesquieu's *Persian Letters* for the format of the dialogue. As we were entering our terminal point, the small town of San Juan Bautista, we were pelted with a shower of stones hurled by an otherwise harmless gang, an event that made later recollections of the pilgrimage more colorful. Without further adventures, we managed to reach the mission, made famous by Hitchcock in his movie *Vertigo*, to celebrate Mass, and then board transportation vehicles that had been organized by Mr. Fessio to drive us back to Santa Clara. The pilgrimage was a stimulating, prayerful, long-remembered experience, as those former students we encounter today are quick to testify.

In 1968, Father Patrick Donohoe was appointed provincial of the California Province, and Father Thomas Terry was elected to take his place as president of the university. Shortly afterward, Mr. Fessio received notice that the provincial wished to see him. Older Fathers might have been taken aback had such a notice been delivered to them, but it was so especially rare for a *scholastic* to receive one that indeed no recorded account of such a summons could be found. Was Father Copeland's wished-for stockade about to become a reality and set up in the old cemetery beside the mission church? Such was the question on Joe's mind, as we drove up to San Francisco, parked the car before the steps that climbed up to the provincial's palatial, foreboding residence on Lyon Street—long since abandoned—rang the bell, and said a Hail Mary as we awaited the opening of the door.

Father Patrick Donohoe was a brilliant, laid-back, kindly, gracious, and somewhat enigmatic Jesuit, spiced with good-natured cynicism. In addition to these qualities, he was a holy priest, which he was quick to cover up with a clinging cloud of cigar smoke. His Jesuit brother had been a missionary in China and afterward exiled to Taiwan, where he was then stationed. Another brother, a bishop, had the same qualities as Patrick, but rather than being hidden, they were ostentatious, giving him the reputation of being a great wit and a shrewd but fatalistic administrator whom one confronted at risk. His sister was a religious of the Sacred Heart—modestly balancing out many of her brothers' qualities—who was mellowed by the sorrowful process of watching her distinguished religious order slowly melt away. Father Donohoe would often joke about his intent on sending a letter to the Jesuit general in Rome suggesting a "redwood curtain" be built about the California Province, protecting it from viruses "blowing in from Woodstock [Maryland], St. Louis, and Wisconsin". Whether he put his intentions into an envelope or not will be the job of future historians to ascertain. He manifested an open distaste for Jesuits who were beginning to sport salon-pampered facial hair, having a special abhorrence for the lone moustache. "Utter decadence", he would say, shrugging his shoulders with a laugh.

Although none of these prejudices were known at the time, Mr. Fessio had instinctively retired his Fu Manchu 'stache and had dressed himself in attire proper for the visit. When we were admitted to his presence, the provincial wanted to know all about the progress of Project 50 and then asked Joe to follow him to the TV room so that he could continue watching a show we had interrupted. Twenty minutes later, Joe rejoined me, ready to go back to Santa Clara. What had happened in that interview? Seated in one comfortable chair, the provincial invited his subject to sit in another. Then during the TV advertisements, he proceeded to joke a bit about Joe's relationship with Father Copeland, assuring him that no potential stockade had been noted on the budget. Next, out of nowhere, with a chuckle, he dropped a bombshell: "Have you ever thought about going to Europe for theology?" Joe's days as a teaching scholastic at Santa Clara would be coming to an end in a few months' time, and his next assignment would be at a house of studies where he would spend four years mastering the science of theology. After the third year, he would be ordained a priest. He offered a respectful negative response to the provincial's question. "Why don't you think about it?"

The subject was then dropped, and abruptly the provincial asked Joe what he thought about next year's prospects for the 49ers. The question went unanswered because the TV ad was over; the show had resumed, gracious adieux were exchanged, and Joe and I found ourselves back in the car headed home. We discussed the topic of theology in France—not Europe—as we drove along the same highway on which, twelve years earlier, he had been distracted by flashing red lights behind him and then, a few years later, he went skidding circles over the double line and back again. France—was there something prescient here? I refrained from telling him that Father Donohoe had spoken to me earlier in an informal, cryptic, surprisingly frank conversation. He realized that the objections to Joe's behavior were of no serious account. In fact, he laughed; they were humorous. Though Joe might have been hippie-like in the exterior, Father Donohoe knew he was orthodox, and he knew that he was intellectually and spiritually gifted to a marked degree. All the more reason, he said, why he should not make his theological studies in the California Province theologate, which he admitted he did not hold in high regard. Confirming this prejudice, he noted the faculty there had already indicated they would not uphold Pope Paul VI's teachings contained in the encyclical *Humanae Vitae*, which had been published the previous year. Before we reached Santa Clara, Joe shouted, "I am going to do theology in France!" Yes, I thought, for Joe it was the *preux* thing to do.

3

HENRI DE LUBAC

Joseph Fessio's new home, the Jesuit theologate, was situated on the crest of the hill of Fourvière, a district within the city of Lyon—*forum vetus* (old forum)—built by the Emperor Trajan, who ruled the Roman Empire from A.D. 98 to 117. From the backside of the building that housed a community of about one hundred Jesuits, there was a panoramic view of the city, the confluence of the Rhône and Saône Rivers, and the far distant mountains to the east. At the end of the sloping garden were the remains of a Roman wall, and less than one hundred yards to the north was the famous Basilica of Notre-Dame de Fourvière that dominates the city. As with its counterpart, the Sacré-Cœur Basilica in Paris, construction on Notre-Dame began in 1870, at the end of the Franco-Prussian War, as a tribute to the Blessed Virgin, who had protected Lyon from a belligerent assault, but the building was not completed until just two years or so before Monsieur Fessio's arrival. The local *Lyonnais* like to remind visitors that this monumental masterpiece of nineteenth-century Romanesque and Byzantine art resembles an elephant lying on its back with its four legs lifted skyward. The early morning bells from the tower of *la Sainte-Vierge* not only had the ability to awaken the newly arrived Monsieur Fessio from his sleep, but, he reckoned, also had the might to knock him out of bed. Like so much of the ambience of his new surroundings, he found it a challenge to absorb all of the history and art that demanded his whirling attention and that distracted him at times from the need to learn, understand, and converse in French. But, as we have seen, Monsieur Fessio thrives on the call to take part in any contest, and so he met that demand with proficiency, if not ease.

From the early 1930s to 1950, the theologate housed a group of Jesuit scholars known as *les nouveaux théologiens*, or members of the Fourvière School, about which more will be noted. The passing into history of this famous group did not affect the religious *modus vivendi* of the theologate, which remained on course in the strict style characteristic of Jesuit houses of study until it sloughed into more relaxed features in the wake of Vatican II. This was evidenced by the abandonment of cassocks, the flexibility of the daily schedule, and a more open-to-the-world syllabus in the classrooms. In the mid-1970s, shortly after Father Joseph left Fourvière, the community moved to Paris. The historic building was sold and became a school of dance—an irony that merits a reverential silence.

Meanwhile, despite the dispersal of the *nouveaux théologiens*, as soon as he arrived, Joe had made a resolution to be a serious student, but flexible, as accommodating as possible in adjusting to French culture. One of the first goals was to comply with a practice he had stubbornly resisted up until now. He would begin drinking wine with his meals, in order to be French with the French. He would not be "singular", as Rodriguez would have put it. Lyon stands at the southern end of the small Beaujolais wine district, and so the seminary's cheap-to-buy *vin ordinaire* would have received the highest recommendations of sommeliers in the most expensive American restaurants. At Fourvière, wine was drunk with characteristic French moderation at the daily principal meal, where silence was no longer observed. Joe began mixing his wine with water, probably much to the amusement, if not horror, of his companions, but he slowly graduated to appreciating it in its pure form as a vehicle for enhancing both conversation and the lyonnaise cuisine. Lyon, indeed, is France's epicurean capital, where the principal meal of the day is served in small-sized courses at unhurried intervals to enhance the social and gastronomical experience. This was not Joe's first culinary adventure, although the ones before had been of a far less satisfying nature. As an underweight high school student, desperate to make the varsity baseball team, he would force himself to eat a dozen eggs, along with his ordinary breakfast, and would then arm himself with a number of fat sandwiches to stuff away at lunch. All of this effort led to no success. He stayed skinny no matter how much he ate. Then in college, he read an article about an experiment in which over a period of time, one set of rats was fed a generous, calorie-filled diet while another was given sparse food of a non-nutritional nature. The first group fared better, but they all died before any from the second group. In a typical Fessio fashion, Joe immediately gave up eating three meals a day, restricting himself to two in austere moderation. During these initial days at Fourvière, he also learned to take advantage of hopping on one of the seminary's many *mobylettes* (mopeds), and with a few companions he would ride out to the countryside to lunch on fruit, cheese, and *charcuterie*. These day-off excursions to small villages, rural areas, and vineyards gave him an appreciation for peasant life as well as for those who lived close to the soil, and, as we shall see, this made an impression that has remained with him ever since. He recalls today, "France to me is a little garden."

However, he had been assigned there to learn theology, even though Father Donohoe probably would not have been too concerned if the young scholastic sometimes put aside his books to feast on *quenelles* and buzz about on his moped. So how was theology taught there in Lyon? Compared to theologates throughout the Catholic world at that time, Fourvière's ratings were far above the average. In the early 1960s, Pope Saint John XXIII, who had the reputation of taking two steps forward and then one backward, had directed that seminary professors should teach their classes in Latin, but because the post–World War II Jesuit professors in France protested that they had either forgotten Latin or had never learned it well, the lectures were given in French. The faculty was orthodox, maintaining a hands-off approach to the ongoing squabbles initiated years earlier in response to their own theologians. While advocating the spirit behind the *aggiornamento*, the Fourvière faculty certainly did not hold that Thomistic Scholasticism was *dépassé*, at least not altogether, or that it had been made irrelevant by the method of Kant and the insights of Darwin, Freud, and Marx. On the contrary, they were, with some exceptions, defenders of Scholasticism, to a degree, as well as quiet and firm supporters of traditional Catholic teaching on moral matters. Joe admitted it took him a longer time to follow the lectures than he had anticipated, but as we have seen, he is a man of hard, systematic discipline, and when he sets his mind to doing something, he does it with persistence. Consequently, much of what he learned of the science of theology was self-taught, and thanks to the rich veins of knowledge flowing through the house library beckoning him to tap into their precious bounty, his experience was as satisfying as it was enjoyable. He also took advantage of German classes given on the French radio because so many of the books and journals in the library were written in that language.

He had the intention necessary to be a good theologian. "From my earliest days," he recalls, "I came to the conclusion that the Catholic faith was true and that the Catholic tradition developed in a way that was rich, and I was just a small part coming into this historically vast Church." He goes on:

> Yes, you can see pictures of me with my guitar and a little cross strung around my neck. So, I did edgy things externally, but internally I was always sound. People ask me, "How were you not affected?" I could never understand those [heterodox] people. I could never understand people who call themselves Catholic, but do not accept the teachings of the Church. What is the problem? Women priests? Don't you get it? Christ is the bridegroom! Homosexual unions? Don't you understand the human body and its reproductive system? It is hard for me to get into the minds of people who think much differently from the way I think. So maybe I have been inoculated against heterodoxy by my lack of ability to understand the positions of other people.

It was perhaps an evaluation more modest than real, but this erstwhile high school star on Bellarmine's debating team remains a formidable force when it comes to supporting objective truth, and he has a style that is as simple and direct as it is unpretentious; yet devastating for those holding an opposing view.

"The year I got to France", he remembers, "was the year the polarization around *Humanae Vitae* in the United States became perceptible. I read the encyclical and said to myself, 'That makes perfect sense.' I got into debates with those who were against it. I listened to their arguments, but I just couldn't go along with their logic." Father Donohoe would have chuckled and approved, and Joe would soon learn that others in his new community would welcome his direct, simple style of argumentation delivered in intelligible, though still bungled French.

One of the warmest welcomes Joe received in his new home was from a seventy-four-year-old priest who lived as a member of the community but did not teach in the classroom, for he had been forbidden to do so. His name was Père Henri de Lubac, and although Joe certainly knew him by reputation—he was the most distinguished of *les nouveaux théologiens*—he had no inkling at the time what influence this charming old man was to have on him, right up to the present day. It might appear curious that Père de Lubac would take much notice of the arrival of one more scholastic whom he would never be able to encounter in a classroom setting, but in the priest's eyes, Joe was exceptional: he was American, and de Lubac had a special place in his heart for Americans. There is a common belief that the French do not like Americans. I have not found that to be true. Just as some New York merchants can become impatient with people not used to big city manners, so some Parisians can be short with American tourists. The farther one gets from metropolitan Paris, the more tolerant Frenchmen seem to be of American ways. Among the older generation, an affection for American GIs lives on, and many who had contact with U.S. soldiers delight in recounting anecdotes about their generosity, humility, and friendliness, in particular about how so many of them attended Mass and participated in the sacraments. Once, an old French Jesuit surprised me by affirming that any people who could turn out the Marx Brothers, Mae West, W. C. Fields, and John Wayne had to be great. Such models may not have engendered an admiration for Americans in Henri de Lubac, but they probably would not have discouraged it, either. Even though he could not speak or understand English, his respect for *la culture anglo-saxonne* was genuine and unapologetic.

Shortly after his meeting with de Lubac, Joe remembers going up to the library alone and picking out a volume containing the writings of Saint Irenaeus, who died in Lyon in A.D. 202. As he sat there relishing the text, he could not help holding back a rush of tears. "It was so beautiful", he recalled. "I felt that Saint Irenaeus was here with me, speaking to me through the text, and I was overwhelmed by the connection of almost eighteen hundred years." Given the character and disposition of Joseph Fessio, people find it hard to believe that he would even know what a teardrop was. Yet simple things, sentimental things, pious things, innocent things affect him deeply, and he is not averse to giving in to what spiritual writers term "the gift of tears". It was a grace with which Saint Ignatius Loyola was generously endowed.

In a very short time, de Lubac and Fessio became like Socrates and Plato. The glue that solidified this union was the topic of the

Fathers of the Church. The younger man would search out the older priest to discuss current theological problems, and he would be given surprising insights into the rich and relatively unknown tradition of the Church. At the same time, he would seek guidance in spiritual matters from his newly found mentor. The older man eventually prevailed upon the younger in more mundane affairs like answering his correspondence and managing his appointments, and then, too, the preceptor would never let his tyro become too serious, a task that was not demanding for de Lubac for he was a very simple Frenchman with a great sense of humor. I recall one time, after he had shared a *pranzo* with Pope Saint John Paul II, someone asked him, as the Catholic world's most renowned theologian, what he was thinking as he sat at table with the Holy Father. He replied, "Le vin était ordinaire et le fromage, vulgaire"—the wine was common table variety, and the cheese, tasteless. So much for the difference between essence and existence.

In order to appreciate Joseph Fessio's development during this period of his Jesuit formation, and to understand better his motivations as a priest, theologian, and publisher, it is essential to become better acquainted with the background and personality of Henri de Lubac. We should give a brief reconstruction of the times, places, and conditions that formed the framework of his world, so as to understand better his resolve to turn to the Fathers of the Church, the *ressourcement*, and to consider certain propositions of modern philosophers as ways of meeting the intellectual and religious challenges of the age in which he was living. The times into which Henri de Lubac was born were complex. They marked an end of an era, some factors of which had been dying for a generation: optimistic faith in scientific, industrial, and economic progress; Romanticism in the arts; and a sharp divide between various classes within society, as well as within the intellectual life of the Church. The French Revolution of 1789 had divided France into two separate worlds, and with the establishment of the Third Republic in 1870 came the triumph of *laïcité*, militantly anti-Catholic secularism that saw Christianity as an enemy of humanity. A besieged political Catholic minority, *les intégraux*, became identified with the reestablishment of crown and altar and found allies in the military, nobility, and some elements of the bourgeoisie. The Dreyfus Affair of

1896–1899, which was the catalyst that solidified *laïcité*, had long since won the allegiance of the press and a sizable majority of the intellectual and artistic classes.

In 1913, the eighteen-year-old de Lubac entered the Jesuits. The novitiate had been set up in Protestant England since 1879, the year in which the Jesuits were exiled from Catholic France. Then, when World War I was declared in 1914, the French government ordered de Lubac and other able-bodied Jesuits back to France and put them in the infantry. Like his confrere Pierre Teilhard de Chardin, young private de Lubac was seriously wounded in the trenches during the Battle of Verdun in 1917, and he never fully regained his health, but he used his long recuperative years with great profit, reading through and studying diligently the 221 volumes of Jacques-Paul Migne's *Patrologia Latina* (which contains the works of Saint Irenaeus), and the 165 volumes of his *Patrologia Graeca*. This monumental opus was published between 1844 and 1858, and its purpose was to make available the original writings of the Fathers of the Church.

The Great War. To this day, such is the designation used in France to distinguish that conflict from World War II. It ended in 1918, after which France tallied up some five million soldiers who either lost their lives or were severely wounded on the battlefields (of the 841 exiled Jesuits compelled to serve in the army, 164 were killed). What was the effect of this zeitgeist on the Catholic Church, which was so wrapped up in her continuous struggle with the secular government and the Modernist crisis, whose proponents had been condemned by Pius X in 1907? Exhausted and disoriented, the intellectual Catholic Right seemed to retreat into a cocoon-like shelter where *les intégraux* of the Action française movement could console themselves with memories of the glorious Middle Ages and take consolation in a particular form of Neo-Thomism, which some Catholic thinkers asserted had become conducive to sterile, abstract, ivory-tower speculation. Since Church-supporting political leaders were still reeling from the consequences of the Dreyfus Affair, they timidly, fitfully attempted a mild reaction against the government in power. Meanwhile, the Catholic Left was drawn to a flirtatious relationship with newly discovered Marxism. Going back as far as 1904, the Catholic Left became vocal in calling attention to the Church's neglect of the social condition of the poor, and it promoted the need for unions and pressed for a more democratic form of government. After the Great War, it became involved in the widely supported Action catholique and the Jeunesse ouvrière chrétienne (JOC), which were social action and religious revolutionary projects.

Prior to 1914, the only Catholic thinker who won a limited respect from the anticlerical university elite was an intellectual named Maurice Blondel, whose integrated philosophy emphasized that man was created for the supernatural, the beatific vision. His influence was not limited to France; he was considered by some to have put the finishing touches on the so-called Catholic Tübingen School in Germany. Prior to the Great War, he had a profound influence on a Jesuit scholastic named Pierre Rousselot, who was later killed on the battlefield. The philosophy of these two men—which some today consider to have sown the seeds of phenomenology and existentialism that flowered after World War II—had a profound and lasting effect on Henri de Lubac and a number of other young Jesuits whose studies were interrupted by the war. They became convinced that the triumph of secularism in France could be met only by abandoning what they considered the fossilized Neoscholasticism that prevailed throughout the Catholic intellectual world. According to the Jesuit theologian Léonce de Grandmaison, who taught young exiled French Jesuits before the Great War, this theology had become ineffectual because the Neoscholastics failed to see the importance of history in the development of dogma. Declining to enter into the fierce debates of the Catholic anti-Modernists, de Grandmaison attempted to reconcile the philosophical tenets of Thomism with the convictions of modern society and the advancement of science. His own pupils in turn would become the professors of the rising stars of la nouvelle théologie, for whom de Lubac was an outstanding spokesman. Father de Lubac would later acknowledge de Grandmaison as "the great master", who in turn was indebted to Blondel's philosophical school of thought. To the young postwar Jesuits like de Lubac, de Grandmaison appeared as a kind of intermediary between Catholic philosophy and laïcité in general, and in particular between the theology and social thinking of the Catholic Right and the Catholic Left. In general, these young Jesuits took a

cautious stand against the older generation of Jesuits, who were proponents of Neoscholasticism, as interpreted by the Suárezian school.
Although these proponents of *la nouvelle théologie* in no way espoused
the tenets of Modernism, they recognized that the Modernists—
even though their answers were wrong—continued to pose relevant questions and that these questions had not yet been given satisfactory answers. They became advocates of making philosophy
and theology more meaningful and attractive in form so that they
again might be effective vehicles for bringing the Gospel message
to men and women in the postwar era of widespread agnosticism
and pessimism.

For these proponents of *la nouvelle théologie*, Neoscholasticism was
a failure. Worse, perhaps *it*, rather than Luther, Descartes, Hegel,
or Kant, had been the real cause of modern materialism. The
Neoscholastics were so intent on proving the existence of a Prime
Mover, a cold God, on proving the triumph of reason, that they
missed the intimate relish of knowing the God who fills and satisfies
the soul. They resisted the philosophy of Saint Thomas Aquinas by
failing to bring his theories up to date with the advance of modern
scientific research. Such was a thesis that de Lubac would later develop. Meanwhile, his wartime experience and that of his confrères
further confirmed for them that Blondel was right when he taught
that the present despairing age called for reassessing the manner and
language of presenting dogmatic truths and theological teachings.
Their experience of living in the trenches confirmed their philosophical convictions. In the trenches, they had been forced to live
in close proximity with comrades from backgrounds very different
from their own, but they came to see that each one, because of
his human nature, had an inbuilt desire for God, for the beatific
vision, even though each one's history and his environment may
have darkened his orientation, leading to skepticism, materialism,
sensualism, and nihilism. In this respect, these men in the trenches
were no different from every human being. Like seeds in a parched
desert that need water to enliven them, these men needed grace,
given by Christ through the sacraments of the Church. The Jesuits
of de Lubac's circle saw there was a certain urgency to mediate that
grace, and this was a persuasion they shared with the Dominican
theologians of the Le Saulchoir School, especially Marie-Dominique
Chenu and Yves Congar, and, in a different manner, with secular

intellectuals after World War II who espoused existentialism. But
the conclusion de Lubac and his friends drew at the time was that
the Church should encourage missionaries, at home and abroad, to
learn about, affirm, and be more willing to appreciate, rather than
condemn, every perspective of modern thinkers and also to be open
to the modern world, while being uncompromising in support of
the Ordinary Magisterium of the Church.[1] The pages that follow
are designed to show how influential this Lubacian background has
been in molding the various projects designed by the missionary
for our times, Father Fessio.

The period after the war was termed the Roaring Twenties in
the United States, and in France it was dubbed *les années folles*, a period of great economic growth and restlessness. It was the age of
Marcel Proust and Dadaism; of the Lost Generation; of Art Deco
and jazz; of Pablo Picasso and Josephine Baker; of the birth of the
French Communist Party and the Front populaire. By that time,
the perennial battles between the Church and the state had come to
resemble a contest between two exhausted wrestlers. This enabled
the Jesuits, many of whom were veterans, to set out with stealthy
steps and settle in soundlessly at Fourvière, re-establishing their theologate. In this house, de Lubac continued preparation for his ordination to the priesthood, which took place in 1938, and Joseph
Fessio eventually made his appearance in 1969. In the meantime, emphasizing the importance of historical *mise-en-scène* in understanding
and appreciating the development of Catholic doctrine, de Lubac
immersed himself in the writings of Saint Thomas Aquinas, while
at the same time recognizing a need to study and appreciate the works
of modern philosophers—Hegel, Husserl, and Kierkegaard—
as well as the artistic accomplishments of novelists, especially
Dostoevsky. Eventually, he and his group became known as proponents of the Fourvière School, or, as their critics dubbed them, devo-
tees of *la nouvelle théologie*, whose philosophy was built on the twin
foundations of classic patristic and medieval theology—soldered
to the New Testament—and a Blondelian anthropology, communicated through a modern idiom. Meanwhile, during these years,

---

[1] This subject is well documented in Jon Kirwan, *An Avant-Garde Theological Generation: The Nouvelle Théologie and the French Crisis of Modernity* (Oxford: Oxford University
Press, 2018).

France watched with mounting terror the military build-up of Germany, and with pessimistic resignation, she saw Hitler occupy the Rhineland in 1926, annex Austria in 1938, and invade Czechoslovakia and Poland in 1939. World War II had begun, and for her it ended quickly.

At the cessation of hostilities in France in 1940, until 1944, the country was divided into spheres, the northern two-thirds occupied by the German army and the southern section governed from Vichy by the hero of the Great War, General Pétain. It was in the Vichy section where Father de Lubac remained, and it was here that he played an important role in the Resistance movement, founding in 1941 the influential journal *Témoignage chrétien* and cooperating conjointly with Communists, Catholic Right patriots, and others who were part of the potpourri underground movement. He was also responsible for the rescue of many Jews. In August of 1944, the war ended, but the joy of that event was significantly modified for him and the members of the Fourvière School by the recent publication of the book *La France, pays de mission?* In it the authors Henri Godin and Yvan Daniel argued convincingly that the Church had lost the working and the economically poor classes in France. As a result, in the post–World War II late 1940s, there was a surge of support for the social action agenda of the Catholic Left that ran in tandem with the popularity of the Left throughout the country. As a result of this sobering sociopolitical situation, de Lubac and the members of the Fourvière School became prominent in the movement for change and sympathetic to the rising tide of existentialism. But there was a price to pay for their seeming chumminess with Communists and enemies of the Church. Beginning in 1946, the Toulouse Dominicans sharply criticized the Fourvière School in their periodical *Revue thomiste*, claiming that the advocates of *la nouvelle théologie* movement were guilty of reasserting Modernist principles and advocating relativism. The result was that in August 1950, Pius XII issued *Humani Generis*, effectively silencing both sides. Father de Lubac's superiors had already given him assignments outside of Lyon. Then in 1958, he returned and was reassigned to teaching, but in a non-Jesuit institution. In 1960, the newly elected Pope John XXIII appointed him a consultant for the Preparatory Theological Commission for the proposed Second Vatican Council. He was a *peritus* during the council and as such exercised considerable influence on mapping out the final decrees of that momentous event.[2]

This short summary of de Lubac's life and historical milieu should offer a better understanding of Father Joseph Fessio's development after the year 1970. Hopefully in the pages to come the reader will detect echoes of Blondel and de Grandmaison, along with more obvious insights from de Lubac and Hans Urs von Balthasar, and perhaps—having seen some of the tensions at work within the Church in France—will better understand what took place in the United States around the 1960s. Could there be a parallel here explaining why, beginning at that time, the Church in the United States lost so many of her Catholic-educated young? If so, might something have been done to prevent it? Are such questions helpful in appreciating better the motives for various projects adopted by Father Fessio that will be described in later chapters? Read on and see.

---

[2] See Henri de Lubac, *Vatican Council Notebooks*, 2 vols., trans. Andrew Stefanelli and Anne Englund Nash (San Francisco: Ignatius Press, 2015–2016).

4

TO INDIA AND BACK

Given Father Henri de Lubac's theological propensities, it should come as no surprise that he took an interest in non-Christian religions. Indeed, he became a recognized authority on Buddhism, after having published three books on the subject between 1951 and 1953. He had also gotten acquainted with l'Abbé Jules Monchanin, a true intellectual with an impressive library of Hindu studies. At the time, Monchanin was serving as a parish priest in Lyon, having retired there after a fruitful life in India, and he soon became a close friend and tutor in Indian studies to a most eager pupil, Henri de Lubac. In 1938, Monchanin and the Benedictine monk Henri Le Saux founded the Saccidananda Ashram in the village of Tanniapalli, Tamil Nadu, India, where they adapted, in imitation of the seventeenth-century Jesuit Roberto de Nobili, the life-style of Hindu holy men. But it soon became evident that each had developed fundamentally different approaches to the principle of adaptation. Monchanin, in accordance with de Lubac's theory of accommodation, believed in Christianizing Hinduism, while Le Saux appeared to be of the opinion that a Christian missionary immersed in Hinduism was equipped rather to Hinduize Christianity.

At a later date, Le Saux separated himself from the ashram to become a hermit, and eventually the English Benedictine Bede Griffiths took his place and began to propagate the belief that all religions were an experience of God and that no one could claim pure truth, which was unknowable, and therefore a broad type of ecumenism was to be fostered. For some, the "spirit of Vatican II" aligned with this thinking, becoming in the United States a kind of Neo-Catholicism. This view explains so much of the late 1960s and early 1970s: religious services in the back rooms of Santa Clara Mission; a Berrigan brother giving the Eucharist to a Muslim, the popularity of Rosemary Ruether. Given this background, it is understandable why Fessio became fascinated by de Lubac's conversations with him on the topic of Hinduism. Then too, we should recall that as a beginning freshman at Santa Clara, he said he was not much interested in theoretical engineering as a study. Rather, he wanted "to test materials, concrete and steel, stone and lumber, that sort of thing". So, it is not surprising that he had to experience, not only learn about, the social and religious culture of India. He wanted to see for himself what tools were best fit for the project of Christianizing the Hindus, "so that at last they may have light", as the Vatican II document expressed it. His opportunity to do so came at the end of the first year at Fourvière, shortly after the return from his venture in Rome with Father de Lubac, which we will explore later. For the present, he was planning an ambitious undertaking that promised to make riding a bike from Chicago to Santa Clara seem minor in comparison. It is also an example that stands in contrast to the theologate's strict regulations of but a few years earlier, when one needed special permission to travel even a short distance from Lyon and when pocket money was given sparingly.

As soon as classes were terminated in the summer of 1970, Joe persuaded two fellow scholastics—an American, Jim Joseph, and a Swiss, Georges Enderle—to drive with him to India. They pooled their resources and purchased a *deux-chevaux* (2CV), which was a marvelous vehicle, a two-cylinder Citroën, small and durable. Because it had collapsible removable rear seating, Joe was able to take out the back seat and lay down in its place a piece of plywood with a mattress on top. This makeshift bed, however, was longer than the car, so it stuck out of the back hatch, enclosed by a low hand-built wall. As we have seen, when he was a student at Santa Clara, he had experienced sleeping on mattress-covered plywood during his flight to Chicago for the bicycle trek, but that bedding was downright luxurious compared to what was now in store for the adventurers. The threesome left Lyon, and, after driving across eastern France and northern Italy, they entered what was then Yugoslavia and then sped through Bulgaria and Turkey to reach and pass through Iran and Afghanistan. From there they made a bumpy way down through Pakistan, finally arriving at their stopover destination, New Delhi. They traveled some 6,000 miles in six days and nights, alternating drivers and stopping only for gas, food, and essentials. Joe did most of the driving while the other two tried to rest or sleep. "I was driving sixteen hours a day," Father Fessio recalls, "and when I got to New Delhi, I just collapsed, I was exhausted. So then we drove to Calcutta and stayed with the Jesuits there." At Calcutta (today Kolkata), "we didn't meet Mother Teresa, but we had heard about her." In later years, Father Fessio and Mother Teresa would forge a close friendship, but that is subject matter for a later chapter. The leg of the journey from New Delhi to Calcutta was a stop-and-go affair, convincing Jim Joseph that he had had enough of driving, and it took little coaxing to convince him to stay there with the hospitable Calcutta Jesuit community to recuperate. But Joe had to visit the Tamil country. So he and Georges squeezed once more into the *deux-chevaux* and headed south. As in the Chicago bike ride, three started, but only two finished.

At Madras, now called Chennai, they met the Jesuit Father Pierre Ceyrac, something of a lesser-known counterpart of Mother Teresa. Ceyrac had arrived in India from his native France in 1937. Before entering the Jesuits, he had studied Sanskrit at the Sorbonne, and in India he received a degree in Tamil enabling him to become a respected professor at a local Jesuit college. But soon he reflected: "How can I philosophize in a university while people are dying right beside the walls?" He then petitioned and obtained permission to leave the classroom and immerse himself in the life of the poor. Thus began his extraordinary career. Ceyrac's question to himself was reminiscent of a similar query addressed to Father Fagothey during a town-and-gown forum when Mr. Fessio was teaching at Santa Clara. "Father," one of the outside invitees asked on that occasion, "you are living in this ivory tower and you're teaching students philosophy. But what about the poor? What are you doing for people who are really hurting in the world?" Unfazed, Fagothey answered: "Everyone is born spiritually and intellectually poor. Someone has to enrich them with wisdom and knowledge, and that is my task." It was a question and answer that Mr. Fessio rehearsed over and over in his memory and would have the effect of inspiring him to take on projects right to the present day.

Father Ceyrac's reflections likewise led him to action. He immersed himself in Indian customs and religions, declaring, "There are many paths to God." He asserted firmly that his particular mission was to eschew all forms of politics. He fought "not for human rights but the right to be human", with the result that he solidified a close friendship with Mahatma Gandhi and won the admiration and encouragement of Jawaharlal Nehru for his work. Eventually he was put in charge of the All India Catholic University Federation in which there were some 100,000 young people, and in 1957 he directed a large number of them to build a town—Cherian Nagar was its name—in which 20,000 Christians, Hindus, and Muslims lived together in peace and growing prosperity. "He was tremendously impressive," Father Fessio recalls, remembering their first meeting in Madras, "[dressed as he was in his] white cassock that was dirty and sweaty because of all the work he did. But he had got the students, the Jesuit students from this college, and gone to the city council in Madras and asked for a piece of land that was abandoned in the middle of the city. He said, 'I want this land, and we're going to build a place for the street people, because the people live on the sidewalks, you know, and die in the gutters.'" They gave it to him. Joe reported: "He wanted to build nice little huts for them. So we wanted him to show that to us. So we went out there." Running well water was the first thing Ceyrac installed in the area. "Not each hut had [water], but there was always a place with a basin and a place to wash and everything, running water and a place to go to the bathrooms. Each hut was made out of bricks four or five feet above the ground, cement floor and then poles and then a thatched roof, very clean, very beautiful." Such was the conclusion of the man whose earlier life had been so influenced by *The Ugly American*. As Ceyrac escorted the two scholastics through the town, people came pouring out to greet him. "They thronged to him," Joe recalls, "bowed down, tried to kiss his feet, he kept trying to push them away, push them away, but they loved him so much." Joe recounted that the nuns who were teaching little girls to sing hymns also had a powerful emotional impact on him, and it is a scene still very much alive in his memory.

The following day, Ceyrac wanted to give him and Georges a look at his newest dream, a cooperative farm called the Thousand Wells Project begun less than two years earlier in Manamadurai, Tamil Nadu, to train mainly poor "untouchables" how to farm on reclaimed land. In order to arrive at their destination, Joe had to persuade the *deux-chevaux* to bump over dry, rocky, roadless land, where soon there would be paved streets, clinics, wells, schools, and colleges in order to accommodate more than 250,000 people in what was to become the largest guava-producing area in India. Father Ceyrac, of course, is not the topic of this study, although his life demands a biography. But because he had so many character traits, aspirations, and ambitions similar to those of Father Fessio, it would be inappropriate to leave him without a brief closure on his later life. In 1980, the Jesuit Refugee Service was established as a response to thousands of Cambodians fleeing the Khmer Rouge, and Ceyrac was sent to the Thailand border to care for them. It was a temporary assignment that lasted—thirteen years! Afterward, he was dispatched to Rwanda and given the same job description. In both places, he gave himself to caring with heroic zeal for a countless number of victims of violence and poverty. Finally, in 1990, he returned to his teaching job at Loyola College in Chennai, where he died in 2012 at the age of 97. Meanwhile, in 2005, the secular French government, recognizing his "eminent merit", had received him into the Légion d'Honneur.

Father Ceyrac's insight was that everyone is born spiritually and materially poor, whereas Father Fagothey's contention was that everyone is born spiritually and intellectually poor. The fact is that everyone is born ontologically poor, and poverty is a lack of a potential good. Both Jesuits would have agreed, and their accomplishments argue well that the challenge is to alleviate poverty, not to sit down and pretend to share it with the poor. The latter is a form of narcissism. Change the condition of the poor by teaching the truth or by training them in manual skills, in both cases "so that at last they may have life", as the Vatican II document *Lumen Gentium* reads. In other words, Christ cannot be left out of the equation, and that is why Catholic education and social action differ only in form, not in essence, and why neither should be identified with purely secular social projects or secular institutions of learning. Such was the lesson Father de Lubac impressed upon his eager pupil, and such was the effective stimulus which that pupil would give to his future ventures and endeavors, as we shall see.

In early October of 1971—more than a year after the little Citroën first sputtered to India—Joseph Fessio was working with Father de Lubac in his room when the telephone rang. "Oh, I'd love to come," Joe heard the older man say into the receiver, "but I really can't this year. No, no, I know you'd like me there. But I can't do it." Then, after a few more niceties, de Lubac hung up the telephone. "So what was that about?" Joe asked. "Well, that was Cardinal Villot, the Secretary of State, and he wants me to come to the International Theological meeting this fall, but I really can't because I'm not well and I just can't go alone and there's no one to come with me." "I'll go with you", Joe responded, and so de Lubac immediately dialed back Jean-Marie Cardinal Villot, his old friend from Lyon, explaining to him that thanks to a young Jesuit scholastic from California, he would be attending the conference after all. As it turns out, this is where he would disassociate himself from his crypto-Modernist allies.

As soon as the two arrived at the Bellarmino, a Jesuit residence near the Pantheon, de Lubac took to his bed. Two or three days later, leaning on Joe's arm, they made a slow quarter-mile walk to the Church of St. Louis des Français, the French national church that butts up against the Piazza Navona. There Henri de Lubac began his talk. Joe, seated next to von Balthasar, beheld the dramatic scene. The church was packed with cardinals, bishops, priests, civil politicians, and ordinary lay people. The feted speaker began his lecture in a hushed, trembling voice that soon dramatically picked up volume, enabling his message to echo throughout the spacious enclosure. His topic was the role of Peter and his immediate successors in the early Church, and he peppered what he said with a multitude of extemporaneous quotes from the early Fathers. A thundering applause followed his final words. Afterward, people were all over him, and he cried out to Joe to rescue him and help him back to the Bellarmino. Joe remembers de Lubac's words as they freed themselves from the crowd: "I've done my duty as a Jesuit. I've defended the pope." The next day, Father Pedro Arrupe, the general of the Society of Jesus, sent word that he would like to welcome Father de Lubac at his residence, but de Lubac's reply was that he was too exhausted and could not leave his bed. Father Arrupe then came to the Bellarmino to greet him, and after he left, the bed-ridden de Lubac confided to Joe what he had told him. After reminding the general that Saint Ignatius had founded the Society to defend the Church, and particularly the Roman pontiff, he asserted that in the postconciliar period, "the Society of Jesus is known internationally as opposition to what comes from Rome and opposition to the pope." Finally, the former *peritus* of Vatican II predicted to his humble superior general: "If you continue to let this happen, you will destroy the Society." Undoubtedly, both men bade their farewells in muted sadness.

Mr. Joseph Fessio had been at Fourvière about two years when the new provincial of formation for the California Province, Father Robert Maloney, encouraged him to take his time looking around for a graduate school where he could pursue studies leading to a doctorate in theology. Quite naturally, the first man he consulted on this matter was Father de Lubac, but the old priest ignored his query about where he should study and said: "I would suggest you write your doctorate on Hans Urs von Balthasar. He's the greatest theologian of our time and perhaps of all time." Young Joseph was startled. He felt he already knew de Lubac well, conversed with him frequently, and had read many of his books. He knew he was a very measured person. Although capable of being enthusiastic, excited in friendly conversations, he was an author whose writing was carefully crafted, a lecturer who gave opinions with nuanced deliberation. But this was different. He was so conclusive. Cautiously, Joe asked: "Then who would be a good director for a thesis on von Balthasar?" It was obviously an anticipated question, and de Lubac had an immediate, definite answer. "There's a young theologian from Regensburg, Father Ratzinger, and he's a friend of mine, I'll write to him on your behalf." By this date, Herr Doktor Ratzinger had become a well-known intellectual, and aspiring doctoral students vied with one another to be accepted into his in-group and study under his direction. So it was thanks to his strong ties of friendship with de Lubac that, in the following year, young Joseph Fessio would be able to claim a chair in Ratzinger's close circle of scholars, but it was also thanks to his talents and persistence that he would be able to convince Ratzinger that his friendship with de Lubac would not be a hindrance in this matter, but would pay off in handsome dividends. Those dividends are still being realized, even to the present day, and our purpose now is to trace how events evolved from Fourvière to Regensburg and beyond. But we are getting ahead of ourselves. Let us turn back to the summer of 1971 to accompany him on another classic romp.

Tom Rausch, a former classmate and good friend of Monsieur Fessio, was at the time pursuing his undergraduate studies at the Jesuit
School of Theology at Berkeley (JSTB). Like Joseph Fessio, he, too,
had been asked to investigate various universities where he could
pursue a doctorate in theology. This search put the two of them
in Joe's 2cv, speeding over the Provence hills while arguing over
matters esoteric, as theologians are wont to do. But in Provence?
Well, one must be thorough to be a theologian. According to Joe,
some of whose adventures at the wheel we have already seen, Tom
was as nice a friend as he was a reckless driver. Often, when at
the wheel and hotly arguing with Joe over matters theological, he
would swish over the dividing lines on curves. Finally, the inevitable
occurred. As they were nearing the abbey of Thoronet in Provence,
Tom spun about a bend in the road and hit a car, causing considerable damage to the back left fender of the *deux-chevaux*. "We kind
of taped it on or something", Joe remembers. "And then we were
going up; he wanted to see Dunkirk and the World War II sites."
Questions by service station attendants on the way convinced Joe
he should remove the fender and store it on the back seat. But leaving France and entering into Belgium in a fenderless vehicle could
cause a long delay, and so Joe determined to seek a roundabout
way, a Bertie Wooster solution that wasted no time researching legal pleasantries. At last, in the black hours of night, he found a small
road, unguarded at night, offering an invitation to cross furtively
over the border into Belgium. Congratulating themselves on their
resourcefulness, the two daring young men parked the wounded
deux-chevaux in a hidden grove, unpacked their sleeping bags in total
blackness, and snuggled their tired bodies onto seemingly feather-
soft soil. Providence had smiled upon them.

Tom remembers being awakened around six o'clock the next
morning by a shoe tapping at his face. He jumped up to see himself and Joe surrounded by police. A long session of *tete-à-tete*-ing
ensued. Certainly the two looked like they might have drugs on
them, with their hippie–kitschy wear and unshaven faces. After all,
who but drugged bums would debouch from an invalid auto and
stretch themselves out for the night on the lawn of one of Belgium's
most famous chateaus? After a long investigation and some seemingly senseless questions, the two American Jesuits were able to re-
claim the 2cv and continue putting along, only to be stopped again

by another policeman, who let them go on but warned Joe to do something about the fender on his car. He took pity on the haggard duo, and after promising to fix the fender, the two then made their way to Amsterdam, where Tom caught his plane back to the States and Joe continued to drive to Aachen. At the German border, he found his passport was not enough. Looking at the *deux-chevaux*, the guard asked, "Where is your international decal?" (Decal patches were necessary on all cars—D for Deutschland, F for France, CH for Switzerland, etc.) "You must have a decal on your fender for identification, and you do not have a fender." Joe assured him he did have one lying on the back seat. An inspection was made. "You pass" was the laconic judgment. It was a great lesson for Joe: the law states a decal must be on the fender, but the law does not define where the fender must be: *Non omne licitum honestum*, not everything permissible is proper. So contemplating the possible application of such a principle for possible future confrontations, Father Fessio headed back to Fourviére.

Just a few months later, Mr. Fessio would be ordained in San Francisco and move to Germany. There were a few adventures that awaited him, and some of these we shall recount later. But now, it is proper to follow him as he takes up his new assignment.

5

5

JOSEPH RATZINGER AND
HANS URS VON BALTHASAR

In early June of 1972, Joe left Lyon and boarded a plane bound
for San Francisco, where he was to be ordained a priest on the
tenth of that month by Archbishop Joseph Thomas McGucken in
San Francisco's St. Mary's Cathedral. The archbishop had been an
admirer from afar of Project 50 and had informally advised us how
to navigate through the canonical shoals to obtain his authority to
celebrate weddings at Mission Santa Clara, a practice that up until
then was forbidden but has since become not just possible but popular. One of the Project 50 counselors was the first person to obtain
that long-sought-after permission, which has proved to be such a
blessing for so many couples ever since. During his brief stay in
the States, Joe was also able to fulfill a request made by Father de
Lubac. Present at the 1970 International Theological Commission
meeting in Rome, already described above, had been a number of
well-known theologians, among whom were Louis Bouyer, Hans
Küng, Karl Rahner, Bernard Lonergan, Yves Congar, Louis-Marie
Billé, Hans Urs von Balthasar, and Joseph Ratzinger. Each of these
scholars had published articles from time to time in a journal named
Concilium, which emerged shortly after Vatican II, with a mission
to define and reflect the spirit of the council. But during the course
of time, irreconcilable differences developed among the contrib-
utors on what precisely that spirit was. The result was that during a lunch break at that iconic international conference, de Lubac,
Bouyer, von Balthasar, and Ratzinger decided that another journal
should be founded as a counterweight to what they considered to
be *Concilium*'s misrepresentative interpretations of the council. Joe
found himself at the luncheon table seated in the company of these

theological giants, and he heard them agree that the mission of this new publication would be "to overcome the polarization between 'modernists' and 'traditionalists'" by "renew[ing] theology in continuity with the Christian tradition".[1] It was to be named *Communio*, and it was to be published in various languages across Europe. Later, as Joe was making ready to return to California for ordination, Father de Lubac commissioned him to see if an English language edition of *Communio* could be launched in the United States. This he did. He arranged a meeting with Andrée Emery, a member of Our Lady of the Way, a secular institute, and the translator of a book by von Balthasar; James Hitchcock, a professor of history at Saint Louis University; and David L. Schindler, Sr., a professor at Notre Dame. In 1974, under Schindler's editorship, the journal's English edition was launched, and today *Communio* continues to enjoy worldwide success with fifteen other editions published in thirteen different languages. However important the *Communio* project was—attesting as it did that the beak of the pelican can hold more than his belly can—it was but a distraction from his ordination.

Now, he was finally to realize his long-nurtured hope. Yet the actual experience of ordination fell a trifle short of what his many meditations had assured him it would be. People milling about him, relatives and guests of his fellow *ordinati*, seemed more excited than he. He had never liked being in the spotlight for adulation, and he looked forward to being alone, away from all the fuss, to contemplate in wonderment and gratitude the gift of that priestly stole entrusted to him.

His stay in the United States was surprisingly short, uncomfortable. He was eager to get going toward the challenges that awaited him in his new assignment in Germany. A few short weeks after ordination, he found himself in Regensburg and delighted at meeting a local philosophy professor named Ferdinand Ulrich, a man he would later describe as "one of the greatest contemporary Catholic philosophers", though his writing, in Joe's estimation, was "so convoluted that it is hard for you to understand it". Ulrich's warmth,

---

[1] "Communio: International Catholic Review", SAGE Publications, last updated January 3, 2010, archived at https://web.archive.org/web/20100103235122/https:/www.sagepub.com/journalsProdDesc.nav?prodId=Journal201746; "About Communio", *Communio*, last visited June 1 2022, https://www.communio-icr.com/about.

hospitality, and encouragement were unequaled. Soon after arriving, Joe began spending most evenings with him and his family, mainly, he asserted, to practice chitchatting in German. (Convoluted chitchat? *In German?*) The two remained good friends until Ulrich's death in early 2020.

Father Fessio also had a room in the historic Schottenkloster St. Jakob, which was founded in the eleventh century by Irish monks and where Thomas Aquinas taught for a stint two centuries later. It was during his time in the Schottenkloster that Joseph began a close association with a young Austrian priest, Christoph von Schönborn, who was not a doctoral student, but was assigned to do some interim studies under Ratzinger. The two hit it off well from the beginning, and Joe's friendship with this future cardinal and editor of the *Catechism of the Catholic Church* would mellow and strengthen during the course of the passing years.

In the fall of 1972, he settled into his own quarters. Regensburg may have been a bit different from his "little garden" in Lyon, but he came quickly to appreciate the German genius and the friendliness of the people who welcomed him. The tuition at the university was also attractive—about $5 per year, a charge he incurred only in order to take advantage of the gymnasium and track field, which were not considered tuition-exempt entities at the university.

There were a few doctoral students who met with Father Ratzinger for weekly sessions at which an assigned student would present a brief reflection and suggest some questions. A lively discussion would follow while the professor sat and listened, seldom saying a word. "It was hard for me because my German wasn't good", Father Fessio admits. "And he'd always say, Oh, Fr. Fessio, what's your contribution here, what do you think about this?" Apparently such challenges were met with mutual satisfaction. Toward the end of each class, the priest-professor would "kind of lean back, look above us all, and give four or five big beautiful German sentences. He would summarize all that we'd done in the two hours. . . . And it was just like a little bit of a masterpiece, like the finale of a symphony, you get all the themes and in the last finale they're all woven together with a big crescendo." Father Fessio often met with his monitor outside of class to clarify various points of discussion from the seminar. "To begin with," he says, "we spoke in French because my French was better than my German and his French is perfect. As time went on, I'd speak more in German. But his English had got better . . . and my German worse and worse, so we'd always speak in English." Joe also recalls that in dealing with him, Father Ratzinger was always "very gentle. Wonderful sense of humor. Sort of a soft-key humor, a little irony."

Joe was determined to finish his dissertation (on the ecclesiology of Hans Urs von Balthasar), get his doctorate, and return to the United States as soon as possible. "I loved Europe, . . . but I just wanted to get back home. And I knew I wasn't going to be a great scholar, but I could maybe be a teacher, and I thought I want to get this thing as fast as I can." He had planned that the master's degree in theology from Fourvière, which he completed after the end of his first year in Regensburg, would be the first part of his doctoral dissertation that he planned to finish the following year. It was certainly an ambitious project. But given that Joe is a dynamo, a take-on-tasker, and an energetic worker, it was not surprising to see that he accomplished what he set out to do. From early morning to late at night, when not participating in the required seminars, he was reading and making notes and flashcards on von Balthasar's works, all of which were written in German. The classes proceeded from fall to summer, after which he felt he needed some space and time away from the university, however satisfying it had been. The opportunity came to him like an answered prayer. A U.S. Army chaplain in nearby Amberg needed help. Could Father Fessio come to his aid? Indeed, he could. Could Father Fessio work on his thesis during his off-hours? Why not?

Military conscription was being phased out in the United States in 1972, and so there was a mixture of drafted and voluntarily enlisted soldiers. The result was that the personnel at the Amberg base was a mixed bag, presenting challenges of a different order to Joe. The volunteer soldiers were easier to deal with than the conscripted. The former had elected to sign up, and if they later discovered that they had made a poor decision, they had to take the consequences. They knew they had to serve and bide their time. They knew they would not like it and could not lump it. And so they put up with it. With the conscripted, it was different. Many of them were emotionally immature. They were in a foreign country with too much time on their hands and too little money in their pockets. And so there were more AWOLs among them—much more work for the chaplain. At the same time, there were extraordinary compensations for Father Fessio, and it did not take him long to find them. He discovered a group, made up of officers and enlisted men, Protestant and Catholic, that got together to read and discuss on a regular basis the writings of C. S. Lewis. Shortly before Father Joseph arrived at the base, they had expanded their area of interest to include praying for the trouble-prone conscripts and working to evangelize them. The group immediately became a source of edification and admiration for the new civilian chaplain, and in a very short time he became friends with each one of these men, whom he judged exceptional and inspiring. He was quick to judge that this was the kind of group that could give witness to an authentic ecumenism, the type de Lubac encouraged. They all wanted to know Jesus better and to follow him more closely, and Joe felt that if they were not one in mind and heart on religious matters, they should discuss the issues that divided them, such as prayer, Mary, Purgatory, Mass, the sacraments, and so forth. Some had been brought up to believe that the Catholic Church was the whore of Babylon, but when he talked to the group as a whole, even the Protestants among them became first interested and then enthusiastic about Father's description of the Spiritual Exercises of Saint Ignatius and how it was possible to put into practice meditation and prayers in an eight-day retreat. After some discussion, they responded that as a group, they would like to discern better God's will in their lives and use part of their annual leave time to try to do this. "OK, let's do this", said Father Fessio. "Let's make a pilgrimage retreat. . . . We'll walk from Florence to Assisi, and we'll make an eight-day retreat while we're walking. We'll meditate for four hours a day." It was a modification of the pilgrimage the Project 50 student counselors made in 1968 from the Old Stage Road to Mission San Juan Bautista. When all was ready, Father Fessio, together with fifteen or twenty U.S. soldiers of various rank, boarded a train bound for Florence. On arrival, they walked up to the Dominican monastery of San Marco. Here along the monastery's walls and corridors were famous frescos by Fra Angelico depicting various events in Christ's life.

Father Fessio certainly seemed to have the qualifications that Ignatius outlined for an apt director of his Spiritual Exercises— someone pliant and responsive, without being a commanding-officer type, and with the spirit of the Exercises ingrained in his thinking.

We can trace how he implemented these directives as this diverse Christian group progressed on their first day from San Marco into the Tuscan countryside. "So it started raining", he recalled. By nightfall, the eager retreatants were soaked through and through; their feet sore, not only because of their heavy mud-clogged boots, but also because each one was loaded down with food and supplies. It was at this point that the director spotted a barn a bit distant from the road. "So we just went into the barn, there was a lot of hay there, and so we just lay down in the hay. And this one soldier, he was from Iowa, he said, 'You know, I'm from a farm, I don't think we should be here. If that farmer finds us here he's not going to be happy.'" A needless distraction: the director's determination was to give the men points for their continued reflection and prayers. Trudging through the rain, they had already reflected on and prayed over Ignatius' first meditation, which was the primary and fundamental aspect of one's life: Why was I created? "I was created to love God, that is, to praise, glorify and serve him and by these means to save my soul." Now it was time to consider the follow-up part of this affirmation, the second meditation: the persons, places, and things in my life. "My relations with others, with all beings that enter my life, including my attitude with respect to situations and events in which I find myself involved." But Joe did not get very far. Screaming and yelling interrupted his considered commentary. The sounds came from a man running down the empty road while brandishing a shotgun in one hand and shaking his fist with the other. "We got up, running down the road. . . . He didn't shoot at us, but we were running down this road . . . and we heard the shot going into the trees. He was firing over our heads." So much for "my relations with others who enter my life". So much for "my attitude in respect to situations and events in which I find myself involved". So much for *la dolce far niente* of the Tuscan way of life!

But when they got up the next morning, the August sun was shining. It was warm, Joe recalled. They were rested. They were alive. And during the seven days that followed, they walked all the way down to Assisi in the scorching sun, finished the retreat there, and then made their way back to Germany. On reflection, they realized it was hard to pray when walking twenty-five miles a day on hard roads while loaded down with a backpack. "Although it was very beautiful." Joe concluded. However, the group agreed that,

profitable as the experience was, too many physical demands compromised the ability to reflect and pray well. There was agreement
on Ignatius' dictum that all positions are conducive for prayer, except walking. But for Joe, minor challenges are simply major advantages. He would reconnoiter the terrain, and next summer the
group would meet again for another encounter with the Ignatian
Spiritual Exercises. Meanwhile, there was another expedition begging to be made before Joe returned to Regensburg to prepare for
his next round of seminar classes.

Across from the Amberg chapel was the post school, directed by
Mr. Letch Connell, a civilian instructor with whom Father Fessio
had become a fast and devoted confrere. What drew them together
was their shared admiration for ancient Greek history, literature,
and philosophy. Connell was popular with his students, and so it
was not difficult for him to engender enthusiasm in some of them
about making a trip to Greece in his antiquated jalopy. The parents
of two boys agreed—the car could fit no more than two—provided
that Father Fessio be a part of the expedition. Would Father agree?
How could he refuse! The group of four tucked themselves into
the road-hopper, and off they sallied to the fields of Thermopylae.
In those halcyon days, there were no large busy freeways, and so
when the driver discovered that the first gear on the age-challenged
vehicle was not low enough to make some of the Alpine climbs, he
had to turn the car around, shift it into reverse and back it up over
the grades that led to Italy. Hannibal with his elephants would have
understood. Meanwhile, the one free adult would walk with the
two students along the crest of the road beside the chugging car in
funereal procession. At the Austro-Italian border, they turned the
car back to normal, everyone climbed in, and they coasted down
toward Greece. Once there, the adventure-seeking Jesuit had to run
off and climb more than 9,000 feet to the top of Mount Olympus,
where none of the gods were on hand to meet him. Then, after
some swimming in the Mediterranean and visits to places about
which Homer, Heraclitus, and Thucydides wrote, the group made
its bumping way back to Amberg.

The northern section of Italy through which they passed, the Alto
Adige, was not entirely unknown to Father Joseph, because during
his first Christmas in France, he ventured down the Fourvière hill,
stuck out his thumb, and was picked up by an obliging truck driver,

who dropped him off at the junction of an abandoned road "somewhere toward the Franco-Italian border". He recounts:

> Night is falling. I'm walking, a pack and everything. It's getting dark and it's very rural. I see lights off way in the distance. I'm thinking "Wow, where's the next truck stop or something." I finally came across a little village and there was a bar in it. A French bar is different from an American bar. It's [a] more convivial place. I go in, there's a bunch of guys there and I said, look, is there a truck stop around here. Oh yes, about two kilometers further ahead. I thanked them. I said to myself, you know something? I'm not sure how much those guys know, how intelligent they are, how much they've been educated. But they knew the one thing I needed and I'm grateful for that. They knew where the truck stop was and that gave me hope in the midst of a nightfall.

Joe got to the truck stop, hitched a ride to the Italian border, and hopped on a train bound for Rome. From there he made it to a lodging where some of the students he had taught at Santa Clara University were staying to complete their junior year. Here, he managed to get a car and drove up to the Alto Adige, to the village from which his paternal grandmother came. "Are there any Bolegos left?" There were, and he learned that Bolego is a corruption of Polacko, and that sometime in the distant past, merchants from Poland (perhaps Jewish) came to do business in the area near the Brenner Pass. "So I've got some Polish blood in me, too", said Joseph.

After his summer adventures in Amberg, Austria, Tuscany, and Greece, he returned to Regensburg intent on giving undivided time to his thesis, a task that had become even more challenging than he had earlier estimated. Fortunately, he was able to find a helpmate in the person of his friend Ferdinand Ulrich, who had been encouraging him and helping him along the way. He admitted, however, there were some days when, after hours of working on some aspect of the opus, he found it difficult to spur on necessary psychic and physical energy necessary to push himself further. Then he remembered what a joy C. S. Lewis was to his soldier friends in Amberg, and this led him to divert time from his thesis to reread many of Lewis' essays for sheer enjoyment and relaxation. Quite by accident one morning, he found a blurb written by C. S. Lewis asserting that the book he was holding in his hand had "words that would pierce like steel and burn like fire". The author of this book was J. R. R. Tolkien. He began skimming through it out of curiosity. Then, he says, "I'd read it for the rest of the day and then I'd get on the bus, and read it on the bus, I'd get off the bus and walk to the apartment, reading it all the way up the elevator up to the apartment." The following day, he took another holiday from the thesis and spent it with Tolkien, seeking out anything written by him. "I got a lot of theological inspiration from Tolkien rather than from some of these theologians." One wonders, whose fault was that—the theologians' or Tolkien's?

It was at this point that Ferdinand Ulrich said to the traumatized scholar: "Let's go to [the Rigi-Hüsli] together for a few days." Rigi is a mountaintop between Lucerne and Zurich where Father von Balthasar and his community, the Johannesgemeinschaft (Community of St. John), had a small house. The area was accessible only by cog railway from Arth Goldau, via Zurich. Set high in the Alps, the peak is bordered on three sides by the majestic Vierwaldstättersee (Lake Lucerne). Here, in this ethereal retreat, Father Joseph had alighted, loaded down with notes and cards assembled from his extensive readings by and about the master, who was now casually seated before him, responding to questions that suddenly seemed ephemeral. Finally, the heavy, lengthy session was winding down, and Joe lightly asked: "Are there any other authors you read with pleasure?" "Yes," the master energetically replied, "I do love reading Agatha Christie. Isn't she a delight? So entertaining!" However surprised, the disciple recovered and humbly admitted he shared his master's taste for Christie's murder mysteries. But he did not care to plumb the depths of that association with his mentor. All he wanted was to be alone. However profitable this particular session was— and there had been other meetings like it in the past—the pupil felt almost as he did after the drive to India. So he picked up a copy of C. S. Lewis' *Perelandra* and walked outside, over to where he could contemplate the majestic view below. It was nearing sunset. Lakes sparkled beneath him. To the west was France, to the north Germany, to the south and east more Alpine peaks. He was reminded of the sign in the Rigi-Hüsli cog-rail station, a quote from the poet Johann Wolfgang von Goethe describing what at present was spread out before him: "Ringsum die Herrlichkeit der Welt" (All around, the glory of the world). Then, picking up his *Perelandra*, Father

Fessio read in a loud voice all of chapter seventeen, the climactic ending of the book, pausing a long time after the passage: "He has no need at all of anything that is made. . . . We also have no need of anything that is made. Love me, my brothers, for I am infinitely superfluous, and your love shall be like His, born neither of your need nor of my deserving, but a plain bounty."[2] The experience made an indelible impression upon him. Standing there in the oncoming twilight, he was overwhelmed by gratitude to God and to all those who had helped to engender this gratitude. It summarized everything he had learned from Fathers de Lubac, Ratzinger, and von Balthasar. It was a powerful insight into what heaven promised. It was the summation of the Spiritual Exercises: the *Contemplatio ad Amorem*, the Contemplation to Attain Divine Love.

The next morning he had to catch a train in Zurich back to Regensburg. Ferdinand decided to stay on. Then he learned the cog-rail train would not get him down to Arth-Goldau in time for him to make his connection in Zurich, and so he decided he had to hike down on the ice- and snow-covered cog-rail tracks. He got a tree branch, put it across his shoulders, and balanced his two suitcases loaded with books and notes on either end, then took off before 5 A.M. in the all-encompassing blackness. The descent down was much steeper than he had calculated. When he got to a trestle high over a ravine, one of the suitcases slipped off the branch, nearly plummeting into the current, but he jumped and grabbed it just before it fell. Physically exhausted, he at last reached the lighted level station, boarded the train, and reflected: "That was just one of those situations when I said to myself: 'I'll just walk down to [Arth-Goldau], no problem, but then I started doing that and I found out that it's a lot more difficult than I anticipated.'" Well could Saint Ignatius congratulate him on his self-knowledge and join with him in his hopes for the future. Did he ever learn? Read on in the following chapters to see.

Meanwhile, there was one adventure that begged closure before he bid his final adieu to Europe: the place for the summer retreat with his Amberg Army group. He finally decided on a monastery in the Val Venosta, in the South Tyrol (Alto Adige) district of Italy, where he had visited during the Christmas break of 1969–1970. Se-

---

[2] C. S. Lewis, *Perelandra* (New York: Scribner, 2003), 186.

questered in the Tyrolean Alps, Monte Maria, or Marienberg, was a monastic foundation that traced its origins back to Charlemagne, and it promised to be an ideal spot for a silent eight-day retreat. So at the beginning of summer 1974, twelve men from the Amberg post, the majority of whom had made the Florence to Assisi trek, gathered together at Monte Maria, anticipating a less torturous Ignatian experience than in the previous year. The majority of the men were Protestants and had a real grasp of the Bible. "I'd go over with them the four times of prayer, an hour each, the next day we'd have and what the themes were", Father Fessio recalled. "And then I'd say, oh what scripture shall we use? And they'd make all these suggestions. . . . That was a beautiful experience with these young men who really loved God, loved the Lord. We've kept some kind of contact ever since." "I don't think any of them at that time became Catholic as a result of my apologetic work, but they became more respectful of the Catholic Church." He also admitted that his retreatants gave him many scriptural suggestions that helped him when he was asked to give future retreats. It was not a one-way street to spiritual growth, for this was the group that introduced its leader to a deeper appreciation of C. S. Lewis, who has maintained a powerful influence on his spiritual and intellectual development ever since.

In the previous summer, the summer of 1973, as Father Fessio was nearing the end of his doctoral courses, he wrote to the provincial for formation, Father Robert Maloney, to advise him of the situation and to ask him where he would be assigned when he returned to the province in the following year. He would probably have to petition admittance to one of three California Jesuit universities for a faculty position, and that would take time. Father Maloney responded to the query with a characteristic Irish answer: "Where would you like to be assigned?" The response: "I've been out of the province for quite some time and I'd just rather be told where to go." The provincial responded: "I appreciate that indifference, which is an Ignatian virtue of indifference in which you leave yourself open to whatever God is going to do, but do you have any preference whatsoever?" "If Mary had gotten her preference," Joe replied, "she'd have been a housewife, and if Luke had his, he'd be a doctor, if Peter had his, he'd be a fisherman. . . . But I suppose, if I had to choose, I would go to USF [the University of

San Francisco], and that was because my friend Father Buckley was there." As he wrote the letter assigning Joe to USF, Father Maloney hid his secret delight, for he had just been given the same assignment.

In the fall of 1974, the soon-to-be decorated doctor of theology (he still had to finish and present his dissertation) purchased the cheapest ticket he could find. It was on Icelandic Airlines from Luxembourg to Oakland. But then there was an emergency. There was a need for a chaplain at Grafenwöhr. Yes, if he came there to say Sunday Masses, he was assured, the Army would get him to Luxembourg to catch his flight. So he took a detour from Regensburg to Grafenwöhr. After the last Mass, he boarded a Huey, a giant helicopter that was awaiting him, and he was flown across Germany at low altitude. Huddled up beside the Karlsruhe train station there was a soccer field, and it was there that the Huey set down. "Here's this Jesuit in my clerical suit getting out, waving off the plane and running across the tracks to the train station. I don't know what those people thought." It was a fitting adieu to Europe for the knight in clerical armor. But what adventures would be in store for him when the plane landed?

6

UNIVERSITY OF SAN FRANCISCO

Nineteen seventy-four was a critical year for the Jesuit-run University of San Francisco (USF) where Father Fessio made his landing, though not quite as dramatically as he had done on the soccer field of Karlsruhe. This time he made his entré onto a turf where the contests resembled more closely the trenches of Verdun than the playing fields of Eton. There were academic, financial, administrative, theological, and philosophical problems, some of which were simmering but had not yet begun to bubble, while others had already reached the boiling point. The faculty was fragmented and confused about the mission of the university and the nature and purpose of a core curriculum. The inflation rate was beginning to grow throughout the country. There was economic stagnation. Money was scarce. The predominantly lay board of trustees was constantly putting pressure on the president, Father William C. McInnes, S.J., to balance the books, reminding him of the short term of office the board had enjoined on his predecessor. Cuts he did indeed make, but the result was that in 1975 the faculty formed a union. Although not solely based on the Marxist model of exploitation and conflict, it was certainly far from the model of Leo XIII, which stressed seeking mutual benefits.

One member of the faculty argued that belonging to the collective bargaining unit ran contrary to his vows as a Jesuit, and he therefore petitioned for an exemption that would allow him to remain a full-time faculty member while abstaining from the union. The petition was refused on the local level and then appealed to the higher union court, which sustained the earlier decision. The case then went to the Superior Court of San Francisco, where the judgment rendered was that there could indeed be a clash between union regulations and the Jesuit vows of poverty and obedience; therefore, at USF, which claimed to be a Jesuit-run institution, any Jesuit who had not already joined the faculty union could request and receive an exemption while maintaining his position as a member of the faculty. It is significant that no Jesuit who has since been assigned to the University of San Francisco has yet taken advantage of this freedom, perhaps giving credence to Freud's observation that the death instinct is stronger than the life instinct. The response to the presence of a union at the university vacillated between indifference and enthusiasm among most of the Jesuit faculty. Some members of the Theology Department were most vociferous in their belief that the picket line was where the "service of faith and the promotion of justice" were exemplified. It was a sign of identification with the exploited masses. As far as the administration was concerned, the voice of any Jesuit superior was muffled, while from the voice muffled there was no retort.

Then there was the 1970 report of the Western Association of Schools and Colleges (WASC), the group responsible for accreditation of public and private universities in the state of California, which lingered over the university like smoke from a put-out brush fire. The visiting committee noted that for a number of years "USF had been in a state of transition from one in which 'Catholics teach Catholics' to one in which a broader spectrum of backgrounds and attitudes characterizes both faculty and students." The growing number of lay faculty and some of the Jesuits welcomed the change, "but there remains a genuine concern by significant elements of the University community about how the Catholic character of the institution is to be manifested." The final report concluded with this ominous statement: "The Committee found little to distinguish this institution from a secular college or university." True, there were some symbolic indicators of a Catholic presence—an occasional Roman collar, some religious images, and the "imposing presence of Saint Ignatius Church. Students and faculty remarked that the University had not found itself since the changes in church and campus life in the 1960s." The spirit of *in loco parentis* had vanished from campus life and had not been replaced. "Furthermore, the traditional Jesuit union of faith and intellect has not found new forms in the curricular inventions of the past few years. . . . Weaknesses in academic advising, failure to articulate how a value-oriented education is to be found in the new courses

and programs, and relaxation of rigorous quality controls may be
seen as products of a fundamental uncertainty of purpose."

Father McInnes, who had promised the world that his ambition
was "to make USF the Harvard of the West", wondered if these
two challenges facing the university—the financial crisis and the
Catholic Jesuit identity—could somehow find a common Band-Aid
remedy. He received some encouragement from one of the part-
time members of the History Department, Monsignor John Tracy
Ellis, an advocate for making USF comparable to the Ivy League universities, but both men agreed that encouragement would never be
enough; action was needed. So, in the spring of 1974, Father President confided his concerns to four priests from the USF Jesuit community, members of the faculty or administration, and asked them
to discuss among themselves the challenges that plagued him and to
suggest possible, realistic solutions. One member of this informal
committee was Father Robert L. Maloney, the former provincial for
formation whom we have already met, who was now a recent addition to the USF administration. The other three were Father Maloney's assistant, Father Theodore Taheny; Father Robert Burns, of
the Department of History; and I, sometime assistant dean, sometime acting dean of the College of Arts and Sciences. The first
item on the committee's agenda was to come up with some plan
that might attract Catholic students to the university, although the
president confessed his primary objective was to discover some way,
any way, to attract more tuition-paying students, irrespective of their
religious beliefs. We met informally on a number occasions, and
the script was always the same: Father Maloney, puffing on one of
his ever-present cigarettes, would reflect long and brilliantly on the
educational philosophy of such preceptors as Thomas Aquinas, Cardinal Newman, Mortimer Adler, Allan Bloom, and Russell Kirk;
then, Father Taheny, like a prosecution lawyer, would bring the
subject back to earth with sharp, incisive queries; next, after some
coaxing, shaking like self-aware Jell-O—his habit when a funny
anecdote was coming to the surface—Father Burns would give examples, rich with ironic details, of how the Ignatian *Ratio Studiorum* had been, at different periods of history, implemented, modified, undermined, and then promptly consigned to the exclusive use
of the universities' publicity departments for future use in alumni

bulletins and recruiting brochures. Father Burns was rightly considered an eminent historian and would soon leave USF for a position at the University of California at Los Angeles (UCLA), where, never appearing without his Roman collar, he lectured to and dealt with M.A. and Ph.D. candidates. His 1974 evaluation of Jesuit university planners and administrators at USF and beyond was harsh: "Resolutely vacillating, a contingent in the growing secularization of Catholic institutions of learning", they "straddle all the primrose paths like a centipede, and with low cunning keep redefining the terms they live by—'Catholic university,' 'Jesuit university'— so as to conform with whatever they are forced to do by the circumstances of a given moment." Eventually this description would also fit the Jesuit high schools from which the Father Flynns had long since made their departure.

Of course, in order to remain in existence, the academic institutions had to have enough financial resources to survive, and USF at that date was a good example of that fact. Their strategy: accommodate the goods to the desire of the buyer. Realistically, one had to recognize that the majority of students at the university believed that in order to get a good job, they had to have a college degree. If that cost money, they were ready to pay. They were not contemptuous of arguments for a "liberal education", but such luxury could wait until later in life. There was an economic crisis. That was a reality, and, in order to attract and retain students, the administrators had to water down requirements in the liberal arts sphere. To educate "under the light of the faith"—*fidem quaerens intellectum*— was an ideal that was no longer practical, even in seminaries, and pushing the Jesuit Catholic theology card too far might risk another set of difficulties. USF was the happy recipient of some state and federal funding. If challenged, where would the money come from to defend the university's position in court? For the nonce, the prudent, realistic policy would be to let sleeping dogs be the bedfellows of *fidem quaerens intellectum*. The members of our committee of four were in agreement on this. But we also recognized that the era of gentility was gone; that it had been succeeded by the age of economics, computers, and the media, that the university existed in the here and now, in the concrete, not some abstract, ideal realm, and that, despite deficiencies, it was doing good for a number of people. Being harsh on the administration was not the realistic path

to take in order to make the university less secular. Was there anything positive that could be done? The members of the committee
discussed this question at length and decided that a college within
the university might be the answer. There were models for this
arrangement in sixteenth-century France when Saint Ignatius was
a student at the University of Paris, and similar colleges exist to
this day at Oxford. We unanimously agreed that setting up a kind
of college within the university might be worth consideration. We
presented the result of our discussions in a memo to the president
and filed a copy of it in a forgotten nook of Plato's cave somewhere
on campus; then we went off to pursue other distractions. What
the president did with his copy is a mystery not worth investigating, much less solving, particularly since the fall semester of 1974
had just begun, bringing with it a conglomerate of distractions of
a more pressing nature.

Once he would learn about such perplexing matters, the newest
member of the Theology Department would be ready and eager to
meet the challenges they offered—and, to his satisfaction, resolve
them. He would never be shy to gorge his pelican beak with a pas-
sel of other peremptory issues that yet lay hidden in the promising
future. Since his arrival at his new assignment, Father Fessio found
himself well ensconced in a corner of a men's student residence hall,
thankful for the years as an undergraduate at Santa Clara that had
taught him to pack only what was essential to preserve the *aequam
mentem* necessary for survival in such a precarious location.

Just about two or three weeks before his arrival, a new rector
was appointed as the religious superior of the USF Jesuits. Father
John Lo Schiavo was the quintessence of the ever-smiling gentleman. Courteous, gracious, obliging, he gave unrestrained expression of these qualities to all. Shoes always polished; trousers ele-
gantly pressed; mannerisms noble yet casual and friendly. In the late
1930s and early 1940s, he had been an all-city basketball star at San
Francisco's Jesuit high school, and now he was an excellent golfer
and could have easily fit into a Giorgio Armani ad, set up to attract
the attention of the sophisticated, athletic man of taste. His parents
were immigrants from the Lipari Island, off the coast of Sicily, but
John was a San Franciscan through and through, with a streak of
undeniable Italian charm. His father had died when he was quite
young, and he had been reared by his mother and his two older

unmarried sisters. No family could have been more tightly knit. John was also an exemplary priest and a devoted religious, whose close relative was a cardinal in Palermo.

Shortly after the fall semester of 1974 began, Father Fessio told me of an encounter he had had with Father Lo Schiavo. He began by saying he had made friends with a student who was housed in the dorm where he had been assigned. His name was Tom Safranek, the eldest brother of some of the most outstanding students in the future Saint Ignatius Institute. Father Fessio and Tom would solidify their newfound friendship by jogging the three and a half miles down to the ocean, plunging into the surf, and taking a bus back to the university in time for classes. One morning after his return, Father Fessio dropped into the refectory at the Jesuit residence where Father Rector was sitting alone having a late breakfast. He pulled up a chair, sat down across from him, and began to regale him with the story of the run that culminated in the exhilarating dive into the cold water known for its dangerous undertow. "You can't do that", was the slow response of his superior, "It's forbidden to swim in that beach." "No, it's not", flashed back the younger man. Pause. "Yes, there's a sign there saying swimming prohibited", retorted the rector with a toothy smile served with a bit of steel in his voice. "John", was the matching reply, "I run down there three times a week. There's no sign there. . . . I run past the wall there. It says 'Dangerous'. But not prohibited." Silence echoed. The superior continued eating. The young subject stole away. The next time he buzzed down to the beach, Father Fessio took special interest in the sign. "Sure enough, it did not say prohibited, it just said dangerous." He adds: "But from that point on, it was just like I was *persona non grata* because I didn't agree with him, because I argued with him." As Father Joseph was recounting this episode, I became aware of a quiet whispering in my ear of the fatal three notes from Bizet's *Carmen* announcing the *finis* of Don José.

If he failed to make a favorable impression on the rector, Father Fessio's classroom efforts to impress some students were at best consistent. I recall having encouraged a friend of mine, whose son had just enrolled in the university, to sign up for a class conducted by Father Fessio. He did; the boy flunked; I lost a friend. The young man's teacher was adamant: he would not change his grade or the grades of others who were equally desperate. The university's pol-

icy at the time was that Catholic students had to take a number
of units of theology as a prerequisite for graduation; non-Catholics
were exempt. The dean was expected to enforce the policy. His
instructions to the students had become similar to those of Diocle-
tian to Roman Christians: deny your faith so that you can graduate,
or else accept the consequences. Did Father Fessio not understand?
Could he not appreciate the students' predicament? Father Fessio
held firm. "I was all enthusiastic," he says, "and I taught my first
class in I think it was Christian Anthropology, and I thought all we
need is Balthasar's book by the same name for this class. I couldn't
understand it, therefore I couldn't make them understand it. Total
disaster." He wanted them to read Chesterton, C. S. Lewis, Plato,
Aquinas. "But they just looked at me whenever I suggested it."
Outside of the classroom, his reputation among students was exceptionally favorable. He was friendly, good-natured, and involved
in athletic contests, and he went out of his way to accept and show
interest in everyone he encountered.

His interests and activity were not limited to the campus. Shortly
after arriving at his new post, he formed a prayer-study group. Small
at first, made up exclusively of people from outside the university,
the participants would meet weekly for Mass and discussion in the
basement of what, until 1969, had been Saint Ignatius Prep School
(now part of the ever-expanding USF complex). One member of
this group was John Galten, a teacher at nearby Presentation High
School pursuing an M.A. in theology at USF, his alma mater. He
had been an Army officer in the Vietnam War and, before that, a star
basketball player at San Francisco's Riordan High School when Father Fessio's Santa Clara roommate, Bill Beasley, was on the school's
freshman team. John was a calm, clear-sighted young family man
with a strikingly beefy and stolid athletic build and undeniable qualities of leadership, a man whose unconscious courage in carrying
out future responsibilities will be described later on. Shortly after
the appearance of John, Frank Filice began showing up at the weekly
Mass and discussions. Frank had been an esteemed and successful
biology professor at USF for a number of years, and after his wife
died and his adult children had been cared for, he embarked on a
path that eventually would lead to his being ordained a priest for
the Archdiocese of San Francisco.

Father Fessio had not been at the university yet a month—he

confessed one day to the prayer group—before he began to see alarming indications on campus pointing to the demise of the traditional Jesuit philosophy of Catholic university education. He attributed this state of affairs to three causes: divisions within the Church; divisions within academia over how to define the nature of a Catholic, Jesuit university; and divisions within the Society of Jesus. As we have seen, these same problems had been vaguely identified and discussed somewhat desultorily by the members of the committee set up by Father McInnes at USF in 1974, but it was Father Fessio who now, speaking before the group, defined more specifically the causes and effects.

After he cited numerous examples, the members of the group agreed that no one would doubt the divisions and polarizations within the Church. There was the liberal-conservative split, the heterodox-orthodox, and the progressive-reactionary, and although it was difficult, if not impossible, to describe such differences honestly and accurately, they were real and remain so to this day. He listed for the group those issues where these divisions were—and continue to be—most readily apparent: the nature of the Church, authority and obedience, freedom of conscience, the Magisterium, papal infallibility, human sexuality and artificial contraception, liturgical practices, interpretation of Scripture, and the existence of moral and doctrinal absolutes. Father Fessio was never eager to disclose his insights into the reasons for such confusion, but when pressed, he placed much of the blame on those leaders who were not handing down the faith, failing to teach the joyful self-surrender so necessary in marriage, the religious life, and the priesthood. He claimed the "loyal opposition" was not only wed to a culture of death and dying, but was inviting many—especially college-aged kids—to join them in their funeral procession.

When it came to addressing the second kind of division—over the nature and mission of a Catholic, Jesuit university—Father Fessio's clipped judgments, often seasoned with irony and humor, were never personal. Still, he and the prayer group lamented the fact that there had been no concerted voice at the university declaring that the norm for faith, morals, and liturgical practices is always anchored in the contemporary teaching of the official Church, of the bishops in union with the pope. This teaching, he reminded them, is summarized in paragraph 25 of the Second Vatican Council's Dogmatic

Constitution on the Church. For this reason, those teaching and ministering to students should be expected to adhere to the principle that, although the Spirit operates in different ways and provides the Church with different gifts, the special charism of the bishops in union with the pope includes that of authoritatively preaching, teaching, and governing the sacramental life of the Church. In matters of faith and morals, the faithful must accept the teaching of the bishops and adhere to it with assent.

Father Fessio's reflections in these prayer group meetings were greatly enhanced by the memory of his many conversations with Father de Lubac on the state of the present-day Church, on the sad history of the Church in France after World War I—how her attempt to cooperate with liberalism and Communism ended in failure—and on his reasons for founding the international periodical *Communio*. When it came to the failures of the Society of Jesus, Father Fessio was less prolix. Although hesitant to make known explicitly his opinion on the subject, he could not forget his mentor's comments about the conversation he had had with Father General Pedro Arrupe after the 1971 International Theological Commission meeting in Rome. Differences of opinion about faith and morals within the Society were then a matter of common knowledge and public record. Father Fessio cited the New England Province procurator's comment to Father Arrupe from June 21, 1970, which appeared in *New England Province News*. Summing up his findings, the procurator wrote that within the Society, "disagreement and disunion . . . is pervasive and reaches three vital areas: theological, philosophical and spiritual (i.e., the spirit of the *Exercises* and the *Constitutions*)." As we can see, this considered conclusion on the part of the procurator coincides with what Father de Lubac had confided to Father Arrupe a few weeks earlier at the Bellarmino in Rome.

These discussions in the prayer group had been going on for some time when at the end of one of the meetings, Father Fessio told his newly formed friends that their interchange of anecdotes, opinions, and experiences had been insightful, even at times amusing, and he asked them for further input on a still-nebulous project that he hoped to explore: how to go about fostering at USF a true Catholic intellectual culture that would be of profit to students interested in the Church's rich tradition, students eager to deepen their faith, broaden their knowledge, and become leaven in a secular world where relativism and a hypersexualized culture prevailed. The group was unanimous in responding that this was a tall order, a challenge that should be met with another corresponding challenge. At this point, Dr. Filice cried out, "We should go to Mexico!" Mexico?! Whatever did Mexico have to do with these discussions? That is a question we will take up in the following chapter.

7

LA GUADALUPANA AND THE INSTITUTE

Frank Filice's peculiar suggestion obliged him to remind the group that the San Francisco vocations director had directed him to work in close coordination with the diocesan director of pro-life activities in Santa Rosa. This venture had put him in contact with a contingent of thirteen committed pro-life, anti-abortion hippies, who had expressed the desire to make a pilgrimage, along with their children, to the shrine of Our Lady of Guadalupe in Mexico. It was to be a journey in thanksgiving to the patroness of the pro-life cause for their recent reception into the Catholic Church. The local bishop had encouraged them from afar, referring them to the prospective seminarian, Dr. Filice. At the same time, he urged Frank to see to it that their ambition be attained in a convenient manner.

It should come as no surprise that as soon as Father Fessio learned of the proposed adventure, he showed immediate interest. Sometime after the 1975 summer classes had come to an end, he found himself speeding up to Santa Rosa to meet Frank and his group. Frank had already clued him in: for some years, this band of aliens from conventional society had been "truth seekers", living together in an open-marriage community while traveling about in various places in the San Francisco area, and they finally ended up in Santa Rosa. They had done a considerable investigation of New Age methods for self-fulfillment and happiness, but they had put this aside to investigate Hinduism and Buddhism. Unconvinced, they then turned their collective attention first to the claims of Judaism and then to those of Christianity. Wanting to go about this properly, they had attempted to teach themselves Hebrew and then Greek, in order to read the Bible in its original languages. One can imagine how well this went. When someone told them that Saint Thomas Aquinas was a good guide to Christian beliefs, they tried their hand at Latin and purchased some of Aquinas' works, giving themselves over to the study of his writing—and meeting with the same success they had had in learning Hebrew and Greek.

At last, though, they came to the unanimous conclusion that God had revealed himself in Jesus. On the Sunday after arriving at this consensus, they went as a group to the nearest Christian church they could find. At the "altar call", the preacher received them warmly, assuring them they were not only welcome, but saved. They were delighted. On the following Sunday they returned, but this time, after responding once more to the call to step forward and be saved, they met a rebuff from the minister: "No, no. You were already saved last week." The spokesman for the group answered, "It can't happen all that fast! We have a whole lifetime of sins to undo." They left the church disappointed, but after considerable prayers on their own, and after discovering the consistent pro-life teaching of the Catholic Church, they presented themselves to a Catholic priest and informed him they wanted to become Catholics, all of them. He looked at them with surmise and informed them, with less equanimity than what had been prescribed in his manual for pastoral care, that it would take months of intense instruction to accommodate their request. Meanwhile, would they not want to separate? No, they would not, answered the group. They were a family, and a family they would remain. What was the matter? Was the Catholic Church against families?! Finally, instructions were successfully completed over the course of six months, and six marriages were regularized. This arrangement left just one woman unclaimed, and so it was decided that, since she had the talents of a mother superior, Theo Stearns would become the dowager matriarch of the group. In thanksgiving for their reception into the Church, the members unanimously decided they had to make a pilgrimage of thanksgiving to the shrine of Our Lady of Guadalupe in Mexico City. Was she not the patroness of the pro-life cause?

Thus Don José Fessio readied himself for another adventure. The noble knight later recalled how when he and Frank Filice arrived at the place where the hippies were living, his eye casually took in the various curiosities of the neighborhood until it fixed on an old bright blue school bus parked in the driveway. On both sides, large white painted graffiti broadcast that "El Aborto Es Muerto", giving evidence that it was ready for the adventure below the border. Frank knocked at the door of the castle of hippie living and high thinking, and immediately Hippie Hal swung it wide open, exposing a gigantic picture of Our Lady of Guadalupe hanging over—indeed almost hiding—the fireplace. When Father Fessio saw it, his first words to Hal were "How would you like to make a pilgrimage to Our Lady of Guadalupe?", to which Hal immediately responded, "When do we leave?"

Summer classes had ended at USF, and Father Fessio was not going to take excuses from John Galten to exempt himself, along with his three kids, from boarding the hippie-filled bus and heading south with him on Highway 5, bound for Mexico. John, always the reliable planner, wisely packed into the bus' baggage compartments some survival needs, including a generous stash of giant-size cans of peanut butter, beer, soft drinks and goat's milk for the kids, and an ample supply of rice, refried beans, awful canned mackerel, and jalapeños—all of which would hopefully keep the pilgrims well fed and safe from "Montezuma's revenge". Once over the border, they bought tortillas and three times a day slathered them with peanut butter, jalapeños, and *frijoles refritos*. When the beer ran out, there was *cerveza* to buy at roadside stations. The bus was transformed into a rolling-along bedroom at night, and a porta-potty, seemingly de-signed to accommodate grade-school children, modestly ensconced at the back for the convenience and need, if not the delight, of all. There was no reason to make stops other than to buy gas and to rest for a day or more on the Mexican *campos*.

Of course, Father Fessio offered Mass each morning for his con-gregation on a makeshift altar set up in a variety of places. He also did more than his share of driving, and on the first day of the odyssey, after traveling a few hundred miles, he stopped near the border to refill the tank. The mechanic in him forced his hand to open the hood, and he was surprised to see a Clorox bottle attached to the carburetor by a piece of baling wire. "What's that?!" he asked. "We add water to the mixture, and it seems to get better mileage" was Hal's reassuring answer. According to John, this was just one dismaying surprise, representative of a number of others, too nu-merous and unreal to narrate, that must have caused the befuddled knight to wonder if in this quest he had stepped through a looking glass to find, not Dulcinea, but the Mad Hatter.

Granted, there was much of the whimsical about the adventure, but it also had a serious side, confirming that the Reverend Fessio's exploits always seem to have the same contextual ingredients as a Mexican margarita, where the sweet, salty, and sour are all mixed together with the fateful blast for the satisfaction of the many. Having begun their pilgrimage from Santa Rosa on August 15, the feast of the Assumption of the Blessed Virgin, the pilgrims arrived at their destination very early in the morning of August 22, the feast of the Queenship of Mary, at a convenient hour for Father Fessio to offer Mass at the Guadalupe altar. During the brief homily, he reminded his hippie friends that he had come with them to this spot to ask for the grace to know how to initiate some kind of a program that would give USF students the option of a true Catholic liberal education in the Jesuit spirit and tradition. He asked his co-pilgrims to add these petitions to their thanksgiving for the grace they had received, through the intercession of Our Lady of Guadalupe, to become members of her Son's Mystical Body, the Catholic Church. This Mass was offered at the old shrine where the famous image of Our Lady, stamped on Saint Juan Diego's *tilma*, was encased above the altar, and Father Fessio, being a tall man, was able to reach up and touch the frame, to the unrestrained delight of his co-pilgrims.

Later in the day he returned to pray alone at the shrine, and it was then and there before the image of Our Lady of Guadalupe—"when the soul is not agitated by different spirits", as Saint Ignatius counseled, "and has free and peaceful use of its natural powers"[1]—that he made the choice he had long been prayerfully considering. Here before the image of Our Lady of Guadalupe, he resolved to flesh out the sketchy design of the committee set up by Father President McInnes to make the university more Catholic, more Jesuit. He reflected on the curriculum of the first Jesuit university, founded in 1547 by Saint Francis Borgia in Gandía, Spain, chiefly for the education of young *moriscos* (newly baptized Muslims). Next, he reflected on the plan of studies of the Gregorian University, founded by Saint Ignatius in 1551 in Rome, primarily to train clerics, and, finally, his thoughts turned to the beginning of the University of San Francisco in 1855. The founding Jesuits in each of these examples shared a common purpose: to educate men in the Ignatian spirit. Yet each adapted his motives to the place, time, and condition of

---

[1] Spiritual Exercises, no. 177, in *The Spiritual Exercises of St. Ignatius of Loyola*, trans. Louis. J. Puhl, S.J. (Chicago: Loyola Press, 1951), 74.

the prospective students. Here Father Fessio saw his challenge: the USF of 1975 was certainly not the USF of 1855, much less was it the University of Gandía in 1547 or the Gregorian University of 1551, and to try to pretend it was or try to make it so would be an exercise in romantic thinking. He was called to form an integrated intellectual, spiritual, and social curriculum in the Catholic, Jesuit way of life for the students at the University of San Francisco, lay men and women who were potentially called to bring Christ into the twenty-first century. He determined to call this "dream child" the Saint Ignatius Institute. How this was to come about he did not know. He ended this memorable prayer time by asking Our Lady of Guadalupe to obtain the grace from her Son to confirm somehow the choices that he had made and to guide him along in this venture. He further asked Saint Ignatius to be his advocate and guide. He recalled later that, in spite of some Bertie Wooster–like dramas on the *camino* back to Santa Rosa, he felt a reassuring peace every time he considered the decision he had made at the Guadalupe altar. Once back in San Francisco at a Mass of Thanksgiving, he mapped out his plans to the joyful approval of the prayer group.[2]

And what happened to the hippies? They moved out to New Hope, Kentucky, where they became active members of the St. Martin de Porres Lay Dominican Community and began a printing and publication project called Catholics United for Life, which expanded into New Hope Publications. They flourished and remained for many years under the direction of Ms. Theo Stearns.

Looked at from a broader perspective, this hippie jaunt, irresistibly funny as it may seem, has some features about it that make it quite compatible with what we might term "the Fessio factor". We have seen that whenever Joseph Fessio meets any opposition to his well-thought-out plans, he is inclined to treat it with either opposition or contempt. Relying on self-confidence and undisputed intelligence, he aspires—Quixote-like—to perform great feats, with little tolerance for any distraction. On the hippie trip, he found himself wondering what might happen to this earthy community of young

---

[2] Years later, after the formation of Ignatius Press, such pilgrimages would become a longstanding tradition for Father Fessio and his staff: to Ireland, Lourdes, Fatima, Santiago de Compostela, Mexico City, among other sites.

couples. They had been living together in polyamorous relationships. Now that they had the sacraments, would they be able simply to turn their lives around? More to the point, he wondered about
the fate of their children. But perhaps this was just impatience. He
had to admit to himself that he did not always accept with an open
heart the things that didn't fit his schemes. Perhaps now was the time
to learn the art of waiting—as Saint Ignatius had done before him.
The young Inigo of Loyola had been the epitome of recklessness,
but later, he became the very embodiment of patience, letting the
weeds grow alongside the wheat. Kneeling at the Guadalupe shrine,
Father Fessio hoped that prayer might work such a change in himself.

The second distinctive feature of the hippie trek that helps defines
the Fessio Factor can be best appreciated by describing an incident
that took place during the Project 50 program in the summer of
1968. One evening, he and one of the student counselors, Patrick
Finley, were driving across the San Mateo toll bridge. In those days,
there was not much traffic, especially at night. As they neared the
exit, Joe confessed he had no money at all with him, not one cent,
and he asked Pat whether he could scrounge up the necessary fare
(much lower than today, of course). Pat searched through his jeans
and shirt pockets and found the exact amount in small change.
"We're really lucky. I do not have anything more", Pat said as he
handed a fistful of coins to Joe, who accepted them with a smile
and then threw the whole amount out of the open window into
the black night, saying: "Let's go for it! Let's see what can happen
now!" Pat was an engineering major at the time, later a lawyer who
would greatly help Ignatius Press. In 1968, he had much of the Joe
Fessio in him—minus the Fu Manchu 'stache—and so, as the two
rolled up to the tollbooth, Pat, recovering from his initial shock,
called back: "Great. Let's go for it!" Then began the drama. They
pulled up to the tollbooth, and after a little smooth talking, joking,
and bargaining with the toll keepers, they were let through with
laughs and good-luck wishes. Over the course of Father Fessio's life,
especially at times when he found himself with empty pockets, this
espièglerie of "Let's go for it! Let's see what can happen now!" would
be repeated innumerable times.

Jumping forward again to 1975, we find ourselves with a good
example. Elated by his pilgrimage adventure to the shrine of Our
Lady of Guadalupe, Father Joseph Fessio returned to his poky room

in the resident hall, made still and quiet by the summer vacation, then whisked over to the library to refresh himself on what Saint Ignatius had to say about the purpose of a Jesuit university. What he found delighted him. Ignatius was clear: "Very special care should be given that those who come to the universities of the Society to obtain knowledge should acquire along with it good and Christian moral habits."[3] Knowledge and Christian moral habits are central to the Jesuit university. This objective was further developed in the *Constitutions*, part IV, and later expanded in the *Ratio Studiorum*. The pursuit of knowledge and the development of Christian virtue, with an emphasis on morals, is the purpose, the mission of a Jesuit university. And the object of the two—virtue and moral habits—is truth. They are like the two blades of a pair of scissors: they work in conjunction to achieve the end for which they were made.

The Institute, he determined, would have an integrated Catholic liberal arts core curriculum and be designed according to the spirit, if not the letter, of the *Ratio Studiorum*, the overall plan of studies for Jesuit colleges and universities. More specifically, he determined that the basis for any policy taken by this inchoate Saint Ignatius Institute would be that of Ignatius' spirituality, outlined in the Spiritual Exercises, and of the educational principles defined or implied in the *Examen*, found in the *Constitutions* of the Society of Jesus. Thus the double-bladed structure had been defined in theory. Now it was time to put it into operation.

Leaving the library, Father Fessio hurried over to the registrar's office, where he picked up a number of brochures describing great books programs at various colleges. There was St. John's at Annapolis and Santa Fe, the general program at Notre Dame in Indiana, and then, especially, Thomas Aquinas College, which had been founded just a few years earlier in San Francisco by some dissenting faculty members of St. Mary's College in Moraga, another Catholic institution of higher learning. Ah, San Francisco! It gave birth to the beatniks in the fifties, the flower children and hippies in the sixties, and now in the seventies yet another counter-establishment movement: great books programs at Thomas Aquinas College and, perhaps, at the Saint Ignatius Institute. Father Fessio obtained much

---

[3] *The Constitutions of the Society of Jesus and Their Complementary Norms*, ed. John W. Padberg, S.J. (Saint Louis: Institute of Jesuit Sources, 1996), pt. IV, no. 481, p. 187.

from these catalogues, but he realized that the Institute had to be different. One might draw an analogy here with the foundation of the Society of Jesus. It adopted many elements from the older religious orders, but it had to adapt its spirit to the times and modify the mode of living of its members to accommodate a rapidly evolving post-Renaissance world. Then there was the example of de Lubac and his band of scholars in *la nouvelle théologie* movement. Did they not also recommend revitalizing Catholic thinking in the context of the prevailing social and intellectual currents, presenting immutable truths in the language of the town square?

In less than two weeks, Father Fessio had drawn up a detailed proposal, which he presented to the president, who in turn appointed a committee to investigate the project and determine whether it would benefit the university. In his oral presentation to the committee, Father Fessio prudently refrained from broaching philosophical and theological convictions, stating the program would be designed to fit into the university curriculum. It would not be an honors program, nor would it be a program solely for liberal arts majors. Rather, he contended, it would be a program intended to attract ordinary students from various majors who were serious about their desire to learn and willing to apply themselves to the Institute's systemic structured program of studies and to acquire a familiarity with Catholic cultural and intellectual life. Its aim was to mold the academic with the spiritual in order to generate a specific culture on the campus and to educate students in the truth. Its purpose was to turn out graduates, competent in their own chosen specialty, with that distinct view of reality that in the past had set apart alumni of Jesuit colleges. To achieve these objectives, the SII would adapt a curriculum based on the great books of Western civilization and on history and art. Although not as deeply focused as the programs in those universities devoted exclusively to the great books curriculum, it would nevertheless provide the students with a solid grounding in the philosophy and theology of Saint Thomas Aquinas as well as give them some basic understanding of science and of a modern European language. It would have an overseas program for students in their junior year.

If Father Fessio prudently refrained from discussing before the board the ideological reasons for approving the Saint Ignatius Institute on campus, he clearly described the academic plan it would follow, and his presentation made it plain that he had done his home-work. He stated that a typical undergraduate student at the univer-sity, irrespective of what college the student was registered in—arts, business, science, nursing—normally carried eighteen units per semester, eight in the courses required by the major and ten units from electives and university required courses. A student who opted to join the Institute would take all of his non-major require-ments in the SII curriculum. That curriculum would be structured in such a way that both the great books seminars—restricted to fif-teen students per section—and the systematic courses in philosophy and theology would be set in historical sequence beginning with the Greco-Roman worlds and passing through Medieval, Renais-sance, Enlightenment, and modern periods, for a total of ten units per semester. Philosophy requirements would include logic, meta-physics, ethics and political philosophy (totaling eighteen units by graduation). Theology courses: Old and New Testament, Fathers of the Church, Christology, Church and sacraments, moral theology, and great spiritual writers (twenty-three units). All courses would be integrated with an emphasis on the history, art, and literature of each period. Members of the university faculty would be en-couraged to apply to teach in the SII, thereby sparing the univer-sity the cost of new hires. After consulting with an advisory com-mittee made up of in-house faculty, administrators, and staff, the director of the Institute would accept or deny applications. There were to be special floors for Institute students in the residence halls. Men living on campus would be assigned rooms on the two floors where Father Fessio and I were the assigned residents. Sister Marie Ignatius Clune, R.S.H.M., of Campus Ministry would eventually be housed with the women students. Since the Institute was to be an integrated program within the university, the students were not to be an isolated group, but encouraged to be the yeast, the salt of the student population. It is peers who best teach peers, and so a limited number of non-Institute students would also be encouraged to live on these floors, but would be expected to live by the SII rules regarding study time. Because there were still separate resident halls for men and women on campus in 1975, this element in the proposal was not considered excessive. Replicas of famous paint-ings would be hung on the walls of the SII floors. On every class day, there would be a non-obligatory 10 P.M. Mass—very different in form if not in time from the Santa Clara Masses—which would be offered in the chapel at the Jesuit residence. These Masses were open to anyone who wished to attend, and for the following two decades, many came to cherish the "SII Mass". Once classes began, voluntary all-night first-Friday Eucharistic Adoration was introduced into the schedule.

It was some Jewish faculty members and administrators who showed the greatest interest in and support for the Institute. One of these men confessed that his experience in secular universities had taught him that the more Catholic the university was, the more one could exchange ideas freely and honestly. The Institute, he said, would keep USF from becoming oppressive like the nearby University of California at Berkeley, where the administration-accepted "politically correct" policy was squashing free speech. As for another Jewish professor, Dr. Alan Calvin of the Business College, not even the members of the prayer group could outdo his enthusiasm for the dreamed-of Institute. This man was particularly helpful to Father Fessio in composing some of the arguments he would deliver to the president's special committee as well as in bringing the young Jesuit's optimism down to earth. For example, Father Fessio worked out a statistic showing how much money the SII would save the university. "I think we can get sixty students to come to the Institute", he told Dr. Calvin. "That would mean $10,000 per student times sixty. That's income without any expenses for the university." Dr. Calvin, soon to be named dean of the Business College, was not impressed. "Don't say sixty. They could hold you hostage. If you get thirty, that's more than enough to force them to take a gamble." Indeed, thirty is the figure Father Fessio gave to the committee, and the reply was simple: "Go for it." However, the chairman loudly broadcast the caveat that if Father Fessio did not produce as many students as he estimated, the committee would be inclined to weigh more carefully the arguments from the opposition, namely, those of the Theology Department. What he quickly perceived, thanks to Dr. Calvin, was that any munificence on the part of the committee depended on how well he could show that the Institute would be a productive financial venture for the university, and it was on this point that he hinged his argument, while leaving the door ajar for explaining how the curriculum could impart knowledge to train the ability to think and foster Christian moral habits.

On December 19, 1975, the campus was quiet. It was raining. The students had departed for Christmas break. Doors on faculty offices were closed. Father Fessio checked his mailbox in the dark, deserted mailroom and found the following message addressed to him from Donald J. MacIntyre, the vice president for academic affairs:

> I am delighted to inform you that Father McInnes has approved for implementation your proposal for the creation of the St. Ignatius Institute. You and those with whom you worked are to be commended for [your] work on this project. It is this kind of creative imaginative program planning that will make USF an even better institution. My heartiest congratulations to you and the others involved in the project. Needless to say, I stand ready to assist you in any way I can in the development of the Institute.

A day or so later, Father Vernon Ruland, one of the senior members of the Theology Department, approached him and told him in a very friendly manner that he had heard rumors about a new program Father Fessio was planning to initiate and that he was interested in learning what it was all about. Flattered by his interest, Father Fessio described the program in detail, outlining its curriculum and explaining the need for its presence on campus. When the lengthy description had ended, Father Ruland smiled and responded: "I will do everything in my power to stifle it." Father Fessio was quick with the retort: "Well, you're too late. It has just been approved." The encounter ended, but Father Fessio felt that both he and his interlocutor were of the same mind: the Saint Ignatius Institute was destined for future confrontation.

Two weeks earlier, an event began to unfold in Rome that would have a profound influence on the mission and development of this new program. It was the Thirty-Second General Congregation of the Society of Jesus. In March, as the elected delegates made their way back to their various parts of the globe, they would bring back with them the joyful report that the new mission of the Society of Jesus throughout the world was "the service of faith [and] the promotion of justice". Social justice would be an absolute requirement for all works of contemporary Jesuit apostolates. Some delegates probably also reflected on the three questions Pope Paul VI posed to the whole Society when he addressed the assembly: "Is the Church able to have faith in [the Jesuits] here and now, the kind of faith it has always had? What will the relationship of the ecclesiastical hierarchy toward the Society be? How will the hierarchy itself in a spirit free from fear be able to trust the Society?"[4] Such papal *dubia* led the California Province's delegate to the Congregation, Reverend Michael J. Buckley, a one-time USF trustee and the rector of the Jesuit School of Theology in Berkeley (JSTB), to comment that never since the suppression of the order in 1773 had a general congregation "been so publicly the object of the uneasiness of the Holy See and for so long a prolonged period". These three papal questions were destined to have a profound influence on Father Fessio's decision-making during his years of directorship at the Institute. But that is a matter for future chapters. Meanwhile, before Christmas break had come to an end in early 1976, Father Fessio borrowed his father's car and took off on an excessive recruiting adventure. It was Rocinante on the road again. "John Galten's wife and my mother made me tins of chocolate chip cookies," he delighted in telling supporters, "and these kept me going." His later class schedule was flexible enough to allow him to show up at every Catholic high school in California and Arizona, as well as some in New Mexico, one hundred and five total. "I would not bother making an appointment. I would just walk into the principal's office and say: 'We've got a new program. Can I talk to your seniors?' I spent the whole spring doing that." He got sixty-four enrollees for the first Saint Ignatius Institute class that began in the fall of that year, and they were an exceptionally gifted, well-balanced group of young men and women.

---

[4] Autograph Letter of His Holiness Paul VI to Father General Pedro Arrupe (1975), in *Jesuit Life and Mission Today: The Decrees and Accompanying Documents of the 31st–35th General Congregations of the Society of Jesus*, ed. John W. Padberg (Saint Louis: Institute of Jesuit Sources, 2009), 392–93.

8

IGNATIUS PRESS

Balance. Father Fessio decided *that* was what was essential to carry out his plans for the St. Ignatius Institute: balance. Was this new liberal arts curriculum not to be a balance between great books/ Catholic studies and the departmental requirements for a student's major? And did not the academic committee, which gave approval to the Institute's presence on campus, not promise to weigh—that is to say, balance—the financial benefits accrued by its presence on campus against the objections from well-established sources? The engineer in him confirmed the importance of balance.

Then, he recalled the hazardous experience he'd had years earlier on Mont Blanc that enabled him to see more clearly the need for balance. This was one more exploit of the knight in him searching for an adventure. It took place during his third year at Fourvière, that is, in the spring of 1971, a few months before the Rausch rambles and one year before his ordination, when he was given the option of going to another Jesuit house for six or seven weeks to prepare for the examination required for obtaining his master's degree in theology. He claimed it was for pious reasons that he requested Annecy, Saint Francis de Sales' home base, as the place of destination. But there may also have been some unspoken reasons for the choice: a beautiful lake, lazy beaches, spectacular views of the Alps glittering in the sun, and a countryside replete with the scents of spring. Francis de Sales would have congratulated him for making such a prudent decision. He was a saint whose writings offer practical suggestions on how to live a well-balanced life, mixing the spiritual with the practical, the ascetical with the beautiful, piety with pleasure. So the aspiring theologian and the two classmates who accompanied him on this exploit spent their mornings glued to their desks, but the afternoons were reserved for swimming, relaxing, and taking in the treasures of the Savoy countryside. On the weekends, Joseph concentrated on getting himself in shape for some serious hiking in the Alps, with his eye focused on conquering an ever-looming challenge—nearby Mont Blanc, the highest peak in Europe. One of the Jesuits in the community where the trio was housed was a certified Alpine guide, having been trained in Yosemite, where he had to climb the granite face of El Capitan in order to get his certification and, presumably, to give witness that the nature of the Jesuit vocation is open to going anywhere, taking on any task for the honor and glory of God and the good of souls. Whether or not aiding others to climb to the crest of Mont Blanc fulfilled the basic, inherent nature of being a Jesuit is a matter for conjecture. But Alphonsus Rodriguez, the Jesuit author whose works Brother Fessio had taken less than gratification in reading during his novitiate days, would agree that it is always good to mix a little mystery in one's ministry, roller coaster rides along with retreats.

On his last Friday at his chosen retreat, he set off with a band of mountain climbers to reach a little cabin some 10,000 feet from sea level, which was inaccessible except by hiking. There, after taking some refreshments and getting a little sleep, he arose at 1 A.M., pushed his feet into a pair of crampons—spiked iron plates that strap on to the sole of one's boots. "I am afraid of heights", he confesses. "So I put these crampons on and I tested them out on the roof of this hut, very steep roof with snow and ice on it. When you have these crampons on, you feel invincible. You can walk on a wall almost. It was great." He then saddled the heavy hiking gear onto his back while savoring the anticipated excitement that lay ahead. Finally, all was ready, and the party set out at 2 A.M. He recollects: "It's a full moon and it's beautiful. It had rained and snowed two days before so the air was perfectly clear, but we're just inching up. I'm just inching up the thing, because you've got a pack on, you're now eleven, twelve, thirteen, fourteen thousand feet." There the small team arrived at a critical point of their destination: a narrow ridge, about two to three feet wide, that dropped down hundreds of feet on both sides and connected one part of the mountain to another. Here the stalwart daredevil confessed he thought he had better stop and begin the descent back. Like Saint Ignatius of Loyola, he suffers from acrophobia. "I am *really* afraid of heights. I just cannot go on", he sorrowfully lamented. But his guide was an expert. He knew exactly what to do. He attached the best hiker on the last place of the line and the second best in front, in the leading position. Father Fessio would be tied in the middle. The guide told him the hiker in back could see everything going on during the march forward. If Joseph would fall, it would probably be to the right, in which case the rear man would jump to the left to ensure that the ropes would latch onto the ridge of the trail; if he fell to the left, the tail man would jump to the right. He was assured that there was nothing to worry about. "So I said OK, I'll give it a try, but I don't know how far I'm going to make it on this thing, you know." Trembling, he did manage, and the party arrived at the 15,781-foot summit between seven and eight in the morning. "Sunrise, perfectly clear air. You could see the Mediterranean, you could see Italy, France, Germany, Switzerland. It was absolutely gloriously spectacular, just unbelievable."

This part of his experience was a kind of prelude to what he would later encounter walking, sliding, and stumbling down the cog train tracks from von Balthasar's Rigi-Hüsli to where he could board the train home. It was also a prefiguration of the role he would play as director of the Saint Ignatius Institute. As he stood contemplating the panorama stretched out before him, he was convinced that he desperately needed two experts to guide him: one who could follow his direction seeing where the venture was going, pushing forward, avoiding obstacles; the other, who could save the director by supporting him, calmly listening to critics both from the left and from the right. Should Father Joseph take a fatal step to the right faction, his associate would willingly throw himself over to the left, and should he veer toward the left, the balance man would throw himself to the mercy of the right. Both supporters would be there should the director sigh: "I don't know how far I'm going to make it on this thing." At this point they would step up to the plate and push him on. Where would Father Fessio find such balance-keepers? He did not have to reflect on this matter long.

There was John Galten, who would make the ideal associate director. Sancho Panza-like, he would loyally stand behind his boss, asking questions and making observations that would keep him anchored in reality as the SII whisked its way into the future. John was a pleasant mixture of temperance and courage. He had a cool head and a keen eye, which would enable him to see the route ahead. Whenever the boss might swerve too far to accommodate parties on the right, John would ready himself to jump into the laps of those on the left; and when it looked as if his boss was cozying up too close to a faction on the left, he would ready himself to bob up and bounce to the right. Such an instinct would enable him to identify, separate, and bring together warring parties wherever they appeared. Always joyful and accommodating, he would keep the director centered, performing his task in readiness and facility. Such were the qualities that would make John the ideal assistant director of the SII machine. Then there was Dennis Bartlett. Dennis had been a scholastic at Mount St. Michael's with Father Fessio and had subsequently left the Society. Married with a growing family, he was living in San Francisco and working for the Office of Naval Intelligence. In addition to his sense of moderation, he was blessed with an innate proclivity to levelheadedness. Instinctively, he kept his socks rolled up in his dresser drawer, neatly matched and carefully separated from the pile of folded, slightly scented handkerchiefs. Following barked directives from his boss, Dennis would be able to forge ahead fast, winding up cliffs and skidding down over the potholes native to that academic Elysium on the correct side of the San Francisco Bay. He and Joseph were thirty-four, and John a year younger. So, reminiscent of one of those three-engine push-pull aircrafts, the SII enterprise took off in the fall of 1976, blending together the quixotic thirst for adventure, the Ignatian way of "the greater glory of God", and the Bertie Wooster "What ho?" manner of meeting crises.

If all of these mixed metaphors are not enough to describe the doings of Father Fessio during this period of his life, we should further comment that our pelican felt there was still ample room in his beak for scooping up more projects, plans, and schemes. For this reason, it was not surprising that plotting and laying out designs for action became part of the study-prayer group's agenda, the first item of which was discussing the works of von Balthasar, a few of which were available in English through Sheed and Ward, as well as Adrienne von Speyr's *Handmaid of the Lord*, already published in a limited run in England. Von Speyr, a Swiss medical doctor, had been a friend and close collaborator of von Balthasar's, producing over sixty books of spirituality and Scripture commentary before her death in 1967. Indeed, von Balthasar openly considered her work and mission to be far more important than his own. Efforts to have her *Handmaid* published in the United States, however, had so far come to naught. Father Fessio recognized a lack. The writings of both von Balthasar and von Speyr needed to be brought somehow to a broader U.S. audience. In the Church, he kept encountering a real enthusiasm for these works, despite their limited availability—not only in his prayer group, but beyond. For example, he met a woman—Carolyn Lemon, the head librarian at Notre Dame des Victoires grade school in San Francisco—who had stumbled across a photocopy of one of von Speyr's books and, moved by it, made a copy for herself, showing it to Father Fessio. He was delighted to share her interest. In another instance, he made the acquaintance of a certain Antje Lawry on a pro-life walk. Though not Catholic herself, this German-born woman had been reading and enjoying von Balthasar's *First Glance at Adrienne von Speyr*. Father Fessio put her in touch with Mrs. Lemon and encouraged her to try her hand at translating the book. Carolyn Lemon quickly became a friend and collaborator, rendering Antje Lawry's translated manuscript into flowing English with the help of Anne Englund. After completing this first book, the two women took on translating von Speyr's *Bereitschaft: Dimensionen christlichen Gehorsams* [*Readiness: Dimensions of Christian obedience*]. Meanwhile, the prayer group took pleasure in discussing all these works with them, although efforts to have them published came to naught. These were days in the wake of Vatican II, after all, and publishers in general were not interested in books written prior to the council, notwithstanding their contribution to the fields of knowledge and scholarship. Reading the Lawry–Lemon translations, John Galten casually declared at the end of one of the prayer sessions, "These books ought to be made known to the public. If no publishing house will print them, we ought to start our own press." No one seemed to pay much attention to such a random assertion at the time—it was not meant seriously—but Father Fessio would not forget it.

Then came a letter from Father von Balthasar to Father Fessio in the early summer of 1977, casually mentioning a young man named Erasmo Leiva-Merikakis, a very good linguist and translator finishing his doctorate at Emory University in Atlanta; perhaps Father Fessio might want to get in touch with him. After a telephone interview, Father Fessio hired him on the spot to teach at the

Institute, and Father mailed him Adrienne von Speyr's book *Sie fol-gten seinem Ruf*, which he translated hurriedly. Father sent the result to Alba House on Staten Island, who liked it and published *They Followed His Call*, the first book translation completed for what one day would become Ignatius Press. Holding the book in his hands, Father Fessio asked rhetorically, "If ever we do start a press, what will we call it?" He quickly added that his two inspired authors had already answered the question. Von Speyr's particular brand of theology, he told his reading group, is best spelled out in von Balthasar's *First Glance at Adrienne von Speyr*. "It can be summed up as an ellipse with two foci: love, exemplified by Saint John the Evangelist, and obedience, the hallmark of Saint Ignatius Loyola", he explained to the group. "So love and obedience go together." He then concluded: "Since von Balthasar's publishing house is Johannes Verlag, John Press, we'll call ours Ignatius Verlag, Ignatius Press. It will reflect the ellipse with two foci, two presses, but it will also testify to the fact that I am a Jesuit." And as a Jesuit, he reminded them, his focus was centered where obedience had missioned him, the University of San Francisco, part of which was the Saint Ignatius Institute. The Institute demanded most of his attention and was the source of his greatest excitement. Between 1975 and 1977, a desk, a typewriter, and a drawer in an SII file cabinet were the only visible signs of the dreamed-of press. Then there would come other undertakings, distractions, pet projects pursued on the side, a few of which deserve a passing nod.

In 1976, not far from the president's office suite in the University Center, was a one-room cubby tucked in between workrooms where busy administrators labored. It was the first headquarters of the SII, occupied by Father Fessio, John Galten, Dennis Bartlett, and their secretary, Julie Beck Ball. Julie was a leftover of the Santa Clara Project 50 adventure in 1968 and now a delightful addition to the balanced trio. From these earliest days of the Institute, one of the great delights enjoyed by those working in the Institute office was experiencing how the drudgery of everyday duty was lightened by a pervasive atmosphere of humor. We have seen how Father Fessio strove to live in a spirit of continuous gratitude for all that he had received and his stark conformity to the will of God— ideals Ignatius spelled out in his Spiritual Exercises. But there was also a certain lightheartedness in Father Fessio's thinking that added a distinctive flavor to the *esprit* of the early sixteenth-century Spaniard's style. Perhaps it was a response to the beauty, richness, and variety of the world he had experienced thanks to the care and encouragement of his superiors. The result was a Thérèsian element in his gratitude and conformity to the will of God that gave him the ability to laugh easily during the most stressful times of his daily duties. John Galten's powerful laugh—mixed with Dennis Bartlett's machine-gun satiric reflections—went far to instill in the office a comic spirit even while serious decisions were being made. It was the *preux* thing to do.

A series of secretaries added to sustaining the all-pervasive gaiety. The first after Julie was Gail Ayala. Before the beginnings of the Press in 1978, the foursome had packed up their expanding files and moved down to share slightly more commodious accommodations in the vacated Saint Ignatius Prep School building, known as Loyola Hall, and there Gail divided time scurrying back and forth between the Institute and the amorphous enterprise that would eventually evolve into the Press. Gail was the daughter of Frank Filice, who would be ordained a priest in 1979. He subsequently moved to Tijuana, Mexico, where for a number of years he ministered to the people in one of its poorest barrios before returning to the Archdiocese of San Francisco.

It was not long before Gail left to become a flight attendant, and Olga Orellana relieved her in dealing exclusively with the Institute. In no time, Olga became the office lion, mixing rough affection with imperiousness in dealing with students and faculty. She eventually found a more financially attractive opportunity, allowing a recent graduate of USF named Barbara Zukin to take over her desk in a newly acquired Institute office on the ground floor of Loyola Hall. Barbara was Jewish and maintained that she knew nothing about Catholics, a confession that enabled her to make observations and pose questions—bordering sometimes on the irreverent—that kept the office rolling in laughter. She had a knack for injecting spontaneous and unrestrained comments at meetings when her Jesuit boss was most seriously engaged with some weighty matter, and—much to the credit of all present—she managed to get away with it. Her contribution for solidifying the "balance" element of the Institute was considerable.

In 1977, a young woman from San Francisco, Karen Summerhays, began helping Barbara, and in July of the following year, Karen became the full-time secretary, a position she held until 1986. Quiet, intelligent, and ever equipoised, she provided the reasonable equilibrium to the operation that kept it on an even keel. From the very beginning, she also gave witness to the veracity of the proverb about the apple not falling far from the tree: her brother Kim was one of the most respected men in the university, a professor of chemistry in the College of Science and an instructor in the Institute until its demise in 2001. After Karen followed Kris Wartner Quispe and Lisa Hamrick.

Besides the Institute and the Press, there was one more factor destined to mold the future Fessio saga. Its provenance lies hidden in the beginning of 1976, as the happenings of the Mexico adventure were becoming pleasant memories. Frank Filice was again the instigator. He had a friend named Paul Ryan who had some connections with a legal tax-exempt group called the Sullivan Reading Program, dedicated to teaching reading skills to children between five and nine years old. Frank talked Paul into using the proceeds of this work to help promote various nonprofit causes. But first, to protect this donation from taxation, a tax-exempt California corporation had to be set up. This was simple enough. They initially received federal—not state—tax-exempt status through their affiliation with the Archdiocese of San Francisco, which had a 501(c)(3) rating. They established a board, of which Father Fessio became an outspoken member. In 1976, thanks to the gratuitous pro bono service of attorney Carl Noelke, Guadalupe Associates Incorporated came into existence. As soon as the entity was legally recognized, Dr. Filice pulled out his wallet and contributed twenty-five dollars to the treasury. This corporation would eventually become the trade name of Ignatius Press, serving as a reminder of that fateful pilgrimage to the shrine of Our Lady of Guadalupe in the summer of 1975.

Father Fessio may be a dreamer, but he is before all else a practical man. So it should not be surprising that when he began to consider if and how Ignatius Press could grow from the soil of Guadalupe Associates, he realized money would be the most essential vehicle to enable it to slide along to success. Meanwhile, the future looked bright, and various signs of hope encouraged the Institute team to move its office from the main campus to Loyola Hall, the building already described that had been home to Saint Ignatius Prep. An old gym locker separated the two entities of the Institute and the Press. If a student came in about an academic matter, Carolyn Lemon, who was now working for the Press, would stop typing, tiptoe over to the locker and stealthily swing open its door to block the noise and insure the student more privacy. In doing so, she had to be careful not to disturb the piles of clothing that had been donated for Vietnamese refugees and stored in the cramped quarters. Eventually, with the arrival of planeloads of "boat people", the clothes found wearers, and the Institute moved from the basement to the third floor, then to larger quarters on the first floor, and eventually up to the center of campus into Campion Hall (since named Kalmanovitz Hall), beneath a large statue of the Blessed Virgin (since removed).

Between 1975 and 1977, a desk, a typewriter, and a file cabinet were the only reminders of the hoped-for Press, a lost dream that became more haunting with the passage of time and with the remarkable success of the Institute. Yet San Francisco in the late 1970s was one of the richest spots in the country for the book industry, and Father Fessio was able to consult easily with typesetters, calligraphers, fine printers, paper makers, and a host of other artists and craftsmen dedicated to the trade. These inquiries also stimulated dormant fund-raising instincts in the Fessio make-up. Eventually he was able to purchase an IBM Selectric typewriter equipped with an element containing the characters needed for optical character recognition (OCR) typesetting. The process demanded maximum patience and was especially time-consuming when an error was made. When finished, the typed pages were sent off to a typesetter, who in turn would return the typeset pages for proofreading. Such progress emphasized the need to purchase more sophisticated equipment. He had been able to collect a number of small donations, but what he needed was a generous handout, and, after studious investigation, he came to the conclusion that the man to approach for the furtherance of this end was Harry G. John.

It was in the early days of 1976 that Father Kenneth Baker, S.J., a well-known theologian and editor of *Homiletic and Pastoral Review*, recommended Harry to Father Fessio as a likely sympathizer of his dream to publish Catholic books. Harry was one of two children who had inherited the Miller Brewing fortune in the late fifties or early sixties. He got 49 percent and his sister 51 percent of the company. When she sold her portion for $32 million, Harry's friends urged him to sell his and catch a similar windfall. But no, he wanted to be involved in its management. He was somewhat of a conundrum: having entered the Trappists (one of the strictest monastic orders of the Catholic Church) at an early age, he later left the monastery, married, and became the father of nine children. In 1972, after a bidding war, he sold his Miller inheritance to the victor, Philip Morris, for $97 million. Meanwhile, he had named his fund the De Rance Foundation, after the seventeenth-century founder of the Trappists, Armand-Jean de Boutbillier de Rancé. Overnight it became the world's largest Catholic charitable foundation, enabling its director to build leprosaria in India, construct water wells in East Africa, and establish seminaries in the Philippines and camps for inner-city children in Milwaukee. He and his wife, Erica, along with Don Gallagher, a college friend and former professor of philosophy, were the trustees of this treasure trove.

Father Fessio's eventual connection with Harry would convince him that the millionaire was a genius in handling money: he would both easily make it, gladly divest it, and then turn around and make more than he had planned on giving away. Before the invention of computers, Harry had two human "calculators" who would rush about evaluating the financials of small businesses, then buy them, invest heavily in them, and sell the stock for a considerable gain. Besides being a successful, capitalist philanthropist, he was also interested in Catholic education, thanks to the influence of Don Gallagher. Together they founded Cardinal Newman College in St. Louis, which unfortunately closed its doors in 1985. Early in 1976, Father Fessio wrote to Harry, giving a brief description of the Institute, suggesting how he could further enrich so worthy a cause. Mr. John responded by inviting his correspondent to come to Wisconsin and discuss the matter face-to-face in his Wauwatosa office. Father Fessio obliged, and with great hope and energy he took a plane to Milwaukee. After some confusion, he managed to make it to Wauwatosa, where he finally found the building for which he had spent some valuable time searching, entered, and approached a lone man in baggy pants and scruffy shoes—obviously the janitor— and asked: "Pardon me, Sir. Could you kindly direct me to Mr. Harry John's office?"

"Who are you and why do you want to talk to him?" was the surprising reply.

"I'm Joe Fessio, Father Joseph Fessio, from San Francisco. Mr. John invited me to come and discuss a personal matter with him."

The man sized him up before saying: "OK, follow me." They walked together upstairs and down a hallway until coming to a private room, which the man unlocked and entered, saying: "I'm Harry John. Sit down. What's your deal? Be quick about it, please." Apparently Father Fessio was quick indeed. In August 1977, the secretary, Karen Summerhays, opened an envelope containing a $25,000 check for the Press and handed it to her boss. His reaction was not recorded, but had it been so, Karen probably would have asserted she did not see him swallow as he contemplated the favorable hand he had been dealt that put the Institute into full gear.

In 1977, USF got a new president, the rector of the Jesuit community, Father John Lo Schiavo, whose dealings with young Father Fessio were recounted earlier. Like so many, I was delighted. I knew that instinctively John would use his new authority very cautiously, reasonably, and never viciously. He was ever the gentleman with a strong sense of sympathy for the oppressed and disadvantaged. But he was also a man determined to achieve his goal, and beware to anyone who would oppose him. These qualities had served him well on the basketball court. He would never flare up, but he could present a potential opponent with the gracious option of making a choice he would not be inclined to refuse. He had not been president long when Father Fessio and four or five of us Jesuits associated with the SII were sent a summons to meet with him, not in a university office, but, significantly, in the conference room of the Jesuit residence. Was this the same room where in January 1976, a few weeks after the Institute had been approved, eight members of the Jesuit community called for a special meeting with the then rector of the community, Father Lo Schiavo? Probably. On that occasion, the group expressed their commonly held fears for the university if Father Fessio continued to be associated with it, and a number of them confessed they were sincerely concerned about his psychological well-being. These Jesuits tried to persuade the rector that Fessio needed psychological or psychiatric attention. Father Lo Schiavo saw at once that such a decision would have dire consequences. As the religious superior, he had to defend one of his subjects who, seemingly, was being bullied. At the same time, he would not alienate himself from a faction whose influence among Jesuits beyond the USF campus was a well-known fact. After that meeting had ended, the rector probably reasoned that time was on his side. He would wait for further developments. A year later, he was spared from making a rector's decision, but now, as president, he had to face the "Fessio Problem" in a new guise, and he was not going to let it deter him from fulfilling the demands of his new assignment. Hence, the consultation with the SII Jesuits was imperative.

The president began by informing the group that word had got around that Father Fessio had said he would like to publish the doctoral thesis of Karol Cardinal Wojtyła on the spirituality of Saint John of the Cross. The president informed the group that repercussions of publishing this opus were registered far and wide, and then, in a calm, friendly, but firm voice, he stated that the Press was in no way to be associated with the university. The two were totally separate, and separate they were to remain. On the following day, he reiterated this policy decision in a letter addressed to the director of the Saint Ignatius Institute. One has to be sympathetic with the newly appointed president in this matter. Whatever he thought personally, his job was to keep peace by accommodating a powerful faction that included some Jesuits from other institutions, especially the Jesuit School of Theology at Berkeley, across the bay. At first, Father Fessio was disappointed, because he had labored under the impression that both the university and the Press would benefit from a close association. "The Ignatius Press of the University of San Francisco" had something attractive about it, and in future years aspiring authors of the USF faculty did indeed bemoan the fact they could not easily publish their scholarly works through such a collegiate publishing house. Later happenings, however, convinced all sympathetic to the mission of the Press what a blessing the president's decision had been. The university could destroy the Institute, but the Press was under a totally separate corporation, completely free to answer the *dubia* of Pope Paul VI in an unadulteratedly Ignatian spirit by making the writings of orthodox theologians and rational philosophers available to all, in particular to young scholars. This ideal was unequivocally and clearly expressed in the mission statement of Guadalupe Associates in their meeting on April 25, 1978, the date when the board members affirmed: "This corporation shall, among its other activities, undertake to prepare translations of foreign language manuscripts and books on theological and philosophical subjects for use in academic courses."

9

THE FESSIO PROBLEM

Here we shall attempt to disentangle some instances that went into forming the "Fessio Problem". In order to do so, we should speed back to November 11, 1976. That was the day Professor Michael Lehmann, the secular-minded president of the Faculty Administration Union, addressed a letter to Father Fessio, the director of the newly established Saint Ignatius Institute. He began: "I have been disappointed in the past that USF was not able to offer a value oriented or theology program to students on an elective rather than compulsory basis." Eventually he concluded: "It seems to me that USF could *best* show its uniqueness by offering such a curriculum, rather than requiring it. It seems you have done the job. I want to commend you on your initiative and drive, and offer you sincere good wishes for the success of your program." Two years later, in the 1978 edition of the *National Jesuit News*, another letter from Dr. Lehmann appeared. Speaking for some of the members of the faculty union, he confessed that certain misgivings about the Saint Ignatius Institute had developed: "There is a fear—not substantiated, but a fear—that the university is fostering the growth of a college which will grow to the point where the rest of the arts college just fades away." So in less than two years, a fear of the Institute, not yet "substantiated", was already beginning to take shape.

If this was a fear, however unsubstantiated, among a very few faculty members in the College of Arts and Sciences, it was indeed limited—the majority could not have cared less—but it had long since solidified substantially in the Theology Department, where the chairman, Father Albert Zabala, S.J., had earlier cheered the arrival of this promising young German-trained theologian, the next Rahner, joining *die Bande der Theologen* at USF. Disappointment, however, soon turned to resentment, then to fear: the promising young scholar became a threat and did so rapidly. Three weeks after receiving Lehmann's complimentary 1976 letter, Father Fessio stood reading a memo from Father Zabala advising him that "it seemed wise, given the many new burdens the Institute is going to place on you, not to add the further burden of serving on department committees." So he was not expected to participate in departmental affairs. At the same time, the chairman instructed him to prepare a course in Christian social teaching. "In my opinion," he stated, "this is more in line with the last General Congregation's decrees [i.e., the 32nd General Congregation of the Society of Jesus] on 'Service of Faith and Promotion of Justice' than courses in Mariology and Thomas Aquinas." There were some who speculated the anointing oils for Jesuit universities were blessed in the name of "promotion of Justice" at that General Congregation. That is debatable, and beyond the scope of this biography. But certain it was that at USF the leitmotif of the upcoming drama was sounded loud and clear, thus defining the wellspring, the source from which the Fessio Problem would grow steadily over the next twenty-five years.

Two other quests in the career of Father Fessio beg for a brief nod. In the spring of 1978, between teaching classes, the demands of the Institute, pickup games of Frisbee and visions for the future of the newly founded Press, Father Fessio stumbled across an essay by Dorothy Sayers entitled "The Lost Tools of Learning". He was fascinated by her description of a program of primary–secondary education based on the traditional trivium. She wrote that what was important for young people was to learn who they were, where they have come from, and where they are ultimately going. To achieve this end, she suggested, an early great books program could be helpful. The result of this conviction caused him to form a circle of more than thirty parents and educators to discuss the possibility of beginning a Catholic school, extending from grades 4 to 11, that would prepare students to qualify later for the Saint Ignatius Institute at USF or for some other college with a great books orientation. He contacted the archdiocesan superintendent of education, who showed considerable interest, and the plan took root right away. Even the place to begin the school was agreed upon, the suppressed Holy Cross Church, one of the oldest churches in San Francisco, presently a Buddhist temple. But to the disappointment of many parents, the venture was spiked. Meanwhile, there were some who wondered how his involvement in such a program aided in his commitment to the university and the Saint Ignatius Institute. Indeed, "A wonderful bird is the pelican."

Then, there was the Classic Books on Tape project. Here, his experience with the fizzled early great books program encouraged him, first of all, to form a committee made up of Saint Ignatius Institute personnel and a few students. Their plan of proceeding was to report back to him on their research and discussions regarding four questions he had proposed: (1) Is there a market for classical-type works in cassette form, and, if so, what great works would lend themselves to this market? (2) What would be involved in accomplishing the agreed-upon agenda? (3) What would be the cost, from the reader to the finished product? (4) Could the profit-making idea be recommended as a feasible venture? The report of the committee was thorough, and its recommendation positive, so he began to put the project into action. But because of a lack of space and personnel, this venture was eventually put on hold. Those proposed questions, however, have ever since played an essential part in his planning projects and plotting adventures, right up to the present day. Later, when the space conditions were more favorable, he began the Catholic Books on Tape project, which proved to be a popular and profitable enterprise for the Press for many years.

Another adventure came in March 1978, a year that was filled with a plethora of activities. Early that month, the Department of Theology and Religious Studies, in conjunction with the Department of Religious Education and the Graduate Coordinating Committee, gave its report to the Faculty Association's Committee on Graduate Studies regarding the proposed Master of Arts in Catholic Studies (MACS) program. If that sounds to today's reader like a gambol on an academic merry-go-round in Disneyland, it certainly was, at least on the surface. A later autopsy would reveal the cause of its demise. The MACS proposal was the child of Father Fessio. Inspired by the fact that over the past decade there had emerged a number of "Ethnic Studies" programs designed to explore the distinctive contributions of individual minorities within Western Civilization—programs that were accepted enthusiastically by universities of that era—Fessio, in conjunction with the Board of Directors of the Saint Ignatius Institute, suggested there should be a

correlative program to the SII offered by the university on one of
Western civilization's great traditions: Catholicism. It should be an
interdisciplinary program—more extensive than a traditional religious studies program.

His justification for the MACS program was that almost a whole
generation of Catholics, both religious and lay, had been educated
without this traditional core. Now many of these individuals were
coming to see there was a profound deficiency in their education.
They began to question whether Vatican II was in reality a repudiation of Catholic tradition, as the popular media and some theologians would have it. They did not know, because they had never
had the opportunity to study systematically the background of their
own long-established beliefs and customs. The director of the Saint
Ignatius Institute now suggested that the study proposed to the graduate programs coordinating committee would provide present-day
students with an opportunity to answer their queries at a level of
sophistication appropriate to their own educational achievements.
He proposed dividing the curriculum of this proposed program into
two levels of courses. At the lower level, there would be two year-
long lecture courses giving a survey of the Catholic Church and of
the Catholic tradition. These courses would be numbered in the
university catalogue at the junior-senior level; at the same time, the
gained units could fulfill some requirements for an M.A. In these
team-taught courses, the faculty members would provide overviews
of Catholicism—one systematic, the other historical. Whether or
not an individual graduate student would have to take one or both
of these surveys would depend upon his background. Hopefully
such courses could also be popular with non-degree students interested in Catholicism. The second level of the curriculum would be
a series of graduate seminars focusing on various aspects of Catholic teaching or the Catholic tradition. The titles of these courses
would be flexible, giving the instructor the freedom to concentrate
on whatever topic in which he felt most competent in directing
research. There would be a dozen or so seminars that would cover
the whole range of Catholic studies and culture—the Catholic tradition in philosophy, literature, social teaching, economics, music,
art, architecture, and the like. One can detect in this proposal the
shadowy presence of Henri de Lubac.

Father Fessio pointed out to the members of the committee that the Saint Ignatius Institute had been established to provide a traditional curriculum for students who had expressed a desire to follow it and that already the Institute was more successful and more financially advantageous for the university than anticipated. There was presently an analogous need to initiate a similar program on the graduate level. He tried to convince the members of the committee that the MACS would prove advantageous to students, teachers, and the university.

In his outline of the typical curriculum a candidate would have to take in order to obtain a MACS degree, Father Fessio refrained from speculating on the amount of homework one would have to do in order to meet questions and objections with expertise. He also wisely encouraged other sympathetic members of the faculty to do most of the explaining. With his donnish manner and biting wit, Dr. Raymond Dennehy of the Philosophy Department defended the MACS proposal in a memorable manner. He was one of the first instructors of the Institute classes, but he was appreciated by a much larger audience at Stanford and, especially, the University of California at Berkeley, where for more than twenty-five years he defended the pro-life cause in celebrated debates. But his arguments had little impact on the course of the tide that carried the MACS discussions to their conclusion. The spokesman for the Theology Department was more persuasive. For the benefit of the committee he read a carefully prepared statement emphasizing that the department

> welcomed Father Fessio's recommendation . . . provided that the "Catholic teaching" phase of the proposed program is wholly assimilated within the present Master of Arts program and its staffing remains entirely subject to [Theology] Department control. We are categorically opposed to the separate implementation of the Master of Arts in Catholic Studies program . . . because it would weaken Departmental control over a degree program under its own sponsorship.

The majority of the members of the department could not restrain their animus when they voted that to add the MACS program "would further accentuate a present polarization between the mainstream Catholic theological community and a group of Catholics

who seemingly arrogate the claim of Catholicity to themselves".
Adhering to the position statement of the Department of Theology
and Religious Studies, the Faculty Association Committee rejected
Father Fessio's proposal.

All of this detailed description might be of little use today, but
what it shows is how thorough Father Fessio was in designing an
academic program for the betterment of both the individual and
the university and why there was consistent opposition to any program initiated by the director of the Saint Ignatius Institute. It further demonstrates that one can be sympathetic with the theology
professors' opposition to the MACS program—he did seem to be
encroaching on the department's defined prerogatives—and understand why they remained so opposed to him. Finally, it witnesses
to the fact that the 1970s were a time when the popularity of non-
directive counseling and "encounter group" workshops militated
in the theology departments of Catholic colleges throughout the
country. This factor played into the MACS game. It was generally conceded by many popular theology professors that for those
of Father Fessio's ilk, religion had to be repressive in order to be
authentic, whereas true religion was freeing. Institute and prospective MACS instructors assumed they knew what was best for a person. This was the reason for their political acts: under the guise of
propagating philosophical and religious truth, they sought to deny
the rights of the individual. The Faculty Union was the godsend
that guarded academic, political, and religious freedom. The secular guru Carl Rogers was everywhere admired for his insights into
how psychology could fit easily into the spirit of Vatican II, freeing
people from the debilitating causes of religious rigorism. It was easy
to see why some regarded Father Fessio as a non-conformist with
respect to the way the Holy Spirit was pointing for membership
in the Church of the future, a Jesuit sincerely in need of psychological help. Finally, these three factors reveal what might appear
to be a shallowness in the disputes between Father Fessio and his
opponents, described in later chapters—a certain de Lubacian ap-
prehension he had of elements attempting to destroy the traditions
of the Church.

With reason, Father President Lo Schiavo was uncomfortable with
what was seen as the Fessio Problem. Fortunately, he saw a way out.
There was a recently hired specialist on campus who was able to

come to his aid. His name was Dr. Michael Scriven. In recognition of his wide-range areas of knowledge, he had been given the prestigious title "University Professor", and at the time he was the director of the university's evaluation institute at the School of Education. Agnostic, if not atheist, he was a man of integrity, careful not to let any of his own prejudices interfere with his judgments in evaluating different programs at the university. He was also conversant with Catholic beliefs as well as with the history of the Church and of the post–Vatican II tensions within the Church. So Father Lo Schiavo, recusing himself and dropping his responsibility for the outcome of the case, commissioned Scriven to do an evaluation of the Saint Ignatius Institute in general and of its problem-causing director in particular. About this same date, the early spring of 1978, the union filed a complaint against the university regarding hiring practices on the part of the Institute. The results of this case and the results of the Scriven report will be given in a subsequent chapter. Our purpose here is to focus in on the personality and the *modus procedendi* of the Director of the Saint Ignatius Institute as the torturous seventies were ending, and in order to make this intent clearer, there is one more anecdote that should be recorded.

Again, I was delighted when the rector of the USF Jesuit community without vanity or arrogance moved his chair to the president's desk at the university. But when I considered what might be the potential rapport between this suave, uncontested Godfather and the newly appointed wave-creating director of the Saint Ignatius Institute, I heard once again deep within me that fateful Don José leitmotif from *Carmen*. Sometime later, those three notes sounded with greater intensity. Shortly after his appointment, Father President Lo Schiavo had hired a specialist to advise him on the economic status of the university he was now commissioned to govern. After some research, the expert was confident that he could draw up a plan that would turn deficits to assets, worries into joys. The president shared his confidence, and he let it be known that he was impressed by his pick and was eager to introduce him and his plan of action to the university's faculty and staff. Representatives of the various colleges and programs were invited to attend small sessions at which the president and the expert jointly spoke. As a member of the board of the SII, I was invited to attend one such conference, and after giving half-hearted interest to what was being said, I was relieved when the president finally thanked the speaker and the attendees, extending hope that all would have an enjoyable luncheon. Scraping of chairs and shuffling of feet followed, but then, along with the others, I sat again when I heard Father Fessio say: "Wait a minute. I have a question." The answer led to another question, and then more comments and questions, until I heard him say, politely but convincingly, that he did not think the expert understood the main problem and that his solutions to the non-problems he presented were not very satisfactory, either. With a toothy smile and frosty eyes, Father Lo Schiavo thanked the director of the Institute for his comments, again assured the invitees how fortunate the university was to have the economic expert with us, and repeated his hope that we would have an enjoyable luncheon. We filed out of the room in silence. The expert stayed on campus as an advisor to the president for a while, but then quietly disappeared, and nothing more was heard of him or of the solution to the problem that had brought him to the university. Could Father Fessio have been responsible for his retirement? No mention of the matter was ever made. But the scene convinced those of us from the Institute that when anyone took on Father Joseph Fessio regarding financial and budgetary matters, he had better know his facts and be ready to defend them. He has a calculator-like mind that deals with numbers in an amazing way. In this instance, his calculations took precedence to prudence, setting the stage for future encounters with the president. One last reflection about the relationship of Fathers Lo Schiavo and Fessio during the development phase of the SII and the Ignatius Press begs comment. The older and the younger man could sit together all alone, buddy-like, in the television room completely engrossed in a sporting event, analyzing plays, criticizing decisions, arguing with one another affably about the talents of the players or coaches, and recalling previous contests. Then, after the game was over, it was back to business as usual. There was something about the interaction of these two shrewd, complicated Italian-American Jesuits that made me sometimes think that I was living in a Godfather movie. The following chapters are designed to show how the drama unfolded.

10

A TIME OF GROWTH

In the midst of all of this turmoil, the Jesuit vice-provincial decided that it was time for Father Fessio to complete his long formation in the Society by making his tertianship, that is, by spending several months or a year away from the active life in order to study in depth the *Constitutions* and *Institute* of the Society of Jesus. High on the agenda of this period of solitude and reflection was making the Ignatian thirty-day Spiritual Exercises. Earlier, Father Fessio requested to make this retreat under the direction of Father de Lubac, who was willing and eager to accommodate him. The vice-provincial could understand his desire to recharge his worn-out spiritual batteries with de Lubac, to make a thirty-day retreat under his guidance, and for this he gave permission. But understandably, he advised him that a decision would be forthcoming on whether or not this experience could substitute for a thirty-day retreat made with his fellow tertians, under the direction of the California Province director. Father Fessio confirmed his desire to meet with de Lubac. So, ever optimistic, in the summer of 1978, he returned to France and placed himself under the direction of his revered former spiritual director, and the two of them retired to Wépion near Namur, Belgium, in order to explore the paths and directions outlined by Saint Ignatius to discern and put into effect God's will. Wépion is nestled in hills that slope steeply down to the soft-flowing Meuse, an ideal place for daily interchange with the beauty of nature and the direction of Father de Lubac, guiding him to become more immersed in the life, death, and Resurrection of Jesus Christ. Following Father Fessio's return to San Francisco, the vice-provincial gave him some news: after much thought and prayer, he had decided—and with good reason—that because Father Fessio was thought to be "singular" enough, he should remake the retreat in the tertianship setting with his peers in California. Sanctity is found in doing the ordinary: a Jesuit axiom.

Father Fessio readily complied, and in the first part of March 1979, he pulled himself away from his many distractions and ventured to Montecito for a few days to join his future companions and their three directors in preparation for beginning tertianship later in the summer. What he found there was extraordinary: Masses with the chief tertian director as celebrant, in which none of the concelebrants wore vestments—"sport clothes only"; alterations in the Canon of the Mass—even in the words of Consecration—and modifications, additions, and omissions throughout the celebration. Father Fessio, though not surprised, was somewhat confused. Later the director, who had been trained in France by recognized specialists in the "new way" to offer Mass, was an obliging, considerate man and a very good priest. So it was not surprising that he approached the candidate to ascertain how he thought he would fit into the community. Father Fessio replied that since there was a difference of opinion between men of good will on these liturgical matters, he thought he should seek clarification from the local ordinary, seeing that as a future tertian he would be concelebrating in this diocese. The local ordinary was Timothy Cardinal Manning, archbishop of Los Angeles. When he returned to San Francisco, Father Fessio wrote a letter to Cardinal Manning, with copies to the vice-provincial and tertian director, respectfully asking the cardinal's answer to three questions. First: "Am I correct in thinking that you as the local ordinary have jurisdiction over these Eucharistic liturgies, even if the celebrants are all Jesuits and the place is a private chapel?" Second: "Do you approve of such liturgies in your archdiocese? If so, under what conditions?" Third: "May I, as a priest who will be concelebrating the Eucharist, participate in or preside at such liturgies?"

He soon received Cardinal Manning's reply to his letter, with copies addressed to the vice-provincial and tertian director. The opening sentence read: "The situation you inquire about is distressing to me, but not unknown where members of the Society gather." Then, after a paragraph explaining why such violations went against liturgical law, he concluded: "With as much insistence as I can communicate, I disapprove of the circumstances you inquire about. I think they are unworthy of the loyalty which the Society holds to the Holy See and a source of scandal to those who are aware of this kind of conduct. God's blessing does not fall upon it, nor mine." Since liturgical practice was expansive in folly and limited in required rubrics among Jesuit houses throughout the archdiocese of San Francisco, Father Fessio, in "a spirit of openness", sent photocopies of the two letters, his and the cardinal's, to Archbishop Quinn. In his response, the archbishop asserted he was "in total accord with the response of Cardinal Manning" and "doubly distressed when these things are perpetrated by Jesuits whose special vocation requires a unique form of loyalty to the Holy See and a unique form of obedience in the Church".

A short missive came to him from the tertian director, too, respectfully advising him that he would probably not be at peace making tertianship at Montecito. Meanwhile, the vice-provincial for education requested that he meet with him at Los Gatos to discuss the copy of the letter addressed to the provincial. He was a tough, Texas-born, no-nonsense negotiator. The two Jesuits now sat facing one another, the older man holding in his hand a copy of the younger man's letter. As Father Fessio remembers, the vice-provincial began the conversation by asking, "Why did you go over my head and write to the cardinal?" He replied, "I didn't go over your head. You are not in the liturgical chain of command. It is the ordinary [bishop] who has authority over all Masses in his diocese." The vice-provincial: "What about charity towards your tertian director?" Father Fessio: "If I were doing something questionable, I think the charitable thing would be to point it out to my superior." The vice-provincial: "I can see you are not psychologically prepared for tertianship." He returned to San Francisco with peace of soul, but with the date of his tertianship put on hold.

The letters from Cardinal Manning and Archbishop Quinn were read by Father Fessio with interest and satisfaction but quickly put aside. He now had other distractions: not only the affairs of the Saint Ignatius Institute, but those of Ignatius Press. Thanks to that $25,000 gift to the Press from the De Rance Foundation, his conversations with salesmen and specialists in the publishing industry had suddenly taken on a tone that differed from the post-prayer-meeting chatter of earlier days, and before long Father Fessio became proficient in one more field of endeavor. He was dealing with hands-on matters like the protagonist of *The Ugly American*, the book that had such an influence on his life. Part of the De Rance money was very soon exchanged for some necessary equipment for printing manuscripts. The first product was a translation of *Humanae Vitae* by Father Marc Calegari, S.J., used at the *Humanae Vitae* symposium Father Fessio would organize in July 1978. However, since Father Fessio wanted his own master's opus to be the first recognized work printed in house by Ignatius Press, von Balthasar's *Heart of the World* was given an ISBN ending in -001 designation (in contrast to a -000 number assigned to the Calegari translation, which actually appeared in print first). But the next book received from the printer was *Woman in the Church* by Father Louis Bouyer, and this was followed in quick succession by Balthasar's *First Glance at Adrienne von Speyr*, Pope John Paul II's doctoral thesis *Faith according to St. John of the Cross* (publishing rights obtained through the influence of Father de Lubac), and *Understanding the Heart* by Rev. Francis Larkin, S.S.C.C., which sold more than 5,000 copies. The Press also published three works by James V. Schall, S.J.: *Christianity and Life*, *The Distinctiveness of Christianity*, and *Liberation Theology*.

These published works owed their existence to the inexperienced, mainly volunteer labor of several women. Carolyn Lemon was particularly conspicuous in this onerous occupation. Many days, after finishing her regular job as a librarian at the Notre Dame des Victoires grade school, she found herself spending hours wrestling, sometimes in tears, with the office technology: first the Selectric/OCR and later a Heathkit H-89 computer—machines she had never heard of just a short time earlier. How she managed we shall see. And as was noted earlier, the cell where her agony transpired was a tiny faculty office, jam-packed high with donated clothing destined for the Vietnamese boat people. Then there was Anne Nash, who began helping the fledgling Press with book design—her field of doctoral study—along with translating, copyediting, and proofreading. She talked her friend Victoria Hoke Lane into doing the cover calligraphy for *Heart of the World* and other titles. Carolyn and Anne have been with the Press for the past forty years. Other helpers were Sandi Ellingwood, who set up the accounting system for the Press, and Julie Ball, mentioned earlier, as well as Darlene Lawless, a student who excelled in typing the new manuscripts. Darlene and her future husband, John O'Rourke, eventually founded Loyola Graphics, which still typesets for Ignatius Press.

A strange coincidence, occurring in the summer of 1980, brought a valuable addition to the Press. Busy at work, as usual, Father Fessio was distracted by a telephone call. On the other end of the line was a woman who identified herself simply as a Quaker. He was looking for a way to hang up quickly without being rude when she proceeded to tell him that she had heard of Saint Ignatius of Loyola but knew nothing about him. "So?" he thought, holding his tongue. She went on. Seeking a solution to her problem, she turned to the telephone directory and looked up "Saint Ignatius", finding there listed the Saint Ignatius Institute. "That sounds Catholic enough", she decided, and she dialed the number. As she explained to her uncommitted interlocutor, she knew a young man, a computer programmer, who was having spiritual problems. She thought the poor fellow ought to speak with a priest. She then asked the unidentified man at the other end of the line whether he knew a priest who would have time to accommodate her request. *A computer programmer!* Father Fessio thought. "Oh yes, I am a priest, and I'll be more than happy to speak with him about his spiritual quandaries."

It did not take much time for Father Fessio to be sitting across from young Steve Canino, counseling him on matters spiritual, interspersed with a query or two about computer programming. Very quickly, with more astonishment than joy, he realized that he was sitting face-to-face with a specialist in basic on-line typesetting and pagination computing. It was just what the Press needed. Soon he and Steve began working on a program for hyphenation and justification (BOLT: Bembo On-Line Typesetting) as well as another for page layout (PAGE: Paste and Glue Eliminator). To aid his spiritual progress, Father recommended that Steve sign on with the Press where he could speak with Father—in between sessions at the computer, *bien sûr*—about his spiritual progress. Steve proved to be an answer to many prayers. He and Father Fessio also devised a way to run a donated piece of typesetting equipment with a Heathkit computer supplying the data. August 1981 saw another valuable player added to the Press' team. Tony Ryan, destined to become the Press' vital marketing manager, was a tough, dedicated family man, who rode his motorcycle more than 120 miles each day, rain or shine, to and from work.

One might have thought that the hustle and bustle from the Press to the Saint Ignatius Institute would be more than enough to keep the director occupied, but just as the beak of the pelican seems never able to be filled, so the director of the Saint Ignatius Institute and editor-publisher of Ignatius Press could not refrain from latching onto a new project that promised social and spiritual satisfaction. About the same time Canino and Ryan joined the personnel at the Press, he decided on a new venture. His time in Europe had introduced him to a travel program used by priests, nuns, and committed Catholics that donated all of its profits to various charitable institutions. Why not launch such an agency here in San Francisco? Hence the birth of PACE (Profits Aid Catholic Education), whose financial earnings would go to support the Saint Ignatius Institute. Father Fessio persuaded Dennis Bartlett's wife, Denise, to assume the managerial role, aided by the wives of some SII professors. The project was greeted with the characteristic enthusiasm of admirers who had already seen how Father Fessio can turn brass into gold. PACE organized a large pilgrimage to the Holy Land, Rome, and Lourdes in 1981. Later, after this flash forward, it flickered a bit, sputtered, and then spun flat, "through no fault of Denise", Father is quick to add. But it was not a complete failure. It gave all the ladies connected with Father Fessio's various projects reason to meet occasionally at lunches to discuss common objectives of greater moment than the progress of PACE, the SII, or the Press. One cannot overestimate the contribution of women to the beginnings of the Press and the Institute.

To the uninitiated, the Press seemed to have had amazing growth. In 1979, three thousand books were sold, and that number doubled each year until 1986, when the ratio tripled to almost one million, and after that it continued to double annually for several more years until the rate finally leveled off. This impressive efflorescence of growth was due to the Press' being a well-organized, well-managed, committed Catholic enterprise, rivaling the businesses booming in nearby Silicon Valley. In 1976, when Father Fessio was still contemplating beginning the Press, he had asked Frank Sheed's advice about plunging ahead on such a risky venture. Frank and his wife, Maisie Ward, were the directors of Sheed and Ward, the best-known

Catholic publishing house in the English-speaking world during the mid-twentieth century. Some of the authors whose works were published under the Sheed and Ward label were G. K. Chesterton, Hilaire Belloc, Christopher Dawson, and Ronald Knox. The headquarters of the company had moved from London to New York in 1933, and Frank used to make frequent trips to Australia, often arranging for a few days' stopover in San Francisco. Here he learned about the Saint Ignatius Institute, and, after 1976, he would give a lecture to students when possible. Frank encouraged Father Fessio and his plan, but warned, "You will have ten years of grief." What was true for the Press was more true for the Institute. In fact, the troubles continued for more than a decade.

If the last year of the 1970s passed with memories of stressful contradictions, the first year of the new decade gave no indication of change. But unlike tornados, earthquakes give no warning when they will strike, and what happened in February 1980 qualifies as an earthquake. Father Joseph's new vice-provincial sent him a four-page letter, with copies to the Jesuit rector at USF and to the Jesuit general in Rome, stating: "As Vice-Provincial for Education, I hereby direct you to resign as Editor of Ignatius Press, resign as Director of Guadalupe Associates, Incorporated, and desist from any other association or official connection with Guadalupe Associates and any and all of that Corporation's enterprises, activities, projects and programs. And I ask you to effect this disassociation [sic] as soon as possible." The author was a man conversant with the Fessio Problem, having formally served as the chief chaplain of USF's campus ministry team. He was a man totally committed to the social apostolate, sympathetic to advocates of liberation theology, and although never a vociferous critic of the Saint Ignatius Institute, it would have been difficult to find anyone else on campus more crammed with quiet, suppressed hostility for what motivated Institute staff members, professors, and students. But caution calls for adjudicating events as he did at the time, rather than seeing them through the focus of present-day knowledge. He was sincerely convinced he was in total sync with the Church and the Society, but this fact was not the reason for his present resolve. "I want to make clear", he wrote in his letter to Father Fessio, "that this decision has nothing to do with your views concerning the Church, your theology or your spirituality. And it is not some sort of punishment or retaliation for your actions of the past." Rather, he reminded Father Fessio: "You were *sent* to U.S.F. in 1974 to be a full time faculty member of the Department of Theology and Religious Studies." Subsequently, wrote the vice-provincial, in becoming involved with Guadalupe Associates and Ignatius Press, Father Fessio had failed to carry out his appointed assignment. But the vice-provincial asserted that his addressee's well-meaning failure to carry out this assignment was not the only reason for his decision. He also did not want him "legally involved with a corporation that is totally independent of and *per se* unaccountable to the Society and the Church, particularly one whose stated primary purpose is: 'to support and operate schools, colleges and universities.'" He concluded: "*What is to be done* has already been decided. The only question is *how to work out the logistics* of your obediential response. I leave this to you and [the Jesuit rector at USF]."

Of course, Father Fessio immediately obeyed. He resigned from the board of Guadalupe Associates. His supporters were dumbfounded by his reaction, which might be described as a "ho, hum, so where do we go now" attitude, certainly not dramatic or revengeful. But shortly afterward, he worked out some wiggle room with his superior, and, in a follow-up letter, the vice-provincial agreed that seeking less involvement in the Press, and no involvement in choosing a new chairman for Guadalupe Associates, did not mean that he should have no connection with the Press. Instead, this involvement should be "on an *ad hoc* basis for contingencies, but only with *toties quoties* permission from the rector of the Jesuit community". He was also allowed "to cheer the members of the Associates and Press from the sidelines" should they request it.

Shortly afterward, a cry for help went up. Previously, the board of Guadalupe Associates had requested that for tax purposes its name be included in the Catholic Directory as a valid association with ties to the San Francisco archdiocese, and this was done. But when the 1980 directory was printed, there was no mention of Guadalupe Associates, and no proper authority could be found to explain the reason for its absence. The problem was given to Father Fessio. All his efforts to discover the reason were met with a polite "no comment" from archdiocesan officials. He then reached out to the bishop of Reno, Norman McFarland, an enthusiastic supporter of the Institute and the Press, asking if he could authorize the inclusion of Guadalupe Associates in the Reno diocese directory. The bishop hesitated because the organization was housed in San Francisco, not Reno, but he volunteered to discover why the archdiocese failed to honor the request. The answer was that the Jesuit vice-provincial for education had made the request to have the Guadalupe name deleted from the directory, even though Father Fessio was no longer associated with the group, and the archdiocese hesitated to ignore a request made by such an authority. Never vanquished, Father Fessio rode off to the tax office in San Francisco to see if Guadalupe Associates might qualify for its own tax exemption. He may have been a little surprised when the official told him that, in fact, it did.

This possibility prompted the erstwhile director of the Press to have recourse to the rector of the Jesuit community to distinguish *"toties"* and *"quoties"* permissions on this ad hoc basis. The rector of the Jesuit community was a scholarly man, but he often experienced difficulties distinguishing his *toties* from his *quoties* in directing the quotidian perambulations on the way to spiritual perfection of the founder of Ignatius Press, who looked for hands-on ways of acting. Thus the Press was able to buzz on as usual. The future of the Institute, however, was not so fortuitous.

11

THE SCRIVEN REPORT

Dr. Scriven's thoroughly researched report on the Saint Ignatius Institute was completed and published in June 1978, one month before the Fessio-organized *Humanae Vitae* symposium began. As a point of departure, Scriven judged that the Saint Ignatius Institute "is not only a worthwhile effort in terms of its secular educational goals, but one that makes excellent sense in terms of USF's special mission as defined in its own public documents". Furthermore, "Father Fessio is a leader, a totally committed person. There is little chance this combination will draw no fire." One such fire, the evaluator recounted, was the accusation that the Institute exerts excessive pressure in recruiting, retaining, and running the lives of the SII students. But he brushed this complaint aside with the comment that students were always free to drop out of the program, with or without broadcasting their decision, at any time they wanted to do so. On the other hand, students in the program who were interviewed confessed that the pressure element generated by some non-SII faculty members and students supported their commitment to the program. At times this pressure could cause them to falter, but the caring interest shown by the Institute's faculty and administrators buoyed up their spirit and their determination to remain in the program. "[Is the SII] unacceptably narrow?" Scriven asked. He reported that during the investigation he had heard the word "narrow" repeated often by the program's critics. He pointed out the Institute does not represent itself as a theology or religious studies department. These areas are already represented on campus. And so: "Is there to be no room for an Asian Culture department which treats Eastern religions, even advocates them on the USF campus? Is USF tied by charter to 'liberal' Catholicism? It is obvious the answer is negative in each case." Conclusion: The position of the critics of the Institute is "far more narrow-minded than that they

project on the SII". Their attacks "showed more clearly than catalogues that liberalism has become the new orthodoxy and hence
that a stronger foundation for presenting the alternative was indeed
desirable". Scriven claimed that he did not focus on the attacks in
the media on Father Fessio and the Institute, but he noted that there
were many, and this substantiated his point about the orthodoxy of
liberalism. It was "obvious", he wrote, "that the critics were vociferous and hostile, while Father Fessio was judicious and temperate."
He concluded: "It is scarcely persuasive for these critics to make it
a major thrust of their criticism that Father Fessio is intolerant and
intemperate and engages in public denigration of those with whom
he disagrees."

If there was reaction to the Scriven Report among the administrators of the university, it was not advertised. Characteristically,
there were no expressions of gloating satisfaction on the part of Father Fessio over the tertianship victory or the Scriven Report. He
simply put the sword noiselessly back into the sheath, anticipating
further skirmishes, and he certainly did not have to wait long.

The first began in the fall of 1976 when some members of the
Theology Department complained they were being excluded from
teaching in the Institute. We briefly noted that the union filed a
grievance against the university and the case was resolved in a letter
of mutual understanding. Part of that agreement was that "all full-
time USF faculty members who are competent to teach the courses
in question will be considered as appropriate candidates for teaching
the course." At the same time, "the University reserves the right to
hire part-time faculty whose competency and suitability for the Institute would significantly add to the quality of the program." Then,
after months of letters exchanged between the union, the university, and the Institute, the union filed a second grievance against
the university for the Institute's failure to provide a class schedule
for the fall semester of 1977. Father Fessio, claiming harassment,
refused to comply, saying the information could be obtained from
the University Registrar. Dr. Donald J. MacIntyre, the academic
vice president, concurred with Father Fessio. The case then went
to arbitration, and the decision was made in favor of the union's
position. In early May of the following year, Father Paul Bernadicou, S.J., as a full-time member of the Theology Department, applied to teach the Institute course Great Figures of Spirituality in

the fall semester of 1978. Father Fessio turned down the request in favor of another candidate, Father Paul Conner, O.P., from the Dominican School of Theology in Berkeley. On May 15, 1978, a few weeks before the symposium began, Father Bernadicou filed an unfair labor practice grievance. Publicity about the case grabbed headlines in the Catholic and secular media. The case was again decided against the university and the Saint Ignatius Institute, and the ruling was then appealed to the National Labor Relations Board (NLRB). The head of the USF board of trustees, Father Richard Hill, S.J., was adamantly opposed to bringing the SII controversy before the board, arguing that it was an administrative problem and not a matter of concern for board members. Father Hill, a noted canon lawyer, was also a past and future president of JSTB, as well as an active member of the USF Jesuit community.

The NLRB arbitration began its sessions—raucous thanks to the audience—on February 5, 1979. In a letter to the arbitrator dated April 5, 1979, the then-chairman of the Theology Department, Dr. Hamilton Hess, had stated: "I have reviewed Father Conner's curriculum vitae and find him to be less qualified than Father Bernadicou's more extensive professional engagement and teaching experience in the field of spiritual theology. . . . I recommend that Father Bernadicou be engaged as instructor for this course." So Dr. Scriven closed the door on one Fessio battle, while the NLRB opened another onto a field destined to host further combat.

12

HUMANAE VITAE SYMPOSIUM

Father Fessio's next project riveted the attention of more than many on both sides of the Atlantic. It was an event designed to celebrate the tenth anniversary of the publication of Pope Paul VI's encyclical *Humanae Vitae*. It began on July 15 and ended on July 22, 1978, one month after publication of the Scriven Report and two months before the first Bernadicou grievance was filed, though it was in the making for months before the opening session. It proved to be a veritable lightning rod in the turbulent atmosphere encircling the Catholic world at the time. In order to stage the event with as much fanfare as possible, Father Fessio contacted the Archbishop of San Francisco, John Raphael Quinn, for moral and some financial support, and then he managed to get approval for hosting the event in the USF sports gymnasium. After that he went big, inviting such luminaries as Mother Teresa of Calcutta, Malcolm Muggeridge and Elizabeth Anscombe, Fathers Louis Bouyer and Hans Urs von Balthasar, Ronda Chervin, Frank Sheed, James Hitchcock, John Kippley, and a number of other noteworthy Catholic intellectuals from around the globe to come to San Francisco and give their considered reflections on the encyclical as well as on the resulting fallout it had left behind. The news of the event evoked responses worldwide. Media around the globe were becoming familiar with the Fessio phenomenon.

The ailing Paul VI's expected death in Rome, which eventually occurred on August 6, also added impetus to the event. Then all of a sudden, the archbishop felt the pressure of disapproval from committed and solicited allies, causing him to insist that the name of Rev. Gerald D. Coleman, S.S., a professor of moral theology and dean at the archdiocesan seminary, be included on the slate of distinguished speakers. He was a disputant of the encyclical's premise; the other panelists were on the same page concerning its message. At the same time, they were aware of the reasons why it generated such strong negative reactions. Prior to the opening of the gathering, an appendicitis attack forced the archbishop to retire to a hospital—*actus Dei nemini facit injuriam*, nobody can be faulted for an act of God—thereby rendering him exempt from criticism in that part of the Catholic media where, later in his career, he would be exalted. At the same time, a reoccurrence of malaria kept Mother Teresa in India. This illness also forced the ticket salesmen to open up their coffers to accommodate a number of the more than three thousand in-and-out attendees, some of whom had purchased tickets solely to hear Mother Teresa speak.

The Saint Louis University historian Dr. James Hitchcock was one of the most impressive speakers. He drew parallels between the crises facing the Church in the early sixteenth century and the present rejection of the papal encyclical. He then proceeded to give various reasons why collusion between the secular and some Catholic media favored such rejection. First, the Church had recently changed her approach to such seemingly immutable practices as Friday abstinence and the Latin liturgy, thus welcoming the prospect of more changes previously thought to be impossible. Second, there were open discussions on subjects that had seldom, if ever, been discussed before, conspicuous among which was the topic of "birth control". Two factors invited this subject to assume importance and relevancy: the new, much-discussed concern about overpopulation and the appearance of the Pill. Both contributed to the full dawning of the "Sexual Revolution", which had been developing since *Les Années folles*, the Roaring Twenties. Result: traditional Catholic teaching about sexuality was judged to be a barrier to human progress. Furthermore, in the ecumenical spirit of Vatican II, Catholics were invited to welcome the philosophies of life of all people, while backwardness, rigidity, and "Phariseeism" were to be eschewed. "The fact that many American Catholics do not accept the teachings reiterated in *Humanae Vitae*", Dr. Hitchcock said, "is often presented as though it represented the admirable and newly acquired ability of these Catholics to think for themselves, independent of hierarchical dictation."[1] Dr. Hitchcock's analysis was also

---

[1] Roberta Ward and Fr. John Penebsky, "1968 Encyclical Focus of Meet", *The Monitor*, July 27, 1978.

a good explanation for the liturgical shenanigans Mr. Fessio experienced as a scholastic at Santa Clara in 1967, and it will serve to explain more events in the coming chapters.

Father Louis Bouyer of the Institut Catholique in Paris, a recognized specialist on matters theological and an author of more than forty books, put much of the blame for Catholics' rejection of papal teachings on dissenting Catholic *bien-pesants*, professors of theology, who seemed intent on passing along to their students their own intellectual authoritarianism and social snobbery. Dr. Elizabeth Anscombe focused on this problem in her own inimitable manner. She was a British philosopher of great repute, an analytical Thomist, a student of and authority on Ludwig Wittgenstein's thinking, and a lady who did not mince words when it came to expressing her opinion. She blasted contemporary bishops and priests for not teaching as they should. "We must pray for them", she said. "The danger of hell is much greater for them" than for dissenting theologians or professional journalists.[2] Reminiscent of Old Testament prophetic rhetoric, she reasserted her conviction that sexual promiscuity was the root of most contemporary moral problems and predicted something that very few at the symposium could believe: that the homosexual agenda would become a central concern in the future.

The Sulpician Father Coleman tried to be as accommodating to the majority of panelists as his contrary position would allow. He stated: "If the mind of the Church is to be accurately gauged, it is right and proper that all the faithful should be consulted by authority. Such consultation adds a dimension to the authority's understanding of the mind of the church." Such was the position defended by John Henry Cardinal Newman, he declared. Calmly developing this idea, he then pointed out that throughout the history of the Church, truth has been discovered; "there is always discovery and the discoverable." Therefore, the faithful "should not be afraid of dissent or questions". Conclusion: "The various reactions to *Humanae Vitae* [should] be sensitively listened to."[3] The reason, he claimed, was this: "The final word is not yet in, and

---

[2] Ward and Penebsky, "1968 Encyclical"

[3] Jeffrey Lewis, " 'Humanae Vitae'—Authority, Dissent", *The Catholic Voice*, July 31, 1978.

thus there can be no simple yes or no reply." He then made a distinction between objective moral norms and pastoral practice and concluded that priests should give absolution to couples "who prudently come to the decision to engage in individual acts of contraceptive intercourse".[4] Someone reading Father Coleman's talk forty years later might be reminded of the controversy that erupted over Pope Francis' encyclical *Amoris Laetitia*. But in 1978, as Father Coleman stepped away from the microphone, Ronda Chervin, the moderator of the forum, a convert from an atheistic Jewish background and a prolific author on theological subjects, took his place and gave an impassioned fifteen-minute rebuttal to just about everything he had said.

Although not in accord with the basic tenets of the other panelists, Father Coleman's reflections were not as radical as those of another theologian who, a short time earlier, had given a lecture on the topic of *Humanae Vitae* across the San Francisco Bay at St. Mary's College in Moraga. "The pope is in error", declared Father Charles Curran, who at that time was a professor of moral theology at the Catholic University in Washington, D.C. But the encyclical "is important," he proclaimed, "because for the first time in recent history it has been widely proposed and accepted that one can dissent from authoritative, noninfallible hierarchical teaching and still be a loyal Roman Catholic." Moreover, he declared, "the specific papal teaching condemning artificial contraception is wrong, and a Roman Catholic can dissent in theory and practice from such a teaching."[5] In developing his position, he noted that the expression "papal magisterium" came into existence in the nineteenth century. It derives from the Latin word *magistri*: teachers, theologians who instructed the pope on theological matters. (Curran was removed from the faculty at Catholic University in 1986.)

The reactions to the symposium were mixed. In a *National Catholic Reporter* article, Reverend John A. Coleman, S.J. (no relation to Reverend Gerald Coleman, S.S., mentioned above), a professor of social and moral theology at the JSTB, bemoaned the fact that dissenters

---

[4] John A. Coleman, S.J., "Dissenters Barred", *National Catholic Reporter*, August 11, 1978.

[5] Lewis, "Authority, Dissent".

were not invited to be on the panel. He repudiated the idea that Catholicism should be equated with the rejection of contraceptive acts, writing that the symposium panelists "seemed enamored of an inexorable domino theory which linked dissent from 'the each and every marriage act' teaching to general approval for contraceptive mentality, promiscuity, homosexuality, abortion and euthanasia". Moreover, he considered parts of Father von Balthasar's presentation "downright silly" and found that Father Bouyer's thesis on the link between Christian marriage and virginity "disintegrated into a harangue at priests and nuns who sought dispensation from vows as undermining marital fidelity".[6]

Less than two months after the *Humanae Vitae* symposium had ended, Father Vernon Ruland, S.J., an associate professor of the Theology Department at USF whom we met earlier, stepped up to the plate to meet the director's challenge in a three-page article entitled "Neo-Catholicism on Campus: The Saint Ignatius Institute", which appeared in the September 9, 1978, issue of *America*. Vernon was a good friend of mine. He was exceptionally intelligent, cultivated, and endowed with a prickly sense of humor. We used to take long walks together through Golden Gate Park, keeping clear of philosophical or theological differences. Our unspoken agreement was that we belonged to the same Society, but to different churches. In the *America* essay, Father Ruland began his diatribe against the Institute, which threatened "to breed legalists, heresy sleuths, religious clones for the generation to come", and he warned that it posed a danger for "the progressively expanding and centering *Tao* of an authentic Catholic humanism" that had long flowered on campus. He saw the conflict as a repetition of the Vatican II clash between "ahistorical and historical orthodoxy. One side with a Platonic ideal of pure, coherent, logical Catholic truth; the other with a developmental truth that is ragged, experimental and uncomfortably fragile." He went on to affirm that the essential argument centered on "the theologian as a mere advocate and interpreter of bishops, versus the theologian as at times the bishops' prophetic co-teacher and admonitor". The theologian was the *magister* who in concert with other theologians made up the Magisterium, as Father

---

[6] Coleman, "Dissenters Barred".

Charles Curran had pointed out. Father Ruland did not exaggerate when he claimed the Institute threatened the *Tao* of what he considered was the pervasive "authentic Catholic humanism", which, presumably, was generated on campus by the Department of Theology and the USF Campus Ministry. Ironically, the nature of the *Tao* is to reverse the order of values by emphasizing the struggle of the weak over the strong, but in these *yin-yang* struggles (ontological vs. phenomenological), it is sometimes difficult to disentangle the *wu* from the *wei*, as any good Taoist would affirm.

Another critic, Father Joseph A. Tetlow, S.J., one of the editors of *America*, echoed some of what Father Ruland had written, but his comments were significant because he was a present trustee of the university and a former president of the JSTB. He was quoted in the September 24, 1978, issue of the *National Catholic Register* as saying: "The St. Ignatius Institute is held together by, and is at the service of, an ultramontanist religious mentality that cherishes consent more than assent and loyalty more than inquiry." He judged that "the mentors" of the Institute "seemed to believe that a constant-care infallible Magisterium is right out of the Bible" and implied that the eminent American Jesuit theologian Avery Dulles would agree with him. (However, Cardinal Dulles at a later date confessed he had the highest regard for the philosophy that had generated the Institute.)

A two-page interview with Father Fessio in the July 23, 1978, issue of *Our Sunday Visitor* was an early medium that equated the theology expressed by the panelists at the symposium with the mission of the Saint Ignatius Institute, personified by its founder and director, thereby making him "The Most Controversial Jesuit in the United States". "I doubt that I am" was his clipped response. "I don't really care if I am controversial or not. I know with our faculty we share a common love for the Church, and we think our program is worthwhile. We are not going to interfere with anybody else, so we expect people not to interfere with us." At the same time, he asserted that if takers-on wanted to engage in a controversy, "That's fine. We'll defend ourselves because we think we've got some 'defensibles'." At the same time, the letter from Jean-Marie Cardinal Villot, the Vatican's Secretary of State, to Archbishop Quinn on behalf of Pope Paul VI, praising the symposium was widely publicized. The cardinal extolled the symposium "as a response to the [Church's] teaching, and as a clarification against certain interpretations that would deprive the Encyclical of its true meaning and in practice distort its application".[7] So, in spite of lightning flashes and peals of thunder, the symposium was an exceptional success, and it became a twofold catalyst: making the name of Reverend Joseph D. Fessio better known in both friendly and decidedly antagonistic quarters.

In early January 1979, John Galten received a letter from Gabriel-Marie Cardinal Garrone of the Congregation of Catholic Institutions in Rome commenting that he and others at the Vatican had been following the "progress and aims of the three-year-old Saint Ignatius Institute", which he claimed "[d]eserve nothing less than praise and commendation". He further asserted: "Devotion to the Magisterium of the Church and to the ideals of Catholic higher education as well as to the noble traditions of the Jesuit Order in higher learning and research is certainly to be rewarded by God with success." He ended his letter by adding: "We would appreciate your continuing to keep us informed from time to time about the developments and progress [of] the Institute and [of] the University." Just how pleased he would be to learn of the tussles and pitfalls of both the Institute and the university during the coming years would be a matter for conjecture.

The curtain of these contradictory years of 1979–1980 fell onto the stage with the opening of the Synod of the Family in Rome. A few days after the first session began on September 26, 1980, Archbishop Quinn, the president of the United States Conference of Catholic Bishops, gave a newsworthy speech before the 200 synod Fathers from more than ninety countries, frustrating some and delighting others. Affirming his personal assent to *Humanae Vitae*, the archbishop, however, then proceeded to give an impressive summary of the arguments of its opponents. He claimed that fewer than 30 percent of American priests supported the encyclical and that a large percentage of the laity did not consider artificial birth control im-

---

[7] Letter of the Holy Father Paul VI to Archbishop John Raphael Quinn (July 21, 1978), https://www.vatican.va/content/paul-vi/en/letters/1978/documents/hf_p-vi_let_19780721_arc-san-francisco.html.

moral. He ended his remarks by recommending a dialogue be set up between theologians and churchmen to establish "guidelines on the possibility and limits of dissent within the church".[8] Father Charles Curran tabbed the pronouncement "a huge step forward", as did many professors in seminaries and American Catholic universities. In November 1981, Pope John Paul II summed up fruits of the synod in his encyclical *Familiaris Consortio* (*The Role of the Christian Family*), in which the recommendations of Archbishop Quinn were not included.

Almost two years after Father Bernadicou's request to teach a course in the SII, as supporters from both sides of the arbitration awaited the NLRB verdict of the Bernadicou case versus the SII, the university decided to host a roundtable discussion on the nature of a Catholic university. It was designed to downplay the anticipated defeat of those Fessio "defensibles". On March 5, 1980, nine days before the announced decision, about two hundred people gathered in the USF auditorium to listen to Archbishop Quinn deliver an address on Pope John Paul II's definition of the role and goals of the Catholic university. The event was chaired jointly by Father Joseph T. Angilella, S.J., the academic vice president of the university, and Father Richard Hill, S.J., mentioned earlier, the chairman of the USF board of trustees. "The vision of the university", said the archbishop in what could have been a definition of the vision of the SII, is "the integration of knowledge rooted in the ultimate unity of truth arrived at in its unique way by each field or discipline in fidelity to its own proper methodology." He emphasized that "theology and philosophy are essential to a well-rounded and integrated education," as a writer for the *Foghorn*[9] expressed it. Dr. Raymond Dennehy of the Philosophy Department and the Saint Ignatius Institute concluded this phase of the program by stressing John Paul's point that the salvation of the Catholic university would come "through the integration of reason and faith". With this summation, the presentations ended; it was now time for

---

[8] "New Approach Needed for Teaching on Contraception, Says Archbishop Quinn", *Catholic News Service*, September 30, 1980.

[9] Angela McNulty, "USF Hosted Symposium on the Catholic University", *San Francisco Foghorn*, March 14, 1980.

questions. The archbishop then stood up and announced that a previous engagement would, sadly, prevent him from remaining. Begging the forgiveness of all, he prudently left the room. The action could not have been more symbolic. Father Angilella went to the lectern and spoke at length, reassuring the audience that USF was meeting the need for social justice integrity, connections with Shanghai Normal University, achievements in theology, and research in fire safety and toxicity. Then, in a panel afterward, he answered a student about Archbishop Quinn's emphasis on the need of philosophy in the curriculum, responding that philosophy is to be found in all classes; when another SII student queried them about the "Catholic identity of USF", Father Andrew Woznicki of the Philosophy Department answered: "USF is in a stage of searching for its identity. We're not lost; just searching."

Nine days later, on March 14, 1980, as indicated earlier in this chapter, the NLRB arbitrator rendered his long-awaited decision on the Bernadicou grievance. The plaintiff was competent to have taught the course and therefore the university had violated the contract. The arbitrator stated that the university could not make teaching assignments on the basis of whether or not a regular faculty's viewpoint is consistent with the stated mission goals of the Institute. The contract states that a teacher may not "use the student audience to gratuitously, deliberately and persistently express views which misrepresent or impugn the authoritative teachings of the Catholic Church". The arbitrator judged there was no evidence that Father Bernadicou was guilty of such infractions. The Faculty Association (also known as the Union) demonstrated that he held views consistent with Catholic teaching, but divergent from those Catholic teachings of Father Fessio and the Institute. Later, Father Fessio questioned the right of the NLRB to have jurisdiction over questions of religious or educational principles. "I think the arbitration decision is ultimately against the U.S. Constitution because it interferes with the Institute's freedom of exercising religion. In effect, the university is not allowed to have any programs which have any religious, philosophical, or professional principles as part of the nature of the program."

The judgment on that part of the agreement was final and binding on both the university and the Association. One can sympathize with the arbitrator Adolph Koven, who, although not even a

Christian, was expected to disentangle Catholic beliefs from secular union arguments. But he was a man of recognized honesty and integrity. During the lengthy and bitter cross-examination of witnesses, it must have often seemed to him as if he were being carried by dark tides to some unknown shore. A decision for or against the Institute would bring him condemnation. There had to be a third way. And there was. The arbitrator noted that the second part of the agreement read: "The university reserves the right to hire part-time faculty whose competency and suitability would significantly add to the quality of the program." Thus the question was, Would the future hiring of Father Louis Bouyer, the latest candidate Father Fessio recommended to teach the Institute course Great Figures in Spirituality, significantly add quality to the Saint Ignatius Institute? Bouyer, a panelist at the *Humanae Vitae* symposium, was one of the best-known and most highly respected theologians in this particular field. So the answer: Indeed, it would add to the quality of courses given at the university! Would the Theology Department pit Father Bernadicou against Father Bouyer? Indeed, it would not! The third rail was found, and the university could rejoice that this French theological giant had become a part-time member of the faculty. Father Fessio is not a polo player or even a fan of the sport. Those who are might have preferred an analogy to a "tail shot" strike— that is, leaning far back over the saddle, the player hits the ball beneath the horse's tail.

After the case was decided, the university's lawyer, John A. Scalone, released a thirty-five-page post-arbitration hearing report of the Bernadicou case. Its purpose was to "highlight some of the points raised in the Hearing", and no report better captures the distilled essence of the Institute position vis-à-vis the Theology Department and the faculty union. After asserting that "there was much rhetoric raised during the Hearing; contentions, allegations and yes, attacks on the University, the SII and in particular, Father Fessio, the Institute Director", the author concluded that "such grandiloquence cannot obfuscate the central and *only* issue in the case: *Did the University's action in not hiring Father Bernadicou to teach the SII course, Great Figures in Spirituality, violate the Contract* [between the university and the union] *as written and expressed?*" Before that question was answered, Mr. Scalone stated that, given that the record was replete with the union's personal attacks on Father Fessio, with a deliberate intent on making *him* personally a defendant, it was imperative to set the record straight in the hope that future grievances and arbitration hearings "will not be encumbered with assumptions and unfounded allegations that Father Fessio, alone, determines the mission, goals and direction; the course selection; course content and selections of faculty to teach the courses". He asserted that in order to distract from the main point in the arbitration, the union side set up Father Fessio as a straw man, a refutable argument not central to the case. "There is no evidence that Father Fessio has ever acted arbitrarily or capriciously in the selection of faculty, nor that these decisions have been made on the basis of his personal opinion only." The basis for this judgment was that Father Fessio, contrary to popular belief, is not the Institute. He directs the Institute in conjunction with a faculty under the direction of a board.

Mr. Scalone argued that the Institute was not the "Hitlerian wedge hammered into the fabric of the University" that the union lawyer claimed it to be, nor should it be considered "a threat of incipient fascism" on campus. He asked: "Does Father Fessio and Father Fessio alone make decisions for the Institute?" and answered: "*Absolutely not.*" Mr. Scalone explained that the Institute is governed by a board answerable to the university's vice president and that from the beginning it was recognized as having different goals from other departments or colleges within the university structure. Moreover, the university's contract with the union did not confer upon faculty members the right to change the mission and goals of the Institute, and yet Father Bernadicou admitted he applied to teach the course of Great Figures in Spirituality not only because he was interested in the course but also because he wanted to give the students a wider view of what Catholic theology entails. He not only criticized the "narrow" approach of the program, but he testified he wanted to change it, to lead it to "a more pluralistic approach". He admitted he had his own viewpoint on how to teach Catholic theology—"a viewpoint he wants to be honored, but he refuses to grant the same consideration to another point of view, even though he agrees that it is a right of the University to establish such an alternative."

The fact that Father Bernadicou and the majority of the members of the Theology Department clearly did not share the defined mission and goals of the Saint Ignatius Institute was understandable, Mr. Scalone asserted. But Father Bernadicou also wanted to "scrap" the Institute, "dismantle it and rebuild it with an approach which he believed to be the best for the students". That was not understandable. Would the union favor the hiring of a recognized philosopher and proponent of Nazism to teach a course on the Jewish people in Germany, even supposing he had the "mechanical and technical" competence to do so (incongruous adjectives used by the union to express Father Bernadicou's ability)? Mr. Scalone gave an example summarizing the union's logic: a contractor hired a carpenter, endowed with "mechanical and technical" competence to do a job. Some might say that no one should care what artistic prejudices might motivate his style. That was no one's business. The man was hired to do the job. That was what was essential. Mr. Scalone pointed out the defective reasoning here:

> Would a contractor who designed a house and was in the process of building hire a carpenter who did not believe in that type of design, criticized it, stating it should be taken apart and rebuilt, and if hired by the contractor, would proceed to rebuild it to suit his beliefs on what was the only house design which was better for buyers, even though the buyers had already chosen the first design? We suggest not.

Father Bernadicou had admitted—as Mr. Scalone proceeded to assert—that he believes the SII's "narrow" approach should be broken down and reconstructed to make it more pluralistic. He believes that the university does not have the right to establish a program such as the SII because it has too limited an approach to Jesuit Catholic higher education and that a faculty member or the union has the right to dismantle it so as to conform it to the view of authentic Jesuit higher education. Mr. Scalone argued that the contract between the university and the union does not confer upon faculty members the right to change a program established by the university, which alone has the right to establish such a program as the Institute.

As Mr. Scalone emphasized, the university does not take the position that Father Bernadicou's form of pluralism should not be taught in the Theology Department or at the university. The SII plan of studies is not a replacement. It is an alternative and should be permitted to retain its integrity. At this point, he mused how ironic it was that the union, propelled by the Theology Department, argued the

Institute should be dismantled because it was not pluralistic! Father Fessio then reiterated his continuously held opinion that he and the Saint Ignatius Institute board never questioned Father Bernadicou's right to teach anywhere else in the university. However, because of the stated mission and goals of the Institute, he should not be permitted to do so in that program. Dr. Hess, chair of the Theology Department, who was an unashamed opponent to the ideas expressed in *Humanae Vitae*, as well as to other orthodox Catholic teachings, was not a competent judge of Father Bernadicou's ability to teach a course in the Institute. Toward the end of the meeting, Father Fessio summed up his ideas on why Bernadicou's application was refused.

> We maintain that the qualifications to teach in the Institute— particularly in the more sensitive areas of philosophy and theology —include not only academic competence but more importantly, for the preservation of the Institute's integrity as an alternative program espousing a well-defined position within the Catholic Church, positive support of the Institute's educational goals and an attitude and practice of obedience with respect to the doctrinal, moral and liturgical directives of the Church.

He then reiterated his position that the Institute's board, which had a strong Jesuit contingent, believed that Father Bernadicou's "whole attitude toward Church and authority did not fit the Institute's approach". He had earlier explained at the pre-arbitration hearings that this "attitude" would have an effect on his interpretation of Catholic spirituality and would be contrary to the philosophy and mission of the Institute. He argued: Father Bernadicou "dissents from the Church's official teachings on artificial contraception in *Humanae Vitae*, teaches this in class and does not consider himself bound by the official liturgical directives of the bishops".

It was only after the verdict of the arbitration had been rendered and the third rail discovered that Father Lo Schiavo emerged from his sequestered space and said, "By and large, I think it is a healthy thing for people in universities to be arguing about ideas and theologies. We've always had disputes in the Church about theologies. I think that is good." The president also knew, although prudence would have cautioned him from broadcasting it, how good the Institute had been for the university. We have seen that thirty-five students of the first class admitted would not have thought of coming to the university had it not been for the Institute. Their presence, along with that of subsequent classes, meant that there was an increase for the university at large; especially for the College of Arts and Sciences including the Department of Theology and Religious Studies. The presence of the Institute also increased income for the university through tuition revenue and gifts. Gifts and grants at the time of the Bernadicou case totaled over $90,000 with $75,000 coming from new sources to the university. Indeed, it was good even for the university to have disputes over theology. But the president was aware that it takes two to have a dispute, and being John Lo Schiavo, he must have realized he had better keep it that way. Let laymen like Michael Scriven and John Scalone defend Father Joseph Fessio, preserve the integrity of the Institute, and define the nature of a Jesuit Catholic university.

13

HEADWINDS

From the beginning, the board and staff of Ignatius Press were in full agreement that any manuscript that the staff judged to be advantageous to the mission of the Church or the betterment of society in regard to the Church was considered apt for publication. It was under this rubric that the Press published a work that plunged the Reverend Director into a swamp of criticism that has lingered on to this day. In the 1980s, San Francisco was a center of the AIDS/HIV plague, and the cause of the virus' spread seemed to be either unknown or kept hidden. In 1986, a Lutheran minister named Gene Antonio submitted a manuscript to the Press entitled *The AIDS Cover-Up? The Real and Alarming Facts about AIDS*, and since the virus presented a danger to bodies and souls, Ignatius Press published it. Some of the author's claims—e.g., that the virus might be spread by mosquito bites, sneezes, or touches—were subsequently discredited, but Antonio's main thesis was that homosexual activity was the chief cause of the spread of the plague in the United States and that pressure from various gay task force groups was responsible for keeping that fact from being known. Bathhouses, breeding pits for the AIDS virus, were multiplying throughout the city. When the book was published, the reactions in the *San Francisco Chronicle* and the *National Catholic Reporter* were predictable. Critics focused on the author's faulty examples for the spread of AIDS, ignoring his main thesis. What the media kept silent, however, was the number of expressions of thanks sent to the Press for having the courage to broadcast information about how AIDS spread and how it could be stopped. It also might have challenged scientists to be more open, less intimidated by pressure groups about the mysterious AIDS virus and how it was spread.

A talk show host named Sean Hannity, who was still in his twenties, invited Antonio as a guest on his hour-long call-in show on

146

the University of California at Santa Barbara (UCSB) radio station. Hannity expressed some of his own judgments against gay pressure groups, but they were balanced and reasonable, designed to encourage honest dialogue. However, he was accused of promoting anti-gay intimidations, of being an enemy to social justice. As a result, he was removed from his post because of the university's anti-discrimination policy. He then took his case to the American Civil Liberties Union, who supported his claim that the university had denied him "freedom of speech". The university was forced to yield, and young Sean Hannity was rehired, only to turn around and quit—a gesture that aided him in his slow climb to becoming one of the top TV–radio hosts in the nation. Then there was the fact that sales from *The AIDS Cover-Up?*, which sold over 200,000 copies, allowed Father Fessio to shift into a higher gear in his race to expand Ignatius Press. Whatever might have been the predictions when it was published, no one had guessed that the sales from this book would wind up being a catalyst for the success for such different entities.

Another book, published by the Press in 1992, is worth noting. This was the first volume of a two-volume study by Father John Becker, a Jesuit sociologist, entitled *Re-Formed Jesuits*. In it, the author attempted to give an analytic description of what the future editor of *America*, Reverend James Martin, S.J., would later refer to as an "explosion" that occurred within the Society of Jesus in the United States between 1975 and 1985. (Might a Californian find the term "earthquake" more cogent, measuring perhaps nine on the Religious Richter scale with continuous aftershocks?) It was in this socio-cultural atmosphere that the Press and the Saint Ignatius Institute would continue to function, and, as we shall see, the challenges were many.

The early years of the Press marked an epoch of tension and strain, but it was also a period motivated by growth and optimism, with signs of a hopeful future. Now it is time to spin the spotlight back on the Institute. To see the starting point of some remarkable changes that evolved there, we must speed back to 1970, the year my provincial assigned me to the joint office of rector and president of Saint Ignatius High School in San Francisco. Obedience does not necessarily engender enthusiasm, and I shared this lack of fervor with some members of my Jesuit community, who greeted me, their new superior, with—one might say—uneasiness. As was stated earlier, this was a period of confusion, even chaos. The job descriptions of the president of the school, his assistant, the principal, and the rector, offices that at one time all belonged to one man, were in a state of flux. Then there was the growing power of the board of trustees; the lessening involvement of the Jesuit provincial; the rise in the number of lay teachers—and what were their beliefs? Did anyone care? As we have seen, the previous year the school had moved from its prior location to a totally new neighborhood. But all of these concerns were minor compared to the anger of a faction of young men within the Jesuit community. The rector at the nearby University of San Francisco, who was a good friend of mine, confided that he, too, had to deal with what he termed "the leftover of tensions from the sixties". But he suggested that one calming remedy for this plague was the vacation house the USF community had in nearby San Rafael, to which the men could retire on weekends and holidays and discover the favorable sides of those whom they had judged harshly. That, I decided, was what would solve all our problems: a vacation hideout in San Rafael! Property taxes were high there, but then there was that old adage about the advantage of having a bird in the hand. In the winter of 1973, I approached Louise M. Davies, a long-term friend of my family, about capturing such a bird. Could she help? She readily agreed, but asked me to try not to go over a million. Suppressing a gasp, I replied: "Louise, I'll try my best!" For the next few months, in the company of a competent real estate agent, I looked at a few places, but none was satisfactory. Finally, I got a call from him on a Thursday afternoon. He had the ideal place. It might cost a little more than the agreed-on price but not much, he said in a reassuring way. It was a "hot buy" and would go fast. What a surprise in store for the community! He and I agreed to meet early in the coming week, but then there was another surprise call from my provincial on Saturday morning telling me he was giving me a new assignment. I was to report to the University of San Francisco for the coming semester. That proverbial bird stayed in the bush.

About three years later, seated comfortably in a beautiful garden, I heard myself ask: "Louise, remember that bird . . . ?" She did, and agreed it was time to net it. Did I have a cage? Indeed I did! From the first days of the Institute, Mrs. Louise Davies took a great interest in its progress, and in 1977 promised to support it with a million-dollar donation (the equivalent of some $8,000,000 in 2024).

At the time, however, this highly revered and well-loved San Francisco celebrity was working to scrape up enough cash to cover payment for her pet project, a concert hall dedicated to the joy of music. She promised she would be as good as her word and give one million as soon as her trusted advisor Mr. Phil Hudner would allow it. Members of the SII board figured the Institute would not need a million dollars to take care of its immediate needs. Why not settle for something like $650,000 and let the financially challenged university have the rest? The Institute and the university were not in competition—on the contrary. But this agreement would guarantee the university would not crush the Institute before the promised gift was made. Time was to the advantage of the Institute as it continued to prosper, bringing in financial bait to the university's coffers, supporting its existence. We on the board admitted it was like blackmail. The compromise would go far in winning the president's approval, perhaps turn the fatal theme from *Carmen* into Der Rosenkavalier Suite and maybe even win the support of the campus neutrals. It would show that the donor of the magnificent $28 million iconic Louise M. Davies Symphony Hall in San Francisco, which opened in 1980, was also a sympathetic benefactress of the modest Saint Ignatius Institute, the recipient of her gift that same year. In hindsight, it was a naïve judgment, a mix-up of roles. It was the president's genius, not Father Fessio's, to make deals one could not refuse, as we shall see. Details for the settlement were worked out on paper by President Lo Schiavo to the satisfaction of all at the time.

Now back to September 1976, the date when Louise Davies made her first formal appearance at the SII. It was then that she came as the honored guest at the first presentation of the Saint Ignatius Institute Lecture Series. After Mass and an informal dinner, attended by students and faculty, she listened to Dr. Raymond Dennehy of the USF Philosophy Department—a professor at the first Institute class—lecturing on "The Significance of Catholic Higher Education in the Contemporary World". She was so impressed that she decided to make her first generous contribution, an off-the-menu hors-d'oeuvre, the *en rapport* prelude to a greater gratification that had yet to be served.

But before Father Fessio could invest her major donation, there were financial problems that demanded attention. In 1981, the university implemented a general plan to eliminate duplication of offices, services, and "unnecessary programs". The objective of the plan was to restore economic well-being to the university, minimize faculty layoffs, and improve services to the students. However beneficial these objectives seemed at the time, it was obvious that the Institute would be affected, and so it was. From the outset, it had been administrated outside the control of any college or school within the university complex, having its own staff, advisors, and counselors. But from now on, it was to be treated as a department within the College of Arts and Sciences and was to become more "cost effective". Specifically, the positions of Dennis Bartlett and John Galten were to be eliminated, and the overseas programs had to meet their own expenses. This academic extension of the SII program had been set up for junior-year students at Oxford and Innsbruck. Father Fessio was determined not to eliminate the positions of Dennis and John and to retain Karen Summerhays as the office secretary. He received the unanimous support from the board backing this position. After lengthy negotiations, an agreement was reached between the Institute and the administration enabling all three positions to be retained, but the salary for each had to be paid from the SII gift account. In a letter to the Dean of the College of Arts and Sciences on August 4, 1981, before the promised Davies bonanza had arrived, Father Fessio assured him that although he regretted having to pay the salaries for these positions from the SII Gift Account, he understood the need to do so. Further, he understood the dean's anxiety about having these positions in that particular account. "But," he concluded, "that is not a source of any great anxiety to me—$70,000 or $80,000 per year is not very much to God, and it is in Him that we place our trust." Such was his variation on "Let's go for it!" Eight days later, the administration announced that the Louise Davies contribution to the SII gift account had been duly filed. And then the real trouble began.

On October 1, Father Fessio wrote another letter to the dean informing him that the SII gift account had been charged for deficits that had nothing to do with the Institute but that it was difficult to pinpoint such irregularities because the Institute office had received no update on the gift account's status since June. By the end of the month, the source of the problem was discovered: a faulty account number concerning the SII overseas program. It seems, however, that the money withdrawn from the fund was never returned. Controversy between the Institute and the university—or, more precisely, between the SII director and the USF president—over how the money in the fund could be spent became more intense until the end of the year. On December 9, 1981, referee-like Louise Davies separated the two sparring partners in a letter stating her purpose in making this gift to the university:

> to enhance the quality of education in the humanities at the university and to raise the ethical and professional standards of future leaders in American public life by offering students at the university an opportunity to study the best in Catholic and Christian thought through the ages, including contemporary Catholic and Christian thought, and to apply this study to modern social, economic and political problems.

She considered there were three different avenues to take in order to achieve this objective: "(1) to bring to the University leaders and thinkers of academic or professional distinction who reflect the Christian tradition in their approach to modern problems . . . (2) to offer an academic program . . . and, if feasible, scholarships . . . and (3) to further the program of the Saint Ignatius Institute." To attain the third objective, she added, the fund given to the Institute "may be expended . . . for any staff salaries of the Saint Ignatius Institute not paid by the University. . . . I intend that the income from this fund be added to the Institute's current level of financial support by the University . . . so that the Institute's program is enhanced by this gift." Father Lo Schiavo responded that the university would not pay the salaries of those employed by the Institute and that therefore in a few years the Davies gift should be "entirely consumed and . . . not have to be replaced [by the University]".

Consequently, by the mid-1980s, there was still no meeting of minds with respect to the advantage the Institute brought to the university. Dr. Scriven's questionnaires to SII students, given in preparation for his report, revealed that 65 to 70 percent of them would not have enrolled at the university had it not been for the SII. Without expatiating on the quality of these students and on the prestige the Institute brought to the university, the tuition revenue alone meant $500,000 per year to the university that would not be otherwise generated. Father Fessio argued that this fact in itself should convince the administration and various departments that they should encourage, not vilify the Institute. In addition to the academic courses, the Institute also provided lecture series, retreats, spiritual programs (such as Masses and all-night Eucharistic Adoration), and a center where students could come for help with academic or personal difficulties. Finally, in addition to these services, the Institute staff spent time in the recruitment of students for both the Institute in particular and the university in general. Father Fessio then complained that the corpus of Mrs. Davies gift had to pay salaries that should have been covered by the normal university budget. He complained that each year money was arbitrarily taken from the SII gift account to make up what he called "the artificially contrived, fossilized SII budget deficit". He further complained that, despite the income the SII brought to the university, every year the Business and Financial Office of the university was nickel-and-diming the Institute by "contrived, irrational, and ethically questionable maneuvering".

We have already seen that Father Fessio is a born fundraiser, and the pages ahead will confirm that fact. So the question is: Why did he not spend time and effort in acquiring monies to supplant the exhausted SII gift account? The answer is simple. He calculated that, given the university's policy regarding budgetary matters, he would have to raise at least $70,000 a year to continue operations. Where would he find the time to fundraise? He was teaching a full load of courses as well as spending time and effort on the expanding Press. Furthermore, he was an explorer, not a settler. Explorers are always moving on, getting shot by arrows, fighting windmills; settlers dig in, improve the terrain, and make friends with neighbors.

Is it possible at this date that he was yearning for new adventures? Like the Santa Clara Project 50 program, he had set up the Institute, and, unlike Project 50, it was a successful undertaking with great potential. But were recurring no-win battles with the faculty union, the in-house Jesuit opposition, and the arbitrary financial manipulations of the budget planners worth the effort? Were there not others who could do a better job? His ties to John Galten and Dennis Bartlett demanded that he remain. Would the university allow either of them to take his place? If he had any thoughts about not remaining on as director during this period, he kept them to himself. What he did frequently state was that the Institute was a vehicle that brought Christ to the spiritually and intellectually deprived, and it was therefore an authentic Ignatian apostolate. It was a real instance of the "service of faith and the promotion of justice" that Pope Paul VI encouraged Jesuits to implement. It was set up to train competent laymen to fight the contemporary "drama of atheist humanism", to quote the title of a book by Henri de Lubac. It was because of this apostolic fixation—as well as his dedication to Father de Lubac's principles—that during the early 1980s, Father Fessio found himself torn between involvement with the Press, teaching classes at the university, and now trying to devise ways to raise money to keep the Institute afloat.

At the beginning of the fall semester of 1983, Father Bernadicou became chairman of the Department of Theology and Religious Studies, and it did not take him long to focus once more on the Institute. In a long letter addressed to the dean, dated October 25 of that year, the newly appointed chairman advised the dean that Father Fessio was guilty of a number of violations against the agreement between the university and the Institute. It must be conceded that, given his position and theological views, Father Bernadicou had a legitimate grievance. He felt that it fit his job description to insist that henceforth all theology majors had to take at least fifteen units in upper division courses from faculty members who were not permitted to teach in the Institute because of their stated theological views. The chairman argued that it was imperative for the department to be able to retain control of its majors, as well as "to insure the appropriate breadth and depth in their education" that they could not get in classes conducted by instructors he considered wedded to a narrow-minded theology. This grievance awakened noble, knight-like reactions in the director of the Saint Ignatius Institute. He had to fight him, if not head on, then at least indirectly. It was the *preux* thing to do.

The first riposte was outlined in a December letter to the dean. In it, Father Fessio outlined his model for a new program. The Saint Ignatius Institute Extension Courses would be offered through the Catholic Home Study Institute (CHSI), a vigorous correspondence course program that was already in the offing. It was designed by the SII for students who wished to gain academic credit from the university for Institute courses. A prospective student would register at the university through the Institute for a fee of $40 per unit of credit, plus a $25 proctor charge. The proceeds would be split between the Institute and the College of Arts and Sciences, and the Institute teachers and staff would do all of the necessary work. Father Fessio did considerable homework in designing the details of this project and proposed that the well-known scholar Father John Hardon, S.J., be made the supervisor and director. He was well aware that Father Hardon, although a well-qualified theologian of renown, would not be accepted by the Theology Department because of his Institute-like views, but he wanted that fact to be publicly acknowledged. The first course was ready to be put into effect in the spring of 1984, that is, in less than two months' time. Father Fessio petitioned the university to offer credit to the students involved. Such authorization would enable him to expand the program for the following fall semester. The petition was quickly vetoed by the department, and therefore the exasperated dean, who had become a supporter of Fessio plans in general, had to refuse it.

Speedily, the director of the Institute proposed another program for the betterment of those involved and for the reputation and financial benefits that would accrue to the university. It was a summer school course of studies for the uncloistered Carmelite Sisters of the Most Sacred Heart of Los Angeles. After lengthy conversations with their superiors, he recommended that the university consider approving a plan offering three summer courses leading to a M.A. for the enrollees. The Sisters' mission consisted in teaching, operating a hospital and retirement center, and running a retreat house. Therefore, having such a degree was advantageous to them. Moreover, he planned that if this program with the small group of Sisters was successful, he would consider setting up a master's degree program in Catholic catechetics. A pyrotechnician, familiar with how a lit match typically reacts with a barrel of gunpowder, would understand how this latest exploit of the bold knight affected the Theology Department. His project was unquestionably and predictably well researched. The proposed courses were outlined in intricate detail. There would be ten Sisters. If they took six units each, at a rate of $216.00 per graduate unit, the total revenue would be $12,960.00. He hammered out a detailed class schedule and recommended classrooms that the Press would provide free of charge. The SII would handle all the publicity for the program. Then there was the price for teaching part-time faculty, which would be the main cost of the program. The bottom line here was $3,600.00, with a net profit to the College of Arts and Sciences of at least $9,360.00. These figures have been given in detail to show how efficient Father Fessio is in evaluating the costs of any operation he sets out to put into effect. In this instance, he informed the dean that he was optimistically confident that he and Father Bernadicou could work out an agreement. He then proceeded to give a long, descriptive outline of the program to Father Bernadicou in part of which he stressed the fact that the Sisters had been going to a summer school in Middleburg, Virginia, and thus could reduce their summer expenses by coming to USF.

The dean judged the proposed program to be beneficial, but advised Father Fessio that he would have to get backing from the vice president before he could give him authorization to implement it. Father Bernadicou voiced sympathy with the concerns of the nuns, but offered arguments against supporting the program. He set up a committee of three—himself and two other tenured Jesuits in the department—to study its proposed offerings. In a letter dated March 22, 1984, he informed Father Fessio of the results of the committee's deliberations. After noting that the program "has no Scripture and incorporates the worst features of pre–Vatican II tractate theology", he further commented: "The program as described runs the serious risk of being a cheap degree which would drag down the reputation U.S.F. has built over the years for quality theological education." And he added that the committee's decision was based on the fact that

> our summer program brings scholars of international reputation in Roman Catholic theology to our campus each year. It would be insulting to their caliber and achievement to bring other less qualified instructors on campus to teach graduate students many of the same courses separately. So it is our judgement that U.S.F. must not run two competing graduate programs during the summer, just as we would not have one orthodox and one unorthodox chemistry program.

After this summation, Father Bernadicou asked: "Why would you not invite the Sisters to join what we already have so effectively going?" No extant reply has yet been found among Father Fessio's papers. The chairman of the Theology Department concluded his letter stating that thanks to the "generosity of the Jesuit community" and the Zabala Foundation, tuition costs could be considerably reduced for the Sisters, should they participate in the present graduate courses instead of the new ones proposed by SII.

Father Bernadicou then suggested an open discussion on the feasibility of the SII program for the Carmelite Sisters. His invitation was made more pressing by the decision of the vice president of academic affairs to set up a committee to study the question in depth. But then March slid into April and April into May, and all the end-of-year activities crowded in to postpone the proposed meeting. Father Fessio remained quiet. Then on June 15, the dean, who had been attending to matters away from the university, sent a short note to William O. Binkley, the vice president for academic affairs, with a copy to the director of the SII: "Father Fessio informed me today that next week some eighteen Carmelite Sisters will arrive on campus for a five-week non-credit program of theological/philosophical instruction under the auspices of the Saint Ignatius Institute." He then added: "I was quite surprised by the news."

Then they arrived. According to a specious legend, sometime in the fourth century, Saint Ursula and her ten thousand virgins came pouring out of the surrounding forests into the city of Cologne, causing wonderment among the inhabitants and dismay among the officials of the city. The problem was solved when Ursula and the ten thousand were beheaded by the civil officials. That put an end to the crisis. Now, if the USF vice president for academic affairs considered a modified "Ursula Option" in responding to the predicament he was facing in June 1984, when the Carmelite Sisters arrived on campus, no reliable record of it has been found. But conjectures abound. At any rate, since it was too late to cancel the Sisters' arrival, the vice president's immediate solution was to assume the direction of the program himself, take it far away from the Institute–Theology Department battlefield, scrap the Fessio-designed courses, and put the proposed project into the hands of the Office of Special Programs. In the end, the Sisters' two-week stay went off without a hitch, as Dean David Harnett himself would later admit.

Some months passed, and in December, Professor Binkley politely but firmly reminded Father Fessio that he could not proceed with such designs without explicit authorization from the university. A quick response from the SII director citing previous correspondence between himself and the dean, as well as a glowing report from Dennis Bartlett, showed that such permission had already been assured. He demanded an apology and even threatened legal action. With this, Father Fessio assumed the problem had been solved. Then there arrived another note from Professor Binkley on January 15, 1985: "To date I have not received a response to my inquiry." With this, Fessio knew the summer program was in danger. He replied with more evidence, attaching the original proposed course listing. When in late February he had still heard nothing from the vice president, he got serious: "If I do not receive a satisfactory response [to my December correspondence] by March 6th, I am going to refer this matter to counsel for further action."

By May, he had obtained the pro bono services of a lawyer friend and had notified Father Paul Belcher, new vice-provincial for education, of his intent, asking his concurrence with the plan. Father Belcher was a long-distance runner in the vanguard of the New Left, a firm advocate of small communities, where two or three Jesuits would choose to live apart from the main community and carry on a life of mutual support for the greater good of all. His doctorate in sociology seems to have provided him with many of the same qualities that characterized the thinking of Dr. Michael Scriven. In dealing with others, he would never allow his own prejudices to get in the way. He had an appreciation for different points of view, always encouraging, and a refreshing cynicism about him that invited cordiality. "In the old days the far-Right superiors gave orders like fascist dictators", he once remarked in a conference of Jesuits. "Today we on the far Left do the same! But we do it with a smile." He had already rescinded his predecessor's orders regarding Father Fessio's relations with the Press. Now, in this matter involving a potential breach-of-contract suit against the vice president for academic affairs of the university, Father Fessio's religious superior calmly advised him "to make sure [you] have exhausted all internal procedures before discussing with him the option of legal action". It was a word of caution, but not a No, and, of course, indifference gives consent. The director of SII had his attorney write to Vice President Binkley. Our knight grabbed his damaged sword and girded up for a fight. He did not have to wait long.

In the Catholic liturgical calendar, May 22 is the feast of Saint Rita of Cascia, the "Patroness of Desperate Causes". Early in the morning of that day, Vice President Bill Binkley was sitting at his desk busy composing two letters, probably not even aware of the existence of Rita of Cascia—and even if he was, it would have made no difference to him anyway. He was in no mood for distractions. He had finished the first letter, addressed to the dean of the College of Arts and Sciences. In it, he had advised his subordinate that because Father Fessio had not met instructions regarding summer school for the Sisters, instructions that had been spelled out in earlier letters with precision and clarity, he was countermanding the dean's approval of the program. Father Fessio, he wrote with less than his customary composure, "cannot make use of the facilities or services of the University including, but not limited to, those provided by the offices or departments of housing, food services," and ten other clearly specified entities. The vice president's second opus was a four-page, single-spaced letter addressed "Dear Joe". In it, he recounted the whole history of the Carmelite summer program's development from the point of view of USF administration, thus demonstrating the speciousness of his cherished correspondent's arguments and, finally, refusing to accept any alternative legal resolution to the problem. The Sisters simply could not use USF facilities. After reading the letter, the plaintiff's pro bono attorney agreed: it would be better not to take legal action. Given the chance, Saint Rita would probably have recused herself.

But what ever happened to the Carmelite Sisters? They arrived in San Francisco eager to begin classes in the summer of 1985, and surprisingly, when they left six weeks later, they were overjoyed by their stay, thanks to the organizational talents of Father Fessio and the cooperation of many. Father managed to find temporary living quarters for them near the Press, and he was able to offer them the same classes that had been promised two years earlier. These classes were taught by members of the former SII faculty, including Father Brian Mullady, O.P., who was joined by his fellow Dominican, Father Quintino Turiel, a noteworthy scholar from Rome. Understandably, the Sisters were not awarded an M.A. degree from the university, but they did earn a Guadalupe Associates certificate in theology, which was later recognized for partial credit by a Catholic university when Sister Judith pursued her graduate degree. Until recently, she served as superior general of the Carmelite community in Alhambra, California. The only sad memory of their second summer stay in San Francisco was the university's dictate forbidding the Sisters entrance—even for a short prayer—into the monumental Saint Ignatius Church, which stands at a corner of the university near the old Press offices and which in those days was canonically designated a college chapel, not a parish church. The exclusion of the Sisters was even more sad, and tellingly symbolic, because at the request of a few Muslim students the church's extensive basement had been converted into a mosque, out from which the phrase *Allahu Akbar* could be heard chanted multiple times each day as an expression of Islamic faith and multicultural commitment.

14

FIRED

It was a packed year, 1985. The final decision on the summer program for the Carmelite Sisters did not seem to satisfy the pelican's bill. It was still far from meeting its fill. Father von Balthasar had organized a symposium on Adrienne von Speyr's life and works that was to take place in Rome from September 27 to 29, and he had invited Father Fessio to give a presentation with the title "How Does One Read Adrienne von Speyr?", So the Jesuit rushed over to his reserved place at this publicized event, read his paper to an admiring audience, and flew back that night for a scheduled class at USF, which was followed by a meeting with a specially formed arts and sciences committee chosen to evaluate the SII curriculum in preparation for the accrediting evaluation by the Western Association of Schools and Colleges (WASC).

He presented the Institute's intent and purpose to the WASC team with what one member later described as rare clarity and expertise—"a pleasure to deal with". He argued for the continuation of the SII's fixed series of studies, explaining how they were divided evenly between courses devoted to the ancient and medieval periods and those devoted to the modern period. He skillfully met objections that the curriculum's courses took too little heed of modern developments. Instinctively, as an apt pupil of Father de Lubac, he carefully explained—to the group's satisfaction—that there was a greater weight given to the modern over the ancient and medieval periods in some courses, such as "Great Figures in Spirituality" and even the systematic courses in philosophy and theology. For this reason, he argued, the curriculum fit easily into the requirements of the various departments for students majoring in different fields. No program in the university was better defined or more closely scrutinized than the Institute, and Father Fessio had become exceptionally agile in making its purpose clearly comprehensible, while at the same time shielding himself from the constant barbs of critics. The WASC evaluators were impressed, and all appreciated the contribution the Institute made to the university at large.

The year before, in 1984, he had become interested in a local broadcasting group, the Catholic School of the Air, whose origins went back to 1969. It featured different speakers explaining various Catholic beliefs and practices, but now the group wanted to offer a new fifteen-minute program called "The Catholic University of the Air" and asked Father Fessio to host it with a commentary on and discussion of the three-volume series *Fundamentals of Catholicism* (1982) written by his friend Father Kenneth Baker, S.J. Here was another opportunity for evangelization. In a December 4 letter addressed to the dean of the College of Arts and Sciences, Father Fessio requested permission to describe the proposed program as "affiliated with the Saint Ignatius Institute of the University of San Francisco". He explained that the USF campus station, KUSF, was willing to lend its facilities to the project for less than $40 a week. The university would have no financial responsibilities, since the sponsoring group was willing to buy the airtime and was willing to bear the cost of using KUSF's facilities. He argued that there would be an added advantage of getting the name of the SII into the surrounding area. Dean Harnett shared Father Fessio's enthusiasm for the project, seeing benefits for both the Institute and the university, and gave him his avid approval to take on the project. "The Catholic University of the Air" met with immediate success, bringing him to the attention of some of the local San Francisco radio stations.

In 1984, KGO-TV was one of the most popular stations in San Francisco. Its editorial director between 1972 and 1982 had been Emmy-winning Father Robert A. Sunderland, S.J., a member of the USF Jesuit community and one of the most enthusiastic, if silent, supporters of the SII and Ignatius Press. The husband-and-wife team Fred LaCosse and Terry Lowry hosted a talk show on the channel called *A.M. San Francisco* that attracted some 300,000 viewers. When they announced that Father Andrew Greeley would be a panelist on November 19, interest became more intense. Greeley at the time was a much-talked-about personality, a priest of the Archdiocese of Chicago who had earned a doctorate in sociology and was a prolific journalist and novelist along with being an obstreperous opponent of *Humanae Vitae*. His 1981 novel *The Cardinal Sins* had given him notoriety and money enough to convince him that writing about celibacy along with sex would be agreeable for a considerable portion of the reading public. His views on the Catholic Church in the United States and Ireland fit in well at times with the editorial columns in *The National Catholic Reporter, Commonweal*, and *America*. The purpose of his appearance on the LaCosse–Lowry show was to promote a book he had co-authored that same year: *How to Save the Catholic Church*.

Father Fessio was invited to be present and bring along two or three supporters. After all, what better way to spark the show than to have the director of the Saint Ignatius Institute pose questions and make comments from his place in the audience? "When you've got a liberal television host and a liberal guest and you're the other person," he informed the KGO-TV staff, "you're in a very vulnerable position. If you are in the audience and they are on the stage, you do not have any kind of a chance to reply." Then, with typical Fessio ratiocination, he continued: "So I'll be there. That's what I go for." Accompanied by two or three students, he made his appearance at the studio about a half hour before the program was to begin. Father Greeley and his sister arrived about the same time. The two priests shook hands, one in good spirits, the other in silence: the younger, a lean six-foot-three, strikingly handsome figure in clerical attire and matching black hair; the older, short and casually dressed, with a fixed frown that seemed to confirm his reputation for a cantankerous disposition. The introductions made, Father Fessio and the students walked over, somewhat self-consciously, to their reserved seats, while Father Greeley and his sister followed Fred LaCosse to their assigned places on stage, where Fred then explained that the two of them would be given the first segment of the show while Father Fessio and his students would have the second segment for questions. Father Greeley and his sister frowned at one another and, after a moment, got up and walked off stage.

The program was scheduled to begin in less than fifteen minutes. The assistant stage manager approached Father Fessio. "Father, we have a problem." Flustered, he then stuttered out: "Father Greeley is refusing to go on, now that he knows you are in the audience." Standing up, Father thought he was being asked to make a quick exit. "Oh no," she replied, "we have an open show and have no

intention of giving in to his ultimatum. It is just that *if* Father Greeley decides to do what he has threatened, what are we going to
do? We have to go on the air. So we're wondering: Would you be°
willing to take his place?" He was, and he did. He mixed seriousness with wit in explaining the Church's position on sex, marriage,
procreation and other issues with which Greeley took exception;
with both levity and understanding, he answered questions from
unsympathetic audience members who had come to hear Father
Greeley. Later in the show, he managed to land a well-aimed dart:
"Liberals talk about open-mindedness, transparency, and dialogue,"
he quipped, "but they do not seem to want to take a question when
it is asked by someone who differs in any way from their dogmas."
He then reflected aloud: "The show was supposed to promote the
book *How to Save the Church* by Andrew Greeley. I think a better
title would have been *How to Save Andrew Greeley* by the Church."
Speeding on to today, we can see Father Greeley in the rearview
mirror as a man, like so many of his admirers, truly dedicated to the
Church he thought had to change in order to be accepted by the
modern world. We can judge how wrong he was in condemning
Humanae Vitae, while still commending him for being the lone voice
in 1989 that condemned bishops and religious superiors for tolerat-
ing what he saw was becoming "the network of active homosexual
priests" along with "Lavender rectories and seminaries".[1] He was
simply not able to connect the dots, as Elizabeth Anscombe had
done at the *Humanae Vitae* symposium, from the encyclical's teaching to those lavender rectories and seminaries. And in all fairness
to Father Greeley, one can argue that at the time of the LaCosse–
Lowry talk show, he had a good reason for walking out when he
did. Later, in a formal complaint to the studio's managers, his sister
noted that she and her brother had known nothing of Father Fessio's
presence before they walked into the studio. They had little to win
and much to lose by remaining, so, understandably, they left.

That 1984 show with Fred LaCosse turned out to be a much
talked-about event. As a result of his strong performance, Father
Fessio began making regular appearances on the TV network—
another Father Sunderland. One KGO celebrity, Jim Eason, whose

[1] "New Approach Needed for Teaching on Contraception, Says Archbishop Quinn",
Catholic News Service, September 30, 1980.

three-hour afternoon show ranked number 1 in the San Francisco area, would frequently have him on his broadcast, and on one occasion in 1986, he was even invited to substitute as host of the program while Jim was out of town. It was during this slot that Father mentioned in passing that "the Jews crucified Christ—but we all crucified Christ"—which generated an uproar. One could hear those three fatal notes from *Carmen* blaring out from the USF president's office. Father Lo Schiavo commissioned Father Ruland to write a refutation of the remark, which was generally interpreted as an anti-Semitic barb. The outcome of the event will be treated in pages to come, but let us first mention one more TV anecdote. Some years later, Father Fessio appeared on a show alongside his fellow California Province Jesuit Father Thomas Reese, taking up the opposing side in a discussion. Former editor of *America* and a senior news analyst at the Religious News Service in Washington, D.C., Father Reese was a delightful man, but certainly not in agreement with Father Fessio on questions religious, social, or philosophical. After the show, one of Father Fessio's friends castigated him for having been so quiet and passive. "You could have steamrolled him into rubble. What happened to you?" Father answered: "I could never humiliate a fellow Jesuit in public, especially not a California Province Jesuit." Bertie Wooster would have agreed that it was the *preux* thing to do.

Back in 1985, there were certainly other things going on in the world, playing a soft second fiddle to the Fessio drama. Excitement was everywhere. President Ronald Reagan declared he would run for a second term of the presidency. After more than one hundred years, the United States and the Vatican re-established full diplomatic relations. Everyone was rushing to the movies to see *Indiana Jones and the Temple of Doom*. Pittsburgh trounced Ohio State in football, too, but no matter: Woody Hayes was still a living legend, even beyond the state of Ohio. Two years earlier, he had been inducted into the College Football Hall of Fame, and two years later, former President Richard Nixon would give the eulogy at his funeral. He was popular not only because of his long successful career with the Ohio State Buckeyes, but also because of his unpredictable, pugnacious personality and many verbal quips. (Once he observed that a pass attempt could go only three ways, two of them bad.) Father Joseph Fessio was involved in many matters, but they were never enough to distract him from the world of sports. He admitted that his attempt to get the Carmelite summer program approved by the campus administration had failed, but he confided to some friends that the case had engrossed the Theology Department enough for him to slip two new teaching positions into the Institute before a formal grievance could be filed. Woody Hayes would have seen that as a successful forward pass. Although Hayes, the expert on the philosophy of football passes, and Saint Rita of Cascia, patroness of desperate causes, lived in different time periods and fraternized with different social sets, they might have found some camaraderie in a few of Father Fessio's projects, which we will now attempt to describe.

Jam-packed 1985 raced into 1986, and in February, the newly named rector of the USF Jesuit community, Father Paul Bernadicou—yes, Father Bernadicou!—called Father Fessio into his office, asking him to give account of two recent displays of boldness, which will be recounted shortly. The fact that he, Father Fessio, was expected to bare his soul to the very man who had been consistently opposing him for the past nine years did not disturb him whatsoever, and this highlights something unique in his personality, something already detectable in his dealings with Father Lo Schiavo: the ability to distinguish between the wrestler and the match—with, it would seem, no conscious deliberation. In Father Fessio's mind, the *person* with whom he differed had no connection with the *issue* at hand. Personal emotions (anger, bitterness) might distract from the end to be achieved, and in his case, such emotions were not simply suppressed: they were not even there to begin with. His dealings with his new religious superior testify to that fact.

Now we will focus in on two notable episodes from the early days under Father Bernadicou, for which Father Fessio was called to give account there in the rector's office. Naturally, being Fessio-related events, both were highlighted by the media. The first was our knight's involvement in a protest in front of a Planned Parenthood facility. Police had been called to clear away a crowd of people praying the Rosary before an abortion clinic (this was at a time before clear directives for such demonstrations had been legally defined). When a considerable number of demonstrators ignored the order to move, the police rounded them up and forced them into a van standing ready to escort them to custody. Father

Fessio and a number of others resisted detainment, and one of them, Ron Maxson, the former Army officer in charge of USF's ROTC program, threw himself under the van and wrapped his powerful arms around the front axle, temporarily delaying its departure until he was forcefully pulled away amidst the cheers of the admiring crowd. Once they finally arrived at the police station, the group was dismissed with a warning not to cause any more trouble.

Not long afterward, a second scene took place; evidently Father Fessio was ready to star in another well-publicized melodrama. Jean-Luc Godard's film *Hail Mary* had just opened at a local movie theatre, a film whose provocative images and subject matter were offensive not only to Catholics, but to Christians in general. So Father Fessio took action. He prevailed on some Italian garbage collectors to park their truck in front of the theatre, it was adorned with a banner reading "Get this trash out of here." He brought with him, too, a bullhorn and an entourage of friends and eager students. With a noisy gas-powered leaf blower in hand, he walked along the line of moviegoers, "cleaning up" the sidewalk. All this managed to attract a crowd of sympathetic protesters—not to mention news crews—to the scene.

Such were the circumstances that galvanized Father Bernadicou's invitation to what was supposed to be an informal get-to-know-you tête-à-tête. At the awkward summation, the rector sat back and read a formal, thoughtfully constructed letter to his miscreant subject. After a paragraph expressing gratitude for Father Fessio's reputed openness and obedience, he carefully read: "Many, both in our Jesuit community and outside it, have spoken to me about their misgivings since you are so obviously identified with the Church, the Society, and the University by reason of your clerical attire and personal affiliations. And yet you represent such a different approach from theirs." He then concluded with the order that Father Fessio was to deliberate with him, his religious superior, *prior* to any future events where the media might be involved. Meanwhile, as rector, Father Bernadicou would be consulting with the provincial to learn whether there was a policy regarding the participation of individual Jesuits in public demonstrations and would later notify Father Fessio of the provincial's mind on the matter.

These adventures, along with others cited above, finally encouraged the provincial to write him a formal letter. Rather than cite passages from this letter, it seems more convenient to cite Father Fessio's written response, dated January 21, 1987. He began: "In our past meetings and in your previous correspondence with me, I have found you to be cordial, extremely understanding, objective and fair. In that light I was surprised by this last letter and inclined to view it as a momentary 'lapsus'." There are not many Jesuits who would accuse their provincial of being guilty of a "lapsus", however momentary. So what were his major superior's concerns? The provincial confessed he was worried about a number of things. First of all, there was a troublesome rumor circulating in Rome. The common talk was that Mrs. Erica John was ready to hand over to Father Fessio one million dollars if he would not interfere in the divorce litigation between her and her husband, Harry John. (The fact that there was such a rumor in Rome causing so much concern is intriguing, but this is no place to speculate.) Father Fessio categorically denied any involvement in this matter. If it was a rumor, it was indeed a false rumor.

The provincial further wanted to know Father Fessio's side of another story. Some said Archbishop Quinn had sent him a message telling him to report immediately to the chancery and answer the accusation that he was the "ringleader" of a group seeking to have the archbishop removed from office. Father Fessio repeated to the provincial what he had already assured the archbishop: there was "no foundation for such an accusation". "I wish I had that power," he remarked, "but even if I did, Archbishop Quinn would not be at the top of my list."

The provincial then informed him that he had been accused of saying "something" at some gathering about the rector of St. Joseph's, the archdiocese's minor seminary. "I am not even aware of what I am supposed to have said", the accused answered. "Apparently you are not, either." Father Fessio then proceeded: "Now I admit that the existence of such spectacular false allegations against me doesn't mean that there might not be some true ones from time to time. However, when accusations are made, I would hope to be considered innocent until proven guilty and, furthermore, that an attempt be made to give a favorable interpretation to what I might have said."

The provincial's final concern was about the outrage Father Fessio had stirred when, on the Jim Eason radio show mentioned earlier, he purportedly accused the Jews of being responsible for the death of Christ. More than one of the 70,000 listeners must have winced, and understandably so. "There are aspects of that remark for which I am sorry," Father Fessio confessed, "and I have publicly apologized." He emphatically denied he was anti-Semitic and insisted, "I said nothing that was theologically inaccurate or which is contrary to the teaching of the Catholic Church." Shortly after the event, he had already told a reporter at the USF *Foghorn*:

> I am not entirely happy with what I said on the air. Coming at the end of the show as [the caller] did, I didn't have time to qualify my comments. . . . When I say the Jews crucified Christ, I am only using shorthand for the historical fact that the authorities of the Jews and those who followed their lead pressed for the death of Christ (cf. Jn 19:6). I don't believe in the collective guilt of any group of people, neither the Jews for crucifying Christ, nor the Germans for massacring the Jews, nor the Church for persecuting the Jews. I do believe in the collective guilt of mankind in the crucifixion of Christ, that I, as a Christian, am *more* responsible when I sin than any Jew in the mob who demanded his death. Jesus asked forgiveness for the Jews who "know not what they do", but as a Christian I know I am killing Christ each time I sin.

Father Fessio's letter to the provincial gives a good insight into how he was judged at this stage of his career, and the incidents singled out by the provincial (along with his reaction to them) offer an insight into the suspicion that many well-meaning people had toward him. The letter also shows how up-front Father Fessio was and how quickly he was to admit guilt when guilt was present. His response to the provincial was frank: "You seem to refer to my seeming delight in taking potshots very frequently, to my being an embarrassment to many of my brothers at USF and the province." Moreover, "you wonder whether or not I have given up completely on serious theological study and reflection. You say my public remarks often sound like a Bible-belt fundamentalist." He continued with a rebuttal:

> As a rule, I try to accentuate the positive in my public talks and statements. I am certainly not in the habit of making public criticisms of St. Joseph's Seminary. But I also do not hold, either in principle or in fact, that it is beyond criticism. If you think this

matter should be pursued, I would be most happy to cooperate in trying to determine what it is I said. And if I have erred, I want to do whatever is appropriate to set matters right. However, the fact that the rector of St. Joseph's was offended by something I am alleged to have said, and of which I am presently unaware, seems a fairly meager basis for a discussion of "appropriate remedies".

The nature of these potential "appropriate remedies" remains a mystery. But one thing is certain: they could have been quickly implemented—and with a smile, too. This conjures up the memory of Father Copeland, the rector at Santa Clara in 1967, whose solution to the Fessio problem lay in constructing a well-built stockade. The bottom line is that in 1987 Father Fessio did not enjoy the unconditional confidence of his secular and religious superiors.

We now return to Woody Hayes' reflections on the trifold nature of the attempted forward pass. Father Fessio did enjoy some successes in his many activities. He succeeded in the TV settlement. It was a good play, one that drove the ball—that is, free selection of part-time teachers at SII—closer to the goal line. The next play, his scrambling attempt at activism on social and religious issues, might be classified as another kind of forward pass: one that went wrong. The heavy defensive line made a great rush, and the ball was dropped. Then, surprisingly, a pass was intercepted. On June 12, 1987, Father Fessio received a letter from "John", president of the University of San Francisco, greeting him as "Dear Joe": "I am terminating you as Director of the Saint Ignatius Institute. The reason for your termination is mismanagement of the Institute's endowment. Contrary to express and written direction, you have completely spent that endowment. Your termination is effective Friday, June 26, 1987."

15

NEW DIRECTIONS

Father Fessio received his termination notice as he was preparing to fly to oversee a section of the SII summer program in France. Before leaving, he typed out a quick reply to Father Lo Schiavo registering his reactions. After a short, desultory introduction, he continued, "Of course I cannot agree with your assertion that I have mismanaged Mrs. Davies' gift to the Institute", knowing that he and the president were in agreement—though not publicly—that this charge was merely a pretext for fending off the problem of the Saint Ignatius Institute in general. There were also echoes here of the 1975 Ocean Beach "Dangerous" sign episode, as must have occurred to one or both parties. After emphasizing the nature and mission of the Institute, Father Fessio then reminded the president, "The Institute is not merely an academic program which has proven its excellence, but a program that has definite spiritual ideals and a clear public commitment to the Church, especially in her capacity of authentic teacher of faith and morals." In his estimation, "whether I or another should be its director is not of any particular importance." What was important, instead, was "to do whatever I can to see that the spiritual and ecclesial as well as the academic ideals of the Institute are not compromised." He was chiefly concerned about who would succeed him as director and, moreover, what would be the fate of John Galten and Dennis Bartlett, "who have been responsible for whatever success the Institute has had" and who "are now understandably anxious" for the welfare of their families. Finally, he reminded the president that for the past thirteen years, fundraising had been a substantial part of his apostolic activity. Now, however, "both my reputation and my further work have been compromised by your accusing me of mismanaging a large sum of money." Therefore, he saw no way of avoiding the moral obligation he had of responding to questions asked of him

170

and giving "as factual and objective an account as I can of the events leading to my removal".

It was quintessentially Fessio: polite but firm. Then the sword was drawn: "I do not at the moment see how I can fulfill this obligation without causing problems for you, since I think you have made a seriously erroneous judgment and this must necessarily be the burden of my account." In the hope of some resolution that would "preserve the integrity of the Institute without compromising either my reputation or yours", he informed the president he was enclosing "a copy of a draft letter and exploratory document I have composed", inviting his "comments and suggestions for emendations".

For those familiar with the attitude of Saint Ignatius in the face of false accusations, this letter should be of particular interest. The discreet and patient Ignatius was frequently under attack from false accusations, and he fought them with no holds barred. When he saw his apostolate threatened, he showed mettle and strength, toughness and dauntless persistence. This man who advocated sufferings, humiliations, and opprobrium became a tiger when it came to threats on his reputation, because such accusations compromised his effectiveness in bringing Christ to others. In the late 1530s, his confreres advised him to suffer such defamation so that he could be more like Christ, who bore calumnies made by false witnesses, but Ignatius would have none of it. Humility is not stupidity. He insisted on bringing the allegations to court. It was the *preux* thing to do. This he did, and he was exonerated. Later in his career, when he and his companions were falsely accused, he again demanded a trial, stating that they would willingly accept a guilty verdict and whatever punishment that entailed, but requesting a formal, written declaration of innocence in the case of a judgment in their favor.[1] Father Fessio's reaction to Father Lo Schiavo's accusations, therefore, was quite Ignatian.

The exploratory document he attached to his letter to the university president encouraged this seasoned Jesuit, who had been so successful in defusing USF's basketball scandals, to negotiate with discretionary prudence. The implication was obvious. In July 1982,

---

[1] José Ignacio Tellechea Idígotas, *Ignatius of Loyola: The Pilgrim Saint*, trans. Cornelius M. Buckley (Chicago: Loyola University Press, 1994), 405–7.

five years before Father Fessio received his termination notice, Father John Lo Schiavo had made history by becoming the first president of a Division I university to shut down completely his school's basketball program. Repeated stories of dishonest, undercover dealings in recruiting and maintaining members of the squad finally spurred him to take drastic action. In San Francisco, college basketball had almost become a substitute religion, and the Dons were judged to be one of the best teams in the nation, making the cut especially tough. There were, however, fortuitous consequences to what some saw as the president's untoward action. Although it put a closure on basketball games, it also silenced all further questions and averted a potentially lengthy fact-finding investigation. With his *ukase* to dissolve the team, the former high school basketball star and San Francisco native won the admiration of the city and the country by declaring that the Dons team "was once a source of inspiration and pride for this university and city", but that the scandals had tarnished that image. The team that had once placed USF in such a favorable light had now led the school to be judged "hypocritical or naïve or inept or duplicitous, or perhaps some combination of all these". A short time afterward, responding to continual questions about restarting the program, Father President answered: "We hope that one day it may be possible to restore a men's intercollegiate basketball team. That possibility will depend on whether those responsible for this university are convinced that the factors that destroyed the program are not going to beset it again."[2]

Such noble, forceful, and self-deprecating pronouncements kept him an international media star. Indeed, at the height of the basketball question, Queen Elizabeth paid a visit to San Francisco, and, at the regal reception, prescinding from her written text, she asked him off the cuff when he was going to restart the basketball program. The reaction was spontaneous applause. The answer to her question was not given until 1985. Meanwhile, in order to guarantee that scandals would not reoccur, the president took the sports program directly under his control. By 1987, Father Lo Schiavo, having gained experience in handling persistent embarrassment to the university and trimming the wings of the sports sector to keep it

---

[2] Gordon G. White, Jr., "San Francisco Drops Its Basketball Program", *New York Times*, Sports Section, July 30, 1982.

tamable, was ready to deal with the fallout from the Fessio firing and the problem of the temporarily decapitated Saint Ignatius Institute. But he also agreed with Father Fessio that any "exploratory documents" about his firing remain unpublicized. This was so especially because Louise Davies stated when she made her gift it was with the proviso that it could be used to finance day-by-day operations. When she learned of the firing, she said: "I just love Father Fessio. Father Lo Schiavo should not have done what he did. I think it's terrible."[3] However, there were many other projects beyond USF that were in line to ease her pain and her purse. Father Lo Schiavo was certainly embarrassed—and his arguments weakened—by her public stance. But former star basketball players are not used to admitting defeat.

Though leaders of businesses and universities shun investigations, they are partial toward committees. Committees create distractions. So Father John formed a committee asking the members to suggest who might replace the deposed director. He decided to keep the group small and manageable. In addition to the four Jesuit members of the SII board of directors, he asked a few executive members of the university community, not connected with the Institute, to serve as well. Then there was Father Richard Spohn, S.J., whom he invited to join the ad hoc group, much to the satisfaction of the members of the Theology Department. Father Spohn was a very popular, vocal, and influential young Jesuit, a professor of moral theology at the Jesuit School of Theology in Berkeley. All who knew him were impressed by his natural intelligence and integrity. From the outset, his solution to the long-troublesome Saint Ignatius Institute was to get rid of it, and he did not hesitate to reaffirm his opinions at the committee meetings. Then there was one of the members of the SII board who told the group that when he was in Rome during the summer of 1982, he received a surprise summons to meet with Father Paolo Dezza, the delegate Pope John Paul II had appointed to govern the Jesuit order after a stroke left Father General Arrupe incapacitated in 1981. They had never met before, but Father Dezza, after quizzing him for a long time about the Institute, ended the conversation saying what hope this model

---

[3] Charlotte Hays, "Institute Founder Fired, Future Uncertain", *National Catholic Register*, July 12, 1987.

gave to American Jesuit colleges everywhere and asked him to encourage those who fostered the Institute's continuance. Set against the strong counterarguments of Father Spohn, attestations of this kind, offered by a number of Jesuits on the board, helped convince the board's token laymen that the Institute was an in-house Jesuit problem, and so for the most part they remained neutral. The president, ever attentive, also kept his silence as we discussed the "Saint Ignatius Institute problem".

His silence, however, was certainly no indication of his sincere desire to put a cap on what had been the most drawn-out predicament of his tenure of office, the nagging, unhappy situation that seemed to find no resolution he was willing to take. He certainly wanted to avoid making the wrong choice—a choice between alternatives that all promised to bring on greater perplexity. He must have remembered the private meeting the Jesuits in the Theology Department insisted on having with him concerning the Fessio problem, where they reminded him of the unspoken claim of their influence in Jesuit communities beyond USF. Then there was the letter he had just received from Father James V. Schall, S.J. Author of many books, Father Schall was a member of the USF Jesuit community and a professor in the Government Department, although he would soon transfer to Georgetown to pursue an outstanding teaching career. His was a voice that had never been heard in the controversies surrounding the Saint Ignatius Institute, and so his three-page, single-spaced letter to Father Lo Schiavo, with copies sent to Father Fessio and Father Charles Dullea, a former president of the university, a present member of the SII advisory board, and a man held in the highest esteem by the city authorities of San Francisco, must have come as a great surprise to the beleaguered president. After a brief introduction in which he tabbed Father Fessio as "something of an entrepreneurial genius", Father Schall commented on his ability to "see spiritual and intellectual needs to be addressed". Such was the main theme he developed in his letter—one with which the president theoretically could have agreed—reminding him that he had heard that opinion expressed many times. But in three separate paragraphs, Father Schall reacted to the president's accusation of Father Fessio's "mismanagement of certain funds". He called this "a most serious charge" and added: "Unless there is some sort of secret evidence which is sustainable in court or legitimate opinion,

I believe you do nothing but damage to yourself and your reputation to make such a charge." The president must have realized
all the more that the shaky reason he had given for Father Fessio's
dismissal was a mistake. He certainly did not want Father Schall's
conclusion bandied about, and all the more did he not want Father
Fessio's "exploratory documents" made public. The truth of the
matter was that they had great personal relations; he probably felt
more at ease watching a 49ers game with Joe Fessio than he did
with all the members of the Theology Department combined. But
his job was to guide, lead, and steer the university, and this present
SII problem was an obstacle to that end. How was he to resolve it?
As in the basketball scandal, he had to stop rumors, but how? Although we cannot know how Father Lo Schiavo ultimately reached
his decision to terminate Father Fessio as director, let us imagine,
for a moment, how this measure may have appeared at the time like
a valid solution to the SII problem.

Four of the five Jesuits who had been commissioned by Father
McInnes in 1974 to draw up the plan that Father Fessio subsequently
crafted into the Institute were present members of the SII advisory
board and had been so since its inception. They now suggested to
the president that he make an additional refinement to the process
of naming a new Institute director. Names of possible candidates
given to the general committee would be submitted to a subcommittee for screening or evaluation. The subcommittee would then
choose one of these names and would present the packet, along with
a written statement giving reason for the choice, to the president
for approval. Should he not approve its choice, the subcommittee
would present another name. This process would continue until the
president finally had a name he could approve. This procedure had
the advantage of keeping the ultimate selection in the hands of the
president while at the same time ensuring that the candidate would
be proposed by those most cognizant of the needs of the Institute.
This was the model used at the Catholic University of America for
the selection of a dean or a department head. The subcommittee
would include selected faculty members who teach full time in the
Institute and all the members of the present advisory board, plus
the founder of the Institute, Father Fessio. Finally, Father Dullea
recommended that the committee vote on a successor to Father
Fessio and that the members of the USF Jesuit community also be

encouraged to make recommendations. Father Lo Schiavo accepted this proposal, and on September 9, 1987, the Dean of the College of Arts and Sciences announced that Father Robert L. Maloney had accepted the president's invitation to become the new Director of the Saint Ignatius Institute. The president then expanded the advisory board's duties to include aiding the new director in his management. A newly created subcommittee was the compromise. The president recognized that the Theology Department would certainly not sing a *Te Deum* in welcoming the new director, and so to sweeten the medicine, he announced that Father Spohn was to be a member of the new advisory board along with two other lay faculty members, one of whom was a tad left of Nancy Pelosi and potentially favorable to the department's agenda. *Divide ut regnes.*

At the time of his appointment, Father Robert Maloney, S.J., was an assistant dean of arts and sciences. As we have recounted earlier, he was also one of the four trailblazers of the Institute project before Father Fessio's arrival on the scene, and he was the provincial who had initially assigned Father to the university. A friendly, modest, cheerful man highly respected and well-liked by members of the faculty and administration, he knew how to cut where he must and to mend where he could. Father Lo Schiavo, always the good priest and the successful administrator, assured all that Father Maloney's background—he was a former Carnegie Fellow at the University of Michigan—gave promise that he would direct the institute in tandem with the university at large, and Father Maloney asserted he would change nothing in the great books program that fostered Catholic doctrine. Father Lo Schiavo reissued another letter praising Father Fessio, mentioning that the two had disagreed on management—saying nothing about funds—and assuring all that Father Maloney would defend the mission of the Institute. On September 9, 1987, Father Fessio addressed a letter to the students, parents, alumni, and friends of the Saint Ignatius Institute explaining why, to the confusion of some, he had maintained a self-imposed silence since his dismissal as director on June 11. He explained: "I did not want to do anything, nor did I want others to do anything, which might prejudice the deliberations by University officials in a way that would be detrimental to the Institute." He proceeded: "It is not only with a sense of relief but of overwhelming joy that I break that silence." And then: "I can understand the enthusiasm and emotion of Zachary in breaking his own silence when I now say to you: 'His name is Robert!' Father Robert Maloney, S.J., is the new Director of the Saint Ignatius Institute. I can honestly say I do not know anyone who would have been a better choice." Father Bernadicou, though relieved by Father Fessio's demise as director, was not altogether appeased by what seemed to be a compromise. He confessed he still wondered about the students: "Does the program, as it is now oriented, do justice to the classics they read, or are they reading from a *parti pris* position?"[4] Perhaps it was to ward off a negative answer to this query, or even to discourage further speculation, that the president had widened the advisory board to guarantee a change of direction for the Institute and put an end to dissension. That was not important at the time. What was important was that the same train was chugging again along the same track. We shall see where it journeyed and how it fared in a later chapter. Meantime, Father Fessio prepared to take off on other quests "far from the madding crowd's ignoble strife".

Less than a month after admitting to "the enthusiasm and emotion of Zachary", Father Fessio was in Rome serving as a *peritus*, that is, a theological advisor to bishops attending the Synod on the Laity that convened on October 1, 1987. Stripped of his Fessio carapace, he found himself flocked with a bevy of cardinals and bishops. In preparation for the general assembly, the participants were divided into linguistic groups. The English speakers were further divided into three alphabetically assigned divisions, seating Father Fessio with those prelates and theological advisors whose names, serendipitously, ranged between and A and F. One item for consideration the American prelates placed on the agenda was the possibility of introducing altar girls into liturgical celebrations. During one discussion, Francis Cardinal Arinze—the letter "A"—explained that in Africa, especially in Nigeria, the practice was for fathers to lead family prayer before a little shrine built in the home; there was a deep patriarchal tradition. Having girls or women play major roles at a liturgical ceremony would go against African culture. At that moment, Joseph Cardinal Bernardin, who was the acting chairman of the group, opined that perhaps regional adaptations would have to be enacted in the matter of girls serving at Mass, to accommodate

---

[4] Ibid.

less developed cultures, as it were. But one thing was certain: it was now time for a long coffee break.

Father Fessio found himself walking out of the room side by side with Cardinal Arinze, telling him that he considered Cardinal Bernardin's remarks condescending, picayunish. He then admitted that he believed that the African culture was more in tune with nature, closer to the soil, to plants, animals, and neighbors; that because Africans were not "technologized", urbanized, they were closer to reality than were those who lived in the environment of modern Western society. The cardinal seemed impressed and asked his companion to write some of these insights down on paper. Father Fessio rushed back to his hotel, sat down, and typed out a page of reflections on the subject; then he ran back to the meeting and handed the cardinal what he had written. The next day, Cardinal Arinze stood before the assembled crowd of clerics to deliver his reactions to the proposal to allow for female Mass servers. He read the very text—no more, no less—that the erstwhile director of the Saint Ignatius Institute had handed him the previous day.

Early in the spring of 2005, when he was again in Rome, Father Fessio paid a visit to the African friend he had made back at the Synod on the Laity in 1987. "Father Fessio, Georgetown University wants me to come and speak at their graduation commencement in May", Cardinal Arinze declared, and then asked: "What do you think I should do?" Father Fessio responded, "They want to use you as a sign of approval for what they are doing." Immediately the cardinal replied with his characteristic smile, "Maybe I will use them." The cardinal's short speech at Georgetown touched off a volcanic eruption. It was a clear mixture of cheeky audacity and careful reasoning. He informed the assembled group that the family today was under siege on a number of fronts: abortion, the homosexual agenda, infanticide, euthanasia, adultery, and pornography. Some faculty members walked off stage and were then joined by a few of the graduates. Later on, seventy members of the faculty signed a letter to the university's president protesting the cardinal's inappropriate, divisive remarks.[5] To be sure, the media took advantage of the uproar. The Nigerian cardinal's text, however, did not sub-

---

[5] James Hitchcock, "Francis Arinze Offends Georgetown", *Catholic Thing*, March 31, 2016, https://thecatholicthing.org/2016/03/31/francis-arinze-offends-georgetown/.

stantially differ from the discourse Father von Balthasar had given at the Institute-sponsored *Humanae Vitae* symposium in 1978— remarks designated "downright silly" by one professor at the Jesuit School of Theology at Berkeley, as already noted in an earlier chapter.

Meanwhile, over the previous five years, the Press had expanded exponentially. In 1982, there were 5,792 books sold, bringing in a total of $39,682, and in 1987, the year Father Fessio was fired from the directorship of the Institute, those figures had increased to 380,553 and $2,606,788. In 1986, the Press hired Institute graduate Roxanne Mei Lum as cover designer and art director, roles she would go on to fill for over thirty-five years and counting. That year of 1986 had been special for Father Fessio: he saw the publication of Henri de Lubac's *The Splendor of the Church* (*Méditation sur l'Église*), adding his own introductory remarks, and in 1988 he published de Lubac's *Catholicism: Christ and the Common Destiny of Man* with a foreword by Joseph Cardinal Ratzinger. André Ravier, S.J., the well-known historian, who had been Father de Lubac's provincial at the time when he wrote *The Splendor of the Church*, stated that although the book may be considered a classic, it was "written in blood", the fruit of the persecutions the author suffered at the hands of his fellow theologians, mainly those in Rome. The translation and publication in English did not elicit exactly the same sanguinary response, but the more success and admiration the publisher met with, the higher rose the wall of hostility from his critics.

The office of the Press was a half-football-field's distance from USF's Saint Ignatius Church, which housed a well-stocked bookstore of religious works. The policy of the church's prefect was that no book published by the Ignatius Press could find a place on its shelves. The presiding student at the bookstore heard it said that Hugh Hefner would find a place there more easily than Joseph Fessio would. At the same time, the Press would donate a copy of each one of its publications to the USF library, and Father Fessio continued to be a part of the Jesuit community. Eventually, however, the community introduced the policy that no Jesuit who was not somehow attached to the university could live in the Jesuit residence, a policy that bred empty rooms. By 1987, the commitment to the Press was so demanding that Father Fessio had been forced to give up his part-time teaching position; so, with the necessary permission from the rector, he purchased a futon and set it up in his Ignatius Press office. He took his meals whenever and wherever he could, mainly in the basement of Taberna, a small house across the street that had been purchased in 1984, which had a stove and a refrigerator in its downstairs meeting rooms. The expansion of the Press showed no signs of slowing during the following decade. In 1999, it hit a new high with the net sales record of 1,013,084 books sold. In 2002, another ceiling was broken when the dollar sales soared to $10,623,618, and nine years later that figure was almost doubled. By then, there were some twelve people working in the sardine-packed offices. The early problems of marketing and distribution had been met and solved, and the works of European theologians had been made available to a worldwide English-speaking audience. What is more, there were historians, novelists, and sociologists, too, who now found their manuscripts in attractive print.

As a side issue, Father Fessio became involved in the publication of four magazines, two of which were short-lived: *Catholic Dossier* and *Catholic Faith*. The former was the inspiration of Dr. Ralph McInerny (of the Philosophy Department at Notre Dame University), beginning in 1995 and expired in 2002. McInerny, a delightful personality whose versatility seemed boundless, authored books on a number of subjects other than philosophy; his Father Dowling mysteries were serialized on American and British TV from 1987 to 1991. The magazine contains some instructive, insightful articles that scholars today would find stimulating and future historians will delight to rediscover, but as a periodical, it was never popular enough to sustain the cost of publication. The life span of *Catholic Faith* was even shorter. Begun in 1999, it was the catechetical product of Father John Hardon, S.J., the author of some forty books and numerous articles on Catholic dogma and spirituality. The last issue appeared in 2001, a few weeks after his death. Then there was the *Homiletic and Pastoral Review*, mentioned above, which made its first appearance in 1900 and has enjoyed a reputation for excellence even beyond the cadre of American priests and bishops for whom it was intended. In 1971, Father Kenneth Baker, S.J., whom we have already met, a scholar of rare ability and a part-time teacher at the Institute, assumed editorship of the review, attracting the very best specialists and authors to vie for space on its pages.

In 1997, when Father Baker wanted to be relieved of the business side of the operation, Ignatius Press purchased the periodical. In 2010, he handed on his editorship to Father David Meconi, S.J., of Saint Louis University. In 2011, Father Fessio and the Press put the magazine online, where it remains to this day.

Finally, when he was in Rome at the 1987 synod, Father Fessio became acquainted with the Italian magazine *30Giorni*. It was love at first sight. He just had to publish an English edition when he returned to San Francisco, and so he did under the title *30 Days*. Unfortunately, tension between the Rome office and the San Francisco headquarters made the continuance of the review impractical, and so in 1991 the relationship was severed—a fiasco we shall recount in a later chapter—but out of the wreckage came a new journal, the *Catholic World Report*, dressed in similar livery and edited by the competent, delightfully readable journalist Philip Lawler. This magazine, now online, has been reaching a large, discerning readership for more than twenty years.

Before his dismissal as the director of the Saint Ignatius Institute, Father Fessio was in the habit of offering the daily Saint Ignatius Institute/Ignatius Press Mass in the Jesuit residence chapel. Ignatius Press employees Glenn and Vivian Dudro would often bring their children along with them. Father Fessio began encouraging their two young boys to serve the Mass, and before long, to the joy of all, the boys were made "official" with small cassocks and surplices. The chapel had been renovated in the late sixties to comply with what were considered the proper Vatican II liturgical norms. The altar had been replaced and then moved, set on a carpeted floor in the middle of the room, flanked by comfortable chairs. This arrangement presented a problem: Where will the two servers kneel? Then, with the gradual introduction of plainchant for the Mass ordinary (*Kyrie, Gloria, Sanctus,* and *Agnus Dei*), the whole arrangement seemed out of sync. The solution was to move across the street to the beautiful Spanish neo-Romanesque chapel in the Carmelite monastery of Cristo Rey, where there was a fixed marble altar, raised up from the stone floor, sheltered by an impressive baldachino; centered on the altar stood a tabernacle, and behind it, on the wall, rose a sculpture of Christ the King. The closed choir for the cloistered Sisters was on a transept beside the sanctuary. The setup required the priest and the people to face the same direction

at Mass, the "liturgical east" (since the chapel actually faces west).
Once there, Father Fessio began saying the Mass in Latin, following
the rubrics of Vatican II, using English for the propers (those parts
that change on a daily basis). Then in his spare time, as he claims,
he began reading and acquainting himself better with the history
and tradition of the Latin Rite Mass.

16

SIBERIA

Father Fessio found himself involved in a number of quests during the early 1990s. Rather than tracing them year by year, it seems better to give attention to how each ultimately developed, even though that may in some cases take us all the way to the twenty-first century.

For starters, in 1987, there took place one seemingly unimportant incident that would have important consequences for the life of the Reverend Joseph Fessio. A recently married former student came to him for some spiritual advice. During the conversation, Father suggested that since he had profited so much from the freshman-year retreat at the Saint Ignatius Institute, conducted at a conference center in the Santa Cruz Mountains, he and his wife might profit from making a retreat together. The young man left the meeting with the address and telephone number of the El Retiro San Iñigo Jesuit Retreat Center at Los Altos stuffed in his pocket. A few days later, he returned. "Father, they ask one hundred and fifty dollars for a weekend retreat", he said. "We can't afford that." "One-hundred and fifty dollars!" Father Fessio replied. The sum was reasonable, even excessively low, but this crafty Jesuit had a proposal: "We'll build our own retreat house, and we won't charge." Such was the resolve of the noble idealist, the knight-errant ever on the lookout for new windmills to conquer.

We speed on now to the fall of 1989. Guadalupe Associates has just completed the purchase of 156 acres in an isolated, magnificent site in the mountainous area north of the Russian River, and it was there that the dreamed-of retreat house was to be built. Here, between his many publishing duties and various other projects, Father Fessio took on the challenge of becoming a self-made architect. Remote as it was, building regulations for that area were restricted to single-family dwellings; no hotels allowed. Eschewing all industrial mass production patterns in favor of a craftsman-style model, he took his hurried sketches to a professional architectural firm, who perfected them and prepared them for implementation. The Sonoma County planning commission approved the blueprints for the rustic hillside residence near Guerneville. The site was far from any human habitation, and the phantom passage up to the construction area may have been even more challenging than the tracks he had persuaded his *deux-chevaux* to climb in rural India. At one point, when driving a group of students up a slick hill, Father Fessio's jeep slid back downhill and flipped over—spewing the students out to safety, but pinning our knight underneath. By the time he untangled himself from the wreckage, he was drenched with gasoline, and he raced with the shaken students back to the shell of the future retreat house, where John Galten, smelling the potent fumes, instantly grabbed a hose and sprayed him down thoroughly, clerical garb and all. Yes, it was one more *déjà-vu* dance of Father Fessio with an automobile. Had William Shakespeare been one of the enraptured onlookers, perhaps with a garden hose in hand, he might have been inclined to whisper: "All's well that ends well."

The retreat house was completed in a few months' time. It had a small, beautiful chapel, later expanded; an expansive kitchen and dining room; and a large great room with a huge fireplace. The building is a stunning example of both rusticity and comfort. Over the years, it has witnessed numerous retreats for priests, religious women, and lay people, who bring their own food and are expected to clean up their spaces before they leave. It also became a place where SII alumni and their families would meet for times of celebration and repose. If Father Fessio could claim no other achievement in life, he would nonetheless be amply blessed for having built Sweetwater, an oasis of spiritual and material wonderment, where hope is rekindled and joy sparkles. He soon introduced sheep and llamas onto the property, partly for wool and meat, but primarily to serve as organic lawn mowers and conversation starters. There is a small creek that runs not too far from the building, and Father Fessio thought it would be nice to dam the stream so as to create a pond. Aided by a work crew, he constructed a long six-inch-high barrier—a concrete wall abutting a large fallen redwood. Father Fessio, never forgetting his earlier aspirations of being a civil engineer, created two sluice gates at the bottom of the dam. The plan was to open them during the heavy winter rains to prevent the pond from silting up. However, when heavy rains came early one year while the Ignatius Press team was warmly sheltered down in San Francisco, there was no one on site to open the sluice gate. When he arrived for the weekend, he found the water of the lovely pond replaced by sand and rock—and the sluice gates buried beyond reach. "The best laid schemes of mice and men . . . "

Another anecdote about the early days of the Sweetwater retreat house: Not far from the residence, Father set up a chair in a sloping field somewhat interrupted by a redwood grove. Beyond the field are acres of oak woodlands. Early one morning, he was seated there on the hillside with his breviary in one hand and a .30–06 hunting rifle in the other, ready to fire at any California wild boar that would be foolish enough to cross his sights and interrupt his prayer. As with most of the unlikely projects he has taken on—smelt netting doesn't count—Father Fessio tends to bring home some token of his successes, and these hunting-chair exploits offered no exception. There have been some who claim they detect a cynical smirk hidden beneath the tusks of the trophy mounted on the wall of the library, but to others the boar's head poses as a kind of memorial to victory.

Around 2010, Father Fessio planted a vineyard at Sweetwater and began making his own wine. The house and the vines nearly burned up in the wildfires of 2020, but were spared, in part thanks to California state firemen who guarded the property, in part thanks to Father Fessio's spontaneous decision to clear the brush months before. Today, the only real vestige of the fire is a vast supply of "2020 smoked chardonnay" in the wine cellar.

We recorded earlier that in 1987, Father Fessio traveled to Rome to serve as a *peritus* in the Synod on the Laity. While there, some young Jesuits studying at the Bellarmino, mostly Americans, requested a meeting with him. Together they expressed their concern about the formation training prevalent within the Society, specifically "about the anti-papal, anti-magisterial, and anti-Roman attitudes on the part of [some of] their formators, and about pervasive liturgical abuses, secularization, homosexuality, and liberal conformism". He brought up this matter when he met a short time later with a Jesuit from Granada, Father Candido Pozo, who had been involved in creating a separate province in Spain during the 1960s, dedicated to the reform of the Society from within. Father Pozo told him that perhaps it was time to reinitiate that lost agenda, suggesting that Father Fessio speak to his friend Cardinal Ratzinger about the encounter he had with the Bellarmino scholastics. He did. He also shared the story with a Jesuit of the French-speaking Belgian province named Father Jacques Servais, a staff member of Cardinal Ratzinger's Congregation for the Doctrine of the Faith, who was also eager to launch a formation reform program within the Society. At the cardinal's suggestion, Fathers Fessio and Servais drew up a proposal for an international Jesuit novitiate with a cardinal protector in Rome. Cardinal Ratzinger also recommended that the two priests talk over the matter with the Jesuit general.

Father Fessio showed some reluctance. Two years earlier, he had already had a meeting with Father Kolvenbach on a similar topic. On that occasion, he told the general that because of faulty formation programs, some older Jesuits were saying they could never recommend a young man to enter the Society. In fact, some went so far as to whisper that, under the present conditions, they would even discourage such a consideration. As a retort, the general quietly informed him that the pope considered the Society to be healthy and then politely shared with him some edifying anecdotes. Later Father Fessio reflected he had been speaking too broadly about the Society, that he should have restricted his remarks to the Society he knew, the Society in the United States. This interview left him a crestfallen warrior, hardly eager to face the general again—even with Father Servais, who was so highly respected—in order to rehash the same matter. It was not worth the risk of another polite, fraternal dismissal. But Father Simon Decloux encouraged him. Like Jacques Servais, Father Decloux was a member of the southern Belgian province. He was also one of the four assistants to the general, the priest in charge of formation programs for young Jesuits throughout the world, and he was eager that the conversation take place.

Father Fessio finally submitted to their persuasive arm-twistings and again met with the general. Afterward, his assessment was that, although cordial, the general was even more reserved than at the

1985 meeting. He listened attentively and interjected some friendly, if terse, comments. He acknowledged there were problems with the formation agenda in the United States, but he gave the impression that he was either unwilling or powerless to do anything about them. On later reflection, Father Fessio concluded that perhaps it was a combination of both. The general recognized that conformation was an effect of American liberalism; his own impression was that, regrettably, no sacrificial choices were presented in the novitiate and that personal problems tended to be approached psychologically, though he admittedly was not well informed on the process of selecting novices or on the character of novice candidates in general. Indeed, alternatives for novitiate training were available in Latin America and Europe, but there were not, he acknowledged, in the United States. He, too, was working for reform. Having consulted with "experts from the left and right", Father Kolvenbach—a systematic theologian, a historian of the Society, and a liturgist—was then in the process of writing a letter on the daily reception of the Eucharist. He informed the two that discussion on the establishment of a special novitiate in Rome was under way, but would not be ready "tomorrow morning", adjoining that even once the institution was formed, its only candidates would be Eastern Europeans or those who would otherwise be part of the Roman delegation. In sum, after agreeing with and even adding to their description and diagnoses of various concrete problems in the Society, he spoke only in the most universal terms of any action that might be taken to address them. Father Fessio assesses, "He seemed to think that problems can be solved by writing letters based on consultation with 'politically' diverse experts." His approach was to admit the general existence of problems and then to deal with what was for him the real problem, namely, the person who brought the problems to his attention. He did this by, first, showing he understood and sympathized with the circumstances of the bearer of bad news and, then, looking for the minimum of assurances or actions needed to reduce the pressure such news generated. Father Fessio later reflected that if Father Decloux had engendered a sense of hope, modest but real, the general left him and Father Servais with the opposite feeling, in spite of the fact that the conversation was friendly and warm. He left the meeting with admiration for the general's ability to say "No!" to their request with such tact and diplomacy.

Shortly afterward, Father Fessio arranged a private meeting at the Gregorian University with Father Servais and Fathers Christoph von Schönborn, O.P., and Marc Ouellet (both future cardinals), in which they discussed founding a house of discernment and formation for young men, and later women, of diverse nationalities who wanted to dedicate themselves to the Lord in the religious or lay life and who were seeking on which path the Lord was calling them to travel. Assisting in this process, the man who had founded the Saint Ignatius Institute and the Ignatius Press in San Francisco now helped his collaborators design the formation program at the Casa Balthasar in Rome. Each candidate would be personally guided through the Spiritual Exercises of Saint Ignatius Loyola as well as through the writings of three great spiritual guides of the modern age: Hans Urs von Balthasar, Adrienne von Speyr, and Henri de Lubac. The program would feature seminars, courses, and study sessions on philosophy, theology, art, and literature, aided by a well-stocked library that over the years has grown to hold some 10,000 volumes; the students would also go on to spearhead public performances of such works as Shakespeare's *Measure for Measure* and Mozart's *The Magic Flute*. The Casa accepted its first residents in 1990 and has continued to this day.

A final note: In January 1990, Father Fessio, responding to a special invitation, was at St. Charles Borromeo Seminary in Baltimore for the installation of Father John Haas as the first holder of the Cardinal Krol chair in moral theology. Cardinal Ratzinger, the prefect of the Congregation for the Doctrine of the Faith, was also present, and during a reception break, he invited his former student to meet him in his room where the two could talk privately. There the cardinal informed him of the fate of his proposal for the international Roman novitiate, which he had drafted in 1987 at the cardinal's request. Ratzinger had personally handed over the proposal to Pope John Paul II, and the pope had even approved it. But now, three years later, Secretary of State Agostino Casaroli had blocked the measure.

Exactly one year later, Father Fessio received a letter from his old Regensburg companion and current board member of the Casa Balthasar, Father von Schönborn, who at that date was living at the Institut Saint-Dominique in Rome and serving as secretary for the Catechism of the Catholic Church Commission. One item in the letter was that Father John Hardon, S.J., and Mr. Tom Monaghan, the founder of Domino's Pizza, had an appointment with Cardinal Ratzinger on how to go about publicizing and distributing the upcoming *Catechism of the Catholic Church*, which was slated to appear the following year, the thirtieth anniversary of the commencement of Vatican II. Mr. Monaghan had already contributed $50,000 to the commission to advance this project, and he was ready to donate more provided there was a realistic plan for the promotion of the *Catechism*. Father von Schönborn wrote that he was now seeking Father Fessio's help in this project.

When it came to the thorny matter of evaluating translations, a number of challenges demanded Father Fessio's assiduous attention. The 1980s and 1990s were the decades wherein a concerted effort was made in the English-speaking world to make so-called inclusive language acceptable. Translators had already revised the New American Bible, the Jerusalem Bible, and the Revised Standard Version. Father Fessio was determined to buck the tide. He began by canvassing English-speaking biblical scholars throughout the world, seeking their opinion on the best, most accurate translation of the Bible in English. The conclusion was that the RSV was superior. At that time, the Press was still struggling, but he put in a call to Mother Angelica, foundress of the Eternal Word Television Network (EWTN). "Mother," he said, "all of these new translations are inclusive language. We would like to reprint the RSV, but we don't have the money. . . . Will you loan us $100,000?" She said, "check's in the mail." It was easy getting permission to republish this version of the Bible because the rights belonged, not to a Catholic group, but to the National Council of the Churches of Christ, the NCCC, which simply wanted the maximum number of Bibles to be circulated. There was no time to re-typeset this Ignatius Press edition, but Thomas Nelson, in Nashville, printed it from their own earlier RSV Catholic edition. This edition proved very popular. Later, the Congregation of Divine Worship in Rome released *Liturgiam Authenticam* on March 28, 2001, a document on liturgical translations. After making some minor changes, such as substituting "you" for "thee" and "thou", the Press published the Second Catholic Edition of the RSV, which they used to produce a full Mass lectionary for the liturgical year. The "RSV2CE" remains the only English Bible translation that conforms with *Liturgiam*

Authenticam. Sales for this "Ignatius Bible" in both editions have been beyond expectations ever since. This happy ending is the prelude to another set of exploits.

First, some background. At the 1985 synod of bishops in Rome, the archbishop of Boston, Bernard Francis Cardinal Law, gave an exhortation (in flawless Latin) to his fellow bishops. He proposed the creation of a "universal catechism", a compendium of Catholic teaching to keep dissenting theologians and post–Vatican II modernists at bay. Pope John Paul II approved the plan, which called for setting up a commission of twelve cardinals and bishops and an auxiliary body of seven bishops and a number of theologians. Finally, Father Christoph von Schönborn was appointed the editorial secretary. After a round of criticism and commentary from over a thousand bishops in November 1989, the final version of the *Catechism* was published—in French—in autumn 1992. Afterward, the drafting of the English edition was entrusted to Cardinal Law and his two translator associates, Monsignor Timothy J. Moran and Father Douglas K. Clark, who announced that they would implement inclusive language in their rendering of the text. A few days later, Father Fessio got a telephone call from a theologian friend, Monsignor Michael Wrenn, who had just landed in New York from Vienna, where he had been consulting with the recently appointed auxiliary bishop, Christoph Schönborn. The monsignor told him that both he and the bishop had been concerned about Cardinal Law's newly submitted English draft and both looked forward to his evaluation. "Fine", said Father Fessio. "FedEx me a copy." "No", was the reply. "I'm catching a flight to San Francisco right away." Father picked him up, and the two spent the next day—Thanksgiving Day—at Sweetwater together. Did reading this manuscript elicit mournful feelings in our knight similar to those he had experienced on another Thanksgiving Day, when, disappointed, he paddled along the Sacramento River through Devil's Canyon? He did not say, but we do know that what Father Fessio read propelled him to the telephone to interrupt the holiday leisure of his friend Francis George, Bishop of Yakima, who besides being an expert in French was also a close associate and friend of Cardinal Law. It was not only a question of inclusive language, he asserted; it went far beyond that. As proof, he read the opening sentence of a paragraph: "*Notre Sainte Mère L'église a toujours ensigné* . . ." ("Our holy mother the Church has always taught"); then the Law version: "It has often been the common opinion that . . ." In short, the phone call was by no means a happy nightcap after a Thanksgiving dinner in Yakima.

On the contrary, the bishop promised Father Fessio that he would telephone Cardinal Law as soon as possible and suggest a meeting between his translators and the Press' translators, and because no one wanted a public debate, he was confident that the problem could be easily solved. Father Fessio admitted that he was so full of joy and hope after the conversation that he wept. Father Donohue would have understood. True to his word, on the following day, Bishop George called back the happy, weepy warrior. "Joe, Bernie told me in a phone call I just had with him that he wants his translation approved. He said it was a good translation, and he does not want to consider any alterations." With the help of others, particularly Bishop James Stephen Sullivan of Fargo, North Dakota, Father Fessio composed a detailed critique of the proposed English translation. During the next few months, Cardinal Law prevailed upon a number of people to pressure Father Fessio into calling off his criticisms. But then one day in January 1993, Bishop Schönborn telephoned Father Fessio telling him that he had shown his critique to Cardinal Ratzinger, who judged that the Law translation should not be published and requested that the Press compose an alternative translation. No sooner said than done.

The director of the Press and two collaborators, Professor Erasmo Leiva-Merikakis of the Saint Ignatius Institute and Doug Bushman, a former author for the Press, immediately set to work on the project, and in nine weeks they had a copy-edited, typeset, proofread, and indexed translation ready to be sent to the Congregation for the Doctrine of the Faith. Fortunately, Cardinal Law was in Rome at the time, and so he, Cardinal Ratzinger, Bishop Schönborn, and a few other carefully selected clerics met to discuss the problem of the two dueling translations. No decision on the question was forthcoming, but all agreed to submit both translations to Archbishop Eric D'Arcy of Hobart, Tasmania, for final evaluation. D'Arcy was a scholar of rare talent, a man of calm and dignified manner, and could serve as a kind of referee in the matter. At a later date, his successor to the see of Hobart remembered him as a man who considered his decisions with great care and would not be rushed into making them, but who, once they were made, would not go back on them. Bishop D'Arcy took several months to finalize his assignment, and the result was an acceptance of the Ignatius Press version, with some minor modifications. The 800-plus-paged English edition was published in May 1994. But that is a development for future consideration.

In the midst of these dramatic episodes regarding the translation of the *Catechism*, there was another episode that illustrates well the personality of the Reverend Father Fessio. In mid-December 1992, he flew out to Milwaukee to concelebrate the funeral Mass of Mr. Harry G. John, the generous benefactor who had played such an important role in the beginnings of the Press. After his divorce, his life had been very unhappy. Then there was the mystery of the disappearance of his huge fortune, which is outside the purview of this study but begs for the reincarnation of Hercule Poirot. The funeral ceremony was scheduled to take place in the Jesuit chapel of Marquette University. The archbishop of Milwaukee, Most Reverend Rembert Weakland, was the presiding prelate at the Mass, and there were about fifteen concelebrants, one of whom was Father Fessio. Before the celebration began, "the woman who ran the church"—Father Fessio's terminology—gave orders that the concelebrants would fill the front two rows on one side of the chapel and that during the Canon of the Mass they would not stand, as was the liturgical practice, but kneel, so as not to appear conspicuous. Providence arranged that Father Fessio was to be in the front pew, seated next to the aisle, where he was free to fidget, unseen and unheard, during what would be a torturous dilemma. He hesitated to go against a liturgical directive, but it was a funeral Mass, and he did not want to create a scene. During the course of the Mass, however, the tension was resolved. One of Harry's daughters read the first reading—fair enough. Another daughter read the second reading—OK, but a bit much. Then, a third daughter read the Gospel, followed by another who gave the homily. If the archbishop appeared to be swimming in a sea of tranquility, Fessio was not inclined to join him. The *Sanctus* bell rang. The concelebrants around him knelt. Later, he admitted it was more anger than piety that encouraged him to stand. After less than a minute, the priest next to him joined him. Soon, there was only one who remained kneeling, the Jesuit in charge of the operation. At Communion, the congregation sang "I Am the Bread of Life" with the words "I will raise *them* up; I will raise *them* up", while Father Fessio belted out the original words: "I will raise *him* up; I will raise *him* up." Today he claims that it was at that moment he declared his "personal war against 'inclusive' language, feminist mistresses-of-ceremonies, and the whole lot".

It must boggle one's imagination, tinged now by awe, to see how Father Fessio had the energy to take on yet another adventure, but his willingness to do so testifies to his endurance and is essential to a proper assessment of his personality. This time the impetus came from his provincial. "Joe," he sighed, "you haven't made tertianship. You know, you cannot take your last vows until you do. After the Montecito debacle, you also realize you will not be accepted to a tertianship program in this province. So find a program on your own." Father Fessio first made inquiries in Chicago, but with much external charity and delicacy, the program turned him down. He was also judged to be a risk in other American provinces, where word got around fast. This rejection prompted him to look abroad. He was eager to learn Spanish, and during his days at Santa Clara he had been drawn to the plight of Spanish-speaking immigrants from across the border. Result: the provincial agreed that doing missionary work in Central America would be good for him, so he wrote a letter to the tertian master in El Salvador recommending that he be accepted in that program. After some *mañana*-time, during which investigation letters were exchanged, the request was refused. "They didn't know me there, but had heard about me, and so they didn't want me." The provincial then told him to do his tertianship studies under the direction of Father Thomas McCormick, the rector of the Jesuit community at USF. Theologically speaking, Father Fessio and Father McCormick were poles apart, but the rector, a devotee of the Enneagram of Personality, was one of the most affable, generous, and charitable men alive. On one occasion, I asked him for $100 for a student who needed it, and without asking me why, he slipped me $500. In another instance, he paid half the tuition for a student he scarcely knew.

What was the plan of action for the aspiring tertian? Besides giving more time for contemplative prayer through the guidance of Saint Ignatius' Spiritual Exercises and considering how one might best adapt to the contemporary social scene in order to continue the evangelizing mission of bringing the Gospel message to others, the Jesuit making tertianship is expected to spend some time "out in the fields". Several weeks are set aside from one's ordinary works to immerse oneself in a completely different ministry. For Father Fessio, the man who felt at home working with "concrete and steel—hands-on kind of things", this challenge was particularly attractive. But where could he put it into effect? A woman named Antonia Willemson gives us the answer. He had met her somewhere along the trail of his many travels. She was the niece of Father Werenfried van Straaten, O.Praem., the founder of Aid to the Church in Need, and she was also the secretary general of that organization, about which unfortunately so little is known in this country. The group was formed as a result of an article, avidly read throughout Europe, that Father van Straaten had written in 1947, appealing for help for the fourteen million Germans who were exiled from East Germany as a result of the Russian takeover after World War II. Among this group were about eight million Protestants and six million Catholics, and they were lodged in open fields and former Nazi concentration camps in West Germany where they struggled with poor nutrition and limited medical aid. They received assistance not only from their fellow German countrymen, who were also struggling to a lesser degree, but also from the citizens of Holland and Belgium, who had suffered so as a result of the Nazi occupation of their lands and from the battles that had brought them freedom. This aid came largely as a result of Father van Straaten's appeals. The Dutch-born Norbertine cleric was given the title "Bacon Priest" by Flemish Catholics because of his constant pleading for meat to feed these refugees. Two books that he wrote describing the history of this apostolic mission were later published by Ignatius Press: *Where God Weeps*, 1989, and a 1991 translation and reprint of the 1960 account *They Call Me the Bacon Priest*. Such was the background of Aid to the Church in Need, whose secretary general, Antonia Willemson, Father Fessio contacted in 1992, inquiring whether there might be a place for his services. Indeed there was. She responded: "The Jesuit bishop in Novosibirsk, Siberia, is desperately in need of help. Would you be able to travel there to assist him?" A typical Fessio response was emailed back: "Since I barely know my 'Da' from my 'Niet', it is not clear to me what earthly (or heavenly) good I could do there. But if it is OK with Father McCormick, sure, I'll go." Father Fessio brought the question to his tertianship director: Would he mission him under obedience to go to Novosibirsk? "Indeed I would", Father McCormick replied. "Sending Joe Fessio to Siberia would make me the envy of every Jesuit superior in the United States."

So, purchasing for himself a visa, a parka, "a mad bomber hat", ice boots, and a roundtrip ticket on Aeroflot, he took off from San Francisco to Novosibirsk, where he arrived in March 1992 and was picked up at the airport by Father Josef Messmer, who was the nephew and assistant of Bishop Joseph Werth, the pastor of the church where he would be working. Father Fessio later described him as "a great man; a wonderful bishop". Both the bishop and the nephew were German–Russians, natives of Kazakhstan, and each had been secretly received into the Society of Jesus in Lithuania, where they had made all their Jesuit training underground. Joseph Werth, who was still in his thirties, had recently been ordained bishop of Novosibirsk, the seat of the largest territorial diocese in the Catholic world—over 5,000 miles from east to west and 3,500 from north to south. After landing and going through a pro forma customs procedure, as Father Fessio recalls: "We [drove] to the [bishop's] residence and chancellery—it's the same thing, a great big dormitory building, one of those Stalin buildings. And the guy takes off the windshield wipers and I said, what are you doing? And he said: 'I can't leave them on, they'll get stolen if I leave them on.' So, in Russia, you just have to tie down everything." Making their exit from the wiper-less car, Father Messmer guided his American guest to what he was given to understand was the joint chancery and Jesuit community residence. "And so I go in and this bishop has four or five rooms", he gasps, and then with an expression of real shock adds, "no telephone!" The recovery from shock was slow in coming: "But there's a chapel and there's a little dining room and an office with a curtain along one side with a bunk in it. That's where [the bishop] slept. I had a guest bed." That first night he suffered from jet lag: "And so about three in the morning, I went into the chapel to pray the office of readings or something and I saw the housekeeper there, kneeling down before the Tabernacle with her arms outstretched in a cross. . . . Beautiful, beautiful devotion on the part of these people."

Who were these "people" designated to discern for him the difference between his "Da" and his "Niet"? They were the descendants of a group of ethnic Germans, some of whom had begun trickling into Russia during the Middle Ages. But it was in 1782 when the trickle turned into a flood. That was the year the Tsarina Catherine the Great invited vast numbers of industrious farmers from her own native land of incorporated Germany to form settlements throughout the extensive Russian Empire. For the most part, the Catholics in Siberia were the *Volynskie* Germans that Stalin had exiled from the Volga region in 1941. Like their confreres from other parts of the former empire, they generally conversed in various fractured German dialects of Swabia, Switzerland, Austria, Holland, and Bavaria, although most were also fluent in Russian. Endowed with the gift of learning languages quickly and easily, Father Fessio, already well conversant in German, quickly picked up enough basic Russian to make himself understood. The result was a curious mélange of German, assorted German dialects, and Russian, spoken to people tolerant of any linguistic mistakes he made. His language was no barrier for expressing his feelings to the readers of *Catholic World Report* about being sent to Siberia. "I can hardly restrain my joy," he wrote, "because the Catholic Church is alive and strong and growing here." Unmentioned was the political figure responsible for this growth: Mikhail Gorbachev. When he came to power in the Soviet Union in March 1985, he had initiated the policy of Glasnost–Perestroika, which meant that people could now practice their religion and businesses could free themselves from communism's economic dogmas. For the Catholic population in Novosibirsk, this meant that—like the oceans of poppies that suddenly appear after the winter rains in Father Fessio's native California—Catholic clubs and meeting houses sprang up all over the land. He reported that some of the people in his new mission had not seen a priest in more than fifty years, while others had never even encountered one. Now they were boldly bringing out into open daylight rosaries fashioned from bones or rocks, along with falling-apart prayer books once used at clandestine meetings in various private houses. "And there are also new converts, who have lived for decades as atheists, now rejoicing in their newfound faith."

About the same time that Father Fessio appeared, another volunteer had joined the mission. He was an older Irish priest from Tipperary who had worked alone for sixteen years in the northern regions of Iceland. Though perhaps not linguistically prepared to take on the only Catholic parish in Krasnoyarsk, the second largest city in Siberia, Father Bob Bradshaw was psychologically and religiously in shape "to work there until I die", as he said. Then there was a reunion with an American priest, Father Myron Effing and his soon-to-be ordained deacon, and later fellow priest, Brother Dan Maurer, who had stopped by the Press on their way back to Vladivostok, where they were stationed, in February 1992. Neither one knew Russian well and relied on an interpreter who traveled with them. When he had first arrived at this far eastern city in November 1991, Father Effing had offered Mass on the steps of a building that had once been the cathedral and now housed the archives of the former Soviet government. It was the first Mass said in that city in fifty-six years. Today, it is again a flourishing Catholic parish.

In his piece for *Catholic World Report*, Father Fessio also mentioned that because he was one of just three priests in the whole diocese —the bishop not included—he was sent to various places beyond Novosibirsk. On one occasion, it was to the small village of Carebropol, forty miles south of Omsk. There he tried to put in a telephone call to Novosibirsk. The local telephone office was three miles from town, which he reached "on a rickety bike down a snow-swept road", but when he finally got there, the phone lines were out of order as usual, and the computer would not work. Back in Carebropol, he recorded: "Every time I walk down the street in this little town, I feel as if I am a character in a long Russian novel." The narrow road was straight and long with about thirty houses lining both sides of the snow-covered way. As he recorded, "they are small, mostly shabby on the outside and very cozy within. The backyards are pretty uniform: a ramshackle stable with two or three cows, chickens, and cats. In some there are also sheep, pigs, and cattle. And there are gardens where tomatoes, cucumbers, peppers, and onions are grown." Then he noted the common fields where the villagers planted beets and potatoes for themselves and hay for the animals.

But his time in Russia ran out, and so with mixed feelings in early May, he waved good-bye to Novosibirsk and set off for San

Francisco, stopping on the way at Vladivostok, where he set up an email system for the two priests there—Dan Maurer had been ordained a priest by that date—giving witness to another Joseph Fessio accomplishment. In an era when high-technology was first budding, he was regarded with respect if not unadulterated wonderment.

Once home, he set out upon a new project, the Fund for Apostolic Works, designed to collect money for the Church in Russia. Part of this venture was mailing between 40,000 to 50,000 donation request letters to people throughout the United States, and since the price of postage was considerably lower in Russia than it was at home, these letters were mailed from Russia bearing postage marks that made the appeal even more dramatic. He was never one to underestimate the effect of going forth with whatever sparkles. At this same time, he sent copies of *Catholic World Report* to the 105 bishops in Eastern Europe and the former Soviet Union to assure them that the Catholics in the United States were solidly behind them. His appeal raised about $60,000, a portion of which was used to purchase and send needed electronic equipment for the two missions. Then sometime in June, he went to a bank and drew out $40,000 of this amount in one hundred dollar bills. "I stuffed it", he explains, "around my belt and in my shoes" and flew to Khabarovsk, which is north of Vladivostok, a short distance from the Chinese border. In those oppressive days, airport custom inspectors did not peek unbidden beneath travelers' apparel, and so in the airport waiting room he unburdened himself of 400 sequestered bills by stuffing them into the suitcase of a man the Fathers in Vladivostok had sent to greet him. The smuggled trove was to be divided between the Vladivostok mission and the new Jesuit church in Irkutsk, a city southeast of Novosibirsk. Most of it went to buying two much-needed automobiles (presumably equipped with removable windshield wipers) for the Fathers at these two mission stations. If he had any sad experiences during his tertianship mission, like Pagliacci, he kept them to himself; he says, "It was kind of fun."

17

CATHOLIC IDENTITY

On September 10, 1987, Father Maloney stepped into what was probably the most peaceful period of the Saint Ignatius Institute's history, although this was only a short-lived and uncharacteristic deviation from the general trend of turbulence. This peace may have come for a number of reasons, the most important of which was the disappearance of the reputedly factious Fessio and the appearance in his place of a man universally regarded with admiration, and even affection. Father Maloney's quintessential trait was his gift of accepting everyone with unassuming pleasure and enviable modesty. On June 10, 1988, at the request of the dean of arts and sciences, he published a ten-page report summing up the newly created advisory board's in-depth evaluation of the Institute. For the most part it was upbeat. However, the board did recommend some changes: (1) an increased treatment of contemporary issues in theology and philosophy classes (phenomenology, American pragmatism, existentialism, liberation, and post–Vatican II theology) and (2) more openness with the board about financial issues on the part of the director. It also suggested that the director take positive steps to inculcate in the students a Christian attitude toward all, eliminating any appearance of condescension and disdain for others. These adjustments aside, the Institute's plan of study should not be altered, but the relationship between the Institute's spiritual activities and those of the university's campus ministry should be improved. Such an ambitious task would require more than expressions of mutual respect or hopeful planning.

In reviewing the history of the Institute, a casual observer might get the impression that, in all of this infighting, the Institute was consistently the loser, that Father Fessio showed more stubbornness than prudence. To see better the program's accomplishments, a cursory study of its graduates might be in order. Nineteen eighty was the year the NLRB arbitrator ruled against the Institute, and 1985 was the year the university administration castigated Father Fessio for his involvement in the unrealized summer program for the Carmelite Sisters. During this five-year period, there were 197 students who graduated from the university with a Saint Ignatius Institute certificate. Of this number, 27 percent continued formal education after graduation; 15 percent were priests, religious, seminarians, or laymen doing Church-related work; 20 percent were in the health professions (22 nurses; 11 MDs or medical school students). Twenty-seven percent were involved in the business world; 6 percent lawyers or lawyers-to-be; 8 percent officers in the various branches of the military service; 9 percent in education; 3 percent in social work; 8 percent housewives and mothers.

Meanwhile, the Institute undergraduate students had been taking more of a conspicuous role in the student body leadership, being elected to student government posts and assuming important roles in the publication of the student newspaper, the *Foghorn*. A few months before the firing of Father Fessio, the head chaplain at Campus Ministry forced the discontinuation of the very popular 10 P.M. Sunday Mass, attended mainly but not exclusively by SII students. The reaction on the part of many students was immediate and fraught with anger. A petition of some 400 names asked that the Mass be reinstated. "The petition fails to give a reason why the Mass is needed", was the response of Campus Ministry.[1] The celebration was judged to be unnecessary and divisive. This decision prompted Andrew Matt, a student who had lately transferred from Harvard to join the SII, to publish a two-part op-ed series in the campus newspaper, the *Foghorn*, entitled "New Breed Buzz Words", a spoof guide to modern Jesuit vocabulary. Here are a few examples:

Ecumenism: the progressive shredding of Catholic beliefs; needed in order to be recognized by the secular establishment, cf. "doing theology".

Pluralism: sacred buzzword which exempts the new breed from publicly defending Catholic principles on the pretext that it would be "imposing one's view on society".

---

[1] "Mass Elimination Protested", *Foghorn*, February 20, 1987.

Catholic University: a secular university sprinkled with token priests; legitimizes itself by compromising its identity.

Building community: banning popular Masses.

Reason for becoming a modern Jesuit: to apologize for two thousand years of Faith, to convert Catholics to the consensus mentality.[2]

While amusing for some, these satirical definitions seemed to many—even to neutral parties—just one more example of the hostile spirit engendered by the Institute and in particular by Father Fessio. But this was a superficial judgment. There were deeper causes behind Matt's op-ed, and this chapter will attempt to identify them.

San Franciscans are familiar with earthquakes and how they are caused by ruptures of geological faults running deep beneath the earth's surface. The reader who has persevered thus far in the biography of Joseph Fessio is aware that there was theological seismic activity rumbling beneath the surface of the University of San Francisco from the day he stepped on the campus and that although its frequency and force varied, its cause remained the same. Father Fessio departed, and Father Maloney took his place, and even though no serious tremors could be detected at that moment, the tectonic forces nevertheless remained. One of those forces was the newly appointed chairman of the Theology and Religious Studies Department, Francis J. Buckley, S.J. Besides being one of the main figures behind the establishment of the Faculty Association Union, proudly picketing during the strike that ensued, he was the author of a number of catechetical books for children, teaching them how to be at home in the liberated post–Vatican II Church. A devout priest and committed religious, he was praised by some for supposedly having the winning solution for the struggles surrounding gay marriage, artificial contraception, and women priests. He was also one of the most outspoken, determined opponents of the Saint Ignatius Institute and especially of its founder; yet there was nothing nasty about him, nothing underhanded. Dressed always in clerics, he was sincere, forthright, confident, logical, optimistic, and probably unaware that he, in his position, was like a tectonic plate at a theological fault line from which mighty forces were ready to burst forth. The first rumblings were discernable in a memo he sent to

---

[2] *Foghorn*, March 6, 1987, p. 6.

the academic vice president in 1988 in which he listed a number
of grievances against Father Maloney, the director of the Institute,
and expressed a request for "appropriate action as soon as possible". His chief complaint was that the application of Dr. Hamilton
Hess, a former Episcopal priest and a convert to Catholicism with
a doctorate in theology from Marquette, had not been approved by
Father Maloney to teach a course in the Institute. Father Maloney's
rationale was simple: Dr. Hess "differs from non-infallible teaching of the Magisterium on the ordination of women". Yet, Father
Buckley maintained, "there are teachers in the Institute who differ
from non-infallible issues, such as social ethics." The chairman complained that Father Maloney's attitude "does serious damage to the
religious formation of undergraduates to shield them from exposure
[to] legitimate dissent within the Roman Catholic Church". As a
consequence of this state of affairs, "the Department of Theology
and Religious Studies formally asks you to approve [our] criteria
for hiring in the area of theology [and] to direct Father Maloney
to stop attempting to set up a second theology department at the
university."

The next year, that is to say in 1989, a tremor from far off would
eventually affect Father Maloney's peaceful reign, plunging the Institute back into the tumultuous state it had known in his predecessor's time. The USF Law School was notoriously anti-Catholic, and
in March of that year some members of the university-chartered
Women's Law School Association posted signs and set up a table
on campus promoting a National Abortion Rights Action League
petition. Some undergraduates led by SII students protested, and
university officials folded the table but promised the group that it
would set up a task force to investigate the matter. Father Lo Schiavo
would order it to "examine the balance between USF's commitment
to the tenets of the Catholic faith and the freedom of expression and
petition". The women in the association were vociferous in claiming that the university had denied their First Amendment rights,
and they sought recourse with the ACLU, whose lawyers advised
waiting until the task force issued its report before taking further action. On February 5 of the following year, the university delivered
its new "Institutional Policy on Freedom of Expression", which
stated: "The University recognizes any student group, regardless of
the cause it espouses. Such support includes full access to university

funding, facilities, professional advice and campus media." Father Lo Schiavo released a statement explaining the new policy: "We are reaffirming the right of every member of the University community to free expression, free association and free exercise of religion. At the same time, as a Catholic university, we are committed to insuring that the Catholic faith and the Church's perspectives on sensitive issues are clearly articulated."[3] The Women's Law School Association was delighted with the new policy, admitting surprise that they had received more than they had initially requested.

Nine days after this announcement was made public, there was a meeting of the Associated Students of the University of San Francisco (ASUSF) to discuss the new policy and the president's endorsement of it. Significantly, the College of Business representative, Aamer Zahid, a Pakistani Muslim, summed up his personal confusion, which was shared by many others: "How can a Catholic University sanction the promotion of abortion on its property when it believes it is murder? It is a scandal that USF is willing to assist the promotion of legalized murder simply to avoid a lawsuit." The combined ASUSF group then voted unanimously "to seek an ecclesiastical decree removing USF from the *Catholic Directory*[,] thereby revoking the sponsorship of the Roman Catholic Church".[4] The vote demonstrated how effective the SII students had become, gaining roles of influence at the *Foghorn* and the ASUSF. The two driving forces of the ASUSF action were Jason Kenney, the chairman of the Student Court, and Jack Smith, both SII students. But Aamer Zahid was quick to assert: "Our resolution against the freedom-of-expression policy was not a spontaneous reaction. Nor was it guided by Jason Kenney, much less Father Fessio."[5] (Like the ghost in *Hamlet*, Fessio hovered over all.) Jason then formed a delegation from the body of the student group to present their petition and objections to the executive committee of the university's board of trustees. Here they registered the complaint that the new policy was directly opposed to USF's mission statement that unambiguously defines the university as "consecrated to the promotion

---

[3] "A Battle on the Bay at the University of San Francisco", *Vita* 4, no. 2 (March 1990): 1.
[4] Ibid.
[5] Ibid.

of justice . . . and the natural rights of all people". This new policy was a violation of justice and supported denying the rights of unborn persons. The elected delegates further complained it was formulated without due process and student input. They pointed out that organizations whose policies are antithetical to the Gospel and USF's mission statement, such as racist, homosexual, or pro-abortion groups, would now be able to use facilities and receive financial resources. This situation was in direct contradiction to USF's mission statement. Jack Smith told a reporter from the San Francisco *Examiner* that earlier the ASUSF had denied a charter to a white supremacist group, but now could no longer do so under the new policy approved by the USF administration. A few days later, Jason and his confreres formally presented copies of the newly adopted statement and the ASUSF resolution to Archbishop John R. Quinn, requesting that he remove the name "Catholic" from the university's title.

Jason admitted he did not think the archbishop would act on it. Some further action was needed, and some further action he would seek. The public information officer for the archdiocese assured the group that the archbishop and archdiocesan canon lawyers were studying the petition. Canon 808 states: "No university shall call itself Catholic without approval from the appropriate ecclesiastical authority." But it does not define who is "the appropriate ecclesiastical authority". Another canon stipulates that the bishop has ninety days to make a decision on such a petition. If he fails to do so, it then goes to the prefect of the Sacred Congregation for Education in Rome, and if there is no decision given there, it goes to the Apostolic Signatura, the equivalent of the Church's Supreme Court. Joseph Alioto, the former mayor of San Francisco, an avid admirer of the Institute, took a great interest in the case, as did State Senator Don Sebastiani, an alumnus of the university, and they offered Jason encouragement and assistance. He further recommended that the USF alumni should be apprised of the commitment the university had made to anti-Catholic causes. Kenney then got legal aid free of charge from the Saint Joseph Foundation in San Antonio, Texas, which provides people with legal guidance on keeping their Catholic institutions Catholic. As it turns out, Archbishop Quinn did task two canonists with investigating the ASUSF complaint. However, after "almost three months of concentrated study", they released a two-page report formally dismissing the matter, declaring the petition lacked "a proper foundation in canon law".

At the time of the momentous ASUSF meeting, Kenney was also the president of the university's chapter of Students United for Life (SUFL). He had earlier declared April to be "Life Month" at USF, asking Father Lo Schiavo to give his blessing to the planned activities. At the time, the president seemed willing, but now he refused to have anything to do with a group in which Kenney was involved. Jason immediately resigned from SUFL, desiring to keep its agenda separate from ASUSF. But even when another SII student, Suzanne Summerhays, took over the SUFL presidency, Father Lo Schiavo still wanted no association whatsoever with the group, whose newly formulated agenda was to promote the pro-life movement with activities in the student dorms. The university's residence hall director was decidedly pro-abortion and encouraged the promotion of lectures on contraception in the women's dorms. Summerhays boldly stated: "We are going to do an educational blitz" on campus. "People need to be educated." The implication was that campus ministry had been faulty in this matter and that it had engendered more bad feelings, setting up higher walls between the Institute and the administration.

Father Lo Schiavo kept a low profile during all of this turmoil, refusing to make any statement and referring all inquiries to Father Jack Clark, S.J., vice president for academic affairs, who was quick to emphasize how courageous the president was. Ever since his first day in office, said Father Clark, "he bucked trends and stood up for principles." Then, as if they had not heard it many times before, the vice president reminded the public of the president's "unpopular decision to shut down the USF basketball program after the National Collegiate Athletic Association cited it for rules violations". Thus began Father Clark's apologia for the president's decision to support the "Institutional Policy on Freedom of Expression", which he argued "reflects the authentic spirit of the post–Vatican II Church." He gave as an example Pope John Paul's meeting with various political leaders with whom he disagreed. "The same goes for USF's relationship with groups on campus." USF is authentically Catholic; otherwise, he said, how could it sponsor a group like the SII on campus? He regretted that the ASUSF officials dealt more "by resolution and ultimatum than by dialogue", and he looked forward to resolving the disagreements, without any hard feelings among the contestants. He reported that he had invited Kenney and his group to "sit down with me around some Cokes and share views", but his invitation went unacknowledged.

One professor, prominent in the faculty union, asked the following question: "If a university doesn't allow all views to be presented— respectable and unrespectable—then what does it exist for?" He was Jewish and of the view that "Nazi party spokesmen should be allowed to speak on campus, then ignored, booed or laughed at." Finally, he called the ASUSF students who voted against the policy "contemptuous . . . self-righteous", and he wondered why they wanted to drag into the mud the name of the institution that will appear on their diplomas forever.[6] Professor Jack Elliot, the head of the honors program, stated: "If these people [SII teachers] just kept to the business of offering a solid education, to think critically, it would be an excellent institute." But what they teach is reflected in the students, who "are swallowing—hook, line and sinker—the party line, and coming on like a bunch of Nazis to everyone else who doesn't agree."[7]

Somewhere in his writings, G. K. Chesterton recorded that there can never be a clear controversy in a skeptical age. The conflicts described above are proof of his insightful judgment. It was only the students who ever mentioned "truth" in their forays against their adversaries, and if they sometimes covered their intent with youthful enthusiasm, the essence of their stance remained. They had become witnesses to the fact that the university was less a hothouse where the growth of reason is cultivated than a swamp where intolerance, irrationality, and prejudice flower. The controversies, however, were not altogether disadvantageous, for they prepared the students to confront "the dictatorship of relativism" they were destined to face after graduation, mud-splashed diplomas in hand. Certainly they were made ready to see that "cafeteria Catholicism" does not lead to some bower of bliss down by the salley gardens, but straight to the *abattoir*. They learned that sharing Cokes with

---

[6] Charles Isenhart, "When Is a Catholic University No Longer Catholic?" *Our Sunday Visitor*, June 3, 1990.

[7] Don Lattin, "Behind the Bitter Free Speech Battle at USF", *San Francisco Chronicle*, June 4, 1990. Also helpful in outlining this whole episode is Dave Manney's piece "A Battle on the Bay".

nice feelings will never be a substitute for seeking and defending the good, the true, and the beautiful—although doing so over a shared Coke can be a pleasant experience. The spring semester was quickly coming to an end, and the customary summer fog flowing through the Golden Gate put a damper on the fights up there on "the Hilltop". Both sides retreated to plan for the contests that would take place once the turning of the leaves would announce the beginning of the fall semester.

That summer of 1990 brought a surprise that promised to intensify future wrangling. In August, Pope John Paul II issued his apostolic constitution on higher education, *Ex Corde Ecclesiae*. His purpose was the renewal of Catholic colleges and universities throughout the world. Some critics judged it to be a reproof of the controversial lay-drafted 1967 Land O'Lakes Statement, which had called for weakening, if not severing, the juridical connection between American Catholic colleges and the hierarchical Church. The very title of the new document—*From the Heart of the Church*—seemed designed to strengthen that connection—and in doing so the pope emphasized the long-held belief that higher education is central to the life of the community. He stated categorically: "The identity of a Catholic University is essentially linked to the quality of its teachers and to respect for Catholic doctrine." The sentence could have been taken out of the Saint Ignatius Institute brochure. But the question was: Who was going to enforce that policy? The pope wrote: "It is the responsibility of the competent Authority to watch over these two fundamental needs." Moreover, Catholic teachers "are to be faithful to . . . Catholic doctrine and morals in their research and teaching, . . . [and] if problems should arise concerning [the] Catholic character, the local Bishop is to take the initiatives necessary to resolve the matter" in conjunction with the university authorities, "and, if necessary, with the help of the Holy See". Jason Kenney, Jack Smith, and their friends congratulated themselves for having been right on target. The message was given very little space in the media, although spokesmen for the leading American bishops were quick to point out that the principle of separation of church and state in American politics made much of what the pope wrote impossible to implement. The federal government could not continue to support Catholic colleges by tax exemption or providing scholarship aid to the enrolled students. This argument had already been anticipated and responded to convincingly by Kenneth Whitehead, former deputy secretary for higher education under President Reagan and a prominent member of the Fellowship of Catholic Scholars. In 1988, Ignatius Press published his well-researched findings in *Catholic Colleges and Federal Funding*. Still, a potential threat from the ACLU seemed to halt USF and other Catholic colleges from filing any claims. At least that was the convenient bogeyman they used to quiet discussion. There was also a clause in the document requiring that all teachers of Catholic theology have a mandate, a sort of "union card" from the local ecclesiastical authority (usually the bishop) *to teach*. This instruction was resisted by many teaching theologians and not enforced by the NCCB. Hence, for all practical purposes, *Ex Corde Ecclesiae* was, and remains, a dead-letter document, and the university continued to let its mission evolve without it, and even against it.

Forty years after the founding of the Ignatius Institute, the University of San Francisco, like a number of other Jesuit universities, now rounds off its Catholic character with a nuance. It advertises itself as a "*Jesuit Catholic*, urban university"[8] whose "core mission . . . is to promote learning in the *Jesuit Catholic tradition*".[9] That tradition "defines USF's approach to learning and to our commitment to welcoming students of every faith and no faith". Just what is that "Jesuit Catholic tradition" of learning? We saw in 1975 how Father Fessio researched Saint Ignatius' writings to discover the essence of that tradition. What he found he used as the mold to fashion the Saint Ignatius Institute. The 1990 conflict between the ASUSF and the administration on the "Institutional Expression on Freedom Policy" testifies to the confusion and inconsistencies meshed together in that term, "Jesuit Catholic tradition". How it will further evolve might be predicted by a policy adopted by the first established Jesuit university in the United States. In 2018, Georgetown announced that it had approved, as one critical reporter put it, "a residential housing option reserved exclusively for students interested in exploring gender and sexuality conundrums beyond the confines

[8] "College of Arts and Sciences", University of San Francisco, last accessed October 26, 2018, https://www.usfca.edu/arts-sciences/about (emphasis added).

[9] "Vision, Mission and Values Statement", University of San Francisco, last accessed October 26, 2018, https://www.usfca.edu/about-usf/who-we-are/vision-mission (emphasis added).

of a seminar room". Sponsored by the university's LGBTQ+ In-
clusivity team, this would be a special Living Learning Community
(LLC) called "Crossroads". The vice president for student affairs
declared that the dorm would uphold "Jesuit values of community
in diversity and educating the whole person". He added: "It is in
keeping with our Catholic and Jesuit values to provide a language,
perspective, and sense of inclusion for deepening our sense of *cura
personalis*."[10] What, you might ask, does this development have to
do with the crisis at USF in 1990? The same *principles* that propelled
USF to approve the "Institutional Policy on Freedom of Expression" led Georgetown to create the Crossroads community in 2018.

There was another incident in 1990 at USF that evolved as a result of the "Freedom of Expression" policy. As soon as this policy
was adopted, a number of highly persuasive individuals circulated
around the campus "not to recruit but simply to explain" that gay
people were not to be feared. They were advocates of freedom, of
acceptance, arguing that it was a sign of tolerance on the part of
the university to acknowledge students' dignity by allowing them
to "come out" and form a gay club. The presence of these advocates and the sympathy they engendered on campus prompted a
number of SII students to prevail upon one of their own, Diane
Barbarini, to head a group dubbed "The Bestiality Club", satiriz-
ing the gay organization. The group wrote up a mission statement
and petitioned to be recognized and subsidized by the university.
They further requested a corner of the library lawn where they
could burrow and roost "furry and feathery things", exemplifying
the reasonability of their mission. At first, they were dismissed, but
when they persisted, the vice president for student affairs realized
she had to take the proposal seriously. She kept Diane in her office,
quizzing her, trying to break her, to force her to admit that the
proposal was a malicious joke. But Diane was a wonderful actress.
She demonstrated Cervantes' dictum that the most difficult character to play in a comedy is the fool, and one cannot be a fool to
play that part well, as Don Quixote demonstrates. Diane did not

---

[10] Maureen Mullarkey, "Georgetown University to Offer 'Jesuit-Approved' LGBTQ-
Only Housing", *The Federalist*, last modified January 9, 2018, http://thefederalist.com/20
18/01/09/georgetown-university-offer-jesuit-approved-lgbtq-housing/ See also: george
town.edu.

crack. Her petition was made strictly in accord with the Freedom of Expression policy. Finally, the vice president agreed to take the proposal to the next step in the recognition process. It was at this moment that the *Foghorn* featured the case, with a large picture of Diane posted on the front page. When her father, an employee of the archdiocese, saw the issue, he was stricken, as he claims, with something similar to a heart attack. Diane was forced to rescind. But the episode, ridiculous as it was, did make a point: any contradictory statement can find a fool to defend it.

It was during these wearisome days of 1991 that Father John Lo Schiavo resigned as president of the university, leaving the SII battlefield in disarray. Shortly afterward, a doughty new champion picked up the splintered mace, promising to take on the challenge with vigor. Father John P. Schlegel was as unpredictable as his predecessor was predictable. In one of his first allocutions to the faculty, the new president asserted he was committed to and driven by the principles of multiculturalism, which meant being a supporter of some left-of-center sociopolitical causes. But he also became an on-and-off advocate of the Saint Ignatius Institute, an admirer of Father Maloney, singling him out for his management skills and his exceptional dedication to the students in his care. He attempted to remain on the sidelines when complaints from the Theology Department about the Institute continuously proliferated in the monthly written reports sent to him from the dean, and he let it be known he was more interested in bettering the campus gardens and finding new benefactors than he was in such problematic matters. That was a job for the academic vice president and the dean. He took great interest in the address by Archbishop Quinn in the April 1991 SII lecture series program. The archbishop was a gifted speaker, and his remarks, designed primarily for the present students in the Institute program, were reminiscent of Mother Teresa's stunning exhortation to the students in April 1986. Father Maloney used the event to reach out further to the archbishop in a follow-up letter. After expressing gratitude for his supportive remarks, he added: "I would also like to meet with you at your convenience to speak about the Institute. The criticism it has received in the secular and liberal Catholic press seems to me unfair." He then informed the archbishop that the Institute was currently "undergoing another of its frequent reviews—this time at the request of the USF Board of

Trustees"—and that "the unstated suggestion" of the investigator is "that the Saint Ignatius Institute *may* have to be terminated". He continued: "It is my belief that the central reason for the negative press and questioning of some members of the Board of Trustees is that the SII clearly states that it is a Catholic program firmly committed to the Ordinary Magisterium of the Catholic Church and expects its faculty and staff to share that commitment. Such a stance evokes criticism from those—on and off campus—who find such a vision antiquated." Finally, he stated that some members of the SII faculty suggest that a condition for being assigned to teach in the Institute would be to take the *mandatum* oath prescribed in *Ex Corde Ecclesiae*. "I'm not certain the University would approve this," he wrote, "and I know that such a decision would evoke further criticism from the same members of the USF Theology Department." He ended his letter: "I would value your direction and counsel in this matter."

On June 11, the archbishop wrote an encouraging reply, asserting: "I do indeed support the concept of the Saint Ignatius Institute. In fact, I would like to see it much more widely used in all Catholic Universities." Naming various secular and Catholic publications that had been very critical of the Institute, he then tried to assure Father Maloney that these had their own agenda and were not worth his attention. The archbishop confessed he was mystified by the hesitation on the part of theology professors—especially Jesuits, given the Constitutions of the Society of Jesus—to make a firm commitment to the Magisterium of the Catholic Church. He signed off telling Father Maloney that his calendar would not permit him to make a visit with him until August, but that if he was still hopeful to speak with him then, an arrangement could be made. There is no record such a meeting ever took place. The archbishop's stance was typical of other bishops at the time. He thoroughly agreed with Pope John Paul's statement in 1987 that bishops were not "external" to Catholic universities—a teaching that was confirmed in *Ex Corde Ecclesiae*. But they seemed powerless to become involved in the "internal" operations of these institutions.[11]

In April 1992, Father Schlegel was pleased to announce that the

---

[11] George Kelly, "Catholic Education: Is it in or out of the Church", *Faith and Reason*, 18, no. 1 (1992).

academic subcommittee of the board of trustees had at last finished its extensive in-depth investigation of the Saint Ignatius Institute and found that it was an excellent program. The investigation committee, however, still recognized a need to define the mission, goals, and successes of the program, and it tasked Dr. Michael Torre, a philosophy teacher in the Institute, with composing one more report on the mission, goals, and achievements of the SII, which had been so highly extolled by Father Schlegel. But the frequent ruptures of theological fault lines during the past six years had taken their toll on Father Maloney's well-being. That fall, while returning from the annual freshman retreat, John Galten was struck by how exhausted the director looked. "Father, do you want me to take over for a while?" Indeed, he did. Father Maloney went back to his former job as the assistant to the dean of arts and sciences, leaving Galten to step into his proverbial boots. This "while" gradually became permanent.

18

REFORM OF THE REFORM

On February 24, 1995, Father Fessio received a letter from his friend Father Louis Bouyer, telling him that he planned to write a book on ecumenism and asking Fessio's permission to dedicate the finished project to him, his good friend who had once invited him to teach classes at the Saint Ignatius Institute. "I would certainly be honored if you were to dedicate a book on ecumenism to me," Father Fessio answered, "but it would be perhaps too ironic. My ecumenical motto is 'Come home to the Catholic Church! It's terrible here!' " This chapter will endeavor to illustrate, through four episodes, why Father Fessio had reason both to think the Church "terrible" and at the same time to grow in love for her and attachment to her. This is certainly part of the Fessio mystique. Over the course of these stories, let us keep in mind that the pelican tends to hold many different morsels simultaneously in its beak, at first keeping each separated with painstaking, assiduous care, but ultimately finding them all meshed together. So it was with Father Fessio's ever vast array of projects. Yet one long saga in particular—lasting from 1990 to 2008—periodically called Father Fessio away from his embroilment in publication affairs, giving him more diversions that, in the last analysis, would spur on his commitment to the publishing apostolate. We shall sketch five exploits that evolved during this period, in a manner more topical than chronological, reminding the reader that although the stories may intertwine, sometimes feeding on one another and seeming to repeat, they are all essential in telling the Fessio epic.

First, one of Father Fessio's distractions during the early years of the 1990s was going to Rome each year to attend a meeting with the board of the Lubac–Balthasar–Speyr Association, which functioned under the direction of Father Jacques Servais, S.J. The group's so-called "cardinal protector" was Cardinal Ratzinger, who always made it a point to be in attendance so that after the formalities of the meeting were over, he could spend the evening conversing informally with the small, select gathering on a number of subjects. Father Fessio delighted in these encounters with his former professor and longtime friend. "It was either in 1990 or 1991", he recalled, "that he told us he was working on a book about the Mass, which I found exciting because, although he had published extensively, he had never written a real book. His published works were mostly collections of his essays, lectures, conferences, homilies and interviews." At subsequent meetings during the following summers, Father would make it a point to ask the cardinal when that promised book would make its appearance. "I don't know", he would answer. "I am working on it. The subject matter is there, but it takes time to work on developing it as I would like." Father Fessio says he knew the Mass was "the heart of his whole life", adding: "But each time I would ask, I would get the same answer. I could tell there was not much progress being made."

In addition to these yearly get-togethers in Rome, there was another meeting of consequence that stole Father Fessio away from his work at the Press. This one took place in Colorado Springs in March 1995, where one of the speakers was the dean of Catholic University in Puerto Rico. He was an Oblate of Wisdom priest, an Australian-born convert named Father Brian Harrison, O.S. The subject of his presentation was a response to the Vatican II declaration calling for a reform of the Roman Rite Mass. Father Fessio recalls listening fascinated as the speaker developed his thesis, the gist of which was that the reformed Mass, which evolved after Vatican II, was in many ways inconsistent with the intentions of the Council Fathers. Father Harrison contended that what was needed now was not a return to the 1962 Tridentine Mass or a more reverent observance of what became known as the Novus Ordo Mass. Rather, they should go back and study the approved rubrics for saying Mass from before the council, examine what kinds of liturgical reforms the council actually called for, and then, finally, "reform the reform".

Ironically, Father Fessio was the celebrant at the Mass that followed the lecture. He found himself at the altar, staring at a ceramic chalice and paten before him that seemed to meet his gaze in defiance. During the homily, he departed from his text and reminded the congregation that the General Instruction of the Roman Missal require the sacred vessels to be made of durable, noble material. Pottery chalices are neither, he quipped. They are unworthy of the Mass. Result: The Reverend Fessio made headlines again, this time in the local diocesan paper where it was asserted that he judged the chalices and patens used in the diocese of Colorado Springs to be unsuitable for Mass. He had developed what he calls the "Fessio suitability test for sacred vessels": after subjecting the chalice and paten to the strictest scrutiny before Mass, the celebrant—or one of the altar boys—should smash them against something solid in the sacristy. If one of them breaks, it means it was not suitable for Mass.

As soon as he returned to San Francisco from Colorado, he wrote a long letter to Cardinal Ratzinger describing the conference and relaying his own reactions to it. In the addressed envelope, he enclosed a printed copy of Father Harrison's paper—thirty-five double-spaced typed pages—and suggested that a grassroots liturgical movement might be in order, though he hesitated to start any such program himself. What would the cardinal think of his beginning a journal in which people in the pews as well as scholars might find information concerning matters liturgical? Cardinal Ratzinger replied in what Father Fessio described as "a beautiful letter". The cardinal assured him: "I unreservedly agree [with Father Harrison]. . . . I believe that we need a new liturgical movement—which, of course, must absolutely be inspired and directed in the right manner. For this reason your idea of a liturgical journal . . . seems to me exactly to correspond to the needs of this hour." In typical Fessio fashion, the abstract became the real, the abstruse turned to "hands-on kind of things". In close collaboration with Father Jerry Pokorsky, a priest of the Arlington diocese, and Helen Hull Hitchcock, president of Women for Faith and Family and the wife of the scholar James Hitchcock (who had delivered such an insightful presentation at the *Humanae Vitae* symposium), the Adoremus Society for the Renewal of the Sacred Liturgy was established, and the corresponding periodical *Adoremus Bulletin* followed suit that same year. Eventually, *Adoremus* would come to reach more than 35,000 subscribers, making it the largest circulation liturgical journal in the world at that time.

By that date, Father Fessio already had concretized his stance on the reform-of-the-reform principle, while continuing to badger Cardinal Ratzinger about completing his book on the Mass. Meanwhile, he could not wait. Confident that the council had legitimately called for a renewal of the liturgy, he began celebrating a more traditional form of the Novus Ordo Mass. One of the characteristics of this new Mass was that it allowed for many options; thus, whenever they could be licitly implemented, he would choose those options most in continuity with the preconciliar Mass. In other words, he would celebrate his Carmelite chapel Masses in the closest conformity possible to those celebrated before the council. Moreover, he would celebrate facing liturgical east, with an altar rail (and never altar girls). There would be Gregorian chant, and he would pray the first Canon in Latin, along with the ordinaries, those parts of the Mass that do not change; the readings, collects, and propers, which change daily, would be in English.

In late 1994, Cardinal Ratzinger was growing in popularity, some whispering that one day he might even become pope. In December, Father Fessio, with foresight, wrote him a letter asking him to give Ignatius Press the legal right to publish the English translation of any and all of his future writings. He did not consider this request excessive, nor evidently did the cardinal, who had already signed contracts with the Press to publish two of his earlier works. According to the Ignatius Press standard contract, that fact automatically should have given the company the right to publish his next work. So Father Fessio's letter was merely a clarification, a reaffirmation of the previous contracts. The cardinal was of like mind and readily granted the requested permission.

At last, in 1999, Father Fessio's pestering paid off. He was holding in his hands the longed-for copy of *Einführung in den Geist der Liturgie* ("Introduction into the Spirit of the Liturgy"), which Ignatius Press translated and published in 2000 under the title *The Spirit of the Liturgy*. He was quick to note that everything from the first to the last page in Cardinal Ratzinger's manuscript confirmed what he had been implementing in his daily Masses. He also confessed that the highpoint of his satisfaction came as he read the chapter entitled "The Direction of Prayer", where the cardinal wrote that in the apostolic tradition of the Church, the priest offering Mass faced east. Father Fessio recalls: "When I read that, I jumped out of my chair and gave the victory sign. Had I been in the NFL,

I would have gotten a penalty for celebrating victory in the end zone." "Anyway," he concluded, "that is how the *Adoremus Bulletin* came to be: through my own liturgical reflection and development of the Mass, with Father Harrison's concurrence and the encouragement and unfailing support of Cardinal Ratzinger."

We speed now to December 2005. This is when Father Fessio was in Rome at a meeting called by the directors of the Libreria Editrice Vaticana (LEV), which is the Vatican publishing arm. Also present were about ten other representatives from various publishers throughout the world that had released translations of Ratzinger's writings. LEV's suave, loquacious president, Monsignor Giuseppi Scotti, chaired the meeting, purposefully seating himself beside his lawyer, *il Signor* Stingone. Smiling wide and raising his arms in a mock *grosso abbraccio* for all those assembled, he began the meeting with the assurance, "We're all family gathered here together." "That made me nervous", Father Fessio remembers. Unabashed, the monsignor proceeded with further calls to trust: "We are all friends, working together." Then he stated that he and Signor Stingone were confident that all present would gladly sign a waiver cancelling any contracts made with Cardinal Ratzinger in favor of new contracts with LEV. Father Fessio recalls that instantly a roar echoed throughout the room. He leaned forward to his microphone and declared: "This proves that we are a family. We are now fighting one another!" Then, with a clear voice through the now quiet room, he continued in Italian: "It seems to me we should first see the proposed LEV contract before we cancel our individual contracts." He further argued that just because all gathered together at the invitation of the reverend monsignor constituted a family, this did not mean that any member should abdicate his rights without knowing what he would be getting in return. The result was unanimous agreement. The meeting eventually broke up, but not before the priest from Ignatius Press was seen by the hosts as an obstacle to their plans, one to be dealt with accordingly.

Six months earlier, on April 19, 2005, Cardinal Ratzinger had been elected pope. Soon, many of his books published by the Press were sold out, emboldening the twice-blessed editor to put in a $50,000 order to purchase reprints. In August 2006, Father Fessio was back in Rome to attend the annual meeting of the *Schülerkreis*, the students' circle. This group had been formed in 1977 when

Ratzinger was appointed archbishop of Munich-Freising and thus gave up his professorship at the University of Regensburg. After his departure, his former students resolved to meet with him yearly as a group to discuss current subjects informally. After he became pope, Benedict insisted these get-togethers continue on as usual, and Father Fessio made it a point to be at as many meetings as possible. One morning, during the 2006 session, in the sacristy after Mass, the pope approached him with the laconic message: "I have finished my book." (The book was *Jesus of Nazareth*.) The circumstances did not lend themselves to further conversation, but Father Fessio reflected: "Why did he tell me that? Obviously because he knows that we will publish the English translation."

Once the final meeting of that year had terminated, Father Fessio decided to pay a visit to the nearby LEV offices and learn from Monsignor Scotti what he could about the status of the contract for the pope's latest book. "We're working on it", was the terse reply to Father's inquiry. Then: "Don't worry. It is slated for you." Again, that was in August 2006. A few months later, in December, Father Fessio was back in Rome, where the lawyer Signor Stingone informed him that Ignatius Press no longer had the publishing rights to Cardinal Ratzinger's books. The reason? *"Il Cardinale Ratzinger non esiste più."* The author of this newly published work, Stingone said, will be Pope Benedict XVI. "Wait a minute", Father Fessio replied. "If he signs a contract for a mortgage on a house, and becomes pope, he still owes the bank money!" The objection was dismissed with a flick of the hand: "That is not Vatican law." The retort: "A contract may not be a contract under Vatican law, but our contracts are under United States law." Stingone rejoined: "Well, Father Fessio, we do not accept the legal obligation, but we recognize the moral obligation. So you will publish the book."

A meeting had preceded these separate interviews with the monsignor and the lawyer, and there it was officially announced that LEV had sold all rights for Pope Benedict's forthcoming books to Rizzoli, one of the largest publishing houses in the world. The conditions of the sale did not affect Verlag Herder, the publishing house that released most of the pope's works in German, and so Father Fessio was naïvely confident that the same terms would apply to Ignatius Press. However, Rizzoli sold the English-language publication rights to Doubleday. Confusing? Indeed! And the reverend monsignor now refused to talk further about the matter with Father Fessio, who was now intent on conferring with the president of Rizzoli. But first, he wanted a lawyer to accompany him. The American ambassador to the Vatican, Francis Rooney, then obligingly stepped onto the scene, sending him the Italian lawyer who represented American causes at the Vatican, who would obligingly accompany Father Fessio to the specially called publishers' meeting. After addressing the group, the Rizzoli representative walked over to a nearby private room where Father Fessio was waiting, in order to consult with him. But at the door, he stopped short and, pointing to the man standing beside Father, asked: "Is he a lawyer?" An affirmative was given, apparently a cue for him to turn about and walk out of the room. It then began to seem as though all those connected with the question had taken a vow of Carthusian silence. Father Fessio headed back to San Francisco and called on his old friend Patrick Finley, the former Project 50 student counselor who had been driving with him when he threw out into the night the coins needed for the San Mateo Bridge toll. Pat, now a highly regarded lawyer in Oakland, filed a lawsuit against LEV, Rizzoli, and Doubleday in the U.S. District Court for Northern California. He did not make a public announcement of the filing, nor did he formally serve the complaint on the defendants, but the Press sent informal copies of the complaint to Rizzoli and LEV. This time the cry was not "Let's go for it!" but "Let's talk!"

Soon afterward, Cardinal Schönborn of Vienna called Father Fessio: "Joe, I understand you're suing the Vatican, what is this?" Father Fessio gave him a brief report and faxed him all of the supporting documents. The cardinal was furious and contacted Monsignor Scotti. "Notice how the Vatican works here", Father Fessio commented to his colleagues at the Press. "They won't talk to me. I wrote them a letter with a threatening lawsuit, they won't talk with me. They're going to go to Cardinal Schönborn, who they knew was my friend, to have him what? Tell me to back off? Let's talk, folks!" The cardinal then got in touch with the monsignor, who admitted he had altered the truth when he told Father Fessio that Pope Benedict himself had made the decision to give Rizzoli all the rights to the book. He argued that he had felt he must do so "to protect the pope". Father Fessio responded, "Do you keep the eighth commandment there in the Vatican?" The cardinal contacted the pope himself, whose reaction was sadness and displeasure. He then asked that the president of the Schülerkreis try to work out an equitable solution. The contract had already been signed with Doubleday, thanks to the actions of LEV and Rizzoli, but would Ignatius Press be satisfied with publishing the paperback edition of volume 1 while Doubleday printed the hardback copy? Ignatius Press also would be given the rights to publish the hardback edition of volume 2. Such is the history of *Jesus of Nazareth*. Doubleday's copy of volume 1 made its appearance in 2007 followed by the Ignatius Press' softbound edition in 2008. The Press printed the hardbound volume 2 in 2011.

We now turn back to 1988 to trace the third act of the Fessio drama that unfolded during the '90s. This was the year the Press began to publish *30 Days*, the English-language version of the Italian *30Giorni*, a monthly magazine of ecclesiastical politics favorably regarded by the Roman curia, a publication that "fully reflects the realistic policies of Vatican diplomacy".[1] It was produced under the direction of one of Italy's "senators for life", Giulio Andreotti, who was considered "the most curial of Italy's veteran politicians".[2] In the late summer of 1990, *30Giorni* published an editorial that coincided with the outbreak of the First Gulf War, in which they asserted that all wars were immoral. Father Fessio refused to run it in the English edition. Shortly afterward, around 5 P.M. one afternoon as the Press was closing shop, Father Fessio got a multi-page faxed complaint summoning him to report to a San Francisco court the following day at noon. He immediately contacted his right-hand lawyer friend Patrick Finley, and the two of them appeared in court with the bulky complaint squeezed into a box. In response to his repudiation of the editorial, the editors of *30Giorni* "were suing the press for something like $100,000 in damages", Father Fessio reports. "They lost, but it cost us a considerable amount just to defend ourselves."

---

[1] Robert Moynihan, "A Tale of Three Magazines", *Catholic World Report*, last updated December 1, 2011, https://www.catholicworldreport.com/2011/12/01/a-tale-of -three-magazines/.

[2] The career and personality of Giulio Andreotti is amusingly interesting beside the characters and incidents in this present biography of Father Fessio. Elizabeth Povoledo, "A Giant of Post-War Politics Is Mourned in Rome", *New York Times*, May 6, 2013, https://www.nytimes.com/2013/05/08/world/europe/08iht-andreotti8.html.

Sometime later, Father Fessio discovered that representatives of the same group had stolen the magazine's mailing list and were using it to solicit subscriptions for their "new" *30 Days*. He immediately consulted with Pat, and the two of them flew to New Jersey to deliver a subpoena to the person Father knew was responsible for the theft. After a rather dramatic hunt, Pat was finally able to serve him, ordering him to appear the following day at 2 P.M. in a Newark court for a deposition. Unfortunately, at the time, neither Father Fessio nor Pat knew that in delivering a subpoena in New Jersey, one is required to give the person deposed enough money to travel to the place of the deposition. The man's attorney appealed to a federal court to quash the writ, and so the following morning, both parties appeared in a courtroom that, as Father Fessio describes, seemed to have been furnished "with pews, an altar rail with a Bible on it, stained glass windows and a judge's bench that looked like an altar". He recalls: "Finally, the judge appeared in flowing robes. The décor was more churchlike than where services were taking place at the time in many Catholic churches." The presiding judge was Maryanne Trump Barry, the elder sister of the man who was to become the 45th president of the United States in 2017. Father Fessio claims he was fascinated watching her preside over a case that preceded theirs. "It was a case", he recollects, between a German auto parts manufacturer and their U.S. distributor. The way she handled the process and the lawyers was, in fact, "awe-inspiring".

During the short recess, the judge met in her quarters with Father Fessio, Pat, the suspect, and the suspect's lawyer. "She knew nothing at all about the case", Father recounts. "So, she turns to Pat and asks, 'Did your client provide the required money when he delivered the subpoena?' 'No, your honor.' Then to the other attorney: 'Would your client be an important witness in this case? And do you know whether I'm going to quash this subpoena because of the irregularity in delivering it?' 'No, your honor.' After a short pause: 'Well then, you show up with your client at 2 P.M. in the designated location. Mr. Finley, you and your client come with a new subpoena for the same time and place, and the required money. Then I will quash the first subpoena." Father confesses: "I actually wept. She was a Daniel. She upheld both justice and the requirements of the law." It was a kind of repetition of his experience of making it through the Belgian border thanks to the decal on his fender—a fender placed where fenders should not be, lying snugly in the back seat of a pitiful *deux-chevaux*.

Father Fessio did not know it at the time, but the judge, who had been the first member of her family to attend college, had a very special place in her heart for the Jesuits. She had lost her parents and her husband in the space of one year, and she confesses that it was her faith and the Jesuits who "quite literally saved my life" in the time that followed. In 2016, when she donated $4 million to Fairfield University as an endowment for the university's Murphy Center for Jesuit Spirituality, she declared, "I love the Jesuits."[3] Had the gallant knight known that fact at the time, he might have been less apt to shed a tear and instead put more energy into informing this Lady Daniel of certain Jesuit spirituality projects in San Francisco.

Now for the fourth episode in the saga. We have seen how enthusiastic Father Fessio became—in response to Father Brian Harrison's talk in 1995—about implementing the reform-of-the-reform movement, one result of which was launching the liturgical publication *Adoremus Bulletin*. Shortly after the first issue made its appearance, he was called upon to give lectures in a number of different locations. One of these places was Irondale, Alabama, within the diocese of Birmingham, where Mother Angelica had launched her television station EWTN in 1981. While visiting the community, Father Fessio offered Mass *ad orientem* in the studio chapel. The local bishop, appointed in 1994, was the Most Reverend David Edward Foley, and he quickly got word of the Mass. Bill Steltemeir, the CEO of the network, reported that after Father Fessio made his departure, the bishop came to the office, threw down a transcript of a lecture Father Fessio had recently delivered in Seattle, and informed Steltemeir that he would have none of Fessio's liturgical buffoonery in his diocese. Shortly afterward, the bishop issued a pastoral forbidding the celebration of the *ad orientem* Mass throughout the diocese and explicitly mentioned a certain unnamed priest who had denied the Holy Spirit because he had criticized the *versus populum* Masses (where the priest faces the people during the Eucharistic Prayer) that had been commonly offered since the 1969

[3] Fred Barbash, "The Other 'Anti Trump'—His Sister", *Toronto Star*, March 8, 2016; Jim Shay, "Trump's Sister Gives $4 Million to Fairfield U", *CTPost*, September 4, 2016.

reforms in the liturgy. The published report prompted Father Fessio to write the bishop asking whether he had been referring to him in the letter and requesting that, if he *had* intended Father Fessio, he either show him how exactly he had been denying the Holy Spirit or else retract what he had written. The letter received no response. The diocesan liturgy director eventually named Father Fessio as the priest the bishop had had in mind when he wrote his pastoral. The article prompted Father Fessio to write a second letter to Bishop Foley challenging him, again, either to show him where he was in error or else to retract his accusation. Again: no response.

Father Fessio now had recourse to a canon lawyer in Rome, who informed him that if such a request is not answered in a stated time, the one accused may appeal to a higher authority. This advice prompted Father Fessio to appeal to the Roman Rota, which responded that such penal cases were under the jurisdiction of the Signatura. But his appeal was not asking for a penalty. Nonetheless, he forwarded the matter to the Signatura. The answer he now received was that his was not a penal case and therefore the Signatura had no jurisdiction. "What wonderful justice in Rome", he said to himself as he filed suit in a federal court in Alabama, using an attorney recommended by the CEO of EWTN. He made it clear that he was not asking the court to decide a matter of doctrine in the complaint he was filing. Both he and the bishop agreed that if he had said the things the bishop accused him of saying, he would be a heretic. Therefore, he asked the court to decide if, indeed, there was any evidence of his saying what the bishop had accused him of saying. He later admitted the judge's reasoning for handing down the decision was remarkable. His Honor quoted Saint Paul, probably 1 Corinthians 6:1, where the apostle writes that Christians should not bring their complaints about one another to a civil authority, but that they should come to a mutual agreement in charity. Case dismissed. That reasoning was based on a principle of American law that Alexis de Tocqueville had failed to record. After Father Fessio's experience with the LEV case, this was not a decision that surprised him, but it was one that prepared him for others, as we shall see, that were to come his way. What would Saint Ignatius say was the *preux* thing to have done in this situation where a Jesuit was accused of preaching heresy? We have seen how Ignatius reacted in the 1530s when his own orthodoxy was contested, when a false accusation could have compromised his effectiveness in bringing Christ to others. He defended his name.

Finally, we turn to a fifth episode that pulled Father Fessio away from his desk at the Press to convince him, as if he needed more conviction, that it's "terrible here" in the Church. In the summer of 1996, the Australian Confraternity of Catholic Clergy in conjunction with the Thomas More Centre of Melbourne extended an invitation to Father Fessio to come to Australia and deliver a series of lectures to Catholics "Down Under". The founder of the Thomas More Centre was Bartholomew Augustine—Bob for short— Santamaria, who had a similar background to that of Father John Lo Schiavo. The parents of both men had emigrated from the Aeolian Islands, those volcanic archipelagic pearls in the Tyrrhenian Sea north of Sicily. Some years before the Lo Schiavos left these islands behind and headed west to California, the Santamarias had bid their *adieux* and moved east to Australia. In 1996, Bob was approaching the final act of his career, which had been spectacular. Lawyer, successful businessman, and editor, he founded the Australian edition of the *Catholic Worker* newspaper, whose approach to the duties and rights of capitalism and labor was based on the teachings of Leo XIII in *Rerum Novarum*. During the 1930s and 1940s, the Labor Party in Australia was seriously flirting with Marxism, and Santamaria is credited with having turned it around. He was against laissez-faire capitalism, against communism, and thus dubbed by his enemies as either a supporter of fascism or a secret communist sympathizer. His Thomas More Centre in Melbourne was created to propagate and defend Catholic teaching, repudiating both extremes.

After obtaining the necessary permission from his provincial, Father Fessio once more boarded a plane. Once there, he met with a combination of both unprecedented adulation and unprecedented criticism. A handsome young priest from the United States—of all places!—and a Jesuit, of all species!—supporting traditional Catholic beliefs—of all things!—was a phenomenon to behold even for natives in the land of the platypus. In Bendigo, he gave an address to his host, the Australian Conference of Catholic Clergy. The local bishop and the leading members of the clergy "were unfortunately not able to attend". He then moved on to Melbourne, where the newly appointed Archbishop George Pell, who would later become a cardinal, welcomed him warmly, forming a friendship that grew stronger until Pell's death in 2023. As ill luck would have it, Camberwell Hall could only accommodate some 1,500 people, who seemed delighted with the American Jesuit's lecture, as did others in the auditoriums where, side-by-side with Archbishop Pell, he received a standing ovation on the topic "Despite Everything: How to Rebuild the Church". In other lectures, he told his Australian audience that while the most common complaint of American Catholics up to about 1980 had been about the undermining of children's faith by Catholic schools, since then the greatest concern had become the liturgy. His contention was based on the fact that Mother Angelica's cable and television network was receiving thousands of calls about liturgical abuses that prevailed throughout the country. Was it the same for Australia? If not, it would be. He stressed to the members of the Confraternity of Catholic Clergy that Vatican II called for a reform of the liturgy and the document *Sacrosanctum Concilium* (*The Constitution on the Sacred Liturgy*), promulgated by Pope Paul VI in 1963, stated that "new forms adopted should in some way grow organically from forms already existing". He held his audience captive by recounting his own involvement in the U.S. liturgical wars that were taking place at the same time Father Brian Harrison was counseling "a reasonable solution" and Cardinal Ratzinger was suggesting that a "true reform of the reform" would require "a new liturgical movement" in the Church. Such persuasive teaching, he explained, had prompted him to action. The result, as he told the audiences, had been his founding *Adoremus Bulletin* in June of 1995, and now, just one year later, it had 15,000 subscribers. By the time he left Australia, that number had increased considerably.

Successful as he was, there was one voice raised in high protest to Father Fessio's brief stay in Australia. Very Reverend W. J. Uren, the provincial superior of the Jesuits in that nation, registered his displeasure in a long letter published in *The Australian*, the largest selling newspaper in the country. He took issue with what he saw as Father Fessio's lack of obedience as well as with his "rather reactionary views". He described the American Jesuit lecturer as one who was probably suspect in his own province, seeing as he was "yet to be admitted to the profession of the final solemn vows". He then criticized him because he had not sought, much less received, permission from him, the provincial, to come to Australia, nor had he even bothered to visit the provincial's office. Father Uren emphasized, "Jesuit statutes require that before [a visiting Jesuit] exercises any public ministry in a Province other than his own he receive the permission of the Provincial Superior of that province." He contrasted Father Fessio's lack of decorum with the behavior of another Jesuit of great repute, Carlo Maria Cardinal Martini, who, being a cardinal, was no longer bound by Jesuit obedience but had nevertheless paid his respects to the provincial before delivering a series of lectures in Australia. The provincial also leveled criticism against the Australian Conference of Catholic Clergy and the Thomas More Centre for their antiquated theology and their apparent disregard for protocol.[4]

The letter created a storm. In an open letter to the editor, B. A. Santamaria opined: "Whether or not the Thomas More Centre . . . is or is not 'normally punctilious' in its adherence to its 'own rather legalistic form of orthodoxy' is a matter of opinion. It depends on whether Father Uren's own view of the limits of papal authority is itself orthodox." He did confess that "this is a rather unusual question for a layman to have to put, especially in relation to a Jesuit." However, he reminded the Australian provincial that Father Fessio's obligation to the order was a matter beyond the purview of the Thomas More Centre. Consequently, the Centre "does not have to apply for . . . permission [from the Society of Jesus] to invite Father Fessio or anyone else to its platform".[5] Father Fessio, too, reacted in print to Father Uren's "preposterous" claim, and his retort was even more cutting. He explained that the protocol for traveling outside one's own province consists in getting permission from one's own superior, not the superior of the place where one is going. And besides, he added, if the Australian provincial had had problems with Father Fessio's coming to Australia, he should have contacted the California provincial or the superior general in Rome. However, the letter went on:

Since Father Uren has publicly challenged me on a procedural protocol that does not exist, let me challenge him on a substantive obligation that does exist: will he affirm publicly that he accepts as authoritative and binding the Church's teaching that artificial contraception is intrinsically a grave evil, that priestly ordination of

[4] *Mercury* [Hobart, Tasmania], December 20, 2005.
[5] "Letters to the Editor", *The Australian*, August 10, 1996.

women is impossible (cf. CCC 1577), that homosexual acts are always gravely morally wrong?

This was a real slap shot. In baseball language, one could call it a confrontation between a fastball pitcher and the home-run hitter. We recall that young Joe Fessio was a home-run hitter in his high school and college days, and it would seem that he had still not lost that gift.

Father Terence Purcell, secretary of the archdiocesan Senate of Priests in Sydney, then sent copies of the newspaper articles to the Father General of the Society of Jesus in Rome. One might imagine Father Kolvenbach whispering to himself, "Will no one rid me of this meddlesome priest?" But Father General's email reply to Father Purcell, which was also printed in the local newspaper, was surprisingly to the point: "Father Fessio acted correctly in asking his own Provincial's permission. If his Provincial had deemed it appropriate, he could/should have informed the Provincial of Australia. But this does not seem to have been the responsibility of Father Fessio." He concluded, stating that he regretted "the upset that the reports had caused" and would "pray peace will soon reign again". He predictably refrained from commenting on Father Fessio's challenge to the Australian provincial's disposition toward certain "substantive obligations".[6] The American Jesuit left Australia with feelings of hope and optimism, and with a new bond of friendship with Archbishop Pell. But his adventures there, along with the reversals described in this chapter, solidified in him a sense of realism that led him to expect new challenges, and the following chapters will demonstrate that these expectations were far from unrealistic.

---

[6] "Visiting Priest Offends Jesuit Protocol", *The Australian*, August 6, 1996.

19

CATHOLIC BROADCASTING

The Fessio-hosted episode of the Jim Eason Show back in 1986 had
certainly kicked up some fuliginous shrapnel in our Jesuit hero's
psyche, but it also sparked optimism, joy, and hope. Thousands
of viewers had watched and listened to what Father Joseph Fessio
said. His ill-considered words may have been unfortunate, but the
number of people who heard them and were affected by them was
considerable. Radio/TV would never be a substitute for the Press
or the SII, but it sometimes seemed there was no better outlet for
propagating the Gospel message in today's world than these media.
In the wake of the crisis, Father Fessio's first reaction was to put
more effort into the "Catholic University of the Air" project; but
then he slowly began to hear that sweet, persistent voice of the media muse, hinting at some new adventure. By 1996, he knew what
it was: he finally had to respond to the invitations sent his way by
the earliest financial supporter of the Press, Mr. Harry John, may
he rest in peace.

He had received the first of several invitations in 1983, a year
before the Father Greeley episode (see chapter 14). Mr. John had
approached and asked him to set up a production facility in San
Francisco to generate news and documentary segments for Santa Fe
Communications' flagship program *Heart of the Nation* and also to feature a one-hour studio show once a week highlighting the apostolic
work of a local Franciscan priest, Father Alfred Boeddeker. Father
Alfred, a close friend of Father Fessio's, was a San Francisco icon,
the founder and director of St. Anthony's Dining Room and Free
Medical Clinic—institutions dedicated to caring for the homeless,
the poor, the street people in San Francisco's Tenderloin district.
Father Fessio had put off Harry's invitation for several months—
between the demands of the Press, the Institute, the classroom, and
small-time radio, he was already way overextended. But Harry per-

sisted, and the rust-gathering armor of the tenacious knight began to itch. Did he not see that there had already been unsuccessful attempts to combine professional quality television and orthodox Catholicism? Yes. Was John's proposal not on too grand a scale? Yes! But these were not barriers, merely challenges that could be met and overcome. "Go for it!" went the familiar echo in his head. He was ready for action.

As the year was coming to an end, he agreed with Harry John to help establish a Catholic television network under the aegis of Guadalupe Associates (GA). He was able to do this by having GA become a partner in purchasing Channel 46, a Spanish-language television station at that time. The De Rance Foundation (DRF) put up $4 million to purchase 40 percent of the station, while lending $4 million to GA so that it was able to purchase another 40 percent, allowing the original owners to keep 20 percent. Why was the DRF so eager to have the GA as its partner in this deal? For two reasons: first, because the Internal Revenue Service (IRS) regulations prevented it from owning more than 40 percent of a nonrelated business; second, because under the Federal Communications Commission (FCC) policy, the buyer of this particular TV station had to be a minority-owned corporation. Such was the identity of the GA, since suddenly two young women of Asian and Latino backgrounds and two Latina religious Sisters had just been elected to serve on the five-member, all-female GA Board! In the following February, Father Fessio arranged with the SFC to hire a director for the San Francisco project, an exceptionally well-educated Catholic and a successful businessman with managerial experience, who in turn hired a business manager. By the end of March, this trio had submitted to Mr. John, as requested, the complete budget for producing a weekly show and ten news or documentary segments. Although the San Francisco Bay Area production facility was the last founded of the SFC units set up across the country, it was the first to submit a budget. From the beginning of the project, Father Fessio had insisted to Mr. John that it would be foolhardy to produce anything that would not give solid hope for recouping at least the actual cost of production. He was quick to set a policy at the San Francisco unit that nothing would be produced without a demonstrable potential for marketing and syndication.

In May, Mr. John advised Father Fessio that he wanted to reduce expenditures; accordingly, the Jesuit decreased the weekly productions from ten segments to three. But he held fast to his initial policy: there would be no compromise on combining quality programming (production side) with orthodox Catholicism (content side). He was satisfied that the unit was faithful in its execution to what it had set out to do, but by September there were ominous signs that could have reminded him of his experience floating down the Sacramento River through Devil's Canyon back in college. The water at that moment had been shallow and placid, but for other well-intentioned adventurers, those same waters had crashed unbridled through the gorge, strewing the remnants of mighty motorboats along the cliffs' sides. Such was the situation that now lay before Father Fessio's eyes at SFC. He was convinced that Mr. John had to reduce his overall operation drastically and continue on a more modest level or else he would be obliged to shut down everything once the money ran out, which Father Fessio calculated would take place in just two or three months, in November or December of 1984. He appraised that the most favorable unit of Mr. John's television empire was the Los Angeles station, where the facilities, equipment, and land promised to remain durable assets. He figured that if properly managed, the station could certainly be made profitable; it could unquestionably be sold for two or three times as much as what had already been invested.

What about San Francisco? The question haunted him, and he determined to look for an answer from an expert, Mr. J. Peter Grace, president and CEO of the W. R. Grace Company in New York, one of the most profitable businesses in the country. Mr. Grace, a committed Catholic, would certainly share the Fessio conviction that Catholic television could offer tremendous opportunities to the Church in the United States. Moreover, he was a man with whom Father Fessio had dealt in the past, a former guest speaker at the Saint Ignatius Institute. This promising relationship with such a giant of the business world gave Reverend Fessio the confidence to address a letter to him on September 10, 1984, asking that he, or someone representing him, come and visit the San Francisco office of the SFC to verify whether it was being run in an efficient, cost-effective, business-like manner, and whether what was being produced was marketable, of professional quality. He explained that operating at the present level, expenses were about $230,000 per month, and, hesitating to divulge his vision of Devil's Canyon, he assured his correspondent that such an amount could be reduced by cutting back news and documentary segments, the most expensive fare on the menu. And so what did he think?

There was something about this very successful New York businessman that resembled another giant of similar circumstances who would later be elected president of the United States. By his ignoring the letter, Mr. Grace let Father Fessio know that wearing a Roman collar did not count for much in the business world. Yes, he was a good Catholic, but he was also a shrewd entrepreneur. The problem was finally solved in Milwaukee, where two of the directors of the De Rance Foundation, Erica John and Donald Gallagher, filed suit to have the third director, Harry John, removed. They claimed that because of his extravagant, foolhardy expenditures, the assets of the foundation were disappearing at a rapid rate. In August 1986, Mr. John was removed from the foundation he had established and funded, and the $15 million sale of the San Francisco station was settled. Guadalupe Associates received $6 million of the total, $4 million of which was paid back to the DRF for the loan it had initially received for the purchase of the station. The remaining $2 million profit was a windfall for the Press, relieving in advance those anticipated pecuniary difficulties Father Fessio always found so bothersome. Back in Milwaukee, Harry and Erica got a divorce. We have seen that Father Fessio's provincial was eager to learn how and why he was rumored to be connected in this sticky business that had become a subject of gossip in the Vatican and an item of concern for Jesuit authorities in Rome and California.

Now we speed ahead to the fall of 1996, ten years after the Jim Eason Show event and the windfall sale of the San Francisco station. Father Fessio had just returned to San Francisco from his Australia venture, infused with generous amounts of enthusiasm that made him vulnerable to other, more alluring siren voices calling from fog-wrapped isles beyond the Press. Ulysses would have understood, perhaps advising him to plug his ears. But Father Fessio was eager to launch out onto that mysteriously seductive sea. After some study of information relevant to the enterprise he was considering, he shared these with those eager to embark with him. He discovered there were almost 14,000 radio stations in the United States, and of this number some 1,800 were owned and managed by various Protestant groups. How many Catholic radio stations were there? Eleven! And these, his research indicated, were Catholic "to a certain degree". His background as the editor-in-chief of Ignatius Press and of a growing number of Catholic monthly magazines had convinced him that the Catholic population in this country was hungry for religious instruction and information, but that Catholic religious leaders had been notoriously baneful in using radio waves to reach the faithful. He concluded that what was needed was to use the medium of radio to complement what Mother Angelica had been doing for years on her EWTN cable television channel.

Now to translate the plan into action, the idea into the real. By May of 1998, he had drawn up a detailed proposal that would be ready to kick off as early as September. Together with Nick Healy, then an executive at Franciscan University at Steubenville, Ohio, he had put together the Catholic Radio Network (CRN), which would bring "faith and values" twenty-four hours a day, seven days a week—in an all-talk format—to major cities with large Catholic populations across the nation, as part of a $71 million deal. By late July, the network had an executive branch well in order. The CEO was John Lynch, a one-time linebacker for the Pittsburgh Steelers who later became president of the Noble Broadcasting Group, which was a network of twelve radio stations that he sold for a nice profit in 1996 to help raise $50 million for CRN. As the *San Francisco Chronicle* put it, one of the goals of the network was to avoid "the strident vitriol of right-wing radio and the fundamentalist zeal of evangelical religious broadcasting". "We want a message of inclusion," Lynch insisted, "not that fire-and-brimstone, in-your-face approach."[1] Frank Hager, the managing director of the brokerage house Morgan Stanley was also an early supporter, as was Tom Monaghan, the founder and CEO of Domino's Pizza, with whom, as we have seen, Father Fessio had spoken to in Rome.

Frank DeFrancesco, the vice president and chief financial officer of the newly established enterprise, said that about 80 percent of the cost had been met to acquire stations thanks to the initial investments of some wealthy Catholics, among whom was John Saeman, the chairman of Medallion Enterprises and the Saeman Foundation

---

[1] Don Lattin, "Catholic Radio Takes to the Air", *San Francisco Chronicle*, October 16, 1999.

in Denver, the city in which CRN would make its debut. Archbishop Charles Chaput of Denver was to be the "episcopal advisor"
of the network, although the archbishop's spokesman made it clear
that no archdiocesan money would be used to fund the enterprise.
The archbishop promised that the content of the network would
not be "polemical or divisive", with the "correct tone" and the
kind of content that pastors and other bishops could be "reassured
about".[2] Father Fessio agreed, emphasizing once more: "We're not
going to be dealing with controversies and divisions between Catholics."[3] Mr. John Neal, another Denver philanthropist, summarized
the philosophy of a number of the board members: "You find a
lot of Catholics today who would be hard-pressed to give answers
about what the Church teaches. They need something more than
Latin, kneeling and penance." Through "stealth evangelism", listeners to the network would get more Christian formation than "a
ten-minute homily" can offer.[4] The CRN would not be something
altogether new for the Church in the United States. It would be a
successor to Archbishop Fulton J. Sheen's *The Catholic Hour*, which,
as one of the nation's most popular programs, had some four million regular listeners since its start in 1951.

On one of the last days of October 1998, Father Fessio bounded
off a plane in Milwaukee and announced to the press that CRN
had just closed the deal to purchase seven more stations from Radio Disney's Children's Broadcasting Corporation, in a $37 million
package deal. But as yet no talk show or host was ready to instruct
the audience that changes made in the so-called spirit of Vatican II
had gone too far. No problem, he assured his listeners: "We'll play
Gregorian chant around the clock until we get something different
to put in there." He was quick to point out that the policy of the
stations would be never to criticize bishops and priests by name,
although the policies of these men would be fair game for criticism.
"We want to work with every bishop, no matter how weak [he]
may be. We think there are ways we can work together. However,
we [will] control the station." When pressed to give his opinion

[2] John L. Allen, Jr., "Talkin' God in Drive Time New Radio Network's Goal", *National Catholic Register*, June 5, 1998.
[3] William Murray, "Trying to Build a Catholic Voice of America", *Our Sunday Visitor*
(May 31, 1998).
[4] "Network Features 'Stealth Evangelism' ", *Denver Post*, July 25, 1998.

of the local archbishop of Milwaukee, Most Reverend Rembert B. Weakland, who had voiced strong opposition to the program, Father Fessio said that earlier during the week he and the archbishop had been together at a meeting of Joseph Cardinal Bernardin's Common Ground, an organization whose mission is to foster peace and unity among factions within the Church. He reported that both he and the archbishop were gracious and respectful to one another, though he did remind the archbishop what the pope had told a group of American bishops earlier in the year about the liturgy, adding, probably with a smile: "I know you have classified me as a papal maximalist, but I can't help it. The pope keeps agreeing with me."[5]

During the rest of the week, there was no lack of excitement in Milwaukee, a fitting prelude to the coming of Halloween. Joint meetings of two Catholic organizations shared headlines with the archbishop and Father Fessio. Father was the keynote speaker at the Wanderer Forum, which also featured Helen Hull Hitchcock, co-founder of the Adoremus Society and founder of Women for Faith and Family, as well as Father John Harvey, O.S.F.S., the founder of Courage, an apostolate that counsels men and women with same-sex attractions to live chaste lives.

Call to Action, an organization that promotes social justice causes, was the second group meeting in Milwaukee that week. Speakers featured the group's president, attorney Linda Pieczynski; feminist theologian Elizabeth Schüssler Fiorenza, co-editor of *Concilium* and editor of the *Journal of Feminist Studies in Religion*; and Riane Eisler, a sociologist and anthropologist of a decidedly leftist orientation. Ms. Pieczynski explained that the purpose of Call to Action was to envision the future, "to look beyond the present repression going on within the Roman Catholic Church against women and men who disagree with the limited role assigned to women". Her group's agenda was to decentralize Vatican authority, give lay people a larger voice in defining faith and morals, ordain women, allow for married priests, and let couples decide for themselves about contraception. Archbishop Weakland declined the invitation to speak at the Call to Action convention, declaring his preference for Joseph Cardinal

---

[5] Tom Heinen, "Catholic Radio Network Beginning Today, Fessio Announces", *Milwaukee Journal Sentinel*, October 31, 1998.

Bernardin's effort with Common Ground to foster unity through the principle of the "seamless garment". But he did offer an opinion on the social action agenda of Call to Action: "It seems to me they give a platform for anyone who disagrees with anything in the Church." He was quick to add that he was refusing to allow CRN in his archdiocese because those connected with the network were too closely associated with Mother Angelica of EWTN. "My feeling is we have enough divisions in the Church", and he added: "I find some of the people involved, especially Father Fessio, have been very divisive."

Father Fessio retorted: the CRN "is basically a group of Catholic laymen. I am the only priest that has been directly involved in it." After pointing out that Archbishop Chaput was a member of the executive committee, he added: "We believe that this will ensure our programming is authentically Catholic." He cited Vatican II legislation that "Catholic laymen have the obligation to sanctify the secular order, and that includes the media", affirming that "there are very strong statements on the media and social communications in the Second Vatican Council wherein laymen are encouraged to support and even buy radio stations." And he concluded: "In every case that I am aware of, the Holy See has confirmed the position that I have taken." Indeed, it had. On a number of occasions, Pope John Paul encouraged Catholics to make use of the media to expand the faith.

At Father Fessio's home base, San Francisco Archbishop William Levada welcomed the arrival of a new network, Catholic Family Radio, but there was a volley of strikes leveled against it because one of the talk-show hosts in the southern part of the state was Dan Lungren, the former attorney general of California and one-time Republican candidate for governor. He favored the death penalty, in contrast to the pope, and criticized the climate change agenda along with the Clintons' marriage. "It is obvious that I am conservative and a Republican", he confessed. "I make that clear. But I also make clear that the Republican conservative position is not necessarily the Catholic position." There were those who claimed that such a statement proved that he was "a cafeteria Catholic". He might have been surprised to learn that the editor of *America*, Father Thomas Reese, would have been on his side. Reese noted at the time: "Everyone is a cafeteria Catholic, whether they're liberal or conservative." Such was the supposed "seamless garment" position of Common Ground. The cafeteria is a place where everyone is free to choose according to one's taste and feelings of the moment. It is not a place to criticize choices of others. Pick your preference on women's ordination, abortion, contraception, the gay life-style. Eschew divisiveness, embrace openness, and live in peace with everyone. That is what is on the menu of the cafeteria Catholic. Father Reese, who, as was earlier noted, is by nature a polite, affable man of strong opinions that differ from those of Father Fessio, then pointed out that the pope and some bishops are even farther left than some far-left Democrats on issues like welfare reform, peace, and justice. "Will this network be Catholic in that sense?" he asked. "That is going to be very difficult to do." Given Reese's criteria, one could question whether the National Council of Catholic Bishops was really Catholic. It was precisely because of the pervasive presence of "cafeteria Catholics" that Pope John Paul II had delivered the apostolic exhortation *Catechesi Tradendae* in October 1979 and encouraged laymen to become involved in the media. But all of this Halloween 1998 infighting in Milwaukee was a diversion from the real life-or-death struggle of CRN, which was taking place under the mask of triumphalism.

Father Philip Bourret was a California Jesuit who had been working in China until the 1945–1949 revolution forced him to take refuge in Taiwan. There he was able to finish a project he had begun on the mainland, a project that grew into (I am told) the largest radio–TV station in the island republic to this day. After Taiwan, he went to the Philippines and there constructed radio stations that beamed waves to underground receivers in China. Finally, he returned to California, but he never seemed to remain in one place very long. With an ever-present briefcase in hand, he was always on the go. When asked, he gladly offered his services to a few American Protestant radio stations making their beginnings. But mostly he seemed to commute between home and various countries in South America, where he used his talents much to the advantage of the Church. After a heavy day's work, he would often board a red-eye flight and settle himself in the back of the plane. Then, once sleep had made everyone around him totally unconcerned which pampas, jungle, or mountain range stretched out beneath them, he would open his briefcase, pull down the tray in front of him, and whisper the Tridentine Mass he had memorized in his China days.

One easily got the impression that he felt most at home thinking in the conditional tense and speaking in the subjunctive mood, in contrast to Father Fessio, who tends to think in the future and, when overcome by weariness, speak in the imperative. One day, Father Phil approached me, and if his speech was not direct, his meaning was nonetheless clear: the Fessio radio project was doomed to implode. Religious networks have to start from the ground up, he said; that way they build a clientele and a network of financial supporters. What Father Fessio is doing, he ventured to suggest, is pouring water into a bottomless hole. The water supply cannot go on forever. At this, I urged him to make an appointment with the CRN architect. He hesitated but said he would try. A few days later, I saw him and asked him if he had spoken to Father Fessio. He had. What did he say? The translated version of Father Bourret's labyrinthine account was that he met him in his office and, while he was standing there trying to explain his case, Father Fessio just kept saying things that reminded him of the TV show *Dragnet*, where Jack Webb would repeat, "Just the facts, ma'am, just the facts." Father finally stood up, told his well-meaning advisor he was busy and to please shut the door when he left. That was it.

The busy man's agenda became more pressing during the following months, and finally on October 28, 1999, one year to the day after Father Fessio made his triumphant entry into Milwaukee, the mail carrier delivered an envelope to him at the Press containing a crescendo to the CRN crisis. "It is with deep regret that I announce my resignation from Catholic Radio Network", wrote the sender, John Lynch, the president and chief executive officer of the network. The reason was financial. The seven studios purchased from Disney, which at one time had been hoisted as symbols of triumph, were draining all the network's funds at a fast clip. John Lynch's experience as a one-time radio executive prompted him to recommend the remedy: secular commercial advertising tweaks between programs. Father Fessio would have none of it. That made the job of the acting chairman, Mr. Gary M. McCausland, simple. All radio stations CRN owned had to be sold immediately for as small a loss to the investors as possible. Back home, the scoreboard marking wins and losses had to be readjusted to account for one more adventure on the part of the noble knight. He knew that jaunty ad spots could never replace Gregorian chant, so he decided to let the siren song of Catholic radio simply fade away into the mist behind him, while the ship sailed on.

20

THE END OF THE INSTITUTE

In the late summer of 2000, Reverend Stephen Arena Privett, S.J., had been in El Salvador on sabbatical leave from Santa Clara University. He had returned to that small republic, which had become almost a second home, to give himself once more to the needs of people made poor by exploitation and the ravages of a perennial civil war. He recalls sitting one day in a chapel where six Jesuit priests and two female workers are memorialized. It was a place he visited often. "Those priests were my friends", Father Privett liked to say. These eight victims had been slain on November 16, 1989, at a dramatic moment in the conflict. Now as he sat there in the chapel, he contemplated whether or not to accept the invitation given him to be president of the University of San Francisco. "There is immense potential for impacting society at a university", he recalls saying to himself. "It would be a real challenge [for me] to realize that potential. . . . Why not give it a shot?"[1] So, on September 15, 2000, that is just what he did: he was inaugurated the twenty-seventh president of the University of San Francisco. That November, surrounded by their life-sized pictures, he offered a memorial Mass in USF's Saint Ignatius Church on the anniversary of the death of these eight victims, asserting that for him "their passion for the truth, and their courage in its telling, continues to be a model and an inspiration."[2] Truth and courage . . .

Before treating how Father Stephen Privett endeavored to put

---

[1] Tanya Schevitz, "New President Brings World to USF", *SFGate*, November 15, 2000, https://www.sfgate.com/education/article/New-President-Brings-World-to-USF-3236561.php.

[2] Ulysses Torassa, "Jesuit Champion of the Poor Inaugurated New USF Head", *SF-Gate*, November 19, 2000, https://www.sfgate.com/bayarea/article/Jesuit-champion-of-the-poor-inaugurated-new-USF-3050908.php.

these ideals into practice as the president of the University of San Francisco, it seems fitting to go backward a bit to appreciate the circumstances that helped form his ideals and ambitions. In 1968, when Mr. Fessio, S.J., was signing up a few fellow Jesuit scholastics as counselors in the Santa Clara University Project 50 program, he placed the name of his good friend, the fun-loving, high-spirited Steve Privett, at the top of his list. It was a fortuitous choice. Mr. Privett brought his spontaneous, optimistic spirit to the venture, and in times of stress his infectious laugh became the glue of cohesion for the group. During the intervening years, his commitment to the social justice apostolate increased in direct proportion to rancor toward "the old ways". In 1968, his path and that of friend and admirer Mr. Fessio ran parallel, down bumpy roads, but over the following twenty-five years or more, they diverged a bit, eventually ending up poles apart. Previous pages in this biography have sketched out an evolution in Father Fessio's thinking; let us now briefly dissect the stages in the life of Father Privett that might have contributed to his distinct philosophy of life.

In 1982, as Louise Davies was composing the conditions for her gift to the Saint Ignatius Institute, which Michael Scriven at the time was busy evaluating, and as people far and wide were admiring Father Lo Schiavo for shutting down the USF basketball program, Father Stephen Privett was traveling and studying in Latin America. At an earlier date, he had spent some time in Bolivia, where he was struck by "extremes of poverty and oppression that most people never see". The country was under martial law, and the same government army that had executed Che Guevara in 1967 continued to exploit the starving people. When he crossed into Chile, which at that time was under the rule of Augusto Pinochet, he shuddered as he witnessed soldiers marching in goose-step formation down the broad boulevards. He saw the same in El Salvador, and, indeed, it was the same everywhere: oppressive armies of fascist governments were terrorizing the people. In 1988, he returned to El Salvador to continue attending to the needs of the victims of the war. His painful recollections of Latin America made him critical of the American government, the number-one seller of arms in these developing countries. "What does El Salvador need with American tanks?" he asked. "What does Chile need with bombers?" he wondered.[3] If the United States insisted on sending items to Latin America, why were they not sending refrigerators and air conditioning units? Why military weapons? His conclusion: Unrest in Central America "clearly arose from repression, not Marxist ideology", and given its consistent support of the wrong side in the various conflicts, it was plain that the American government was largely responsible for such repression. "Our political system is a bunch of interest groups, each scrambling for a piece of the pie, and never addressing the common good" was his considered opinion. "People grumble about taxes, but I haven't heard one person say, 'Taxes are a way to support people who can't afford to live without our help.'" He affirmed that Jesuits have not ceased to ask themselves the same question: "How can one be human in a world where the total assets of the world's wealthiest 358 people exceeds the combined annual income of the poorest 45 percent of the world's population?" "It should not be this way", he added. But education was a means to change this. "Reading and writing are probably the world's most powerful tools for social justice."[4]

Not all of Father Privett's time had been spent in Latin America. During the height of the rebellious era in Jesuit communities between 1973 and 1975, he had been a part-time formation director for novices. Then he was assigned to Father Fessio's high school alma mater, Bellarmine College Preparatory in San Jose, where eventually he assumed the toga of the celebrated principal Father Gerald Flynn and inspired the faculty there enough to have his tenure of office dubbed "the Camelot years at Bellarmine". In April 1978, when attempting to create the master's program in Catholic Studies at USF, Father Fessio addressed letters to principals in all the Catholic schools inquiring if any of their faculty members might be interested in the program. Father Privett wrote a reply addressed to "Gentlemen". After declaring that no one on his faculty would be interested in the program, he continued:

The adverse publicity the St. Ignatius Institute has received in recent publications has led to some serious questions regarding the

[3] Ruth Ashley, "Champion of the Downtrodden", *Marin Independent Journal*, September 3, 2001, F1.
[4] Ibid.

whole orientation of your program. It is caricatured as defensive, self-righteous and terribly narrow in its discussion of contemporary Theological questions.

It would certainly be in your best interests to correct these mis-perceptions of the St. Ignatius Institute.

In 1981, he moved to Washington, D.C., at the Catholic University of America to pursue a Ph.D. in catechetics with an emphasis on Hispanic communities, and the following year, he became the vice president for academic affairs at Santa Clara University as well as a member of the Theology and Religious Studies Department. He channeled his outrage over what he had witnessed in Latin America into classes he chose to teach, the textbooks he assigned, and the lectures he gave. "If people (outside the university) asked me to speak" about such matters, "I could never say no." In 1999, while remaining a professor in the Religious Studies Department, he assumed the rank of university provost. His fast rise to such a prestigious position is a testimony to his abilities, as well as his ambition to awaken the seemingly self-satisfied Santa Clara Broncos to the plight of the poor and distressed.

His close associate, Reverend Gerdenio "Sonny" Manuel, S.J., a few years his junior, observed that for Father Privett, social justice was the central element in the university's mission. The careers of the two men had much in common. Beginning in 1994, Father Manuel, a professional counseling psychologist, had served as assistant provincial for formation and vocation director in the California Province—with Father Bernadicou as his assistant—and in 2004, he would become the rector of the Jesuit community at Santa Clara. During Father Privett's term as provost, Father Manuel served as his assistant while continuing to teach classes as a member of the Psychology Department, and according to him, members of the faculty and staff joined forces with some alumni in wondering if Father Privett intended to turn the university into a "soup kitchen".[5] He would take students and faculty members down with him to El Salvador as pilgrims to visit the shrine where his inspirational heroes were honored. During his tenure at Santa Clara, Father Privett was a supporter of the "Eastside Project", which was sort of a continuation of Project 50, minus the Catholic orientation—

that essential element which, according to Father de Lubac, defined social justice in the Jesuit tradition. This brief description of Father Privett's background seems necessary to understand the events that began at the University of San Francisco on Tuesday, January 16, 2001.

That was the date Mr. Galten received notice from the dean that he was to report to his office at 10 A.M. on the following Friday. Friday arrived. Standing there before the seated dean, who seemed to be suppressing his emotions, he was informed that he was fired and that he was to have his office cleared and be off campus by 5 P.M. the next working day, which was Monday. Ten minutes later, John was walking back to his office. At 10:30, associate director John Hamlon was standing in the same place and given the same notice. Handshakes were given, an about-face was made, and the assistant director was off to join his former boss. Later that day, the dean met with four of the tenured core members of the Institute faculty: Professors Tom Cavanaugh, Raymond Dennehy, Kim Summerhays and Michael Torre. He advised them of the president's decision. The four—later joined by Professor Erasmo Leiva-Merikakis, who was out of town at the time—agreed to hold classes during the coming semester, which was to begin in three days, but they could not in conscience continue to be associated with the SII after the semester ended.

On the day of the firings, Father Privett announced that Dr. Paul Murphy would assume the joint positions vacated by Mr. Galten and Mr. Hamlon. Dr. Murphy was a young, competent, obliging, nontenured member of the History Department who, in addition to having a heavy class load, also directed the Catholic Studies Program. This entity was a relatively new, eclectic assemblage of seven courses, somewhat like an interdisciplinary minor. Being still virtually untried, it had neither the reputation nor the achievements of the Saint Ignatius Institute. On this same occasion, the president issued a statement directed to the students that was printed in the February 1 *Foghorn*. He stressed the fact that the Institute "has a major role to play in shaping the overall campus learning environment and in promoting what Pope John Paul II refers to as 'the increasingly necessary encounter of the Church with the development of the sciences and the cultures of our age' (*Ex Corde Ecclesiae*)."

Father Privett then explained how financial problems facing the university made it imperative to improve coordination of the university's programs and to consolidate its space for the continued betterment of academic quality. In a separate statement, he said that the amalgamation of the SII with the Catholic Studies Program would save the university "about $100,000". He explained that putting both under the directorship of Professor Paul Murphy would help them to merge, enabling them to draw together into "a more synergistic relationship that enriches and strengthens both programs, broadens the influence of Catholic thought across campus, amplifies the University of San Francisco's voice in the inter-cultural dialogue that Pope John Paul II called for in his New Year's message and earns the University national recognition for its contributions to Catholic intellectual life". He finally thanked the students for their cooperation and support "as USF moves to improve the SII and Catholic Studies Program in its ongoing effort to be a community where understanding is joined to commitment, where the search for truth is informed by a sense of responsibility for society and where academic excellence partners with the cultivation of virtue".

Father Privett seems to have a liking for the word "synergy". What does the term mean in this context, and what is a perspective that might enable one to grasp the president's meaning better? Synergy comes about when two or more agents or entities interact to produce an effect greater than the sum of their parts. It is the opposite of antagonism. It is also a much-used term—along with "the strength of the small" and "the option for the poor"—of the Bolivia-born Father Gustavo Gutiérrez, O.P., one of the founders of Liberation Theology. There is no hard conclusion that should be drawn from this observation other than that Father Privett's penchant for solving the plight of the disadvantaged and exploited poor in Latin America was perhaps applied in his approach to the Institute problem at USF.

Father Fessio's initial reaction to the scrape was typical: nothing personal, observations purely factual. A few weeks after the decision was broadcast, in the midst of the uproar it generated, he congratulated Father Privett for recognizing and making public the financial problems of the university and for mapping out clear ways to remedy the situation. He differed, however, with the president's statement that the suppression of the Institute would save money for the university, and with typical Fessio acumen in budgetary matters, he convincingly demonstrated that the president's SII decision would in fact lose considerable income for the university. The number of tuition-paying students would decrease. He said he would fight to the finish Father Privett's decision to modify the Institute. In a later chapter, we shall see how he kept his word in this matter.

On the afternoon of the firing, six lay, tenured, core members of the Institute faculty (this included Erasmo Leiva and Rosemarie Deist) addressed an open letter to the administration. It began: "For over twenty-five years the Saint Ignatius Institute has attracted to the University of San Francisco many of its finest students." After giving some details to support this statement and insisting that "the Institute has remained faithful to the vision of its founding Jesuit priests", the letter summed up this section by stating: "These graduates continue to leaven the world, and we who have been privileged to contribute to this program take great pride and consolation in their accomplishments." The authors then pointed out that Mr. John Galten, who had served the Institute since its inception and who had been its director during the past years, and Mr. John Hamlon, who had been with the program for over six years, had been hastily fired. Despite their "wisdom and courage", theirs had still been "a difficult task because certain individuals within the Jesuit community and the university have maintained a relentless assault on the Institute, trying to undermine its integrity". The letter writers proceeded to give a critical account of these Jesuits: "Representative of that liberality which can abide all things but orthodoxy, they have employed every means available to discredit the program and its personnel and to deny it resources." And the conclusion: "Regretfully these forces have now succeeded."

The reason for the firing, though unspoken, was clear: "[T]he University administration plans to alter fundamentally the character of the Institute." And in light of this fact: "[I]n good conscience we cannot countenance this injustice. Neither can we support an Institute whose nature will be dramatically different from the vision of its founders." Thus the authors concluded: "As honorable men and women we will go forward with the course offerings of the Spring 2001 term, but thereafter will no longer voluntarily teach in this program or its surrogates."

Meanwhile, on Monday, January 22, in compliance with the

dean's order, the two former officials of the SII cleared out of their offices, and, before leaving, they met with students at 5 P.M. to offer their good-byes. John Galten invited Professor Murphy to be present at the gathering. He went out of his way to praise his replacement and asked the students to cooperate with him. The following day, the provost, James L. Wiser, wrote a letter to the university community admitting that, although the firing was not according to "the preferred procedure", nevertheless, all should know that the university's intention was not to deemphasize the Institute, but rather to build something even better upon its strong foundation. Father Privett was also quick to explain his action. He confessed that "from day one" of his being appointed president, "I found the anomaly of a staff person running an academic program of Saint Ignatius' stature unacceptable." It would be unfair not to mention here that like John Galten, Father Maloney had not been a member of the faculty but was, rather, a member of the administration staff, and for fourteen years the Institute had been directed by staff personnel. But then, given what we have learned about Father Privett's long-standing opinion of the Institute and his notion of the purpose of a university—particularly a *Jesuit* university—we ask: Could this instead have been the motivating impetus for his "reorganizing" the Saint Ignatius Institute? It is a question to consider while reading about the consequences that followed.

John Galten issued a printed statement shortly after his termination. The document began with a short summation of the origins of the Institute and its academic, spiritual, and communal orientation. He then touched briefly on the reasons why it had been, since its inception, a subject of controversy and concluded:

> Perhaps some expect me to be bitter, but I am not. With God's grace we have been able to form, and to send forth to leaven this world, an entire generation of men and women of sound education and noble character. With Saint Paul the faculty and staff of the Saint Ignatius Institute can proclaim, "We have fought the good fight; we have finished the course; we have kept the faith." Please remember us in your prayers.

Then within a week, the Institute faculty spoke out again—at length.

21

THE FACULTY RESIST

On January 29, five core members (Tom Cavanaugh, Raymond Dennehy, Erasmo Leiva, Kim Summerhays, and Michael Torre) wrote a ten-page open letter to the president giving their assessment of the causes and effects of the current crisis facing the Institute. Stephen Roddy, a non-Catholic faculty member of the Institute, also added a statement, appended. Even independent of the message, the text was as balanced as it was instructive. Father Vernon Ruland of the Theology Department was delighted by the president's decision, but even he admitted the arguments of the faculty members who had signed the document were reasonable and properly adjusted to the grievance. This chapter gives a lengthy summary of this powerful letter, for two reasons. First, this document became the chief cause of the case's wide popularity in the media. Second, the text should enable the reader to appreciate better Father Fessio's role in this complicated drama as it unfolded.

As the authors state, the president had emphasized that "fiscal challenge[s]" in the university were compounding with "limited resources", making it necessary to trim the Institute's administrative staff. He had announced that the firing would save the university money. Yet Mr. Hamlon's salary came, not from the university coffers, but "from donations solicited, in part, in order to cover his position". He was an able administrator and a much-beloved advisor and advocate for students beyond those in the Institute, an instructor and coordinator for the overseas program. "In firing him," wrote the professors, "you sacrificed all that service and got nothing in return. Or rather, as in the firing of Mr. Galten, so, here you did get something: you got rid of a man of proven character—a voice, an energy, an advocate, and . . . a staunch defender of the ordinary Magisterium of the Church." As for Mr. Galten, he was simply to be replaced by another paid director, Professor Murphy.

Furthermore, the bad press surrounding the new reforms may well discourage new students from enrolling at USF. "Father President," the writers judged, "you have not saved the University money. The far greater likelihood is that your act will cost the University financially, and not in a small way. . . . You must have known this was possible, yet acted anyway. This is to act recklessly, and in a way that should rightly alarm many trustees." No one familiar with the twenty-five-year history of the Institute and its connection with the university could claim that mere ignorance had been the cause of this ill-advised act on the part of the new president, and the letter writers made that point clear. The firing was simply the last nail driven into the coffin.

The five critics then turned to another one of the president's stated reasons for his action toward the Institute, which we touched upon earlier: "coordinating and concentrating" academic resources, by drawing the Institute and the Catholic Studies Certificate program into "a more synergistic relationship". As a matter of fact, he even hoped to realize the Institute's "potential to be the premier residential Catholic Studies Program in the nation". Yet the professors voiced two objections here: "To begin with, Father President, we regard that . . . statement as disloyal to the Institute faculty, and thereby to the University as well. The Saint Ignatius Institute already is arguably the nation's premier Catholic Studies Program. You have publically insinuated otherwise, and to those outside the confines of the University. We find your rhetoric careless and misguided." Moreover, in their judgment, he acted contrary to the Jesuit ideal of *cura personalis*, since the students would no longer be receiving the care and attention they had gotten from the devoted Mr. Galten, whose sole professional responsibility was the direction of the Institute. "[I]t is perfect nonsense" for the president to believe he would advance the SII by replacing two full-time positions with one "non-tenured faculty member who perforce must be busy with his research and teaching, and is already directing another program". Although a good man, Professor Murphy certainly will not have the same hard-won confidence or enjoy the same faculty support as Galten, a man with twenty-five years of experience in dealing with students and USF faculty.

As for the fusion of the SII with the Catholic Studies program, this simply would not take. The letter proceeded:

The stated reason for having the Catholic Studies Certificate program and the Institute enter into a more 'synergistic' relationship under [one director's] common leadership is disingenuous, as anyone who is familiar with the two programs knows well. The Certificate is a relatively eclectic assemblage of 7 courses, rather like an interdisciplinary Minor; the Institute is a highly coordinated alternate General Education Curriculum. The first is a relatively new creation on campus, a virtually untried program, with neither reputation nor achievement. The Institute, by contrast, is one of the most successful academic programs on campus, with a national reputation. To compare the two is like comparing apples and oranges: they are quite different, serving different University needs and students. To "combine" them is both administrative and academic recklessness.

The faculty members also brushed aside the president's claim that firing the SII directors would ultimately "further the academic excellence of the Institute or the University" as just one more "not. . . credible assertion", labeling the action "an offense to justice as well as to charity". They reminded him of the Catholic social-ethical teaching that "the longer an employee has been with an organization, the greater must be the case for dismissing him". As for the president, he "had no such case" and his "action is manifestly unjust". They redescribed the firings:

> [Mr. Galten and Mr. Hamlon] were summarily dismissed, each in a ten minute conversation, without warning and with no reasonable explanation. No effort was initially made to discuss perceived difficulties with them and work out some solution. . . . Instead, they were cast out of the University to fend for themselves in their early 60s. No appeal to the need for administrators to take "hard decisions" could possibly justify the egregiously unjust nature of your action.

The authors then delivered a chilling judgment: "Father President, you speak of justice for all. You talk the talk, but do not walk the walk." In this document, one can easily sense the intense emotion that went into its writing and thus better understand the tenacious and protracted attitudes that would be adopted by both sides over the next twelve months.

The emotion by no means slackened as the letter went on. The professors likened the president's recent actions to a kind of institutional murder, as though the Institute had been a living being, with its own vibrant spirit:

> In addition to the direct and pernicious consequences of your actions—and precisely because of them—you now find yourself with the added consequence of having so alienated the core faculty of the Institute as to be without those men and women who created and nurtured it, and gave it that vaunted Jesuit ideal of *magis* to a program they loved and to the students they served. With full deliberation, you took aim at and killed its head, and have thus managed to eviscerate its guts and heart. For the Institute was far more than an assemblage of integrated courses; it has always been a readily recognizable moral person, with harmonious structure and spontaneous cooperation of its members. By striking at the head, you find yourself with a lifeless corpse. . . . [Y]ou used deadly force against the Institute. That you succeeded in killing what it was, therefore, must be laid squarely on your shoulders, and on yours alone.

They did not hesitate to describe directly their own profound affection for and commitment to the Institute—the real motive for their resignation: "Nor was our action (not continuing to teach in the Institute) unpredictable. On the contrary, on more than one occasion we had informed the Dean that our deep love for the Institute and what it stood for could lead us to this act, if provoked. It is hard to believe that you did not foresee this possibility."

In all of its public statements on the Institute reforms, the administration avoided any mention of the deep underlying cause. But it was no secret that from its inception, the Institute had been a lightning rod for controversy. "Its main adversaries", the professors reminded the President, "have been a group of your fellow Jesuits, especially some members of the Theology Department." This has always been a cause of wonder and surprise. "Why would Jesuits feel inclined relentlessly to attack the one program on campus everyone recognizes as most identifiably Catholic?" The animosity of these Jesuits lies "in their differing vision of Catholic theology and the Catholic Church". This may be a statement that Jesuits would be inclined to ignore or deny, but the facts speak for themselves.

> [T]he Institute came into being when some Catholic theologians argued for, and put into practice, the idea of a "loyal dissent" to the ordinary teachings of the Church; that is, they argued one could

listen respectfully to what a pope taught in an encyclical letter, and then choose publically to disagree with that teaching. By contrast, the core faculty of the Institute argued for, and put into practice, the idea of "loyal assent" to the ordinary teaching of the Church; that is, it argued that Catholics should assent to what a pope taught in an encyclical letter, as is affirmed in the central document of Vatican II on the Church.

At bottom, *this* disagreement, which dates from the earliest days of the Institute, is what set many USF Jesuits at odds with the program.

But the Institute never showed intolerance. Later in the document, the five professors will stress that the SII faculty "never sought, in any way, to prevent theologians who did not share its position from holding their own views or from advocating them." Rather, the Institute wanted only to "hold its view and to advocate its own position . . . in a way that was respectful of others and that was cognizant of the kind of dialogue and disagreement proper to a university community." Yet this was never enough for the opponents.

They have constantly characterized the Institute as narrow, "dogmatic" and intolerant, and have sought ways to undermine its stand on this matter or to silence its voice. Although you yourself, Father President, have only been on campus a brief period of time, we can assure you that what we have just written will come as absolutely no news to anyone who has been at the University for any length of time. The long-standing quarrel is common knowledge.

The writers reminded the president that the task of advocating the full teaching of the Church's Magisterium invites controversy and attack within Catholic universities, and for this reason it requires many virtues to maintain that advocacy prudently, yet forcefully, "to bear witness to its full truth, without alienating those who think otherwise, sometimes, quite passionately". This means a director of the Institute "must not only possess the virtues of courage and wisdom, temperance and justice, but must also possess a deep fidelity to and love of the Church". This was the same policy Fathers Fessio and Maloney and Mr. Galten adopted as their own and put into practice during their terms of office. The letter writers further asserted: "When passions are calmed in future ages, historians might marvel at such a judgment only to have their reactions further stimulated by what the reaction on the part of laymen to such Jesuitical thinking was in an American Jesuit university at the end of the twentieth century."

The composers of the letter pointed out that many if not most of the faculty members and administrators at USF were not Catholic, or at least not practicing Catholics, and yet "the majority would accord [the Saint Ignatius Institute] at least a grudging respect, if not admiration." Over the years, the faculty and administrators—save for some Jesuits—had come to accept the SII, feeling it had earned a place on campus. The letter writers were quick to admit that at times Father Lo Schiavo and Father Schlegel did not agree with some policy or action on the part of the Institute, and yet each ever agreed the Institute "had a right to go about its business according to its own lights, and that it was a 'good citizen' on the USF campus. You, Father President, after a brief few months at USF, have deemed otherwise. You have moved swiftly to fire its leaders and to reduce its administration from two full-time positions, to one part-time administrator. This is an academic putsch." They then pointed out that the essential character of the Institute, as was approved by the board of trustees, is based on three legs: academic, social, and religious. "You have destroyed all that. By placing the Institute as one academic program among several, . . . you have basically removed two of its legs, treating it only as an academic program. This is to change it substantially in a way that exceeds your given authority."

From this point, they waxed even stronger:

> We cannot but believe that you intended precisely to still a voice on campus and a theological point of view that you—for whatever false and misguided reasons—found noxious to your presidency. As a cleric, you have decided not to tolerate a program of lay Catholics, as they conceived it and carried it out, because you did not like the Institute's religious vision. Your action thus goes precisely against the stated Apostolic Goals of your Jesuit Province. It does not foster partnership with your lay colleagues, nor help evangelize contemporary culture, but the exact opposite. It responds to the diversity within your Province by reducing and silencing one of its voices. And, insofar as it may disillusion and drive away many of its students, who generously reached out in service to the marginalized of San Francisco, it does not strengthen but rather weakens solidarity

with the poor. There is something terribly wrong with this picture, as there ever has been with Jesuits relentlessly attacking their fellow lay Catholics, who have sought to serve students in the Institute.

The five readily confessed that at times some presently enrolled students and alumni had behaved in ways that many considered excessively conservative. "We know this, because we ourselves have found that behavior wrong at times, and have ourselves sought to temper their excesses." However, as they argued, to saddle the Institute with the excesses of a few is not just; it is to accuse the whole of guilt by association. Students are free to think and act in ways the directors and faculty do not approve. Their behavior is not the fault of the Institute and to suggest otherwise is unfair. In fact, the president's own recent decisions regarding the SII might be regarded as "intolerant and illiberal", breaching "the right of your lay brothers and sisters to express fully their religious convictions in an academic program".

The authors rounded off their letter with a bullet-point list of their chief grievances against the president. First of all, he fired the directors "in a shockingly precipitous manner, and without following established procedures". What is more, they asserted, he illegitimately tampered with an academic program that was conceived and maintained by its core faculty. He also curtailed the faculty's freedom of expression by hiring a probationary faculty member to guide the future of the program, damaging the Institute's capacity to "advocate and defend its theological position". After reiterating that many students and alumni now felt alienated, they added that the president's action, which bypassed the advisory board of both the SII and the Catholic Studies program, brazenly violated the due process policy established by previous presidents of the university. Then the last charge: by changing an academic program without the approval of the USF board of *trustees*, the president had violated the university faculty contract—an abuse of power and a misuse of authority. In short, in the process of pushing his agenda, Father Privett had acted in an autocratic, high-handed manner.

Because the protest of the five authors involved matters related to their Catholic faith, they refrained from involving non-Catholic faculty members in the letter, allowing them instead to express their opinions separately, though as mentioned above, one non-Catholic,

Professor Stephen Roddy, signed and submitted an attached statement. A number of others had also served notice that they would not voluntarily teach in the Institute during the coming year. The writers acknowledged this. "We are thankful for their show of solidarity with us in our own conscientious objection." The group concluded with the following statement:

> Father President, you have chosen to use your power to reach down into a past faculty dispute that was not your [concern] and that had grown quiet. Furthermore, as a Jesuit president committed to supporting the stated commitment of this University to "the educational mission of the Roman Catholic Church," you have managed effectively to undermine what most regarded as a very significant Catholic element of its curriculum. This is no way to deal with the kind of interchange of ideas, and the balance of differing forces, proper to a multicultural university. We dissent.

But they could not properly dissent without having first included the following words, which attest to the group's integrity and committed objectivity.

> We say nothing against your person or your presidency, to both of which we wish well. We protest only your act. You made a serious mistake. It should not be allowed to stand. . . . There are two versions of the event that has just occurred: yours and ours. According to the Administration, it intended the good of the Institute and its greater presence on campus. According to this faculty, you intended substantively to alter what it was by ways of reducing both its independence and its resources. We stand by our story.

The content of this lengthy message to the new president on campus made a splash in the media, and he was forced to defend himself. He rebutted, for instance, that neither prior consultation with the Institute faculty nor going the extra mile with the terminated parties would have served any purpose. Perhaps. Yet it strikes us that this conclusion is hard to reconcile with the good Jesuit father's own inaugural motto, "Education for a Just Society". At any rate, the letter made its rounds. *Verba volant, scripta manent.*

For the administration, the fallout from this declaration was as unprecedented as it was challenging, and perhaps the most damaging factor was how quickly the story spread throughout the country. An editorial in the influential weekend edition of the *Wall Street Journal* took up the issue, even though San Franciscans had considered it an in-house matter. "Ever notice the contrast in today's campuses between the talk about diversity and the actual practice of it?" was the opening sentence. "Well look no further than the Jesuit-run University of San Francisco." The lamentation continued on for roughly 350 words before concluding with the following paragraph:

Time will tell whether the Institute survives and prospers, as the university promises, or whether the change at the top signals the crippling of a program whose existence added real diversity to what USF offered. Much has been made of the lack of credentials of the fired Institute directors, but the university concedes that in their able hands the Institute stood out at USF for its excellence. In the light of that record it strikes us that if Father Privett was determined to make an example, he might have more profitably done so with those parts of USF that are operating below standard rather than with the one so clearly operating above.[1]

We shall now examine the reactions of other figures and see how the president himself defended his resolve to reconstitute the Saint Ignatius Institute.

---

[1] Editorial, "Ignatius of Dis-Loyola", *Wall Street Journal*, February 9, 2001.

APPEAL TO THE VATICAN

One might well wonder what part Father Fessio was playing in this tense drama. Shelved away, he remained silent. This seeming passive silence is all the more incongruous when we take into account his natural choleric impulses and when we recall that no one was more devoted to the Institute than he, who had courageously founded it, and that no one had suffered more than he, who had long defended it. But this new posture did not indicate inactivity. Mole-like, he was exploring ways to undermine such an offense against ordinary justice, which ran contrary to papal desires for Catholic higher education and to young people's freedom to discover truth. The day after the firings, he put aside publicizing some of the Press' recent bestsellers, including Cardinal Ratzinger's *The Spirit of the Liturgy*, to meet with the core teachers and staff of the Institute. The main thing on the agenda was to draft a statement delineating the "Minimum Policies Necessary to Restore, Protect and Strengthen the Saint Ignatius Institute at the University of San Francisco". After some discussion, the group unanimously agreed that "without these seven policies or enactments, the Institute will cease to exist as an authentic Catholic program."

Specifically, it was necessary that (a) the *Ex Corde Ecclesiae* mandate be required of all who teach theology in the Institute; (b) qualified Jesuits and other priests invited by the Institute be permitted to assume teaching positions in the Institute; (c) the Institute be able to hire qualified part-time and full-time faculty deemed necessary by the Institute advisory board; (d) the Institute curriculum continue to satisfy the university's general education curriculum requirements; (e) the existing, university-approved advisory board, as a self-perpetuating board, have the right to advise and consent in all matters regarding staff, faculty, curriculum, and liturgy; (f) the director, associate director, and faculty of the Institute be reinstated; and (g) these policies remain in effect until abrogated by the Holy See. It was a *malo mori quam foedari* (I prefer death over disgrace) decree before the president's non-compromise stance.

Experience with the university's administration had taught Father Fessio always to ask for more rather than less. It was again that pelican instinct, scooping up a greater beak-full than he can swallow. He had long since learned the hard way that his world had grown so bad that wrens may prey where eagles dare not perch.[1] Not that he had ever been mistaken for a preying wren—a scooping pelican perhaps, but not a preying wren—but now he had to make sure that he was entering a territory from which powerful Roman eagles might be inclined to take timorous flight. The first step would be to show that the Minimum Policies were in no way contrary to American civil law, and he met this challenge with the aid of four experts in the field, all professors of law: Bernard Dobranski, Stephen Safranek (the younger brother of Tom Safranek, Father Fessio's regular companion to the "dangerous" beach in San Francisco in 1975), Richard Myers, and Gerald Bradley. After meeting at the Jesuit-run University of Detroit Mercy, Dobranski, Safranek, and Myers had teamed up to help found Tom Monaghan's Ave Maria School of Law in Ann Arbor, Michigan, where Dobranski was now dean, having already served as law dean at both Catholic University and Detroit Mercy. In 1994, Cardinal Maida of Detroit had solicited assistance from the three lawyers in answering a hostile memorandum issued by a law firm to Jesuit universities regarding the implementation of *Ex Corde Ecclesiae*, and they lived through four years of anti-Catholic resistance at the Detroit Mercy School of Law. Gerald Bradley, for his part, was a recognized authority on constitutional law regarding church and state, a professor at Notre Dame School of Law, the chair of the Legal Affairs Committee of the Catholic League, and the president of the Fellowship of Catholic Scholars, an organization to which Father Fessio had belonged since its foundation.[2] At the 1999 meeting of the National Council of Catholic Bishops, Bradley was singled out by Cardinal Bevilacqua as having given the bishops significant help in passing *An Application*

---

[1] Cf. William Shakespeare, *The Tragedy of King Richard the Third*, 1:3, 70.

[2] Daniel Wuerl, "Fellowship of Catholic Scholars", *l'Osservatore Romano*, February 2, 1978, 11.

of Ex Corde Ecclesiae in the United States, which took a stand contrary to that same memorandum which Dobranski, Safranek, and Myers had fought from Detroit.[3]

On February 2, 2001, while these four experts in church-state matters were mulling over the Minimum Policies, Father Fessio faxed letters to two of his friends, Joseph Cardinal Ratzinger, prefect of the papal Congregation for the Doctrine of Faith, and Christoph Cardinal Schönborn of Vienna. The content of both missives was essentially the same. It was a factual, dispassionate report of events taking place at the University of San Francisco. After a brief account of the commotion caused by the president's action, he advised the cardinals: "The SII is the only part of USF which is in full and wholehearted compliance with *Ex Corde Ecclesiae*. And it is precisely for this reason that so many Jesuits, especially in the Theology Department, have been hostile to it for all of its 25 years' existence." He was then quick to add that not all members of the society shared such hostility, particularly not "the five academically qualified Jesuit priests, who wanted to come to teach in the SII, but were forbidden do so by their own provincials or by the California provincial— even though they had no other assignments!"

He further reported that the present crisis had impelled him to seek the advice of the archbishop of San Francisco, Most Reverend William Levada, "who is sympathetic with the SII". Prudently, the archbishop thought that because the action on the part of the president "was so precipitous, it might be possible to restore the SII by working within the University community". Father Fessio also brought up the matter with the California provincial, asking him to intervene in support of the seven stated policies needed to restore and protect the Institute. Despite being sympathetic and pleasant, the provincial was not inclined to become involved.

Father Fessio stressed to both cardinals that although he had been fired from the directorship and was no longer a teacher at the university, he thought it would be "a serious loss for the Church and the University itself if the SII [were] allowed to disappear (in substance if not in name)." Then, because of the shortage of time, he confessed he was under considerable pressure to know, "should

---

[3] See Gerald V. Bradley, *Church-State Relationships in America* (Santa Barbara, Calif.: Greenwood Press, 1987).

the solution *ad intra* fail", what further step he should take. He was seriously considering bringing the matter to the attention of Father General Kolvenbach, asking him, "in virtue of the fourth vow of special service to the Holy See, to restore the SII and provide it with the necessary safeguards against unwarranted attacks on it". But past experience did not incline him to be hopeful in this venture. In summing up the situation, he reminded his correspondents:

> The SII faculty has labored for 25 years to explain and defend the Magisterium, and the teachings of John Paul II in particular. This is in fact the reason why they have aroused so much hostility from the Theology Department, especially its Jesuit members. The essence of the appeal would be: Holy Father, these men and women have served and defended you faithfully for 25 years: *tantum dic verbo et sanabitur* ["only say the word and it shall be healed"].

He concluded the letters by saying that he would be in Rome the following week for the annual meeting of the directors of the Lubac–Balthasar–Speyr Association and that if either one of them would also be present, he would appreciate their counsel.

Two week weeks later, on Monday, February 26, he had a half-hour meeting with Father Kolvenbach in the curia of the Jesuit Generalate in Rome. In an email message to the core members of the Institute faculty, Father Fessio wrote that the meeting was "very cordial, as I knew it would be". He proceeded to inform them that the general had conferred with Cardinal Ratzinger about the crisis and had written letters to the California provincial, Father Thomas Smolich, and to Archbishop Levada expressing "his desire that the SII be maintained according to its original principles". The general then told Father Fessio that the assistant to the general for the United States was presently in the States and would be speaking personally with Father Smolich about the problem. Father Fessio warned the general that Father Privett had claimed he intended to maintain the SII as it had been but in fact clearly intended to change it.

> [He] then asked me if I had a concrete proposal. I said I did: the SII is something that transcends USF and the California Province; [Father General] should make it clear that this is a work of the Society of Jesus, insist that the status quo ante be restored, and that the SII be protected against further attempts to undermine it.
>
> He said that the President is under the authority of the Board of

Trustees. I replied that he is also under the vow of obedience, as are the Jesuit Board members.

He went on to say that it was unfortunate that the six faculty members resigned, suggesting that had they remained they could have helped the Institute retain its integrity. To this Father Fessio said, "I explained to him why they had to resign." He countered that their number was small compared to the seventeen members on the faculty. Father Fessio recalled that this remark, along with a few others like it, surprised him, for it revealed how cognizant the general was of intricate details concerning the Institute. But he answered that five of the faculty members who retired "had eighty years of experience between them and . . . taught 85 to 90% of the classes", though as he confessed, "[t]hat was a guess." At this, the general changed the subject. "He asked if an independent program could be set up outside the university. I said it could; that it would have some advantages, but more disadvantages." The two concluded their conversation with Father Fessio reiterating the reason why there was such a sharp division between the Institute and its adversaries. Then, "I argued the SII had a right to exist according to its founding principles." Finally, "I said that I was reluctant to ask him to discipline a fellow Jesuit, but that the disappointment of the one person had to be weighed against the good of so many students, the Church, the Society of Jesus, and the University itself." On that note, the meeting ended.

Father Fessio had not long been back in his cramped office with a futon when he received a letter, dated March 5, from the provincial, Father Tom Smolich. It was nicely crafted, considerate, containing three marked points. After advising him that he and the general's assistant had met and discussed the Institute business, he continued: "Through [the assistant], Father General has communicated his perspective to me, and I have weighed all of this before responding to you." Point one: Founding principles, he contested, are important, but all institutions evolve and there is a danger in becoming static in the process of growth and change. "While clearly the SII will change in response to new leadership, etc.", he wrote, "as far as I can tell, there is nothing proposed that will violate its founding principles." Point two: This being the case, there is no reason for a religious superior to become involved in a case that has been decided by the president and affirmed by the university trustees. Point three: The decision has been made. The president "is not interested in talking with you about restoring the SII as it was, and I believe he is prepared to weather the storm whatever complications develop from his decision." So, in other words, Fessio should be realistic: come to terms with what is, what has evolved. It must have been the day after he received the letter from the provincial, March 9, that Father Fessio faxed the letter, along with his comments and further suggestions, to Cardinal Ratzinger.

He began his commentary by taking strong exception to the provincial's assertion that "there is nothing proposed that will violate [the SII's] founding principles." This statement elicited a strong retort: "*Everyone* involved in establishing and implementing those principles knows this is entirely false, the very opposite of the truth." After recounting the general's favorable statements about the Institute to the conversation the cardinal had had with him, and after expressing his gratitude for his consideration, Father Fessio took up the provincial's claim that dismantling the Institute is "consistent" with "respect[ing] the Institute's theological and pastoral contribution to the Church". This assertion, coupled with Father Privett's own refusal to discuss the matter despite his penchant for "dialogue", led him to a grim observation about the attitude "typical of the new *modus operandi* of the Society of Jesus: say one thing while doing precisely the opposite". He expounded on this point: "There is a chasm between what the SII has been and what it is now becoming. Simply put: the SII has publicly supported the Magisterium; it is now overseen by those who dissent from the Magisterium; its liturgies were celebrated by priests who followed the Church's liturgical regulations; it will now be celebrated by priests who ignore or abuse them." He had already given examples aplenty of theological abuse, and then, after citing scandals within campus ministry, he continued: "It is now clear that the only way the SII can be saved—for the good of its future students, of the university, and of Catholic higher education in the U.S.—is if the Holy Father himself requires prompt and specific action by Father Kolvenbach. Essentially, all the Holy Father has to say is: *Sit ut erat* [Let it be as it was]. So once again I presume upon your goodness and generosity." After making suggestions on what could be done before the meeting of the university board of trustees on March 23—that is, almost

two weeks from the date Cardinal Ratzinger received this appeal—
he asserted that, all evidence seemingly to the contrary, he was not
asking for anything extraordinary. To prove his point, he cited *Ex-
posit Debitum*, the sixteenth-century papal bull proclaiming the Jesuit
order's validity,[4] and underlined the part dealing with the special
fourth vow Jesuits were expected to take "to carry out whatever
the present and future Roman pontiffs may order which pertains
to the progress of souls and the propagation of the faith". Finally,
he reminded the cardinal that *Ex Corde Ecclesiae* had been published
in 1991, and after some ten years of struggle between Rome and
American Catholic university presidents, no major Catholic university had yet enforced it. On the contrary, it has been met with
quiet defiance. Conclusion: "If the widely publicized suppression
of the SII is allowed to stand, [*Ex Corde Ecclesiae*] will not only be un-
enforced; it will be unenforceable." Finally: "Cardinal Schönborn
has called me and said he would be speaking with you again about
the SII. We continue to pray with Esther: 'Hear the voice of the
despairing and save us from the hands of evildoers.'"

On Friday, March 16, 2001, at a private meeting, Cardinal Ratzinger
presented the Holy Father with an appeal letter to restore the Saint
Ignatius Institute. Cardinal Schönborn then advised Father Fessio
that the Holy Father accepted the appeal and was now in the process of commissioning the Congregation for Catholic Education to
implement the specified policies requested in the appeal. The eagles
were readying themselves to perch! He cautioned Father Fessio to
keep the matter as much out of the press as possible, although the
following points could be mentioned: (1) Cardinals Ratzinger and
Schönborn had presented an appeal to the Holy Father on behalf of
the SII, (2) the Holy Father granted the appeal, and (3) the appeal
requested the restoration and the strengthening of the SII according
to *Ex Corde Ecclesiae*. With mixed emotions, four days later, Tuesday, March 20, Father Fessio fired off a message to his friend "dear
Christoph" telling him that the trustees' meeting was scheduled
to take place March 23 and that if there were not enough time to
speak to the general, the provincial, and the university trustees before the meeting, it would be difficult to restore the Institute, even
if the Holy Father desires it. Moreover, incoming and continuing

---

[4] Approved by Julius III, July 21, 1550, and known also as *Formula Instituti* no. 3.

students soon have to make decisions about the upcoming year, not to mention tuition deposits. The trustees would not meet again for three months. Time is of the essence. He received an immediate reply basically telling him to handle the situation in the way he thought best. The following day, Wednesday, Father Fessio fired off an email to the general, asking to speak to him about the papal intervention, and he soon had a conversation with Mr. Dominic Tarantino, the chairman of the board of trustees. Fifteen minutes on the telephone is already a long time spent for Father Fessio, but this conversation lasted three hours! He later informed Cardinal Schönborn that he was impressed by Mr. Tarantino: "a good man, a good Catholic, but like many successful businessmen, he doesn't understand what is at issue here." The chairman wanted to find a solution without publicizing that the Holy Father had requested it, saying he would like to have something more substantial than just Father Fessio's reflections to present to the board. Father then requested that the cardinal speak with him. Cardinal Schönborn invited Mr. Tarantino to call him and hear his cautious opinion, but the chairman predicted that a telephone conversation would not be sufficient or satisfactory. He was obviously getting advice from a canon lawyer.

On the previous Sunday—March 18—there had been another maelstrom. It was a full-page ad in the weekend edition of the *San Francisco Chronicle* reading: "Save Liberal Education; Save Saint Ignatius Institute". At the bottom: "Paid for by Friends of the Saint Ignatius Institute". It began:

> We, the undersigned, protest actions which we believe have seriously damaged one of our nation's premier Great Books programs. . . .
> We further believe that the effective gutting of one of the country's finest centers of Catholic liberal education by administrators at the University of San Francisco (USF) teaches a sad lesson about the growing exclusion from our colleges and universities of even the most fair-minded traditional religious educators.

It was signed by such notables as George Weigel, Robert George, Michael Novak, Deal Hudson, Richard John Neuhaus, Stanley Kurtz, Robert Royal, and a number of others, as well as representatives from Princeton, Notre Dame, University of Texas, University of California at Berkeley, Valparaiso, University of Chicago, and a number of important institutes and journals. William Bennett, the Secretary of Education under President Reagan from 1985 to 1988, also identified with the group, which was composed of secularists, Catholics, Protestants, and Jews alike. After praising the "the award-winning Great Books program" that had been "a model[,] blending Catholic education and liberal learning" and "exposed its students to all points of view, secular and religious, while emphasizing traditional Catholic theology", the protestors bemoaned the fact that its directors had been summarily dismissed. Petitioning the USF trustees "to rehire the fired administrators and to return the Saint Ignatius Institute to its former status", they rounded off their protest by asserting that the actions of President Stephen A. Privett, S.J., "grossly violate USF's professed commitment to diversity".

One of the most articulate members of the group was Stanley Kurtz, a fellow of the Hudson Institute, who told reporters that this seemingly isolated action on the part of Father Privett had "broad implications for academics". A March 20 article in the *Washington Times* recapitulated the Institute drama for a national audience, finishing with a few observations from Kurtz.[5] "To me," he explained, "this is a question of liberal education, one that truly represents all thought." Father Privett "doesn't want this program to exist as a coherent, alternative theological voice for the students. He is trying to get rid of that alternative voice." (In the months to come, as the SII problem became more of a media event, Kurtz would go on to write a number of articles on this same subject.) Others quoted in this same *Washington Times* piece had sharper words for the president. Winfield Myers, senior editor at the Intercollegiate Studies Institute—today director of the Middle East Forum's *Campus Watch*—called the reform "a blow against curricular integrity, intellectual honesty and tradition" and "a slap in the face of *Ex Corde Ecclesiae*", since the SII had served both as "a haven for students interested in a rigorous liberal arts education" and as a support for "the mission of the Church in higher education". The author also briefly mentioned that the SII's old guard had reached out to the Vatican, but did not go into detail. The university board would meet at the end of the week, as the article relayed, but clearly Myers' and Kurtz'

---

[5] Andrea Billups, "USF Trustees Urged to Ax President's Reorganization", *Washington Times*, March 20, 2001, A3.

criticisms—though probably accurate—were not quite designed to butter up the trustees.

On March 22, Father Fessio again had recourse to Cardinal Ratzinger, telling him the board meeting was scheduled for the following day and advising him that the chairman said the board needed word from "an official channel", that is, from Archbishop Levada, who was out of town and could not be reached by telephone. Before a response could arrive, the 23rd came—a Friday. A few hours before Mr. Tarantino would call the group to order, Father Fessio addressed a fax message to Father General Peter-Hans Kolvenbach. Mixed with a modicum of confidence and a maximum of desperation, he began: "I'm sure you must know by now that the appeal to the Holy Father on behalf of the Saint Ignatius Institute has been granted and transmitted to the Congregation for Catholic Education." He then proceeded to inform his major superior that he had spoken with Mr. Tarantino, who agreed it would be to the best interest of the university and the Society that restoration of the Institute be done "quietly and quickly". Understandably, however, the chairman would not be able to recommend some definite action until he had received official verification that the appeal had been granted. "We [sic] are committed to working cooperatively with the President and the members of the Board", he wrote. "But the longer it takes for them to be notified, the more embarrassing, even humiliating it will be for them to implement" the papal directive to reinstate the Saint Ignatius Institute. He concluded his message by informing the general that the board would be meeting that very day at 10 A.M. (7 P.M. Rome time), that is, in less than two hours. And then: "I believe if you, or [the American assistant] in your name, simply communicate to Father Privett or Mr. Tarantino that the Holy Father has granted the appeal, they will be able to resolve the crisis in a manner which will put the best face on this, saving embarrassment for themselves and the Society." He signed off by informing the general that "even during the meeting", he or his assistant could telephone a particular sympathetic third party whose telephone would be ready to receive such a message during the course of the meeting. The call never came. Today one might wonder if the old country western song "When the Phone Don't Ring It'll Be Me" was one of the top ten tunes in Rome at the time. Idle speculation.

The board was made up of forty members, fourteen of whom were Jesuits, many of whose names have already appeared in this chronicle. On this occasion, since a number of lay members had absented themselves—not necessarily because of the agenda—the total number in attendance was thirty-two. The chairman began by announcing that the Vatican Congregation for Catholic Education would review the papal intervention regarding the Institute for its conformity with both canon and civil law. Father Privett informed the group that a canon lawyer had judged that two of the seven items in the Minimum Policies declaration violated canon law; one violated civil law. The canon lawyer advised that the board should not act until it received an authentic document issued through official channels. One Jesuit board member, the president of the Weston School of Theology, instructed the others that what Father Fessio had done was a direct violation of the rules of the Society of Jesus. Of course, this was a false judgment, because Father Fessio had spoken first with his provincial and then with the general; when each refused to grant his request, he told them he would exercise his right as a Jesuit to appeal to a higher superior. Both the general and the provincial agreed Father Fessio was not disobedient. One influential Jesuit board member said the situation was like the U.S. Energy Department giving directions to the U.S. State Department, but in reality the step Father Fessio had taken was more like the Energy Department making a request to the president through the secretary of state, which was a reasonable and proper way to act. This board member also urged Father Privett to keep in touch with Archbishop Giuseppe Pittau, the Jesuit secretary of the Congregation for Education, who could be a close ally. The meeting ended with the board voting 30-2 in support of the president's decision regarding the Institute, giving "full confidence to its new director".

The following day, Father Fessio finally received a reply from the general thanking him for the fax, adding: "I could not communicate anything to the Board of Trustees at USF because I have heard nothing from the Congregation." As it turns out, on the day of the meeting, Father Kolvenbach's assistant had emailed a message to the California provincial telling him the general did not want him to silence Father Fessio after that initial *Washington Times* article, and the message was forwarded to Father Privett, who received it before the board meeting was called to order. The general was quoted as having said: "Let [Father Fessio] go to the press. It will be very counterproductive for him. If the U.S. college and university presidents see that the Vatican is trying to impose things from Rome, the *Ex Corde* norms will go up in smoke." That communiqué may have been from his hand, but it was not his voice, not his style. Father Kolvenbach's assistant further reported that the Vatican secretary of state, Angelo Cardinal Sodano, who was also the dean of the College of Cardinals, had asked Archbishop Pittau for information on the SII case, but since the archbishop had misplaced Father Privett's question-and-answer sheet, he wanted another copy to send to the cardinal. There was no mention, of course, of the SII professors' open letter. "Pittau mentioned that Schönborn and Ratzinger had submitted something," the assistant continued, "but [he] did not give any specifics. In the end [Archbishop Pittau] said there was nothing to worry about." He continued the message by telling the provincial that Father Fessio "has no right to say anything to the Board of Trustees without a written statement from the Pope. A letter from Cardinal Ratzinger is not sufficient." Finally, the general was quoted: "The University should not give [Father Fessio] a finger of attention without a written document. (Anything from the Pope will come first to Father General anyway.)"

That Sunday, March 25, there arrived the first gales of a new media storm. An account of the Vatican's emerging role in the Saint Ignatius Institute crisis appeared in the *Washington Times*, entitled "Pope Intervenes in San Francisco Campus Dispute".[6] The reporter argued that the intervention on the part of the Vatican was especially newsworthy because it is "believed Rome's first action to uphold orthodoxy on a Roman Catholic campus since the bishops legislated the policy" contained in *Ex Corde Ecclesiae*. Speaking for the university, however, the provost James Wiser said he knew of no such directive. But the same article quoted Father Fessio as well: "I am still hopeful that [USF] is a university where diversity can allow different voices to prevail and there might be a way to resolve this problem internally." He then clarified what precisely "internal resolution" meant in this case: "The Catholic-related university, loyal to the church and academic freedom, wants to make its own

---

[6] *Washington Times*, March 25, 2001.

decision—without being forced by Rome." Father Fessio's quotes in the article were factual and unemotional.

Two days later (March 27), a follow-up article appeared in the *Times'* Tuesday edition called "Jesuit School Chief: No Rift with Vatican",[7] and it caused some concern at the university, though it rehashed many of the same claims. "We have heard absolutely nothing" about a papal letter concerning the Institute, the president was quoted as saying. "Nobody has heard anything from any ecclesiastical authorities." And even if we did, Father Privett contended, "free-lance messages, even if they are from Rome, have no official standing", as his canon lawyer had advised him. Father Fessio was also quoted: "An appeal has been made through the proper channels, and the pope is aware of the situation." But this same news echoed in another corner of the media world, this time with stronger words from the president. On March 28, the *San Francisco Chronicle* published a long piece in which Father Privett accused Father Fessio and his cohorts of using "McCarthyite" tactics to advance a losing cause.[8] He assured the author that he "has checked with his Jesuit superiors and found no indication that Rome has intervened in the bitter theological dispute". Speaking of his adversary, the president predicted matter-of-factly that "he'll produce no document" to advance his cause.

The next day, even the *Catholic News Service* took up the story and confirmed some of Father Privett's statements.[9] As the article relayed, "Jesuit officials in Rome said there is no indication that the Vatican has been or will be involved in the controversy over the Saint Ignatius Institute at the Jesuit-run University of San Francisco." However, after reporting Father Fessio's claim that Cardinal Ratzinger had appealed to the pope to intervene, the article disclosed, "[Father Kolvenbach's assistant] said that as of March 29, officials at the Jesuit headquarters in Rome had no indication that the Vatican was considering Father Fessio's request." The assistant had added: "It would be very unusual for the Vatican to get in-

[7] *Washington Times*, March 27, 2001.

[8] Don Lattin and Elizabeth Fernandez, "Pope's Help Sought in Theology Clash at USF—School Protests over Orthodox Institute", *San Francisco Chronicle*, March 28, 2001.

[9] Cindy Wooden, "Officials: Vatican Won't Be Involved in San Francisco Controversy", *Catholic News Service*, March 29, 2001.

volved in the matter without informing the Jesuits." Furthermore:
"The Jesuit superior general's position is that the matter must be
resolved locally. He has encouraged them [sic] however, to protect
and maintain the unique character of the institute, which they are
trying to do." The head of the university section of the Congregation for Catholic Education, Msgr. Walter Edyvean, for whom
Father Fessio had the highest respect, "would not comment on the
San Francisco situation".

Father Privett had this last news item—in edited form—printed
and distributed to the university community.

23

THE CARDINALS WEIGH IN

Rome is always an exciting place to be, but on April 4-5, 2001, less than two weeks after the board meeting at the University of San Francisco sealed the fate of the Saint Ignatius Institute, the exhilaration was centered around the Gregorian University, which was celebrating its 450th birthday. On April 6, the pontifical institution's two thousand or more students and faculty members joggled alongside cardinals, bishops, diplomats, ambassadors, and even the president of Argentina to find the optimum place for hearing Pope John Paul II put into words what the celebration meant to him: gratitude for what the university had achieved in the past and the need for its renewal in the present so as to assure fidelity to its original mission in the future. The pope began his discourse by reminding his audience what Saint Ignatius had wanted the university to be: a center of studies, open to all, "at work in Rome, next to the Vicar of Christ, linked to him by close bonds of fidelity, and at the service of the Churches in every part of the world". Its mission was to promote "reasoned and systematic reflection on the faith in order to foster the correct preaching of the Gospel, and the cause of Catholic unity in a social context marked by serious divisions and troubling seeds of disintegration". He then addressed the Jesuits who operated the university: "Given the challenges of today's society, this is the moment for a courageous relaunching of your institution." Expanding on this theme, he continued: "It is the occasion for reconfirming a total fidelity to the Ignatian insight and for undertaking a courageous renewal, so that the memory of the past will not be limited to contemplation of what was done before, but become a commitment in the present and prophecy for the future." He made two proposals for realizing this objective, and it would almost seem—if one did not know better—that he had taken a page from the mission statement of the Saint Ignatius Institute to develop the primary item. "First of all, complete fidelity to the Magisterium. This is a condition that, as can be seen from your centuries-old experience, does not stifle but fosters even more the ecclesial service of theological research and of teaching."[1] The second pertained more to the specific teaching of future professors of theology, so that they may be faithful to the Church's Magisterium.

After the pope's exhortation, Father Jacques Servais, the director of the Casa Balthasar, ran into Father Kolvenbach quite by chance. In an email to Father Fessio, Father Servais reported that the general seemed weary and not at all inclined to take on any confrontation. However, Father Kolvenbach had injected the subject of the Institute into their small talk, saying that he appreciated all that the president had been doing to assure its present and future integrity. At the same time, the general confessed that he regretted the long negotiations to reach an agreed-upon conclusion. Father Fessio's reaction was predictable. Writing to Cardinal Schönborn, he expressed his wonder about who was responsible for these "long negotiations". It was certainly not "we here and the two cardinals who made the request!" But more to the point: "The Holy Father has granted the request for the 'immediate implementation' by the [Council of Catholic Education (CCE)] of the seven specific policies; that request has been transmitted to the CCE: What's to negotiate?" In a letter dated January 3, 2002—that is, about one year after the firing of Mr. Galten and Mr. Hamlon—to Cardinal Zenon Grocholewski, the prefect of the CCE, five core members of the Institute registered, among other matters, their disappointment at the method used in resolving the SII grievance. On February 18, the prefect together with his assistant, Archbishop Pittau—who apparently was the chief respondent—addressed their reply to Professor Thomas Cavanaugh, the first name signed on the grievance. The archbishop began by informing Professor Cavanaugh that this letter was really a reply to all the letters the core professors had mailed to the CCE during the past year. He then instructed his correspondent that, according to Roman curial practice, when the pope issues a decree to be followed—apart from magisterial matters—it is

[1] Address of Pope John Paul II to the Administration, Faculty, Students, and Staff of the Pontifical Gregorian University, April 6, 2001.

automatically forwarded to the dicastery whose business it is to deal with the subject. This was the reason why the pope's decree concerning the Institute was sent to the CCE for study. Moreover, he wrote that canon law legislates that after this process is completed, the matter should be referred to the local bishop for more in-depth investigation. This principle was reiterated in the apostolic constitution *Ex Corde Ecclesiae*, which states, "If problems should arise concerning [the] Catholic character [of a university], the local Bishop is to take the initiatives necessary to resolve the matter, working with the competent university authorities in accordance with established procedures and, if necessary, with the help of the Holy See."[2] In his letter to Dr. Cavanaugh, to which we shall return at the end of this chapter, the archbishop could have suggested to his correspondent that Father Fessio must be aware of this policy. And given the validity of this premise, the archbishop's judgment was as reasonable as it was correct. We recounted earlier in this study that in 1987 the pope had signed Father Fessio's request for setting up an international novitiate in Rome, but then after "long negotiations", the secretary of state, Cardinal Casaroli, blocked it in 1991. But the pope had signed it! Yes, but the pope is not a dictator. Fuller investigation at the time showed that the project would not be advantageous to the Holy See. The archbishop further wrote that he was most gracious to Dr. Cavanaugh and his cohorts for their letter because it gave him the opportunity to clarify the position of the CCE. At the same time, others in Rome lamented that the SII debacle had been leaked to the press.

Picking up on this last point, Father Fessio reminded the SII team—the core members and staff of the former Institute—what the sources and circumstances of that leakage were. The cardinal's letter had been delivered to the pope on March 16. Father President Privett learned about the papal intervention soon afterward and gave a report about its contents to the chairman of the board of trustees. Exactly one week later, the chairman in turn advised the assembled board that the CCE would be reviewing the case. At the same meeting, Father Privett informed those present that both his canonist and Archbishop Levada had counseled him to "go slow", and the chairman informed the members that no action would be taken

---

[2] *Ex Corde Ecclesiae*, General Norms, 5:2.

until the board received an authenticated document through official channels. Father President then informed the group that it would take a long time—months or more—for closure. After the meeting, he was quoted in the press, which had begun to investigate rumors, saying that there was "no indication" from "anyone" that such an intervention on the part of Rome existed. Later, he learned that the policy matter could not be denied but that nevertheless, thanks to the cooperation of Archbishop Pittau, the Jesuits in Rome were not expecting any Vatican action. At this juncture, the Fessio team expressed the desire to work cooperatively with the university administration. The university refused. Archbishop Levada likewise counseled letting the process take its course. By that date, there could be no redress without its becoming publically known. And what about the president? The CCE encouraged him to settle the matter in consultation with Archbishop Levada, who had absolutely no authority over the university. It was precisely for that reason the two cardinals in their appeal to the Holy Father had asked him "to commission the Congregation for Catholic Education to work directly with Father Kolvenbach".

The year rolled on. Was legal action an alternative? The answer to that question begs background. Early in February 2001, a year prior, the four law professors from whom Father Fessio had requested comments on the Minimum Policies proposal had composed a four-page typed letter addressed to Cardinal Ratzinger broaching their collective opinion on the matter. "Given the limited time and the information given to us," they concluded, "we cannot state with any certainty what the civil law implications of a requirement like [the Minimum Policies] would be." They cautiously asserted that nothing would prevent a request from being made in this regard. However, there was still one question begging for an answer: To what degree are "the affairs at a Jesuit University [still] 'Church' affairs"? "Because American Catholic Universities have largely turned over control of themselves to lay boards of trustees, they may no longer be considered entities subject to Church control." So, from the earliest days of the conflict, a yellow light of caution had flashed in Rome encouraging a policy to let wrens prey where eagles would hesitate to intrude. Rome had a good memory, and that old fear on the part of many nineteenth-century Americans that the pope would take over the Republic with the help of Catholic immigrants, bizarre as it seems today, spurred them on to prudence. Somehow, there is still something about America that remains a mystery to the Vatican mind. Then in late March 2001, when the SII conflict had captured the attention of the press throughout the country, Professor Robert A. Destro of the Columbus School of Law at the Catholic University of America, wrote an unsolicited letter to Father Fessio suggesting actions to avoid. Destro was recognized as one of the country's chief authorities on Church-related civil law. He granted that the SII case was *the* challenge to *Ex Corde Ecclesiae*. But he discouraged any type of litigation in a civil court, not only because American bishops would not approve, but also because the university has the first amendment right to define its own religious identity. Moreover, courts are loath to intervene in academic disputes, and the cost would be far greater than the friends of the Institute could meet.

Meanwhile, Father Fessio had a number of conferences with his team, chiefly in reference to the seven "Minimum Policies Necessary" for insuring the integrity of the Institute. On April 11, he reminded his two cardinal friends in Rome that the Minimum Policies document was a mission statement drawn up "with great care" and that "any attempt to achieve the goal of restoring and protecting the Institute . . . with other or less specific means will surely fail." Those hostile to the Institute might deny that such is the case. "Is there some way to ensure that Cardinal Grocholewski is aware of this?" he asked. "If he is not, I am afraid all past efforts will have been in vain." Cardinal Ratzinger replied advising Father Fessio to send the statement by fax directly to the cardinal prefect, and this he did that same day. Of course, the letter would first land on the desk of his assistant, Archbishop Pittau, and from there eventually get neatly folded into the "Saint Ignatius Institute" file. There is no record that the cardinal ever responded.

A few days later, on Easter Monday, the president of the Fellowship of Catholic Scholars, Professor Gerald Bradley of Notre Dame, addressed an unsolicited letter to Cardinal Grocholewski. He said that their encounter in Rome during the September Jubilee festivities for university teachers had encouraged him to bring to the cardinal's attention the seriousness of the Saint Ignatius Institute controversy. "Why", he asked, "is the fate of a small institute at one of America's 235 Catholic colleges so important?" And he offered an answer: "Because circumstances such as timing (the eve of application of [*Ex Corde Ecclesiae*] to the U.S.); the involvement of a *Jesuit* educational apostolate; the high visibility of the SII as a redoubt of faithfulness; and the known interest of Cardinal Ratzinger and the Holy Father combine to make the SII *the* test case of ECE in America. There is no choice as to this fact." He then ventured that the enemies of the SII are the enemies of *Ex Corde Ecclesiae*, and the friends of the SII are the constitution's friends. He further insisted that "the friends of ECE did not instigate this conflict. But the conflict is upon us, and the only matter left to the fate of choice is, who shall prevail—the supporters of ECE, or its avowed opponents." At this point, he reaffirmed what he and his three soon-to-be Ave Maria colleagues had addressed in their February letter to Cardinals Ratzinger and Schönborn, namely, "there is *no* civil law impediment to implementation of the policies the Pope has approved." Professor Bradley could state this judgment to Cardinal Grocholewski with confidence because the American bishops recognized him as an expert on and advocate of *Ex Corde Ecclesiae*. In addition to being president of the Fellowship of Catholic Scholars, the professor was also the chair of the Legal Affairs Committee of the Catholic League. At the 1999 meeting of the National Council of Catholic Bishops, he was formally singled out by Cardinal Bevilacqua as having given the bishops significant help in passing *An Application of Ex Corde Ecclesiae in the United States*, which took a stand contrary to the memorandum set out to guide the policy of Jesuit universities.[3] Moreover, he had led a consortium of expert lawyers "who have pledged to represent, *pro bono*, any Catholic college which implements *Ex Corde Ecclesiae*, should that faithfulness cause public authority to discriminate against the faithful school". Professor Bradley completed this part of his letter with a statement that should have captured the attention of Cardinal Grocholewski and his assistant, Archbishop Pittau: "I would organize a similar legal team to aid USF, should the need arise." He then succinctly summarized his convictions regarding the Saint Ignatius Institute case:

---

[3] Daniel Wuerl, "Fellowship of Catholic Scholars", *L'Osservatore Romano*, February 2, 1978, 11; Gerald V. Bradley, *Church-State Relationships in America* (Santa Barbara, Calif.: Greenwood Press, 1987).

Nothing less than the *full* measure of the policies approved by the Holy Father will do. Why? Because the enemies of the SII do not accept the principles of Catholic higher education as articulated in *Ex Corde Ecclesiae*, and as promulgated in the Code of Canon Law. They will exploit every gap, weakness, and loose end to undermine the intention and spirit of any negotiated or tapered-down resolution. They must be made to comply fully with the intentions of the Pope, and that can only be done by obliging them, in conscience, to adhere to the letter of the Minimum Policies Necessary. And, given that the appeal to the Pope is known to have been granted, anything less than the full measure will now be claimed as a victory by the enemies of the SII. Then the test case will have been lost.

The letter shows that there was certainly an interest, if not agreement, among committed Catholic American jurists on how to handle what was becoming a far more important matter than the squabble between Jesuits at USF. Father Fessio, however, in spite of his quixotic forays, was basically a realist, and so he easily concluded that for him to bring a civil suit against the university was not a hands-on, workable way to achieve what would be needed to restore the SII. If others chose to do so, that would be fine; he would cooperate.

Snail-like spring turned into summer 2002. Classes ended; it was like the calm before the storm. Around the first day of July, Archbishop Levada contacted Father Fessio saying that he would like to talk with any one of the core members of the former Institute faculty. This news called for an emergency coming together of the team, which met for an extended time on July 5. Professor Michael Torre was chosen to represent the group with the archbishop scheduled for the following day. Dr. Torre had been the chief composer of the January 29 letter to the president, a document whose effects were still being felt on both sides of the Atlantic. The initial encounter between the two was warm and friendly. Then, after obtaining answers from the archbishop to such questions as What is your role? Mediator? Implementer? How do you understand the line of authority: pope through the CCE; general, president, Jesuit trustees, provincial? What do you know about what went from the CCE to the Jesuit general?, Torre discussed the principles contained in the Minimum Policies document, a copy of which had been mailed earlier to the archbishop. He then stressed the fact that the contents of the appeal letter, signed by Cardinals Ratzinger and Schönborn and approved by the pope on March 16, were not exclusively those of Father Fessio. It had been composed in consultation with the core faculty members and then affirmed by the two cardinals. It prescribed the seven "minimum policies necessary" that these faculty members believed were essential for defining the Institute. He further explained the faculty members believed these fundamental and paramount characteristics of the Institute had been explicitly stated in the letter delivered to the pope. Finally, Torre proceeded to explain to the archbishop that, though some non-essential accommodations could be negotiated, the substance of the document had to be maintained, if only for the integrity of the two cardinals. This fact did not mean that no compromises could be made with the university in order to reconstruct the Institute. There was what was essential and what was accidental. For example, the members could be open to a compromise regarding a reappointment of the director and assistant director by the SII board. But there could be no bargaining on what was essential to the nature of the Institute. Then there was the matter of the Institute's future composition within the structure of the university, and here Father Fessio had done considerable homework in finding a model. His research led him to study the construction of the Hoover Institution at Stanford University. As it turns out, many of the procedures used in that organization, particularly their advisory board's prudent way of appointing a director, could serve as a model for another SII-like entity at some Jesuit university in the future.

Passing on to another subject, Professor Torre assured the archbishop that the faculty was aware of his earlier statement: "Give the president's mandate a chance. How do you know it will not work?" If this was still his point of view, there was no advantage in continuing the dialogue. The professor then quietly but firmly stated: "All those most closely involved with the SII and who value it for what it has been for over 25 years—students, alumni, parents, advisory board, benefactors, friends, core faculty—are convinced what Father Privett has done will substantially alter the SII." As it had begun, the meeting ended with expressions of cordiality and respect.

On July 17, Archbishop Levada notified Father Fessio by mail that the Congregation of Catholic Education had asked him to be the "outside facilitator" whose function would be to jump-start "a more serene dialogue" in the wake of President Privett's reorganization of the Saint Ignatius Institute. He invited him to participate in this assignment, joining four other clerics he had already selected for the same purpose: Reverend Gerald D. Coleman, S.S., the president/rector of St. Patrick's Seminary in Menlo Park and (as we have already seen) a speaker at the 1978 *Humanae Vitae* symposium; Reverend Antoninus Wall, O.P., acting president of the Dominican School of Philosophy and Theology in Berkeley; Brother Mel Anderson, F.S.C., former president of St. Mary's College in Moraga; and Reverend Milton Walsh, academic vice president at St. Patrick's Seminary. Their function was to gather data from interviews with persons familiar with the SII case, later synthesizing it all into a final report to be sent to the CCE. In addition to this foursome, there were three Jesuits slated to be interviewed, and their input would be added to that of a number of others in order to compose the final synthesis to be submitted to the CCE in Rome. The Jesuits were two members of the Theology Department and the rector of the USF Jesuit community, who was also a member of the board of trustees and a future associate of a campus ministry program. The archbishop ended his letter saying that in his conversation with Father Privett, the president "expressed his hope that the process called for by the Congregation of Catholic Education would not contribute to a renewal of a spirit of contention, which has marked many of the reports of the differences of opinion that have surrounded this matter." For this reason, he expressed his hope "that the present process will be able to make a positive contribution to the esteem in which the University of San Francisco and its Saint Ignatius Institute are held." The archbishop's final report was issued on September 21, 2001.[4]

After a few weeks, the archbishop laid out his recommendations for the Institute at a two-hour meeting. He began by stressing the point that he "was asked by the CCE to facilitate a dialogue". As soon as Father Fessio heard these words, he groaned inside, as he explained in a letter to Cardinal Ratzinger: "If that was all he was asked to do, he has done it. But this is not at all what was requested

---

[4] Victoria Leon Guerrero, "Ex-Director of SII Awarded", *Foghorn*, September 29, 2001.

in the appeal to the Holy Father." By the end of the meeting, he could say with decision: "It is clear that there is no intent on the part of the archbishop to maintain the integrity of the SII." And why should there be? The problem was an in-house Jesuit matter; prudence required the archbishop to refrain from acknowledging that the emperor was wearing no clothes.

The group continued their dialogue, willfully ignoring the elephant sitting there poised among them. Afterward, Professor Torre sat in his office typing out a letter of thanks to the archbishop for meeting with him. After gracious sentences of praise eloquently expressed, with characteristic clarity and precision, the professor then stated the position of the core faculty members, responding to each of the advisory group's four recommendations. Principally, he focused on the faculty members' appeal "personally supported by Cardinals and the Holy Father himself". He admitted:

> We realize full well that your charge was not, and could not be, the task of enforcing the appeal. We also realize that the goal your team has set—of creating understanding and good will—can indeed aid in helping to carry it out. We do not regard a participation in the dialogue you are attempting to create as opposed to that appeal; on the contrary, it can act in synergy with it. We regard the two, however, as separate. We do not think this dialogue can effect our return to the program, and we will continue to rely upon the substance of the appeal in order to protect and strengthen the Institute and thus to effect our return.

On December 7 (Pearl Harbor Day), 2001, Cardinal Schönborn received a letter—in English—from Cardinal Grocholewski, co-signed by Archbishop Pittau, bringing him up to date on the progress that Archbishop Levada was making in his investigation. Cardinal Ratzinger received a copy as well. "We are grateful for your concern for this Institute", they assured him, "and are in agreement with you as to its importance in setting a standard for maintaining the Catholic identity of educational institutions in the United States." They then reminded Cardinal Schönborn that Archbishop Levada's job description was "to serve as a facilitator between concerned parties and to propose possible solutions", and they let him know they had just written to the archbishop inquiring whether any feasible solutions had been proposed. Both Cardinal Schönborn and

Cardinal Ratzinger expressed disappointment in the letter and recommended the representative core faculty members address a letter to both the prefect and the assistant of the CCE, as well as to Archbishop Levada. This they did on January 3. The letter to the archbishop contained much of the information and requests detailed in Professor Torre's earlier attestation. The longer letter to Cardinal Grocholewski and Archbishop Pittau was more to the point. After stating that the entire SII community was disappointed in the Levada group's September report, and at the same time showing an understanding of why it was so feeble, the authors repeated the injustice of the president's action and then added:

> But the real problem lies even deeper than this. Despite public statements by university administrators, and despite the ordinary's carefully worded report, everyone involved here knows, Cardinals Ratzinger and Schönborn know, and we believe you also know there are two mutually incompatible views of Catholic education at stake here. We are not interested in making public accusations, for we do not believe that serves the Church. But this is, in our view, precisely the kind of situation where the exercise of authority by Rome can best support local authority beset by understandable pressures. This is why, from the beginning, we supported and relied upon a direct appeal to the Holy Father. We did not think then that the Institute could be preserved in any other way, and our conviction has been confirmed by events.

They concluded by stating their policy so far has been not to respond to strong pressures from the press, since they "believe this problem should be solved internally". At the same time: "Everyone in the Catholic academic community in the U.S. knows what is at stake. And they also know the Holy Father has approved the original appeal to restore the Institute. If the only result is more dialogue, those who overtly or covertly resist the implementation of *Ex Corde Ecclesiae* will feel, with justification, that they need fear no action by the Holy See that would give it any effect." The CCE issued its final decision on January 25, 2002. Designed to please both sides, its content had much in common with what a press release from the Oracle at Delphi might encapsulate, should the Oracle be inclined to go encapsulating anything that goes on in San Francisco. After analyzing the text, Dr. Torre, who was used to reading the complexities and esoterica of Kant, Hegel, and Sartre, commented, "My understanding is that the SII matter is not resolved, but rather that the Congregation is asking all sides to continue the dialogue that was begun last October."[5] Then, with a Nietzschean interpretation, he continued: "I and other former SII faculty members are willing to continue that dialogue, but we doubt that the University is willing to change the new and—we believe—the false direction it wishes to impart to the SII."[6] Archbishop Levada attempted to assure all concerned that "Cardinal Zenon Grocholewski, prefect of the Congregation of Catholic Education, was grateful for the report on the progress of the 'dialog' that I was able to provide during my visit to the Holy See in January, on the occasion of the Plenary Meeting of the Congregation for the Doctrine of the Faith, of which I am a member."[7] Seemingly spurred on by a spirit of optimism, he continued: "The cardinal has asked me to continue my efforts in accord with the role envisioned for the diocesan bishop by the apostolic Constitution Ex Corde Ecclesiae to support the mission, values and goals of the Saint Ignatius Institute at the University of San Francisco."[8] The official press release from the university succinctly stated that the letter from the CCE "supports the University of San Francisco's Saint Ignatius Institute" and "places trust in San Francisco's Archbishop William Levada and University President Father Stephen Privett, S.J."[9] Understandably, the president's reaction was confident and sanguine. "It is clear that the Vatican supports the Saint Ignatius Institute and its new director, Dr. Paul Murphy."[10] As far as the controversy was concerned, "we are grateful that we can finally put this behind us", and he acknowledged gratitude for "the role the congregation has played in helping us do so".[11] Freed from attacks by dissenters and, as a corollary, empowered by ecclesiastical approval, he could declare: "As the congregation makes clear, the task now is to consign all disagreements to the past and to devote our full energy to developing this program into the premier

---

[5] Patrick Joyce, "Vatican Responds to St. Ignatius Institute Dispute", *Catholic San Francisco*, March 8, 2002, 3.

[6] Joyce, "Vatican Responds".

[7] Joyce, "Vatican Responds".

[8] Joyce, "Vatican Responds".

[9] Joyce, "Vatican Responds".

[10] Joyce, "Vatican Responds".

[11] Joyce, "Vatican Responds".

Catholic Great Books program in the country." The stated hope of Father William C. McInnes, his predecessor, to make USF the Harvard of the West pales in comparison to what the victorious president planned for the Saint Ignatius Institute: "[to] expand its voice and realize its hopes of becoming the premier program of its kind in the nation and in the world".[12]

A historian one hundred years from now might be struck by the minutes of the Theology Department meeting that took place on November 16, 1994. This was about the time when John Galten took the reins as the Institute's director from the beleaguered Father Robert Maloney. The minutes record how the members were discussing ways to deal with the Saint Ignatius Institute. On this occasion, the chair, Father Frank Buckley, encouraged the group to keep applying to teach SII courses "until the Department has control". They did, and they prevailed. By January 25, 2002, it was theirs. The cord on the ventilator that had kept the SII alive for over a year, pumping it with rhetorical illusions, was now snapped. Administrators at Catholic colleges throughout the country were now free to ignore the *Ex Corde* mandatum, and at USF, preparations for the coming of Ash Wednesday began with a quiet presentation of *The Vagina Monologues*. In Rome, the eagles were resting. The next chapter will deal with the fate of the wrens.

---

[12] Joyce, "Vatican Responds".

24

CAMPION COLLEGE

On a February night in 2002 shortly after the fate of the Institute became known, Father Fessio picked up the telephone and called John Galten. "John. Let's drive up to Sweetwater and talk about what's happened." The very next morning, there was a rare California snowfall in the Russian River Valley, dusting the higher peaks around the retreat house. The two old friends decided to hike up one of them for a panoramic view of this crisp winter scene. They stood before a landscape that was familiar, yet different. The silence was intense, broken only by a faint birdcall while the whitewash spread before them seemed to hold back something mysterious, unexpected. On their way back, probably along some path where drops of water from the high branches of trees were just beginning to mix with melting snow and drain into patches of the now-visible slush, John stopped and asked: "Father, did you ever think of starting up a new college?" Father Fessio admitted he had certainly played with the idea of beginning an inexpensive, unashamedly Catholic two-year college, a feeder school for Jesuit universities, but the idea had been filed away some place in that old, over-exploited Plato's cave. John now drew it out again. Later on, Father Fessio would charm his auditors by informing them that John's question about starting a new press had been the beginning of Ignatius Press, and that his inquiry about the feasibility of beginning a new college set into motion Campion College.

The sketch plans for Campion were completed on the hike that afternoon. The snow had melted, leaving no trace of its presence, save for the mud that made the tires spin as the Don accompanied by his Sancho sped down a hill, not far from where years earlier he had turned over a jeep. The college would be named after the sixteenth-century English Jesuit martyr Saint Edmund Campion. Like the original Saint Ignatius Institute, it would be built on twin pillars: faith and truth. For two reasons, it would be a junior college. First, experience had taught both men that the first two years in college presented a crisis point in which students often either develop or relinquish their Catholic faith as well as cultivate a respect and desire for the intellectual life. It had further convinced them that the difference between what students learned in the classrooms, in the dorms, and in the general environment of Catholic and non-Catholic colleges tended, with some exceptions, to be minimal. Second, Catholic colleges were more expensive than state schools and many private secular institutions, which placed terrible pressures on families. Why not solve the problem by beginning a two-year junior college where students could take core curriculum classes required for fulfilling a major at a four-year college of their choice, while being immersed in a solid religious environment? There would be a chapel, a food management center, and separate living quarters for male and female students.

The car had scarcely pulled up in front of the Press office when Father Fessio jumped out and began a begging campaign that would allow classes to begin in late August. Two weeks later, a website had been created, and an unsolicited $500,000 donation arrived—just the backing that the administrators of the new Campion College needed. We speed now to the first week of August. Twenty-five students had been accepted for the first class. A makeshift classroom was fitted out and some of the former Institute teachers had volunteered to conduct classes while other teachers were being hired. It was the SII *redivivus*! The two founders had long since devised a statement broadcasting to the world the appearance of "A New College of Catholic Liberal Arts in San Francisco". A blurb accompanying these tidings defined the college's mission: "to provide talented, committed students with the solid formation of an integrated, two-year Catholic liberal arts and great books curriculum". It then expanded on the ways this mission would be achieved by the curriculum and the spiritual and social life of the students. There was more information on the website introducing the president and his assistant and their connection with the former SII at USF. The Campion team had neither time nor money to acquire facilities for the new college, so classes were taught at Taberna, the house across the street from Ignatius Press. Students were housed in several locations, farther away from USF but still in the nearby

Richmond District. Understandably, the proximity to the university, and especially to the Jesuit residence, did not render benevolent some in the Jesuit community. But by August, Father Fessio was already far from the new college where John Galten was serving as president. So let's back up a bit to see what happened to Father Fessio, zooming back to February 18, a day or two after his return from Sweetwater, when he sat down and emailed a letter to his provincial, Father Thomas Smolich, with a copy to Father General Peter Hans Kolvenbach in Rome.

The letter was a remarkably straightforward attestation in which he recorded his deepest feelings with an openness and candor that certainly would have met with the approval of Saint Ignatius. His opening sentences: "I know you and Father General were disappointed when I took the appeal to restore the Saint Ignatius Institute to the Holy Father. At the same time, you both acknowledged that appealing to a higher superior is part of the Society's manner of proceeding and the right of any Jesuit." He then made mention of his disappointments. The first: "Despite the ambiguous language in the letter [addressed to Professor Cavanaugh and the core faculty by Cardinal Grocholewski and Archbishop Pittau], I still believe that the appeal was in fact granted by the Holy Father and transmitted to the Congregation of Catholic Education to be implemented." He further confessed his disappointment that "some Jesuits in positions of authority knowingly made false public statements about the appeal, some of which called my personal integrity into question." Finally, he was cynically amused that USF, which had no room for the SII, did have room for individuals, namely, those mentioned above in his letter to Cardinal Ratzinger, who advocated morals contrary to Catholic teaching. "However," he concluded, "having done all that I believe I was in conscience to do, I am praying to discern what it is Our Lord intends, for me and for others, in all of this."

He then waded into deeper waters. "As you know, I am temperamentally a problem solver. One problem that I have had to address over the years and again now is: how can I support the work of the Society when I disagree fundamentally in how it is carried out in some important aspects." He then began cataloging a number of examples that had caused him problems. He explained that, when he began the Institute, he saw it as contributing to the Jesuit spirit, a mission "to help souls", transmitting to others what God had entrusted to him. It would be a humanism rooted in the Spiritual Exercises and lived out in practice according to the precepts of his model and guide, Henri de Lubac. If he was disillusioned here, he nonetheless found encouragement elsewhere: "From its beginning, the Casa Balthasar experiment functioned as an Ignatian exemplar," he stated, "and it continues to do so. It not only gives a very intense Ignatian formation to young men discerning their vocation, but it has already prepared five or six young men who have entered or will be soon entering the Society." He next reminded his readers how in 2001 Father General asked him if the Institute could not somehow continue independently from the university. The answer was that for the good of the students and of USF, it would be better if the SII were restored to what it was as a distinct program within the university. "Now that is not possible for the foreseeable future", he stated, and so "those who have staffed and supported the Institute in the past are exploring the option of an independent program." With a clear reference to what had taken place at Sweetwater a few days prior, he continued:

> Naturally they are asking my advice and support and I am giving it. However I wanted you to know that my intention is to explore ways of going forward which will complement and support the Society's mission, and even its institutions. (This is not meant to disguise the fact that I remain vigorously opposed to those who publically dissent from the Church's ordinary magisterium. But if our universities want to claim pluralism and celebrate diversity, then there should be room for a civil debate on these issues).

He spent considerable space telling his two major superiors how for some time he and his close associates had been discussing the advantages of a new concept in Catholic higher education: two-year junior colleges, possible feeder schools for Catholic universities. One advantage, among others, was that graduates from a Catholic junior college, having been exposed to doctrinal and moral concepts of the Catholic faith, would be better prepared to enter a pluralistic and secular environment, which in fact is what our colleges have become. They could be "leaven", or at least present another point of view. He ended this letter by admitting he also had other plans in starting such colleges, but "for now I just wanted to inform you of my activities, explain my intention to go forward in a way that

I think will be complementary to the work of the Society, and ask your blessing." Some three weeks later, on March 4, he sent a copy of this letter off to Cardinal Ratzinger, adding two items in the plan he had not included in his letter to the provincial and general. The first was that he was working in close collaboration with the administration of the newly opened Ave Maria College in Ann Arbor, Michigan, for acceptance of credits from Campion. Second, he explained that someday in the future, Campion could possibly be integrated into USF as a semi-autonomous program. This was an eventuality that would certainly please Cardinal Ratzinger, since his CDF office was admittedly concerned about what was being taught in Jesuit institutions around the world. Without mentioning the Stanford–Hoover Institution agreement by name, he succinctly stated: "There are precedents for this at prestigious secular universities."

Meanwhile, such feeble rays of hope and optimism quickly smashed against impediments, leading to disappointment and dismay. The first, while predictable, was more annoying than catastrophic. The Media Relations Department of USF issued an official announcement that served as a press release. It began with the proclamation: "The University of San Francisco is pleased that the Vatican supports both us and the Saint Ignatius Institute [SII] and the leadership of University President Stephen A. Privett, S.J." Furthermore, it declared: "The Congregation of Education expressed its approval of the SII and raised no question about the University's decision to name a new director and to integrate it more thoroughly into the life of the University." Given this fact, "the University of San Francisco is disappointed that the leaders of the newly formed Campion College have chosen to disregard the Congregation's directive." Despite this detriment on the part of those responsible, the public should understand that "USF will not support a program that duplicates its own." It declared that students should be aware of the fact that in California, "they already have the option of studying a Great Books curriculum in the Catholic, humanist tradition at two institutions: at USF in the Saint Ignatius Institute or Thomas Aquinas College in Santa Paula." Parents also should be aware that Campion College is not an accredited institution, implying they would be wasting money by sending their sons and daughters there. Then, after describing the extraordinary advantages USF offers to students who would end up disappointed at Campion, should they imprudently opt to enroll there, the notice terminated with the following statement: "The University of San Francisco is proud of its Saint Ignatius Institute and will continue to devote its energies to developing this program into the premier Catholic Great Books program in the country."

Simultaneous with this announcement, Father Fessio received a letter from the general counsel of the university ordering him to "cease and desist" declaring on the website that Campion College "arose" from the Saint Ignatius Institute. To the lawyer's injunction, Father Fessio responded that the statement described reflected a historic reality and therefore was truthful. At the same time, he admitted the reasonableness of the university's wanting to protect its name and image, and so if the phrase was offensive, he was willing to make a change, "though I do want to indicate in a truthful manner the factual genesis of Campion College". Before responding to other complaints the general counsel had included in her dictate, Father Fessio asked her to allow him to make a few points that might help move toward "an amicable, or at least a civil relationship between USF and Campion College". The style and thinking give a good insight into the character of the commentator. The fact that he wrote his response within just a few hours of receiving the letter indicates that he could count courtroom skill among his many other endowments. He wrote:

> As you know, there is a very strong difference of opinion within the USF community itself about whether the St. Ignatius Institute under its changed leadership has remained faithful to its original purpose and character. Both sides of the dispute have very strong convictions and the dispute has gone well beyond the USF community, reaching to the highest levels of the Catholic Church. So it is no surprise that emotions are strong.

He then stated: "Perhaps paradoxically, I think these strong differences can actually be the basis of a reasonable and civil relationship." He stated that during his tenure as the director of the SII, he regularly took surveys and found that the majority of the students were at USF because of the Institute, and, were it not for the Institute, they would not have been there at all. His conclusion was that, given the differences between the USF and Campion students, it was reasonable to conclude that Campion would draw no prospective student away from USF. But, he wondered if it was not likewise reasonable to suggest that, after matriculating from Campion, a student might want to complete his degree at USF. He proceeded with his argument: "You ask that we 'immediately and permanently desist from claiming to have any connection with SII and USF.' This seems to me overbroad. There is certainly an historical connection" between the two, and he reminded the general counsel that "USF made the decision about the SII and that decision has been a source of great anger and disappointment—as USF must have foreseen it would be." Next, he referred to a statement in the university's recent official publicity blurb, which he judged "false and at least by innuendo defamatory". It was the assertion that "the leaders of Campion College have chosen to disregard the Congregation's directive." Reminding his correspondent that those leaders were John Galten and himself, he wrote: "The letter of the Congregation was written to neither of us, nor are we under any obligation to comply with it. The letter does, however, ask the university administration to collaborate with the other USF parties to the dispute. I have seen no evidence on the part of the USF administration for any genuine collaboration." He continued his apologia by asserting that ever since the controversy with the SII and university became widely broadcast, he has avoided any public comment about the controversy. "But just as you are rightly zealous to protect USF's name and reputation, so John Galten and I are zealous to protect Campion's and our own." Meanwhile, "I have been contacted by one major secular and one Catholic publication. I have told them both I am not going to respond to the allegations made against Campion and me until I have had a chance to seek a peaceful resolution with USF." In conclusion, he repeated that his goal in this latest upheaval was to create "a civil relationship, and I am willing to accommodate reasonable requests."

Less than three weeks after Father Fessio mailed his long February letter to Father Smolich, the provincial sent a reply inviting him to drive down to his office in Los Gatos where the two of them could meet in a more informal manner. Father Fessio remembered the only other occasion he had been summoned for a conference with a provincial was when Father Donohoe wanted to ask him his thoughts about the 49ers' playing in the NFC Championship and about studying theology in Europe. Instinctively, he imagined that Father Smolich was probably not calling him down to get his prognostications on anything to do with the coming football season. "So I prepared for the meeting", he recalls, "by going out and buying a little audio recorder, because later on I wanted play back exactly what he said to me." Although his intuition about the provincial's lack of interest in the 49ers was right, he had to admit later that he had wasted money purchasing the recorder. He walked into the office. There was no small talk. The provincial invited him to sit in a chair arranged for the occasion and handed him a letter. He was invited to read it, which he was able to do in less than thirty seconds. It stated: "Campion College was not and is not part of your assignment from the Society of Jesus, as determined by me, your provincial." The wording is uncannily similar to the letter he had received from an earlier provincial separating him from the Ignatius Press. Father Smolich continued: "You are to have no role, public or private, in Campion College, just as Campion has no relationship with the Society of Jesus." The letter then informed him that "if your work as director of Ignatius Press cannot be kept separate from the affairs of Campion College, I likely will not permit you to continue with Ignatius Press." He was given a new assignment: assistant chaplain at Santa Teresita Hospital in Duarte, about 450 miles south of San Francisco.

During the course of the conversation, Father Fessio reminded his superior of the email he had sent him with a copy to Father General Kolvenbach, in which he had stated: "I would like to ask for formal approval from you and from Father General—whose approval I request that you solicit on my behalf—for me to participate actively in the establishment and operation of this new college, and to accept the position of its chief executive officer." He asked Father Smolich if the general knew about and approved his new assignment. Father Smolich confirmed that such was the case. The new assignment was clear. Some details were exchanged, hands were shaken, and the erstwhile president of Campion College was back in the car headed for San Francisco. There he called for a meeting with the personnel of the College, who elected John Galten as the new president. Shortly thereafter, the board of Ignatius Press met as well, cancelling two financially limp magazines, *Catholic Faith* and *Catholic Dossier*, while deciding to move two others online, *Catholic*

World Report and *Homiletic and Pastoral Review*. Mr. Mark Brumley, a close collaborator during the Catholic Radio Network project, was elected president of Guadalupe Associates, a position he has held with distinction ever since.

The news of Father Fessio's removal as president of Campion College became a cause of celebration or mourning for journalists throughout the country: the news of the transfer was a hot story to print. His reassignment "will not stop Campion College in any way", said Professor Raymond Dennehy, one of the core members of the former SII. "The curriculum is set up, the faculty are in place, the website is up, the money is there, and they already have had many inquiries from interested students."[1] Stanley Kurtz devoted considerable space in the *National Review Online* to pointing out the irony that Father Fessio and his allies were berated for supporting "Papal tyranny" while it is the liberals "who are acting as the real oppressors". He summed up what in the minds of many was so curious about the situation: "The old St. Ignatius Institute consisted of 150 souls in a university of 7,000—a mere 2% of the students at USF. The program was entirely voluntary, and students at SII could and did take courses on Catholic theology from liberal Jesuits at the larger university. And now a two-year college offering the same curriculum to a mere 15 is under assault from the forces of 'diversity'." Other news stories predictably followed the policies of the publications in which they appeared.[2] There was one, however, that merits recognition. The detailed, dramatic, approximately 500-word Fessio saga was picked up and printed in a French Catholic magazine, describing him—photographed for all to marvel at—as having a "passionately unwavering personality": the virile, intellectual counterpart to Mother Angelica. A one-time intimate friend of Père de Lubac, he had just been "sent to Siberia" by his provincial, with the approval of the Jesuit general.[3]

"I am a Jesuit. I go where I am missioned" was the clipped phrase he used in describing his reassignment to the reporters. And when pressed, he added that his reassignment came from his religious

---

[1] Quoted in Tim Drake, "Father Fessio Barred at San Francisco College", *National Catholic Register*, March 24–30, 2002, 1.

[2] For a number of references, see Lou Marano, "Jesuit Degeneracy", *UPI*, March 22, 2002.

[3] "Père Joseph Fessio: Un Jésuite dans la tourmente", *L'Homme Nouveau*, May 5, 2002.

superior, his provincial, with the approval of the general in Rome. Rome made a knee-jerk reaction to this *obiter dictum*. On March 15, the general's assistant sent him an email stating: "I want to correct the matter in what has been given to the press and others regarding your new assignment." He then informed him that Father General did not "approve" the move, "since he never 'approves' formally those decisions that belong properly to the Provincials." He further explained that Father General knew the provincial was "thinking about a new mission for you and did not express any objections to your being reassigned. This is not the same thing as approving it." That same day Father Fessio registered his response. After citing the email sent to the provincial with a copy to the general, whose contents were the center of the discussion at the recent meeting with the provincial, he informed Father Frank Case, assistant to the general, that the provincial had told him of the new assignment and that he had approved. Father Case had asked him if he wanted to speak with the general. He thought it was not necessary; however, he did ask that the general review his request to initiate Campion College in the light of three documents. First: A review of the original appeal made to the Holy Father by Cardinals Ratzinger and Schönborn and presented to the Holy Father on March 16, 2001. Second: The letter addressed to Father General from Cardinal Schönborn, dated February 13, 2002. Third: The most recent letter sent to him by the same two cardinals, the date and copy of which he did not have. He then cited some passages from the Jesuit Constitutions concerning the relationship that should exist between the Society and the Holy Father and ended his letter with the following paragraph:

> Because of recent discussions in the Plenaria of the Congregation for the Doctrine of the Faith on the subject of Jesuit education, I think Cardinal Ratzinger is in a particularly good position to comment on the mind of the Holy Father in regard to an initiative like Campion College. I realize he has already expressed his support for the restoration of the St. Ignatius Institute. But since he discussed the Institute personally with the Holy Father, this is itself another reason why his opinion would be especially helpful in discerning the mind of the Holy Father.

In years to come, when it will be possible to perform an impassionate autopsy on *Ex Corde Ecclesiae*, there will undoubtedly be traces of the Campion cancer. But before this chapter is ended, there is one topic that begs recognition. Given the reaction of the university to the genesis of Campion, it was impossible to think that Father Fessio could remain in San Francisco. Even if he gave up being president and dedicated himself exclusively to the Press, it was simply not realistic. The provincial had to contend with the university as well as with higher officials in Rome. If he had toyed with the idea of giving Father Fessio a one-way ticket back to Novosibirsk, few would have faulted him. But irrespective of what his personal and political prejudices may have been, his decision to mission him to Duarte argues well that he was not only pragmatic and shrewd, but also a man of delicacy and understanding. Where better could he be sent? The chaplain stationed there, yours truly, found it difficult to meet unaided all the demands of his ministry, and since he was a close friend of Father Fessio, he would welcome him with a double measure of joy. Then there were the Sisters. They were members of the same community that Father had done so much for by trying to place them at USF in the mid-1980s. They would give him a hero's welcome. Finally, the hospital was relatively close to San Francisco, yet far enough away for him not to become a threat to the university community, without any rector on hand to play the *toties quoties* game with him, as had been the case when he was removed from the board of Ignatius Press years before.

25

CHANCELLOR OF
AVE MARIA UNIVERSITY

"I was shocked", confessed Tom Monaghan, founder of Domino's Pizza and chairman of the Ave Maria Foundation, about hearing the news of Father Fessio's new assignment. "I just don't understand it." Tom had been involved with the new chaplain at Santa Teresita on a number of projects and considered him "one of the most famous Jesuits" in the United States, "with the possible exception of Cardinal Avery Dulles, and he is practically being silenced."[1] But in spring of 2002, Father Fessio was slowly adjusting to his new post. At first he reminded me of a stallion sequestered in a sheep's pen, but gradually he got accustomed to the routine of daily visiting the sick, of responding to middle-of-the-night calls from the emergency room and the intensive care unit. Then there were the "age-challenged" patients—ladies mainly—in the extended-care building who looked forward each day to recounting laundered anecdotes of the past and frustrations of the present. We would offer weekday Masses in the expansive chapel, mainly for the Sisters. On Sundays there would be crowds of local people who would contribute to making the chapel overflow with radiated joy.

One day Father said to me: "I'm going to start saying Sunday Masses *ad orientem*."

"No, don't. Cardinal Mahony has forbidden it."

"He can't forbid it."

I tried to make him see that the basis of his argument against the Santa Barbara tertian director in 1979 had been that the bishop

---

[1] Tim Drake, "Father Fessio Barred at San Francisco College", *National Catholic Register*, March 24, 2002.

was the head liturgist in his own diocese. Cardinal Mahony was the head liturgist in ours. But what I was really thinking was that it was Father Fessio who had fed Mother Angelica the chief talking points of her well-publicized confrontation with the cardinal, who might have been well aware of the identity of the prompter. Father Fessio could not afford two banishments by his religious superior. And if the cardinal should ask him to go elsewhere, far from the Archdiocese of Los Angeles, to seek a pillow upon which to lay his head, where would he turn? I never learned the details or the outcome of that drama because I rushed off to give a thirty-day directed retreat in Nebraska to seminarians from the Archdiocese of Denver, and by the time I returned to Duarte in late June, a great change had occurred.

Along with the Ave Maria School of Law that Tom Monaghan had opened in Ann Arbor, he began a corresponding liberal arts college a few miles away in Ypsilanti. Classes were conducted in a former grade school, situated a few blocks from Eastern Michigan University. In 2002, he enticed Mr. Nick Healy to give up his position as vice president of university relations at Franciscan University in Steubenville to become president of the new undergraduate college. As an aside, we might mention that before Mr. Healy assumed his office, the administrators at EMU had suggested that a closer connection between the two institutions might be worked out to the advantage of both. According to the plan, a select number of EMU students would take philosophy classes at Ave Maria, while a number of Ave Maria students could enroll for classes at EMU. At the same time, all Ave Maria students would have free access to the recreational facilities on the EMU campus. Some optimists saw this proposal as a modified SII program on a secular campus, where it could thrive with less hostility than on a Catholic college campus. But Tom Monaghan would have nothing to do with it, and he received the support of his college administrators. He was, however, interested in getting Father Fessio assigned to Ave Maria, persuading Mr. Healy to look into the possibility. Mr. Healy contacted Cardinal Schönborn, who, as we have seen, was an admirer of Mr. Monaghan, indebted to him for his past generosity. Accordingly, the cardinal brought the petition to Cardinal Ratzinger, who in turn spoke about it with Father General Kolvenbach. In a matter of hours, Father Smolich contacted Father Fessio informing him that he was to have a new assignment: assistant to Mr. Monaghan, effective immediately.

The assignment was seen by admirers of both men as a symbiosis of two designer minds: Tom Monaghan, the founder of Domino's Pizza, and Joseph Fessio, the instigator of a number of productions. When Father Fessio arrived at his post in June 2002, there was not much for him to do at the college. Would Father be able to look over proposed plans for an addition on a convent that had been putting strain on Mr. Monaghan's time and pocketbook? Indeed, he would. He had learned a great deal about reading blueprints when building Sweetwater, and he was confident that he could cut costs on any proposed building. In addition to this advantage, experience had taught him it was a singular blessing to be of service to nuns, whose innocence sometimes led others to exploit them. So by taking on this project, he would be doing a favor not only for Tom, but for the nuns as well. Tom had a special connection with these religious women. In 1997, he coaxed them away from New York, where they had been working with Cardinal O'Connor, who established several new congregations of religious women. Four Sisters had left the Dominicans in Nashville to form a separate Dominican group, designated the Sisters of Mary, Mother of the Eucharist. After their canonical establishment, they were invited to come to Michigan. From the time they arrived in Ann Arbor, their number began to increase, at first slowly and then by leaps and bounds. Mr. Monaghan had built them a convent with a magnificent chapel, but already they were forced to change the kitchen and other parts of the convent into bedrooms at night to accommodate their expanding numbers. Their superior, Mother Mary Assumpta Long, had been putting pressure, gentle but constant, on Mr. Monaghan to remedy the situation. His response was to ask her and the Sisters to draw up plans to accommodate their needs. When she did so, he was flabbergasted by the cost, which would be arriving just at the time when he was strapped by the expenses involved in moving Ave Maria College to Florida. It was at this crucial moment that Father Fessio made his entrance on the scene. Tom asked him if he could pursue this quest of bringing satisfaction to all concerned. Of course he could!

In true Fessio style, he gave himself completely to the business at hand, studying the blueprints, comparing them with similar constructions; getting the price on all the building materials, analyzing the terrain, comparing bids, and so on. He at last completed the plan and was delighted to inform Mr. Monaghan that the cost was significantly lower than that estimated by the Sisters. Tom was relieved to hear the good news. Mother Assumpta demurred. Like a number of great Catholic nuns of the past—Saint Teresa of Ávila, Saint Teresa of Calcutta, Mother Angelica of EWTN—she combined piety and sweetness with a business sense that would make some Wall Street moguls look like inept Monopoly players by comparison. She also knew how and when to play the trump card she held sequestered deep in her Dominican habit. After evaluating his plan "and praying over it", she informed him with great delicacy and in so many words that he did not know the first thing about convent life and that imitating the structure of standard Nevada desert-type motels with their cardboard-quality walls was no way to construct cells for religious women. Her assistant summed up her reaction in a more succinct manner. With a smooth, soft Tennessee drawl, coupled with the appellation she uses to all listeners, she said: "Honey, that Father Fessio fella doesn't know up from down. We'll pray for him." Mr. Monaghan ended up opting for the Sisters' plan, assuring them they would have the requested modest cells. At the same time, after a bit of arm twisting, he agreed to have an indoor basketball court constructed within the convent walls. This new amenity would be visited often during the long, cold Ann Arbor winters. The number of Sisters has grown from 4 in 1997 to almost 160 today, suggesting their chief medical complaint these days must be acne and proving that millennial women attracted to the religious life look for challenges, community, a distinctive religious habit, and unashamed devotions to the Eucharist and the Blessed Virgin.

When Father Fessio left Duarte, he could scarcely contain his joy, thinking about how his new role would enable him to fulfill better the Jesuit mission of "bringing Christ to others". Then he was given his first assignment. If the challenge of redesigning a convent to accommodate the multiplication of nuns and the reduction of expenses had caused him some surprise, he did not say, but had he read Voltaire—which he had not—he would have agreed that usually only one step separates the sublime from the ridiculous. But that is often a two-way step, and before he recovered from the put-down Mother Assumpta's sweet smile had delivered to him, he received an uplifting piece of news: he had been approved to receive his final vows.

Normally, a Jesuit is called to take these vows three or four years after his ordination to the priesthood. Father Fessio had been waiting in the wings thirty-three years before being called to become a full-fledged Jesuit. That time lapse argues better for the complexity of the Fessio elegy than anything else the reader may have unearthed from the saga so far. It was his provincial in California, Father Smolich, who initiated the request, arguing that Father Fessio was a good, obedient Jesuit, and the general in Rome approved the recommendation that he be fully incorporated into the order he had loved and served for so many years. Now the question was where the ceremony would take place. Every Jesuit, no matter where he is working, belongs to a specific community, governed by an appointed superior. When he left San Francisco for Duarte in spring 2002, Father Fessio was assigned to the Jesuit community at Loyola High School in Los Angeles, and there he remained during his assignment at Ave Maria. It is doubtful that during these years he ever visited the community, and so pronouncing his vows there was not an attractive option, but he could not think of any other community in California where the members would feel, if not overjoyed, at least comfortable in hosting such an event. So he requested he be allowed to take his vows in Rome. The request was granted. The date set was Tuesday, May 31, 2005, and Father General Peter Hans Kolvenbach himself volunteered to be the main celebrant at the Mass, scheduled to take place at the gilded tomb of Saint Ignatius in the ornate Baroque Church of the Gesù.

Of course, it would not be a Fessio event without drama. Father Fessio and a group of friends from IP and AMU, who had first spent a few days in Norcia, got stuck in a traffic jam coming into Rome. They managed to arrive at the steps of the Gesù just about the time the ceremony was scheduled to begin. "Will the Mass be in English or Italian?" asked Father General, who had judiciously journeyed across town in ample time for the ceremony to begin. "Neither", still breathless Father Fessio answered. "It is to be in Latin with the first canon." No sooner had the Mass begun than it became obvious the General was not used to being the main celebrant at a first canon Novus Ordo Latin Mass. Father Fessio later related that he and Father Paul Mankowski, a professor at the nearby Pontifical Biblical Institute, ended up alternating the role of main celebrant, while Father Kolvenbach stumbled into the parts assigned to the concelebrant. The fact that the general volunteered to be there is testimony enough to his kindness, modesty, humility, and patience, and the scene could have reminded Father Fessio of a similar event he had witnessed some thirty-four years earlier, when Father General Arrupe made a similar cross-town trip to accommodate Father de Lubac. A few months after Father Fessio's vow Mass, Father Kolvenbach announced his intention of retiring from the office as general, making him only the second man to do so. Saint Ignatius' idea was that the general should serve for life, chiefly because electing a new general necessitated forming committees, to which he was adamantly opposed. Jesuits, Ignatius believed, should be dedicated to the work they were assigned and not waste time attending meetings.

Ave Maria College moved in 2003 from Ypsilanti to Naples, Florida, where, adding a master's program, it became Ave Maria University, and accompanying the move was the Rev. Joseph D. Fessio, S.J., the college's chancellor, professor of theology, and head chaplain. When he took the job, he told Tom he did not want a salary; just a bicycle for exercise, a banjo for self-education, and a once-a-month ticket back to San Francisco for business. Tom agreed. He also liked to give his employees bonuses, and so some time before moving to Florida, Father Joseph asked him to send the $25,000 he offered him to Kolbe Academy in Napa, seeing that the directors of this Catholic school, which had remote ties with the Press, were facing serious financial problems. Then, with characteristic force, constancy, and attention to the end to be achieved, the newly named chancellor threw himself into a host of new activities, launching out far beyond the designated expectations of the president. However, as yet he had not assigned duties beyond mingling with the students, offering daily Mass, and suggesting to the less than sympathetic administration ways the university could and should raise funds.

In 2007, the university moved about seventeen miles east of Naples to the planned town of Ave Maria. Here, Father Fessio was given a little cabana as living quarters. It was situated next to the swimming pool, a little beyond three student dorms joined together by a twisted walkway. He had just gotten settled when, one night around 9 P.M., human shadows seemed to be coming from the dorms and gathering on the path. Curiosity compelled him to investigate. He had not gotten too far when a young man stopped him saying: "Hi, Father. We're going to say the Rosary. Do you want to lead us?" He declined, suggesting the students do the leading; he would follow. So began a practice that grew in popularity with the students during the next five or six years he was with them, and each night the crowd increased, walking around the campus in the dark of the night reciting the Rosary with the chancellor in tow. The Florida climate allowed the practice to continue throughout the year. This nocturnal Rosary branded an indelible impression on him, the first of many enabling him to affirm tearfully in later years: "Ave Maria was a tremendous blessing for me. I have never met a group of young people who were so good, so talented, so full of faith, so zealous." He has always had an extraordinary talent for seeing the good in others, and especially in perceiving hidden qualities in young people, as his experience with Project 50 at Santa Clara and the Saint Ignatius Institute at USF testify. He is blessed with a way of attracting young men and women and then, like a football coach with his team during the halftime of an important game, challenging them to reach *ad astra* (to the stars), to what Saint Ignatius termed the *magis*, the greater. He reflected on the students: "God has given me the ability to appreciate goodness and quality, even though I cannot produce it myself." The realization of this gift enabled him to assert further: "It is like publishing. What does 'publishing' mean? It means: 'to make public'. I do not write books, but I can judge a good book."

In that first academic year on the new Florida campus, there were only about one hundred undergraduates, and of this number more than seventy-five were freshmen. Thus, the student body was made up almost entirely of younger legal adults. Some of these students who displayed such enthusiasm for the chancellor were from Catholic families in Ann Arbor, and had been influenced by the Charismatic Renewal in their devotions and religious practices. For them, external demonstrations of Catholic piety were more spontaneous than for students from other ordinary Catholic backgrounds. But when it came to the Mass, Father Fessio decided the charismatic students were in need of liturgical training. He had not requested to be head chaplain—a dangerous position, after all, for a priest with Father Fessio's endowments *and* deficiencies—but as a matter of fact he was, and he was not shy about using the prerogatives of his office to implement what he considered to be the Church's tradition for matters liturgical in the reform-of-the-reform movement. When the school moved to Florida, he began explaining to the students at his daily Masses why something was missing in the chapel—an altar rail—and why he was going to build one. Had he forgotten the place the yet unfinished monumental chapel had in the hierarchy of Mr. Monaghan's architectural priorities? No, he simply explained: "Despite what you may have heard, everyone is at liberty to receive the Eucharist in the hand or on the tongue, kneeling or standing. It is your choice." Who could logically argue with that?

It did not take long for the majority of the students to begin receiving the Host on their tongues while kneeling at the head chaplain's improvised altar rail. This fact caused him to state at a Sunday Mass before the large crowd: "Young people, when they are zealous, know that when I say 'This is my Body', they should be on their knees." But his fellow chaplains were not in agreement, nor were they supportive of his celebrating daily Mass *ad orientem*. He hired a friend from San Francisco, Diana Silva, with an impressive background in music, to develop a choir, to take charge of liturgical music, and to create a program for teaching sacred music. At the same time, he taught the students how to sing simple chant at his Masses: *Kyrie*, *Sanctus*, and *Agnus Dei*. He recalls that they learned all of this music well; it was beautiful. He encouraged them to progress to the next step: chanting the *Orbis factor* Mass. This demanded talent, but surprisingly the students took to it well—to the delight of many at the university, but not of all! The Mass had become the focal point of dissention. The president, Nick Healy, and his wife were in favor of "praise and worship" Masses and ignored the altar rail altogether. Finally, a compromise was hammered out: Father Fessio would offer the morning Mass; one of the other two chaplains would say the noon Mass, at which the priest was careful to walk around the altar rail to distribute the Eucharist to all, standing. It was at this time when Father Fessio began working on a book with his friend Cardinal Arinze, the prefect of the Congregation of Divine Worship in Rome, a fact that necessitated his speaking with the cardinal on a regular basis. At the end of one conversation, business matters having been put to sleep, he said: "By the way, Cardinal, they are trying to outlaw kneeling here at daily Mass." The cardinal's response was: "Tell them to join the Taliban!"

The liturgy continued to be a growing point of tension, but it was not the only cause of discord. We shall single out two typical examples. In 2005, an administrator close to the president persuaded him to invite a particular speaker to address the community. (By that date, Father Fessio had yielded his title of chancellor to Tom Monaghan, while he was given the title of provost.) When the new provost learned that the man believed Catholics should support homosexual civil unions, among a number of other unorthodox views, he used his authority to cancel the lecture, with the result that an important individual in the administration resigned, and animosities were strengthened. Then there were disagreements on how to handle the university's growing financial problem. Academically, the university started out very well. The average SAT scores for incoming freshmen gradually climbed from 1140 to 1225 (old scale), putting the university among the top 3 or 4 percent of schools in terms of average scores. But the income for the university was not enough to pay all the expenses, and Tom was worried about running out of money for building up the campus. His solution was a 50 percent increase in freshman enrollment per annum. Father Fessio disagreed for two reasons: the quality of the students would decrease, and the college, which was presently losing money on every student accepted, would not gain net revenue by increasing the intake. He further argued that, although the university prided itself on giving scholarships, these were not true scholarships, but discounts. After all, there was not any real scholarship fund at AMU. At one meeting, he gave Tom and other administrators the following scenario to consider. Suppose tuition were $20,000 per annum and the university offered an $8,000 scholarship to a sought-for student to enroll in the freshman class. In reality, that student would be charged $12,000.

Father Fessio worked with Gabriel Martinez, the chairman of the (one-man) Economics Department, to compare the net revenues for an incoming class that increased by 15 percent with one that increased by 50 percent. The result was that the net revenues for the larger freshman class would be a million dollars higher. However, there remained a question: Is it more realistic to increase the freshman enrollment by 50 percent or to raise a million dollars in the affluent Naples area? He then boldly posed two questions to this man who had made more than a billion dollars selling pizza: "First: Wouldn't you be happy with a company that grew 15 percent each year? Second: Isn't the solution to the university's economic problem found rather in raising real money?" He concluded: "Tom, I think it is easier to get a 15 percent larger freshman class and $1 million than to get a 50 percent growth with phantom scholarships." There is no record of the answers he may have been given, but one can imagine that the questions might well have been heard with the accompaniment of those three fatal notes from *Carmen* that seem to have become Father Fessio's theme song.

Father Fessio was not dismayed. He left the meeting re-energized to find specific ways to solve Ave Maria's economic problem. "As we left the room together," he recalls, "I said to [Tom]: 'Let's start a Founders Club and invite people to help us found this new Catholic university.'" Tom agreed, and eventually a director was hired to steam up the project. The alumni list was minimal, but the confident provost volunteered to use the Ignatius Press mailing list and others to reach people who would be honored to join the venture. He composed the first letter and had his own picture posted on the packet. The director objected, saying that an image of Pope John Paul II would be more appropriate. Father had no argument that the pope was better than he, but the fact was that the appeal letter was being sent to supporters of the Ignatius Press, and therefore his face would be more effective. People constantly get begging letters enclosed in envelopes adorned with pictures of the pope. But the director was not convinced, and so Father Fessio offered a deal. "I'll tell you what," he said, "let's do a test. Let's do 5,000 of one, and 5,000 of the other and we'll do the other 90,000 with whatever works best." (The dialogue is reminiscent of the wagers he would make with opponents when he was a student at Santa Clara.) He later summed up the results thus: "And of course, mine worked better." So off went the additional 90,000 dunning letters with an image of the half-smiling face of the Reverend Fessio broadcast on each envelope. In the first year, the Founders Club and other *Fessified* projects raised between one and two million dollars, and there were now more than 40,000 donors whose net worth was in the billions.

Meanwhile, there were more untapped mines begging to be exploited by Father, and he wasted no time doing so. Naples was the university's nearest metropolis, and Naples is a wealthy town. After some investigation, Father Fessio learned that a few years before the college moved from Ypsilanti, a man and his wife had raised eighteen million dollars in just one weekend wine festival. Then there was the owner of the largest jewelry store in town. She and the wine festival lady had joint-chaired a committee that drew up a list of 245 wealthy Catholics living in Naples. After a little coaxing, they shared the list with Father Fessio, and he quickly put it to use for the benefit of the university. At this point of his career, he was encouraged that everything, apart from the nagging chapel conflicts, was going along extremely well, and the prospects of making it all better goaded him on daily to greater exploits, totally oblivious to the paradoxes of history.

26

TWO TERMINATIONS

It was Wednesday, March 21, 2007. Mr. Monaghan had just requested that Father Fessio come to his office. He did. Standing there, he heard his employer say: "I want you to resign." Surprised, he replied: "Why would I resign?"

"Resign, or otherwise I'll fire you."

"Go ahead, but may I ask you the reason?"

"I'm not giving you reasons."

The surprise had turned into shock, and standing here he thought: "I have worked five years here without a salary; have raised millions of dollars for the university through the Founders Club, and now I am being fired without being given a reason, although I know the reason. It's a long story."

This brief reflection was interrupted by: "I want you to leave the campus immediately."

"The only vehicle I have belongs to the University."

Pause.

"You can use it for one more day. And don't tell anyone you're leaving."

"Look. I love these students. I just can't leave without saying good-bye."

The interview ended. Dazed, Father Fessio took his leave. Had Clio, the muse of history, been seated there playing her lyre, she might have recalled Talleyrand's observation after Napoleon had the young Duke of Enghien untimely shot dead: "It was worse than a crime; it was a mistake."

But however well Clio might have understood people and situations, her observation was far from the thoughts of the stripped provost of AMU as he rambled back to his quarters. Once there, he contacted his friends Roger and Priscilla McCaffrey, asking if he could take advantage of their hospitality for a day or so. They lived directly across the street from the campus—an ironic reminiscence of the contiguous relationship of the Press office with the USF campus. He then sat down at his computer and emailed the student body: "I have been asked to resign my position as provost and leave the campus immediately. I will miss Ave Maria and the many of you whom I hold dear." A few hours later, the school's public relations firm issued a cryptic notice announcing that Father Fessio "was asked to step down as Provost of the University as a result of irreconcilable differences over administrative policies and practices". The AMU staff was asked not to comment to reporters about the controversy. By then, a student protest was already beginning to take shape. First, more than one hundred gathered in front of the president's office, and then from there they processed, rosaries in hand, to Father Fessio's cabana, where the outcast, who had been packing his belongings, greeted them in a good-natured, joking manner that morphed into a tearful blessing. The protest had grown much larger by 4:30 P.M., when the administration called for an emergency faculty and staff meeting. Because of the growing pressure from the protesters, a delegation of students was allowed entrance, and finally, as an ad hoc damage control measure, the doors were opened to all students. Three to four hundred rushed into the auditorium—where fortunately there were no rafters to hang from—searching for adequate seating or standing room. Every time the Fessio name was mentioned, there were emotional ovations that seemed to shake the room. Except for an absence of violence, the performance seemed patterned on the beginnings of the French Revolution.

Some of the bolder members among the stirred-up crowd stood up and vowed to the administrators, seated in silent astonishment, that they were prepared "to vote with their feet", meaning they would not be returning to AMU the next semester unless the injustice were righted. If nothing else had caused panic, this dire threat did. It was like a virus that could spread quickly. Added to this threatening behavior was the beginning of an inundation of emails from anxious parents and excited newscasters filling the president's inbox. Night fell; the students went back to their dorms discussing what further steps they should take in the morning, while the chief administrators met endeavoring to untangle the knotted-up notices they had issued, realizing that they had a serious crisis on their hands. And it could not have happened at a worse time. The admissions office had been in high gear recruiting candidates for the upcoming semester; Father Fessio was scheduled to be in Washington, D.C., for induction into the Catholic Education Foundation's Hall of Fame, and on the very day of the firing, donors had received a three-page letter written by Tom Monaghan requesting donations. Although informative, it was generally conceded that the letter lacked the spiffy style of the originator of the Founders Club. For the media, the silence on the part of the university over the cause of the firing became fodder for speculation. Finally, that evening the president issued a statement that caused more confusion than enlightenment. The "irreconcilable differences" of two days ago had been reconciled, and Father Fessio, as "a sign of our esteem for his great gifts and abilities", would now remain on campus, not as chancellor, professor of theology, or head chaplain, but as "a theologian".

After Father Fessio had transferred his few belongings back into the cabana that same evening, Friday, March 22, he decided to wander over and watch a rehearsal of Lerner and Loewe's *My Fair Lady*, which the students would be performing the following night. One of the chief singers in the production was the regular cantor at Father Fessio's Mass, while his lector would be playing another leading role in the 1950s musical hit. He reported being fascinated by the coincidence, and then on the following weekend while he was celebrating the Easter vigil along with the two performers mentioned above, he could not banish the distracting thought that the university needed a proper theatre where the students could put on plays and musicals. For the moment, they were simply hosting the events in the AMU student center. He soon contacted Mr. Monaghan, who did not want a campaign started to build a theatre on campus: it would conflict with his plans to construct an athletic gym. "Well, OK, I'll raise money to do one off campus", Father Fessio said to himself. He then quickly borrowed money from Guadalupe Associates to hire an architect to make a cost estimate on the proposed theatre. A few days later he got a call from Jack Donahue, the founder of Federated Investors, Inc., and president of the AMU board of trustees. "I want to help you, Father. . . . Do you have any projects?" (Imagine asking Father Fessio such a question!) Father was quick to tell him about the dreamed-about theatre. "How much is it going to cost?"

"I think maybe $4 million."

"I'll give you $500,000", he said, which would also cover the Guadalupe Associates loan. But Father said he would first want to talk to Tom about the matter. A week later, Father got a telephone call from the university's development director. "Father Fessio, Would you consider building the theater on campus?" Of course—that had been his original idea, after all—but only provided Mr. Donohue gives the university his promised gift, "as long as Guadalupe is reimbursed for its expenses and I'm still in charge of organizing." Years later, AMU refused to make the payment to Guadalupe Associates. A suit was filed. AMU prevailed because of a Florida law regarding verbal contracts.

One of the important visitors to Ave Maria at this time in 2008 was Cardinal Arinze, and his welcome presence gave Father Fessio the opportunity to demonstrate, particularly to the Praise and Worship faction, how the Mass should be properly and reverently offered. The event was to take place in the newly constructed multipurpose building designed by Father Fessio, which could be used as a theatre, auditorium, and chapel. His original plan was that the building should face the east, but when the plans were finalized, he was surprised to learn that the architect, taking advantage of the topography and potential view, had the building facing west. This was not at all satisfactory, and so new plans had to be drawn up to accommodate "reform of the reform" specifications. Ultimately, it did get built. When Cardinal Arinze came, Mass was offered on the stage of this sleek auditorium. The cardinal, however, had not been warned to incense the altar with moderation, and a cloud of curling smoke wafted upward, where it set off a fire alarm accompanied by a frantic, repeating, prerecorded announcement: "You must leave the building." Father Fessio contravened, yelling: "No, you don't. It is not Armageddon!" So most of the congregation sat waiting for ten minutes before the siren finally turned off. Dramatic as it was, it may have allowed the cardinal to experience how "reform of the reform" Masses in the United States can differ from those celebrated in Africa. Furthermore, there was something in the experience that could make one wonder whether God has, among his other recognized attributes, a sense of humor. If so, it was not a divine quality readily recognized by the administration.

There were other events that pointed to the growing rupture between the university and its theologian. In November 2008, the same year a swinging censer had touched off the auditorium's shrieking alarm, the university's board of directors was scheduled to meet. No longer provost, Father Fessio was not on the roster, but he had heard that one of the chief agenda items would be to seek approval for a present and future budget plan. This news set him off, perhaps armed with a calculator, to immerse himself in a sea of figures, thus giving himself over to one of his favorite pastimes. As might be expected, he concluded that the plan was not only faulty, but dangerous for the university. The complex details of these findings are of little interest here, but they indicated clearly that the administration was involved—unconsciously, of course—in a shell game. His findings urged him to make a telephone call that rang in the pocket of the board's chairman, Jack Donohue, and without much ado, he proceeded to describe his insight for his benefit, for the good of the university. After listening to a lengthy monologue, the chairman, who had made a fortune in business dealings, interrupted to say: "Father, don't just tell me I'm going to hell. Tell me how to avoid it." The recently appointed AMU theologian responded: "I just want you and the board to look carefully at the financials and see what the real situation is. That's it." Goodbyes were cordially exchanged.

Getting word of Father Fessio's audacity, Mr. Monaghan and President Healy reacted swiftly. Father tried to defend himself by declaring his conversation with Mr. Donohue had been private, but in addition to this fact, he reminded them that he was a member of the faculty and as such had a right, if not a duty, to speak to the chairman of the board on such an important matter. He certainly had not broadcasted his opinion about the budget, nor did he intend to do so in the future. But faculty members at Ave Maria, where there was no tenure, were perhaps more like employees at Domino's than vested dons of a privileged class. The immediate crisis passed, but it left in its wake an atmosphere of strained expectancy for a coming storm. Tom Monaghan was a businessman; Nick Healy, a lawyer. Surely they were resolved on taking action. This designation is in no way meant to disparage them; it simply reports a fact, one of a number of reasons why the alliance between them and Father Fessio gradually and inevitably disintegrated.

But in reality, the chief bone of contention between Father Fessio and Tom Monaghan was probably the liturgy. Tom is a committed and generous Catholic, whose preference at that time was to stay clear of liturgical battles. Unlike Nick, he was not a charismatic, although many of his friends and supporters were. He remained indifferent to "Praise and Worship" and healing Masses; at the same time, the Latin language, Gregorian chant, polyphony, chapel veils, and alarm-setting incense were equally lost on him. He liked Masses the way they were offered in the Marine Corps. However, he did find the spirit manifested in Michigan's Word of God community attractive. The prospect of remodeling the interior of his Frank Lloyd Wright–style church to include altar rails did not appeal to him, and as for the division the liturgy had created in the community ever since the college moved to Florida, he was not inclined to tolerate this at all. To make matters worse, ripples of the infighting went beyond the university, right up to the local bishop's office, and the bishop, who had already seemed cool toward the invasion of Ave Maria into his diocese, was no aficionado of the "reform of the reform" movement. Tom was eager to have good relations with the bishop, and Father Fessio, with his liturgical tastes, seemed to be the principal block to realizing that objective. Then there were the Fessio projects, good in themselves perhaps, bringing in millions, but they seemed to make him the primary mover in realizing the defined goals of Ave Maria University. His unquestioned popularity among the students was also a detriment to campus peace. Finally, there was his seeming arrogance in matters financial that derailed confidence sought and expected among the administrators and members of the board of trustees. The mixing of these Fessio features with the administrative culture created atmospheric conditions at the university that tend to generate tornadoes—wind shear and instability, along with an eerie calm before the storm hits. Such was the near-unanalyzable quality that hovered long on the AMU campus during the spring term of 2009.

In July 2009, Father Fessio returned to San Francisco for his vacation, which he spent at Ignatius Press—not exactly a Club Med destination. Recently, in April, it had moved from its cramped quarters to a spacious, quaint late-nineteenth-century firehouse, replete with a Victorian-style tower for drying hoses. The need to make renovations on the new acquisition and the adjoining house put Father Fessio back in the architect's heaven, redesigning rooms and installing a chapel (the altar faces east) near the remains of the fireman's pole that once challenged hardy men to slide down and perform acts of bravery throughout the city. In the midst of these many demands on his renewed energies and latent talents, he received a telephone call from the academic vice president of AMU, Jack Sites, an educator whom Father Fessio highly admired, declaring him "a very good, competent, Southern gentlemanly Episcopalian, who always supported the Catholicity of Ave". Jack expressed his desire to fly to San Francisco to pay him a visit. As soon as he put down the receiver, Father Fessio knew that he could soon boast of having been fired twice from Ave Maria University. Upon arrival, Jack confirmed Father's intuition. It was easier the second time around. Neither the students nor the theologian were on campus. Was this definitive separation from Ave Maria a tragedy? Father Fessio admitted that he would miss the students, but there was peace. "God's will is that I work elsewhere, and so I am happy to do so." Needless to say, Tom was happy as well. Having two alpha-male grizzlies in the same den never works out well for either—or for the other bears in the forest.

At that point, Campion College was no longer a distraction. In hindsight, one can see that it had been set up to blaze, not to burn. After just two years, finances—dwindling income and mounting expenses—had been enough to smother the idealist dreams that once had been talked out in detail along the mixed snow-and-mud paths of Sweetwater. Then there had been the matter of accreditation. But still, the young men and women had seemed content with their investment, confidently enrolling as continuing students in some of the country's most prestigious universities. John Galten moved on to take up a new commitment within the diocese of Santa Rosa, while Father Fessio, when he was not at his desk mulling over blueprints for remodeling or reading manuscripts for future books, was planning new projects with relentless concentration. If the Ave Maria undertaking ended up in the Stygian depths along with the bones of some of his other enterprises, he had still not abandoned the courage and confidence to respond once again to that sweet siren voice bidding him to take on more adventures. This was the first year since the beginning of the Press that he was free to give himself unreservedly to its demands. The first of these was working in conjunction with the magazine *Magnificat* to release translations of children's books originally published by the Fleurus-Mame group in France.

This was not the Press' first connection with a publisher of children's books. It had also worked in conjunction with Bethlehem Books, run by the Bethlehem Community of Benedictine Oblates in Bathgate, North Dakota. The history, structure, and mission of this lay group is one of the most fascinating untold stories of Catholicism in the United States from the 1970s to the present date, not unlike that of the San Rafael hippies (later, third-order Dominicans) who had accompanied Father Fessio to Mexico in 1975, though also very different. Bethlehem Community sprouted from a young adult "House Ministries" initiative of 1971 under Bethlehem Baptist Church of Portland, Oregon. In this movement, a number of local young people, led by church members, formed houses of Christian discipleship across the area. In several of these houses, the residents shared their income, a practice that seemed pretty radical at the time.

By 1981, some members clustered near Portland State University had decided to establish together a lifetime community. No longer linked with the Baptist Church, they took steps to incorporate legally under their own identity. The group consisted of five lifetime members, a number of novices seriously considering the life, and another group of "disciples" with one to three years' commitment. Over the next ten years, the new Bethlehem Covenant Community worked at establishing their forms of living, moving to a better location, and, above all, finding an answer to the question: "Where do we belong in the Church?" First, the community decided to leave behind gainful jobs in the working world and start a bakery business (located in an ex-motel) in order to support themselves communally. The members developed many living practices to meet their different needs, and families began to homeschool their children, assisted by some of the single women in the community. Then high downtown taxes pushed the group to relocate to Vancouver, Washington, where they had already established their bakery. Finally, though, the question of where they fit in the Church came to a head. What denomination would allow them the space to live and practice the Christian life as they did?

They found one vital contemporary expression of faith in the

Bruderhof, an Anabaptist German group (now international) who had come to the American East Coast in the mid-twentieth century and was associated with the Hutterians, living lives of radical Christian communion and discipleship. But around 1991, one of Bethlehem Community's members proposed another possibility: "Is God perhaps leading us into the Catholic Church? Let's take a year and study it together. Let's see if any of its teachings really block our following this lead." During that year, the members read, pondered, talked to a few Catholics, including a Holy Cross priest from the University of Portland, and visited Mount Angel Benedictine Abbey in Oregon. Their search—in moments both serious and humorous—led them down strange paths of discovery, and eventually they got their answer. During the Easter Vigil of 1993, twenty-five community members were received into the Catholic Church (four married couples with their children, along with four single women).

Shortly after entering the Church, Jack, Jean Ann, and Peter Sharpe, interested in reprinting quality children's books, visited Ignatius Press and met Father Fessio, Carolyn Lemon, Roxanne Lum, Donna Fong, and others for the first time. Later, a group of Ignatius Press folk visited the community's Vancouver bakery/home en route to eastern Oregon. Father Fessio was very frank with them about how much time and money it took to break into the world of publishing. In fact, appreciating the bakery's products, he outright suggested the community stick to baking.

Nevertheless, that following November, having sold their bakery, Bethlehem Books published three thousand copies of their first children's book, a reprint of Alan French's *Rolf and the Viking Bow*, which was followed soon after by a second edition of Laura Berquist's *Designing Your Own Classical Curriculum*, which would become a classic for the growing number of homeschool teachers. In 1998, the rights to this title were taken over by Ignatius Press, and the book was reprinted in a new edition.

The work of Bethlehem Books, begun on a shoestring, was soon supplemented by a welcome job offer from Father Fessio. In February 1994, the community became the 800-number phone order answering service for Ignatius Press, a tie that remained for more than twenty years.

After selling the bakery building in the fall of 1994 in order to publish their first book, the community hoped to relocate near Mount Angel Benedictine Abbey, where they were becoming oblates. When nothing opened up, however, the group responded to an invitation from John and Sheila Kippley to wait on a prospect in the Cincinnati diocese. In January 1995, traveling 2,300 miles in a variety of trucks and vans, the community had just arrived in Cincinnati when Father Fessio called and said to Jack Sharpe, "Don't unpack; I think I may have found a place for you." Father Fessio had persuaded his good friend Bishop James Sullivan of Fargo, North Dakota, to welcome the community to his diocese, where they have remained ever since, first in a partially renovated convent and later in a larger building that once housed the state school for the blind.

In the spring of 1995, an ongoing partnership was forged between the fledgling company and Ignatius Press, allowing Bethlehem to advertise their works in the Ignatius catalogue as well as benefit from the relative expertise of IP staff members. Bethlehem Books still continues their apostolate to get good books into the hands of children, seeing this as a way to lay a foundation of truth and beauty that potentially leads into a deeper knowledge of Christ. One former member of the Bethlehem community, John Herreid, has worked at Ignatius Press since 2003, designing ads, catalogues, and some extraordinary book covers.

There have been other projects for young people. In 2006, Cardinal Schönborn began working on an edition of the *Catechism* for children and teenagers, the *YOUCAT* (*Jugendkatechismus der Katholischen Kirche* [*Youth Catechism of the Catholic Church*]), which appeared in 2011. Father Fessio was, of course, interested in the cardinal's newest apostolic venture, but other distractions prevented him from focusing on the possibilities that *YOUCAT* might offer. One of these in particular took him away from his flurry of activity at the Press for just a short time, less than a week, but nonetheless proved decisive. He went to Poland to deliver a paper at Torun. After this presentation before a number of Catholic writers and publishers, the editor of the German magazine *Vatikan* approached him, curious about Ignatius Press. During the informal conversation, Father related an incident that had occurred to him shortly after he completed his studies in Germany: He gave a retreat to a group of nuns, and at question time, near the end, one of the Sisters thanked him for introducing them to all the great theologians he had met in Europe, then asked him who he considered to be the greatest American theologians. Thinking for a moment, he replied:

> Sister, before I got to Europe, I didn't drink beer or wine. When I got to France, I learned to drink wine with a meal, and then when I got to Bavaria in Germany, I began drinking beer, and I discovered thirteen different kinds of beer—Bock, double bock, weizenbier, dunkelweizen, you name it. Not brands, but different kinds of beer. And I said, when I came back to the United States, I had my first American beer and took a sip and I spit it out. I said, if this is beer, I need a different name for what I had in Bavaria. . . . And I said, we don't have any theologians. If you're going to call them theologians, I need another name for what I experienced in Europe.

The editor and the small crowd of eavesdroppers in Torun were highly amused, and the next edition of *Vatican* printed Father Fessio's comparison of theologians to beer. Shortly afterward, Bernhard Meuser, chief coordinator of the German-language edition of *YOUCAT*, made contact with Father Fessio, asking him to publish the English translation of the youth catechism. Naturally, Father assumed Cardinal Schönborn had been the *éminence grise* directing the offer, but no, he discovered that it had been his beer story that convinced the board they should do some serious research on Ignatius Press, since its editor seemed to be the kind of man they could work with. Their in-depth study of the Press confirmed their intuition. Father Fessio gladly accepted the deal. The first edition of *YOUCAT* appeared in nineteen languages at World Youth Day in Madrid on March 25, 2011. Subsequently, more than two million copies in these same languages have been purchased, and of that total, Ignatius Press has sold almost a million. In 2014, new *YOUCAT* projects were undertaken—titles on prayer, Confirmation, Catholic social teaching—and the books appear to be as popular now as they were when they were first produced.

Then there was Universities of Western Civilization, an online liberal arts program Father Fessio began the same year of 1995. It offered both high school and college credits to young students. A special recording station was set up in the Press, giving Father Fessio an excuse to pull out some of the notes he had used in his Saint Ignatius Institute classes. This program still continues under the name of Angelicum Academy. The Press was also involved in an online platform called My Catholic Faith Delivered. It is tailored for dioceses, parishes, schools, and individuals, providing courses to help Catholics "grow, communicate, learn, and evangelize the beauty and truth of our faith". The company eventually changed its name to Five Stones and entered into a deeper partnership with Ignatius Press, managing its large Illinois warehouse, which, as we will see later, was replaced by one that Father Fessio designed.

One large apostolic effort that Father Fessio took on at this time was the African Missal/Lectionary Project, a collaboration that proved most advantageous for the Press as well as for the Church in a number of dioceses in Botswana, Ghana, Lesotho, Nigeria, South Africa, Swaziland, Uganda, Zimbabwe, and a few other English-speaking areas where local bishops had given approval to promote the Ignatius Press Lectionary. The Press used the Ignatius Bible (Revised Standard Version Second Catholic Edition) to prepare a Mass lectionary for the liturgical year. In the United States, the only approved lectionary drew from the New American Bible, thus the Ignatius Lectionary could not be approved for liturgical use in the United States. However, the Episcopal Conference of the Antilles accepted it for liturgical worship. Father Fessio was quick to take advantage of this opening, making a special trip to Africa to sponsor the African Lectionary, which uses the Ignatius Bible. With the approval of the bishops, this missal, too, is based almost entirely on the Ignatius Lectionary, except that it uses the Grail translation of the Psalms. The Press also began the massive undertaking of developing a study Bible, periodically releasing booklets on individual books of Scripture, complete with commentary and study aids. In 2010, the full New Testament installment of the Ignatius Press Study Bible was published.

Then there are the book fairs. Since 1981, children's publishing giant Scholastic Books has been hosting annual sales at elementary and middle schools across the United States, reaching some 120,000 schools and some 35 million students as of 2024.[1] They have long been known as "a wonderful provider of materials for young people," as the competitive Father Fessio admits, if reluctantly. Indeed, one would be hard-pressed to find an American student who has

---

[1] "Our History," Scholastic, accessed May 15, 2024, https://www.scholastic.com/aboutscholastic/history/.

not bought something from a Scholastic fair. Yet Fessio, with the mind of a publisher, could not shake a creeping feeling about the multibillion-dollar company. *What kinds of books are these children reading nowadays?* he asked himself. Eventually, he found the source of the stench. Scholastic had begun introducing titles such as *My Moms Love Me* and *Welcome to St. Hell: My Trans Teen Adventure* into its school fairs—a book market on which it has long had a "near-monopoly."[2] Of course, Don José, now over eighty years old, trembled with excitement as he glimpsed the crisp outline of another windmill on the horizon. But the closer he got, the more certain he was that, this time, the enemy was real, and mighty indeed. Victory would require some backup, a few alliances. By the time Scholastic's gender re-education project finally came to light in news outlets in 2023, the Ignatius Book Fairs were ready to deploy.

The Book Fairs project, spearheaded by Father Fessio and his old collaborator Mark Middendorf, is a joint venture between Ignatius Press, Ave Maria University, and an array of children's book publishers across the United States, including many of Ignatius' old competitors, such as Tan, Sophia Institute, and even Penguin Random House. These school-wide events—crafted for children from ages four to thirteen, as well as for their teachers—give America the first viable alternative to Scholastic, offering excellent literature of all kinds, from Newbery and Caldecott Medal winners to books on microscopes and caterpillars to comic-style biographies of Saint Bernadette. Each title is vetted by the Ignatius Book Fairs team, but the selection is tailored by each school to fit their curriculum, whether Catholic or secular. Naturally, the idea has resonated with parents and teachers alike. Within two months of the first fair, which took place in Florida in January 2024, over eighty schools nationwide had signed up for the event—from New York to Louisiana to Illinois to sunny California. Who knows whether this momentum will continue? As of this writing, it is still brand new, yet with Fessio at the helm, we can bet on a great deal of activity. Besides, as he likes to say, if just one soul finds its way because of the work, it will have been well worth the time.

---

[2] Joy Press, "Inside the Succession Drama at Scholastic, Where Harry Potter and Clifford Hang in the Balance," *Vanity Fair*, March 10, 2022, https://www.vanityfair.com/style/2022/03/inside-the-succession-drama-at-scholastic.

Readers of the above pages will not be surprised by Father Fessio's approach to the future. They have been introduced to him as a strong-willed, exceptionally talented man, spurred on by the desire of achieving whatever goal—academic, athletic, social, entrepreneurial—he confidently, quietly, or sometimes loudly sets out to achieve. A born leader, he easily attracts followers to his various causes. Above all, deeply integrated into these characteristics stands Father Fessio's commitment to doing God's will in all matters, while seeking a closer union with him in prayer and contemplation.

As a coda, let us note that the once cracked relationship between Father Fessio and Tom Monaghan has since been mended—and perhaps even taken on new vigor. In the decade after the Jesuit's messy departure from the university, the visions of these two strong-headed men began to converge. Since 2023, Fessio has even begun strolling the powerfully air-conditioned hallways of Ave Maria from time to time, joining his old friend Joseph Pearce to teach courses on G. K. Chesterton and C. S. Lewis. Mark Middendorf, who became president of AMU in 2022, says that the reunion of Fessio and Monaghan has "enriched the academic environment and deepened the university's dedication to its core values". All this should come as no surprise. Even our old companion Bertie Wooster sometimes butted heads with his right hand Jeeves over practical matters. "When two men of iron will live in close association with one another," he observes in *The Code of the Woosters*, "there are bound to be occasional clashes." But once the sabers quiet down, Bertie, a gentleman at heart, is never afraid to admit the truth: "Jeeves was right." It is the *preux* thing to do.

Fr. Fessio's father,
Joseph Dean Fessio, Sr.

Mother, Florence Miller Fessio

One month old

Around age 3 or 4

Around age 5

*Little brother, Vince, around age 5.
There was about a six-year age
difference between the Fessio boys.*

*Italian grandmother, Maria Bolego.
Grandma Bolego settled in
Wyoming and Utah.*

Boy Scout

Little League baseball player, age 12. Joe played first base.

Trout fishing with his father in British Columbia, age 13

*Goofing around with his little
brother, Vince, July 1957*

Age 17, in an oversized suit

*Age 19, with Vince in his 1953 MG TD, in Menlo Park, California.
This was Joe's third used car, after a 1941 Buick convertible, which he fixed
up at and sold, and a 1948 Studebaker convertible.*

Deer hunting, age 19
January, 1960
Joe used to hunt with his Bellarmine
high school friend, Barry Christina

2,700-mile, 27-day bicycle trip from
Chicago to San Francisco, with
Bob Helmholz, summer 1960

At the Continental Divide on his
Chicago to San Francisco bicycle trip,
summer 1960

Age 20

At his Santa Clara University junior prom with girlfriend Nancy, 1961

Joe Fessio, Sr., who worked for Pan American World Airways, arranged for a trip for Joe (20) and Vince (14) to southeast Asia and Tahiti in the summer of 1961, just before he entered the Jesuits

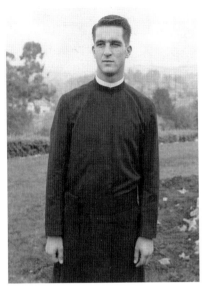

Jesuit novice, 1961

Jesuit Juniorate band, with Joe on upright bass, 1963

Jesuit Philosophate, 1964, "The New Breed",
Joe Fessio in top row, center, fourth from left (holding his head)

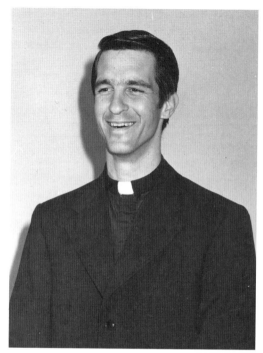

Jesuit Scholastic, 1964–65

*Being fed a sandwich as a Jesuit Scholastic at Saint Mary's
Indian Mission in Omak, Washington, 1965–66*

MR. JOE Fessio, S. J., Bea House, Gonzaga university, borrowed a Burgess 30-338 rifle from Mike Riggs and used it to bag this big mule deer near Kalispel Creek, just inside the Washington line on the Petit Lake road. He got it at 50 yards. Chris Douglass, S. J., and Bill Sullivan, S. J., were hunting with Mr. Fessio. The rifle was custom built in the Spokane valley. "Mike loaned it to me all sighted in and ready to go," Mr. Fessio said. "It really shot true."

The butcher said weighed 350 lb on hoof

Scholastic Mr. Fessio borrows a friend's rifle and bags a 4-point buck

Graduation from Gonzaga University with a master's in philosophy, 1967

Explaining how to do a land survey for "The Land Grant Game"
for students of Project 50, in 1968. This game illustrated the usefulness and
importance of mathematics and English skills in an occupational situation.

Project 50, 1968, a program for promising but underpriveleged 8th grade students
that was started by Joe Fessio and author Fr. C. M. Buckley when Fessio was back
at Santa Clara University as a Jesuit Scholastic. The program helped students to
prepare for high school and to go on to college, if they wished to pursue that path.

With a student and author Fr. Cornelius Buckley, S.J., at a Santa Clara wedding, 1968

Playing guitar for kids of Project 50, 1968

Studying in Europe, early 1970s

Ordination to the priesthood at Saint Mary's Cathedral in San Francisco, June 10, 1972

With his mom and dad after ordination, June 10, 1972

After ordination, meeting up with his old girlfriend, who had become a Holy Cross sister

Studying for final exams around 1973, Annecy, France

At the Rigi in Switzerland, with Georges Chantraine, S.J. (left),
Hans Urs von Balthasar (second from left), Henri de Lubac, S.J. (right),
and fellow student Gerd Haeffner, S.J. (foreground), 1974

In the early days of the St. Ignatius Institute, with secretary Karen Summerhays, around 1981

With friend and colleague Dennis Bartlett's young son, Brendan, in the St. Ignatius Institute's office, early 1980s

With Ignatius Press colleague editor Carolyn Lemon, around 1980

Fr. Fessio at Channel 46, a Catholic television initiative he was involved in, around 1981

At a Vatican symposium on Adrienne von Speyr, 1985

*Ignatius Press (right), was in a house owned
by the Carmelites on McAllister Street*

*Staff pilgrimage to the Shrine of
Our Lady of Guadalupe, 1985*

*Fr. Fessio in the Saint Ignatius Institute
office, April 26, 1986, age 45*

Meeting Pope John Paul II, Vatican Synod on the Laity, October 1987

Left: *With colleague Lisa Caputi's daughter, Maria, in the Ignatius Press offices, early 1990s*

Below, left: *At his desk, 1990s*

Below, right: *Marketing director Tony Ryan and Lisa Hamrick in the McAllister Street offices, early 1990s*

With the young men of Casa Balthasar, Rome, 1991, on a summer trip to Retz, Austria, to visit Fr. Christoph Schönborn, O.P.

One of the Casa Balthasar's Volkswagen van trips, August 1991

Easter in Siberia, 1992, the first public Mass in this small village since the fall of Soviet Communism. There were Catholics in this region whose ancestors originally came from Germany (the "Volga Deutsch") and who had not had access to the sacraments for many decades.

Fr. Fessio visiting with scientists at an institute in Novosibirsk, 1992. He helped set up internet communications for Catholic missionaries in Russia

On the way back from Siberia, 1992, visiting with Fr. Myron Effing (red coat), Br. Dan Mauer (left) and their local helper, Igor. The two had recently re-founded the Catholic Church in Vladivostok, Far East Russia.

With John Galten (left) and James Hitchcock on the occasion of the 25th anniversary of his priesthood

With Archbishop George Pell of Melbourne, Australia, who visited Ignatius Press in 1997

Fr. Fessio with Fr. John Hardon, S.J., late 1990s

At a Mass dedicating the offices of Radio Guadalupe, a Catholic Spanish-language radio station Fr. Fessio helped found in Fresno, California, 1999

Radio Guadalupe equipment

With Joseph Cardinal Ratzinger, who visited the offices of Ignatius Press and the Carmelite Monastery of Cristo Rey, 1999

Cardinal Ratzinger with some students of the Saint Ignatius Institute and Ignatius Press staff, in front of the Carmelite Monastery of Cristo Rey, 1999

Fr. Fessio attends a tense meeting of St. Ignatius Institute students in 2001, after USF suddenly changed the administration and nature of the SII

A visit from Christoph Cardinal Schönborn of Vienna, 2001

Fr. Fessio at the tomb of Saint Ignatius at the Gesù church in Rome, before his final Jesuit vows ceremony, 2005

Celebrating with Fr. Paul Mankowski, S.J., after his final vows

Fr. Fessio at a sing-along with students at Ave Maria University around 2007

Fr. Fessio enjoying a visit with friend Ferdinand Ulrich in Regensburg, 2010

Presenting Pope Benedict XVI with an English-language lectionary produced by Ignatius Press for the Bishops' Conference of the Antilles, 2012

*Trout fishing with Panther-Martin lures in the Imnaha River,
eastern Oregon, at the Driver family cabin, around 1989*

*Rebuilding a hanging bridge at the
Driver family cabin, 1989–90*

*Hiking in Yosemite with
friend Jim Holman*

More hiking in the Sierras, with Jim Holman,
Penelope Boldrick and Chris Veneklase

Leading a work detail with staff and friends
building the Sweetwater retreat house, 1991

Fr. Fessio thanking the construction crew

"Sweetwater"

*Thanksgiving touch football game with Ignatius Press families
at Sweetwater, 1990s*

Fr. Fessio tagging Vince Marsella

Fr. Fessio hunting wild boar, 1990

Bottle feeding lambs at Sweetwater

Jeep flip at Sweetwater (see p. 184)

Jeep flip at Sweetwater (see p. 184)

With Artie, the cat

With Daisy the goat and Buddy the dog (Eva Muntean's dog)

Playing banjo tunes with Eva and Roxanne of Ignatius Press

"Let bygones be bygones": Fr. Fessio enjoys a surprise birthday party hosted by Tom Monaghan while visiting Ave Maria University, January 2024

When George Muntean (right) challenged Fr. Fessio, who is afraid of heights, to join his family for skydiving, Fessio said he'd only do it if George made a confession and returned to the sacraments. George did, and Fr. Fessio kept his promise, even after George told him he didn't have to jump.

Crushing grapes to make wine, Sweetwater, early 2020s

A worker in the vineyard

27

THE SETTLER

The years 2011 and 2012 were productive for Ignatius Press in more ways than one. Father Fessio and his entourage presented the first English translation of *YOUCAT* to the Holy Father in March 2011, expanded their Faith and Life catechetical series (endorsed enthusiastically by many American bishops for its adherence to the Church's official *Catechism*), and released a bolstered edition of the *Adoremus Hymnal*. They had also joined up with Magnificat to create a children's book division and partnered with pilgrimage guide Steve Ray to produce a massive video series, The Footprints of God. But our readers will recall that Father Fessio—ever since he had read about the pedal-operated pumps and enhanced brooms in *The Ugly American* during his college years—he had sensed his life's task was really to help people "make it on their own", in practical ways. Now seventy years old, he needed to provide for the future of the Press. So turning his eyes away for a time from the distant windmills and looking down at the dirt, he decided to till the ground and plant some seeds—both metaphorically, with a number of publishing partnerships, and literally, with fruits and vegetables. He finally became a settler.

Ignatius Press began working with Mark Middendorf, co-founder of Lighthouse Catholic Media. Lighthouse produced inexpensive CDs on Catholic formation and apologetics, which were distributed through more than 7,500 parish kiosks across the United States, a fairly massive operation. First, the group began abridging a few Ignatius Press books to sell in these kiosks, and eventually, Ignatius also handed over to Lighthouse its association with the Catholic Truth Society, since both groups had a similar mission. A little later, Father Fessio also became a matchmaker between Lighthouse and the Augustine Institute, a major producer of Catholic spiritual and educational media, as well as an accredited graduate school for theology—one of the primary formators of Catholic theologians and catechists in the United States. In a joint venture, Ignatius Press and Lighthouse became the sole distributors of Augustine Institute materials, and shortly afterward, Lighthouse and Augustine merged their book publishing arms, with the Ignatius production team playing a key role. The other activities of Lighthouse were taken over by a new company, 5 Stones. Meanwhile, the Augustine Institute, in conjunction with the Press, began Formed, an online platform providing Catholic resources, digital books, podcasts, and films to subscribing parishes and their members.

Then there was the retirement of Neil McCaffrey, the famously blunt New Yorker who owned and ran the Colorado-based warehouse used for decades by the Press. When he announced he would be closing his doors, Father Fessio, ever eager to play engineer, decided it was time to design a warehouse of his own. It would be large enough to accommodate the needs of Ignatius Press, Augustine Institute, and other producers of Catholic media, and it would have the latest equipment, including eventually an automated box maker and a print-on-demand machine. The building was completed in 2017, in Sycamore, Illinois, where 5 Stones moved their offices and assumed the management and the staffing of the facility.

Amid this flurry of activities, Father Fessio began cultivating the land at Sweetwater. We saw in earlier chapters that Guadalupe Associates had bought the hilly, wooded property in Sonoma County in 1990 as a retreat house and a place for both work and refreshment away from the city for the employees and friends of Ignatius Press, particularly the co-founder Carolyn Lemon, who loved the countryside and had been diagnosed with a terminal illness (since conquered). Though he had herded his share of sheep, goats, and llamas over the years, Father Fessio had never considered farming the land of Sweetwater until one day his friend Father Robert McTeigue, S.J., showed him a grim video: impending shortages of credit, energy, arable land, and potable water. As a Jesuit, already poor by definition, Father Fessio had no worries about his own future, but he felt a jolt of responsibility. "Ignatius Press is a family of families," he said. "They don't have the buffer I do." So in 2012 he planted a vineyard, an orchard, and a vegetable garden, hoping to give his people a way to sustain themselves should society come tumbling down. The crash has yet to come, but the crops remain.

The vineyard consists of 1,347 vines of eight varieties of grape. (A mnemonic device for this figure: 1347 is the year Saint Catherine of Siena was born.) Father planned the grounds on the advice of Carmine Indindoli, a retired engineer turned vineyard consultant, who also taught him the art of winemaking. With the help of Ignatius Press employees, friends, and hired workers, Father Fessio still tends the plants, picks the grapes, presses the juice, ages the wine, and bottles it, all while wearing his perennial Roman collar. Sweetwater produces around 840 unlabeled bottles per year, and whatever Ignatius Press does not drink, the Jesuit vintner gives away to friends. In tending to these vines, "I've taken a near vow of stability," he likes to say.

In the Sweetwater orchard, too, are a hundred apple and pear trees. The different varieties ripen successively, such that edible fruit can be picked from June to November. The farming techniques Father Fessio employed came from John Jeavons, the father of modern biointensive agriculture, whose method he had seen in action in Europe. The result: His trees, trained to be short and spindly, "grow fruit, not wood". Then came the vegetable garden—also planted using biointensive techniques. It was so productive that the Press could neither eat nor give away all of their vegetables, so they let it go. The next year, Father sowed wheat instead, which after harvesting, threshing, and milling (in a blender) he now sends to the Carmel of the Immaculate Heart of Mary in Utah, to be shaped into Eucharistic hosts.

Wine and bread—two things necessary for Mass. In these endeavors, at least, the pelican has not gobbled up more than he can swallow.

28

IN CONCLUSION

Father Fessio has been blessed with a complex personality, more adaptable to analogy than definition. In the former pages he has been depicted wearing a variety of masks: a pelican, Don Quixote, the toreador Don José, Bertie Wooster, and a number of passing, whispering images. In order to focus better on learning just who he is, this final chapter will provide a few anecdotal adventures to those already recounted and will end with a final analysis.

In 2018, Eva Muntean of the Press marketing department began to dream of skydiving. The desire to jump out of a high-flying plane, flutter weightless a bit, and then float down and gently land on the earth below haunted her waking hours. Finally she took the jump —and she never wanted to do it again. Yet her father, George, now in his mid-eighties, had a bucket list to take care of, and he asked her to join him in another round of freefalling. How could she say no? But then the robust Hungarian threw another card on the table: "Tell Father Fessio I want him to jump with me, too." Now, if anything terrifies the Reverend Fessio, it is the prospect of falling like a brick from on high—making his mountain-climbing trips a bit bittersweet, as we have earlier seen. Not a chance, thought Eva. Nevertheless, she dialed up Father to ask whether he would jump with George. "No way", he said immediately, hanging up. But after a few minutes, Eva's phone rang again. He raised the bet: "Tell your dad if he'll go to Confession and Communion first, I'll jump with him." Fat chance. George had not been to Confession or Communion in more than sixty years. Eva rolled her eyes and emailed her father to give him Fessio's terms. But George lit up. "Set it up!" So Father Fessio was bound for another hair-raising adventure, this time to bring back a wandering sheep into the fold. Within a week, George came to confess his sins there at the Ignatius Press Firehouse chapel, and he knelt down for Communion beside his daughter. Afterward, remembering Father Fessio's profound terror of heights, George took him aside and reassured him: "You know you don't have to do this. It's all right." "No," the Jesuit replied, "a deal's a deal." They all drove together to the California countryside to find their plane. Though Father Fessio insisted that no cameras film him, there is a single shot where one can detect, in the far recesses of the plane, the seventy-seven-year-old Father Joseph Fessio, dressed in his clerical wear, seated upright between a couple of young tandem aides who would assist him in his whirling exit from the plane. He jumped. How did he land? He did not say. In typical Fessio fashion, the account of the event remained dry and vague. For him, it was just one of those everyday happenings, a distraction, and if it has been remembered by many with exciting emotions, in no way did it ever intrude on the co-performer's agenda of the moment.

There was another happening that he seems to regard as just one more ho-hum affair, indifferent to the reaction of those who learn about it. But those who know him well agree that it is a classic Fessio adventure. It began at Sweetwater—where TVs and radios are taboo—on a Saturday afternoon, when the San Francisco 49ers were playing a championship game. How could he miss that? He decided he would go to some bar in town and watch the televised game, seated with an awful-tasting American beer before him as a penance. A bit bizarre perhaps, but not unheard-of, except for two details. From his earliest days at USF, he had decided never to appear anywhere without a Roman collar, even attached to a parachute, as we have seen. It was the symbol that reminded him who he was, and at the same time it was a clarion trumpet announcing to others the same message: "I am a priest." At Sweetwater, he sheared sheep, corralled llamas, worked in the garden, and did housework with the perennial collar about his neck. The second animadversion in this account is that the closest town to Sweetwater is Guerneville, which over the years has become a recreation spot for San Francisco's diverse echelon gay community—a fact that had no effect whatsoever on the retreat director at Sweetwater.

On this particular Saturday, spurred on by the prospect of witnessing a 49er victory, he zipped into the first bar he saw and announced to the bartender that he wanted a place where he could watch the game and have a beer. "We're not open!" was the snappy reply. "Look, those guys seated there have been served" was his riposte, as every eye of the biker clientele was riveted on him. "We're not open", repeated the bartender. "Go down the street. There are bars serving customers there." So, he made his exit and while walking along the street, he became conscious that hot feelings of anger were swiftly replacing those of disappointment and causing the sheathed, quixotic sword at his side to rattle. Bars were numerous in the small town and crowded on weekends. So in his fast search for another, perhaps he remembered what Saint Ignatius once wrote: "A little anger is very helpful." Encouraged, he walked into another bar and made the same request: a seat at a table, a beer, and a TV showing the game. The bartender, a seemingly polite man, was sympathetic, but he was worried. "Father," he said, "this is a gay bar. I don't know if . . ." He was cut off by the invader's strong reaction: "That's the trouble with you people. You're always claiming that everybody discriminates against you. Well, you're discriminating against me! All I want is to watch the game." Seated, he would have remembered the rest of Ignatius' insight: yes, a little anger is a good thing "provided it is moderated by reason and the fear of God. It is enough to be careful to restrain it and repress it so that it does not burst forth."[1] The beer was awful; the game was terrible; the 49ers lost. But before he left, he made sure he singled out the bartender and thank him, wishing him well. It was the *preux* thing to do. He then speeded back to Sweetwater conscious that the pelican's bill seemed empty. He couldn't do much about the 49ers fumbling, but he could stop the pelican's belly rumbling. Among other things, the event typifies his ability to cut off every distraction when focusing on an objective he intends to achieve. It also testifies to an extraordinary ability to refrain from judging anyone with whom he is dealing. The person involved in the deal never distracts from the deal or from the matter at hand itself.

Another episode, recounted by the late *Communio* editor David L. Schindler, illustrates this point well.

A well-known reporter who publicly identified himself as gay wrote very critical articles regarding Fessio in the Catholic press. At least one major criticism appeared on the front page of a leading Catholic newspaper, calling attention to Father Fessio's relation to Rome and

---

[1] Quoted in Paul Doncoeur, *The Heart of Ignatius*, trans. Henry St. C. Lavin, (Baltimore, Md.: Helicon, 1958), p. 107.

in particular to then Cardinal Ratzinger. I do not recall the details
of the exchange(s) between Father Fessio and this reporter. I know
only that in the course of the controversy, Father Fessio apparently
communicated with this man in a manner that projected the gen-
uineness of Father Fessio's priesthood, assuring him that there was
no personal animus on his part, that he had been concerned simply
with the issue and not this man's person. Sometime after the controversy, this reporter had contracted AIDS and was dying. He had
gone for care in his last months to a home run by the Missionaries
of Charity. He called Father Fessio when he was near death and
asked Fessio if he would come and administer to him the last rites
and hear his last confession so that he could die in peace, in the
Church. Father Fessio went to him, and that is how the controversy
ended.[1]

His intensification of attention, joined with force, intelligence,
and constancy, has enabled him to achieve nearly every impossible
goal to which he has aspired. We have witnessed many examples
of this fact cited in earlier pages. Whether it was reading a map
for a pilgrimage while arranging adequate provisions for a crowd of
students or recruiting potential freshmen for the first SII freshman
class or becoming a professional publisher and amateur vintner of
note or laying out blueprints for the Press' storage depot—it was
all part of the same intensity. Part of his success (and we have recounted failures, too) comes from a prodigious memory for detailed facts and an ability to calculate a budget. In addition to these
natural talents that have made him a theologian, a linguist, and a
quick radio host, he has never been dissuaded by hours of labor,
sleepless nights, and hostile criticism. Although he does not deny
his God-given talents, he is quick to add that the chief source of
his inspiration comes from his religious life.

When he entered the novitiate in 1961, the custom was that when
the wake-up bell rang at 5 A.M., the cubicle beadle would call out
"*Benedicamus Domino*", and the seven other cubicle sleepers would
respond "*Deo Gratias*". So the theme of the day was set by the invocation "Let us bless the Lord" for all that occurs until we close

[1] David L. Schindler, "Father Joseph Fessio, S.J.: A Personal Memoir", in *Ressource-ment after Vatican II: Essays in Honor of Joseph Fessio, S.J.*, ed. Nicholas Healy Jr. and Matthew Levering (San Francisco: Ignatius Press, 2019), p. 25.

our eyes at night, and the response was "Thanks be to God" for another day to praise him, glorify him, and thank him. Father Fessio has never forgotten that invocation and its response, and he calls them out as soon as he awakens in the morning. Pulling himself out of bed and struggling to get into his clothes, he continues these few words with the invocation from the Divine Office: "Lord, open my lips, / And my mouth will proclaim your praise." He confesses that he says this prayer as an introduction to the Morning Offering because he wants to integrate all that happens to him during the day with the liturgical life of the Church. It was during his days in France that he developed a great love for the Divine Office, which contains the prayers priests are obliged to say each day. When he was in Germany serving as chaplain at the Army base, he found himself inundated with duties and distractions while at the same time trying to fit in preparation work for his doctoral degree. The result was that often he found himself trying to cram the Office into his agenda before midnight. Then one day, he remembers walking across the compound, and he said to himself: "No. You got it all wrong. You are trying to fit the Office into all of your activities. Make the Office your framework and sandwich your activities into it." Ever since that day, he has followed out that principle. "It is a beautiful way to structure your week with Sunday and the week-days, and to structure your day as well. The various hours of the Office have ever since been a kind of framework for my day."

His preference is to offer Mass in the morning because it works better into his daily schedule and also because he opts to fast from midnight before beginning the celebration. Such fasting is no longer required, except for the one hour before Mass begins, but he finds it more devotional to do so. When he is obliged to say Mass at noon or afternoon, he does not fast. He has the habit of making an hour meditation before beginning Mass, using either the scriptural readings for the Mass of the day or various psalms or readings from the Office. He regularly offers Mass in the Ignatius Press Firehouse chapel, which many of the Press staff members attend. As of 2020, the Jesuit has missed saying Mass only two days since his ordination in 1972.

He claims he has always had a devotion to Mary, expressed in saying a daily rosary, but until he was thirty-five, it was for the most part perfunctory. It then became more intense. "My name is

Joseph", he quips. "I'm named after Saint Joseph. We don't know much about him, but I figure he took Mary to be his wife when he was about thirty-five. So, maybe I'm following his path. Who knows?" Whatever. Mary became more of an intimate, daily presence when he was forming the Institute and the Press, and she has remained a central yet quiet presence in his spiritual life ever since. He can trace back the pilgrimage to Guadalupe with the hippies in 1975 as an incentive to his deeper Marian devotion and to subsequent pilgrimages taken with members of the Press, to Guadalupe, and to a number of European Marian shrines that have served to enhance his relationship with her. Except for his morning quiet hour, his day is full of distractions, with little time to contemplate long the presence of the Sacred Heart or Mary in between his activities. But he has been consoled by Saint Thomas Aquinas' insight that "a greater charity is shown when one sacrifices the consolation of contemplation to seek the glory of God in the conversion of sinners as human friendship seeks more the good of the friend than the pleasure resulting from his presence."[2] As a novice, he learned that the ideal for a Jesuit is to be "a contemplative in action", seeking to find God "in all things" and trying to do all *ad majorem Dei gloriam* [for the greater glory of God]. So with these two saints by his side— Thomas and Ignatius—he strives to give himself completely to the Ignatian principle of *age quod agis*, "do what you should be doing", when and how you should be doing it, each moment of the day and night.[3]

He is quick to point out that where he has been and what he has done have had a profound effect on him, have changed his perspective, opening up new vistas he never dreamed existed; yet such plans were never consciously made. Here we cite two examples. First: never in his wildest imaginings was Ave Maria University an option for him; it was something he was pushed into; something someone else chose for him. Then he admits the surprise it offered. "Ave Maria, it was a tremendous blessing for me. I tell you the greatest blessing for me at Ave Maria, like my whole life, is the people I've gotten to be around. . . . I've never met a group of young

---

[2] Thomas Aquinas, *Commentary on the Sentences*, bk. 3, dist. 35, q. 1, a. 4 (translated by author).

[3] Cf. Ignatius of Loyola, *Spiritual Exercises*, nos. 23, 319.

people that were so good, so talented, so loving, so full of faith, so zealous, and had so many different abilities." They were able to sing, dance, act on stage, and do all sorts of things he claimed he was unable to do, and they inspired him to think about starting a club for people like himself, unable to do what these students were so proficient in doing. It would be a group whose mission would be to keep encouraging young people to do even better, to strive *ad astra*, to reach for the stars. "I figured that's one thing God has made me do", he recounted. "He's given me the ability to appreciate goodness and quality, even though I can't produce it myself. So it's like publishing. What does publishing mean? To make public. I don't write books. But I can tell a good book." He expanded on this affirmation by asserting: "At Ignatius Press we all love books, but you know what we do when we get a manuscript? If we like it, we publish it. We don't have a focus group or do a marketing survey. We just say, 'Hey, this is a good book. It helps the Church. Let's do it.'" How he was able to equate his admiration for the students he met at Ave Maria with the publishing policy of the Ignatius Press, based on the criterion of "helping the Church", gives one food for thought. All of this adulation and encouragement for young people might help one appreciate how one of these Ave Maria students saw him in kind: "He is awesome. I mean, like, totally a master ninja."

Father Fessio had a friendly bond with young people, but there was also another group with whom he had formed strong ties: women religious. Cloistered Carmelite nuns in convents throughout the United States and far beyond its shores have offered prayers for him and his intentions on a daily basis. Every time Mother Teresa passed through San Francisco, she made it a point to visit him, sometimes making a special trip to the Press, to assure him of her prayers for him and his valuable apostolate in the Church, prayers that are joined with those of other Missionaries of Charity in the many convents where he is well known. Another example of the prayers of religious women was a letter addressed to him from Maryknoll, New York, on August 8, 1976, before he had become a celebrity. After the customary salutation, it began:

A long time ago [1961], a young man whose father worked for an airline got a free ticket to Manila and visited the Jesuits at the

Ateneo University and the Maryknoll sisters next door. He told a Maryknoll sister that he was entering [the Jesuit novitiate] that fall. The sister has a special devotion for priestly vocations, and so she inscribed the name of the boy on a holy card in her breviary, and through the years prayed for him and wondered if he made it. His name was Joe Fessio. Did he make it? I thought you would like to know that I'll be praying for Joe Fessio wherever he is.

It was signed "Sister Aquinata Brennan", and it summarizes well the cause for the success of Father Fessio: constant prayers of known and unknown religious women for him and his apostolate.

What the author of Maccabees wrote of Judas Maccabeus might also well apply to Joseph Fessio: "Now the rest of the acts of Judas, and his wars and the brave deeds that he did, and his greatness, have not been recorded, for they were very many."[4] Obviously, Father Joseph Dean Fessio is a talented, successful man, and we have recounted above much of what he has done, describing the battles in which he has been engaged. But he made his debut and prepares his exit at a time when talent, reputation, and success have little or no lasting value. It is a time when monuments of once-regarded heroes like Christopher Columbus are unceremoniously retired from their pedestals of honor, when universities rush to tear down names like Serra from campus streets, or with buckets of tears wipe away such defamatory tags as Flannery O'Connor from buildings that for years had calmly displayed such designations. What does it matter if in generations to come Father Fessio is regarded a sociopolitical saint or a disreputable scoundrel, or, more likely, not remembered at all? As with us all, it will be God who judges him on his fidelity and gratitude to the Church and on his care for others.

The purpose of this biography has been to demonstrate how Joseph D. Fessio—with the grace of God and the approval of his religious superiors—has been faithful to his commitment as priest, Jesuit, and home missionary. To support this, we have given two major examples, sprinkled with an occasional bit of salt: his founding of the Saint Ignatius Institute and his fathering of Ignatius Press. We have also attempted to show how his natural talents and special training qualified him to take on these two projects. As a young Jesuit, before his priestly ordination, he was a specially formed protégé

---

[4] 1 Mac 9:22.

of Henri de Lubac, S.J., who trained him to capture the Ignatian spirit. Then as a graduate student, thanks to the direction of his tutors Hans Urs von Balthasar and Joseph Ratzinger, later Pope Benedict XVI, he was whittled into a philosopher and theologian of repute.

His gratitude for this stellar education motivated him to launch the Saint Ignatius Institute, a program of studies harking back to the one followed by the early Jesuit universities, but set within a modern Jesuit university. Such an ambitious undertaking led him all the way back to the year 1547, the year when the Society of Jesus' first university was founded—seven years after the establishment of the Jesuits and nine years before the death of its founder, Saint Ignatius Loyola. The place was Gandía, Spain, and the founder was Francis Borgia, a layman, who later became a Jesuit, and eventually a saint. The courses were taught by Jesuits, the student body made up men from different social strata, including Jesuits in training. Its mission was that of the medieval universities: the pursuit of the good, true, and beautiful through the media of faith and reason. The curriculum was close to that of the University of Paris, where the founding Jesuits had studied.[1] The model worked. By 1710, the Jesuits ran 612 colleges and universities throughout the world, one the largest networks in history, all sharing a standardized plan of studies with slight modifications, based on the Jesuit *Ratio Studiorum* of 1599. A recent study has shown what a contribution these institutions have made to forming and sustaining western civilization.[2]

Realist that he is, Father Fessio was aware that the late twentieth century in the United States was vastly different from the mid-sixteenth century or the early eighteenth century in Europe. It was idle dreaming to think that an exact replica of the earlier Jesuit mode could define the mission of the modern American Jesuit university. Some adaptation was not only needed, but, to implement the unstated goals of the modern Jesuit university, imperative. Still, he asked, why could there not be some place within the contemporary, expansive, multicultural Jesuit university for a program based

[1] Cándido de Dalmases, *Francis Borgia: Grandee of Spain, Jesuit Saint*, trans. Cornelius Michael Buckley, S.J. (Saint Louis: Institute of Jesuit Sources, 1985), 62–67.

[2] See Markus Friedrich, *The Jesuits: A History*, trans. John Noël Dillon (Princeton, N.J.: Princeton University Press, 2022).

on that of the original Jesuit universities—a modern-day operation taught by experts in their fields and dedicated to upholding both the magisterium of the Catholic Church and the foundations of reason? The answer to this question was given in the above chapters. The SII experiment failed. But not altogether. Even though Father Fessio, while director, may have stuck his lance into a few windmills, the Institute did unquantifiable good for many college students and paved the way for new Catholic colleges, founded by laymen.

The inevitable course that followed the fall of the Institute had no effect on the direction of Father Fessio's second major project: Ignatius Press. Its progress was, and remains, a vivid illustration of the maxim *per aspera ad astra*, "through hardships to the stars". Beginning in a makeshift closet, shared with boxes of clothes, the Press is now one of the largest—if not the largest—English-language Catholic publishing houses in the world. Its main office is in a remodeled firehouse in San Francisco, where daily Mass and the liturgy of the hours are held in a Fessio-designed chapel for the ever-busy dozen-or-so employees who work there. Beyond the headquarters, there are contract workers scattered throughout the country, along with an exceptionally large warehouse in Illinois that houses and mails out the different products the Press makes available to an appreciative public. It publishes some forty new books a year, ranging from impenetrable theological studies to children's coloring books, along with everything in between: novels, histories, bibles, missals, biographies, and philosophical texts, not to mention two popular online magazines.

The philosophy of the Press is the same that animated the Institute: the pursuit of the true, the good, and the beautiful through faith and reason. Its presence therefore is needed today. As of 2022, various research centers report the number of Catholics in the United States has plumped, but "woke" weeds proliferate even more, particularly in the field of education. In his interview book *Salt of the Earth*, published by the Press in 1997, Pope Benedict predicted that such would be the coming scenario throughout the world, and he emphasized the need for trained workers to sow the seeds of faith. Father Fessio had anticipated that call. If the soil at the University of San Francisco was no longer open for seeding, all the more important for the Press to train willing lay people to plant the faith in the silicon soil of our electronic age. The Press is committed to that goal.

Given the extraordinary expansion of Ignatius Press, Father Fessio, although still the editor-in-chief, is not as involved as he once was in the details of the operation. A board of directors and a competent president, Mr. Mark Brumley, direct and operate the enterprise, while Father Fessio spends most of his daylight hours evaluating manuscripts in a small office, fueled by a jar of almonds. Just down the hall is a Murphy bed for the needs of the night. Yet even when he escapes to the retreat house at Sweetwater, he remains the *éminence grise* of the whole operation, a shadow hovering, sometimes unobtrusively, at other times obtrusively, and at all times humorously, making certain the original spirit of the Press is not modified or compromised, *ad majorem Dei gloriam*, for the greater glory of God.

He turned eighty in 2021, and with courage, confidence, steadfastness, and poverty of spirit, he pushes on, awaiting the call to lay down his arms. Meanwhile, he attends his vineyard at his Sweetwater retreat house—unlike Montaigne, who wanted death to find him planting his self-satisfying cabbages, and unlike Voltaire's Candide, who gardened for the time it gave him to engage in philosophical speculation. Father Fessio tends his vines for a radically different reason. We have seen that as a Jesuit novice, Brother Fessio was introduced not only to the nourishment he could never seem to find in the three volumes of Alphonsus Rodriguez' *Practice of Perfection and Christian Virtues* but also to the satisfaction he acquired lugging boxes of harvested grapes from the vineyards to be sent to the Jesuit winery. Later at Fourvière, he divided time between the companionship of his beloved Henri de Lubac and excursions through the Beaujolais countryside mounted on his *mobylette*.

It is no wonder, then, that in his declining years, he finds time to reflect on his indebtedness to the Society of Jesus along with energy to care for the Sweetwater grapevines and to turn their virtues into a bottled product that brings satisfaction and joy to the lives of others. Each year the harvest is abundant, and bottles are given away by the dozens. For him, handing out such gifts is just one more *preux*—and pious—thing to do, and that is what really matters.

NOTE ON SOURCES

Except where otherwise noted, the author has drawn his material from the Ignatius Press Archive (San Francisco), from a private interview with Father Fessio by Mark Middendorf, and from his own memory as a professor at the University of San Francisco.

INDEX OF PERSONS

SUBJECT INDEX

abortion, 165–66, 202–3, 204. *See also* pro-life movement
Action catholique, 51
Adoremus Bulletin (periodical), 215, 217, 225
Adoremus Hymnal, 319
Adoremus Society for the Renewal of the Sacred Liturgy, 215
African culture, 178
African Missal/Lectionary Project, 316
The AIDS Cover-Up? (Antonio), 146–47
AIDS/HIV plague, 146
Aid to the Church in Need, 194
Alameda Naval Hospital, 15
All India Catholic University Federation, 59
Alto Adige, Italy, 72
Amberg Army Airfield, Germany, 68–69, 71
America (magazine), 235
American Civil Liberties Union, 147
Amoris Laetitia (Francis), 135
Angelicum Academy, 315
anti-Semitism, 164, 168
The Art of Worldly Wisdom (Gracián), 33
Associated Students of the University of San Francisco (ASUSF), 203–5
Augustine Institute, 319–20
Australian Confraternity of Catholic Clergy, 224–26
Ave Maria College, 287
Ave Maria Foundation, 294
Ave Maria School of Law, 295
Ave Maria University, 294–96, 299–304, 308–10
  Cardinal Arinze visit (2008), 308
  Fessio asked to resign, 305–7

Battle of Verdun (1917), 50
Bellarmine College Preparatory School, 18, 19, 241
Bereitschaft (von Speyr), 103
Bethlehem Books, 312–13
Bethlehem Covenant Community, 312–13
Bible translations and inclusive language, 189–90
birth control (contraception), 133–35, 138–39
Bolivia, 240
Bruderhof, 313
Buddhism, 56, 87

Call to Action, 234–35
Campion College, 283–93
Cardinal Newman College, 108
The Cardinal Sins (Greeley), 162
Carmelite Sisters of the Most Sacred Heart of Los Angeles, 154–59
Casa Balthasar, Rome, 188, 271, 286
Catechesi Tradendae (John Paul II), 236
Catechism of the Catholic Church, 189, 191–92
Catholic Books on Tape project, 114
Catholic broadcasting, 228–38
Catholic Church. *See also* Vatican II
  ad orientem Mass, 222, 294–95, 301
  Catholic Left, 50–51, 54
  divisions within, 84–85, 134, 162–63
  Fathers of the Church, 49, 50
  la nouvelle théologie movement, 51–53, 54, 94
  Le Saulchoir School, 52–53
  Libreria Editrice Vaticana (LEV), 217